WRITING WITH POWER

WRITING WITH POWER

POWER

Techniques for Mastering
the Writing Process

Peter Elbow
The Evergreen State College

New York Oxford
OXFORD UNIVERSITY PRESS

Oxford University Press

Oxford   London   Glasgow
New York   Toronto   Melbourne   Wellington
Nairobi   Dar es Salaam   Cape Town
Kuala Lumpur   Singapore   Jakarta   Hong Kong   Tokyo
Delhi   Bombay   Calcutta   Madras   Karachi

Library of Congress Cataloging in Publication Data

Elbow, Peter.
  Writing with power.

  Bibliography: p.
  Includes index.
  1. English language—Rhetoric.   I. Title.
PE1408.E39   808'.042   81-1597
ISBN 0-19-502912-7   AACR2
ISBN 0-19-502913-5 (pbk.)

printing, last digit: 29 28 27 26 25

Printed in the United States of America

I dedicate this book
to Cami
with my love

NOTE TO THE READER

Writing with power means getting power over words and readers; writing clearly and correctly; writing what is true or real or interesting; and writing persuasively or making some kind of contact with your readers so that they actually experience your meaning or vision. In this book I am trying to help you write in all these ways.

But writing with power also means getting power over yourself and over the writing process; knowing what you are doing as you write; being in charge; having control; not feeling stuck or helpless or intimidated. I am particularly interested in this second kind of power in writing and I have found that without it you seldom achieve the first kind.

ACKNOWLEDGMENTS

In the long process of writing this book, I have learned much about writing from many people: fellow teachers, fellow thinkers about writing, readers, students, and kin. I am grateful to the following people for what a writer needs most, honest helpful reactions to parts of the manuscript at various stages: Gloria Campbell, Thad Curtz, Joy and Don Dybeck, Anne Enquist, Lee Graham, Gerald Grant, Burt Hatlen, Susan Hubbuch, Criseyde Jones, Cecile Kalkwarf, Ellen Nold, Margaret Proctor, Eugene Smith, Joanne Turpin, Mary Wakeman, and Bernice Youtz.

I hope that the students I have worked with over these last years here at The Evergreen State College, and the teachers here and elsewhere, know how much I have learned from them and will accept my thanks. I am grateful to the students whose writing I quote here for their permission to do so.

I did some of my final revising during a trip, and due to the kind hospitality of the following people I found myself working in a succession of particularly gracious rooms, each with a lovely prospect: Jean and Joan Cordier, Rex and Celia Frayling, Malcolm and Gay Harper, Helena Knapp.

Deep thanks to my editor at Oxford, John Wright, who helped sustain me in countless ways through many unmet deadlines. Also to Curtis Church, copy editor. I was fortunate to have Janis Maddox as typist.

My greatest debt in writing this book is to my wife Cami for the love and support that made it possible and the incisive editorial comment that made it better.

P.E.

Olympia, Washington
September 1980

Contents

WRITING WITH POWER

SOME ESSENTIALS

INTRODUCTION: A MAP OF THE BOOK

I have designed this book so you can either read it straight through or else skip around. That is, I have arranged it in what seems to me the most logical order; you will find some cumulative benefits from reading it in the normal sequence. But I have also made each section and chapter fairly complete in itself so you can thread your own path and find the chapters you need for your particular writing tasks or for your own particular temperament or skills. By reading Section I and the short introductions to the remaining five sections, you will get a good sense of how the whole book works. In addition, almost every chapter ends with a short summary or section of advice which you can consult for more information about what the chapter treats.

• • •

There is no hiding the fact that writing well is a complex, difficult, and time-consuming process. Indeed I fear I may even heighten that impression by writing a book so full of analysis and advice. In this first section, therefore, I want to emphasize that the essential activities underlying good writing and the essential exercises promoting it are not difficult at all.

In addition this first section serves as a kind of introduction to the whole book. Chapter 1 explains the approach to writing that I take. Chapters 2 and 3, "Freewriting" and "Sharing," present two ways of working on your writing that are at once simpler and more powerful than any other ways I know. Chapters 4 and 5, "The Direct Writing Process" and "Quick Revising," comprise together a simple and practical method for getting something written—a method particularly suitable if you are working under a tight deadline. I call Chapter 6 "The Dangerous Method" because I discuss there that common and tempting practice of trying to write something right the first time.

Sections II and III, "More Ways To Get Words on Paper" and "More Ways To Revise," could together be entitled "Getting Power over the Writing Process" since they focus on the actual steps used in writing something. These two practical, step-by-step sections constitute what is probably the core of the book.

Section IV, "Audience," could be called "Getting Power over Others," yet one of the main themes is the power others have over us as we try to write to them. I suggest ways to use the power of an audience to your benefit instead of letting it get in your way. I also analyze the difficulties of some particular audiences or writing situations and suggest ways to overcome these difficulties.

Section V, "Feedback," could be called "Getting Power through the Help of Others" because I show you how to figure out what kind of feedback you need for your particular writing situation and then how to get readers actually to give it to you.

Section VI, finally, is about a mystery, power in writing: not correctness in usage or clarity in language or validity in thinking or truth in conclusions, but that extra something—or that inner something—that makes readers *experience* what you are talking about, not just understand it. When this mysterious power is absent your writing makes no dent on most readers, however correct, clear, valid, or true it may be. Needless to say, this section is more speculative and theoretical than the others—and longer—but it also contains specific practical advice. It contains the ideas about writing that are most exciting to me as I write. If you love theory, you might wish to start with this section. If you are in a hurry just to get things written competently, and that's all, you can skip this final section.

A note on gender. In some chapters I call people "he" and in others I call them "she." I do so because I believe that "he" refers to men more than it does to women, despite the convention that says it can refer equally to both sexes. Of course the ideal pronoun arrangement would not distract any of a reader's attention away from the main message of the sentence—as I fear mine sometimes does. But I can't imagine a really ideal arrangement until we finish the process of relinquishing cultural habits of male primacy.

An Approach
to Writing

I direct this book to a very broad audience. I'm not trying to tailor my words to beginning or advanced writers in particular, or to students, novelists, professional people, pleasure writers, or poets. Perhaps I shouldn't try to talk to so many different kinds of people, yet in truth I feel my audience is very specific. I am talking to that person inside everyone who has ever written or tried to write: that someone who has wrestled with words, who seeks power in words, who has often gotten discouraged, but who also senses the possibility of achieving real writing power.

> I've learned how to take more control over my writing while still giving it free rein. . . . I've learned the value of not expecting a twelve year old child to come out when you're giving birth to a baby; that any writing needs time after its birth so it can change and grow and eventually reach its potential. I've come to realize that you most probably won't find a pearl if you only pick up oysters once a year. So I will try to write a lot—a whole lot—and not expect that every piece emerge a gem. I'll learn to put up with (maybe even enjoy) the bad stuff, remembering that the more I do of it, the closer I get to coming out with something good. When I feel that a good idea has emerged, but I don't know where to follow it, I won't feel that it's a lost cause— that its moment has passed. I'll let it sit for a while and then go back to it with renewed energy until I can make something whole out of it, or decide that I've gone as far as I can with it.
>
> JOANNE PILGRIM

This is part of a self-evaluation written by a student at the end of a course I recently taught. It says what I hope readers will be able to say after reading and working with this book. It reflects my interest in the writing *process*. That is, I think I can best help you improve your writing by talking not only about the words you should end up with on paper but also about the processes that should occur on the way to that final draft. Sometimes, in fact, when people think too much during the early stages about what they want to end up with, that preoccupation with the final product keeps them from attaining it.

Three themes run through this book.

1. A view of the writing process. Writing calls on two skills that are so different that they usually conflict with each other: creating and criticizing. In other words, writing calls on the ability to create words and ideas out of yourself, but it also calls on the ability to criticize them in order to decide which ones to use. It is true that these opposite mental processes can go on at the same time. When they do, you find yourself writing words that are at once inventive and rich, yet also shrewd, toughminded, and well ordered. But such magical sessions are rare. Most of the time it helps to separate the creating and criticizing processes so they don't interfere with each other: first write freely and uncritically so that you can generate as many words and ideas as possible without worrying whether they are good; then turn around and adopt a critical frame of mind and thoroughly revise what you have written—taking what's good and discarding what isn't and shaping what's left into something strong. You'll discover that the two mentalities needed for these two processes—an inventive fecundity and a tough critical-mindedness—flower most when they get a chance to operate separately.

2. An assumption that virtually everyone has available great skill with words. That is, everyone can, under certain conditions, speak with clarity and power. These conditions usually involve a topic of personal importance and an urgent occasion. But the fact that everyone can sometimes rise to an urgent occasion shows that the capacity for spoken eloquence is there. Most readers of this book have probably had at some time the experience of writing with great power. And as a teacher I have had the opportunity to see that even people with marginal writing ability can sometimes muster their eloquence on paper.

Needless to say, however, much writing, most writing—indeed most published writing—is pretty bad. Not only does the meaning usually fail to come through to the reader lively and clear; the meaning that comes through usually differs from what the writer had in mind. People often sound dumber and more incoherent on paper than they really are. Nevertheless, I have found that people improve their writing much more quickly and easily when they realize that they already have many of the crucial skills they need— even if these skills are hard to mobilize on paper. It helps to realize that learning to write well is not so much like learning to speak a new language as it is like learning to speak to a new person or in a new situation

3. A strategic decision about how best to solve the following problem: on the one hand I think you should take complete charge of yourself as you write (and not accept any of the helpless feelings that writing so often arouses), yet on the other hand I think you should follow my directions since I have lots of good advice here. My solution has been to adopt a kind of cookbook strategy. In most sections I give you a choice among different recipes: various recipes for getting words down on paper, for revising, for dealing with your audience, for getting feedback on your writing, and still other recipes for approaching the mystery of power in writing. I provide choice among them, but within any given recipe I have not hesitated to spell out in explicit detail the steps you should follow. My theme in the end is that you should take charge of yourelf by practicing the different recipes till you have them at your disposal (and can tinker with them). You will end up able to exert great choice and control as you work on any particular writing task.

A Two-step Writing Process

When you begin to realize how writing calls on the two opposite skills of creativity and critical thinking you get a better understanding of its difficulties. If you are trying to be inventive and come up with lots of interesting new ideas, it's usually the worst thing in the world if someone comes along and starts being critical. Thus, the power of brainstorming: no one is allowed to criticize *any* idea or suggestion that is offered—no matter how stupid, impractical, or useless it seems. You can't get the good ones and the fruitful interaction among the odd ones unless you welcome the terrible ones. Besides, you don't really know which ideas are good or terrible till later. Similarly, if you are trying to be tough-mindedly critical and find the weaknesses in your own thinking, you will be impeded if someone comes along and makes you dream up lots of fresh new ideas. To be critical, you have to be doubting, detached, uninvested in the idea to be criticized; to come up with fresh new ideas you have to invest yourself and be believing.

No wonder writing is hard. And no wonder writing skills are distributed in the following pattern. At one extreme many people are tied in knots by trying to be creative and critical at the same time and so they write wretchedly or not at all. At the other extreme there are a few people who write extremely well—who manage gracefully to pat their heads and rub their bellies at the same time—but they give remarkably contradictory accounts of what they're doing. "It's all inspiration!" "It's all perspiration!" "It's all system!" "It's all magic and serendipity!" Just what you might expect if people were explaining a complex skill which they happened to have learned, but which violates normal patterns of explanation. And as for the rest in the middle—those who manage to write but don't write especially well—they don't write especially well *because* the two writing muscles operate at cross purposes: creativity is strong only if criticial thinking is weak, or vice versa. Thus, these ordinary writers fall into two camps. Either creativity has won out and produced writers who are rich but undisciplined, who can turn out lots of stuff with good bits in it, but who are poor at evaluating, pruning, and shaping. Or else critical thinking has won out and produced writers who are careful but cramped. They have great difficulty writing because they see faults in everything as they are trying to put it down on paper. What they end up with is disciplined and of good quality but it is thin and tight and it was purchased at disproportionate cost. And in addition it lacks the brilliance or excitement that comes from unhampered creativity.

But you don't have to give in to this dilemma of creativity versus critical thinking and submit to the dominance of one muscle and lose the benefits of the other. If you separate the writing process into two stages, you can exploit these opposing muscles one at a time: first be loose and accepting as you do fast early writing; then be critically toughminded as you revise what you have produced. What you'll discover is that these two skills used alternately don't undermine each other at all, they enhance each other.

For it turns out, paradoxically, that you increase your creativity by working on critical thinking. What prevents most people from being inventive and creative is fear of looking foolish. After all, if you just let words and ideas come out without checking them first, some may indeed be stupid. But when you know that this is just the first of two stages, and that you are getting more and more critical in the second stage, you feel safer writing freely, tapping intuition, and going out on limbs. You will be more creative.

Similarly, you will increase critical revising skills by working on creativity. For what prevents most people from being really critical of their own writing is the fear of having to throw away *everything*. If I only have one and a half ideas in this draft and I must finish tonight, I'm not as hawkeyed at seeing the problems as I would be if I had eleven interesting ideas and had to pare them down to three or four. Most people start shaping and revising what they have written once they get one pretty good idea. "Yes that's it, now I've figured out what I want to say." That's terrible. You shouldn't start revising till you have more good stuff than you can use. (And it won't take long to get it if you make your early writing into a free brainstorming session.) That way you'll *have* to be critical and throw away genuinely good stuff just to trim your piece down to the right length.

The conflict between the opposing skills important in writing is really just an instance of the larger conflict between opposing temperaments important in most of living. It's a rare person who is, for example, both highly intuitive and highly organized. Most people have to settle for strength in one or the other—or mediocrity in both. If you follow the suggestions in this book for working on writing in two stages—being first creative and then critical— you will get practice in the larger skill of moving back and forth between conflicting temperaments so they enhance each other instead of fighting each other.

By saying that *you* should go through two stages when you write I don't mean to suggest that every scrap of *writing* must go through two stages. For if you get yourself to write freely during the first stage you will warm up *all* your faculties and some passages will come out just right the first time. You will achieve a kind of focus and concentration so that these passages—sometimes even entire pieces—will cook perfectly in your head. They grow out of that magic which some excellent writers can call on at will: simultaneous creativity and critical thinking. As I get more experienced in my own writing, for example, I find that my raw writing (first stage writing) gets to be more of a mess, but that there are more passages scattered in it that need little or no revising. And the quality of these good bits gradually improves.

Creative Writing and the Other Kind

What is usually called "creative writing"—poems, stories, novels— feels very different to most people from what is usually called "nonfiction" or "expository writing"—essays, reports, memos, biography, and so on. Without trying to deny all differences between these two broad categories of writing I will nevertheless minimize the distinction in this book. I want to underline the fact that a good essay or biography requires just as much creativity as a good poem; and that a good poem requires just as much truth as a good essay. (See Chapter 28, "Breathing Experience into Expository Writing," for more about this.)

But because the distinction between these two kinds of writing is so widely felt, people have drifted into emphasizing a difference in the writing process used for each. People are apt to assume that when you write poems and stories it is appropriate to operate intuitively—and in particular to organize and revise in terms of an unconscious center of gravity or an intuitive sense of what feels right. Similarly, people are apt to assume that when you produce nonfiction or expository writing you should be completely conscious of what you are doing—and in particular that you should revise and organize your piece around an idea that is fully conscious, fully verbalized, fully worked out.

But it's no good giving creative writing a monopoly on the benefits of intuition or giving nonfiction writing a monopoly on the benefits of conscious awareness. That's why I stress the intuitive processes in the first half of the writing cycle and conscious awareness or critical discrimination in the second half.

It's true that some of my language in the book may seem to apply more obviously to expository or nonfiction writing than to creative writing: phrases like "figuring out your main idea" or "deciding what you want to say." I have more experience writing expository or nonfiction prose than anything else, and I assume that all my readers will have to do writing of that sort and only some of you will also write poetry and fiction. Yet because I put so much emphasis on tapping intuitions and standing out of imagination's way in my approach to writing, readers and listeners sometimes think I am only talking about creative writing. In certain chapters in fact, especially those in the last section, the language will seem to apply more obviously to creative writing than to expository writing.

The important point is that you should exploit both intuition and conscious control, whichever kind of writing you are doing. Conscious control needn't undermine the intuition you may use in writing poems and stories: you can conclude with critical thinking that the poem you wrote last night hangs together beautifully (perhaps even according to a principle you can't yet articulate) and by all means leave it alone. Similarly intuition needn't blunt your conscious awareness as you revise your essay today, just because last night you wrote seven nonstop pages that came from feelings and perceptions you didn't know you had. You can consciously and critically build your essay today out of insights you could only arrive at by relinquishing critical thinking last night.

Freewriting

2

Freewriting is the easiest way to get words on paper and the best all-around practice in writing that I know. To do a freewriting exercise, simply force yourself to write without stopping for ten minutes. Sometimes you will produce good writing, but that's not the goal. Sometimes you will produce garbage, but that's not the goal either. You may stay on one topic, you may flip repeatedly from one to another: it doesn't matter. Sometimes you will produce a good record of your stream of consciousness, but often you can't keep up. Speed is not the goal, though sometimes the process revs you up. If you can't think of anything to write, write about how that feels or repeat over and over "I have nothing to write" or "Nonsense" or "No." If you get stuck in the middle of a sentence or thought, just repeat the last word or phrase till something comes along. The only point is to keep writing.

Or rather, that's the first point. For there are lots of goals of freewriting, but they are best served if, while you are doing it, you accept this single, simple, mechanical goal of simply not stopping. When you produce an exciting piece of writing, it doesn't mean you did it better than the time before when you wrote one sentence over and over for ten minutes. Both times you freewrote perfectly. The goal of freewriting is in the process, not the product.

Here is an example of freewriting—this one done in a group led by an experienced writer but not a writing teacher:

The second class of no teacher and I'm finding it hard to see how anything will come of it without someone who *knows* something being here. I really mean who knows *some*thing about writing. I know a little about writing, even that speed writing cramps the muscles just inside the thenar curve and I know the grip on my pen is too tight. I know what sounds right when I write right or when someone else writes right. But, is that right just because I hear it right or someone else's right writing listens right. If no one who knows what is right is here to right what we write rightly to our own ears, how will we know who's right really?

The sound of "-ite" and "-ight" and "r's" rolling around is pleasant or sibilant I believe is the right word to describe writing by rule rightly for right writers to hear or rule on. Does sibilant have to have "s's" hissing or are "r's" running rapidly reasonably rationale for sibilance without "s's". My cramp is gaining on me even though I remember my father writing my mother all "f's" in a letter from Frankfurt in the days when "f's" had other meaning than what my youngest son at eight called the "King of Swears."

"Dear Effie," he wrote from Frankfurt. "Four foolish fellows followed me from fearful . . ." I can't go on with it. To follow my original thought, "It doesn't sound right." And with the cramp now slowing me down and running off the paper, I'm hoping our non-leader tells us to stop. She did.

RUSSELL HOXSIE, M.D.

The Benefits of Freewriting

Freewriting makes writing easier by helping you with the root psychological or existential difficulty in writing: finding words in your head and putting them down on a blank piece of paper. So much writing time and energy is spent *not* writing: wondering, worrying, crossing out, having second, third, and fourth thoughts. And it's easy to get stopped even in the middle of a piece. (This is why Hemingway made a rule for himself never to end one sheet and start a new one except in the middle of a sentence.) Frequent freewriting exercises help you learn simply to *get on with it* and not be held back by worries about whether these words are good words or the right words.

Thus, freewriting is the best way to learn—in practice, not just in theory—to separate the producing process from the revising process. Freewriting exercises are push-ups in withholding judgment as you produce so that afterwards you can judge better.

Freewriting for ten minutes is a good way to warm up when you sit down to write something. You won't waste so much time getting started when you turn to your real writing task and you won't have to struggle so hard to find words. Writing almost always goes better when you are already started: now you'll be able to start off already started.

Freewriting helps you learn to write when you don't feel like writing. It is practice in setting deadlines for yourself, taking charge of yourself, and learning gradually how to get that special energy that sometimes comes when you work fast under pressure.

Freewriting teaches you to write without thinking about writing. We can usually speak without thinking about speech—without thinking about how to form words in the mouth and pronounce them and the rules of syntax we unconsciously obey—and as a result we can give undivided attention to what we say. Not so writing. Or at least most people are considerably distracted from their meaning by considerations of spelling, grammar, rules, errors. Most people experience an awkward and sometimes paralyzing *translating* process in writing: "Let's see, how shall I say this." Freewriting helps you learn to *just say* it. Regular freewriting helps make the writing process *transparent*.

Freewriting is a useful outlet. We have lots in our heads that makes it hard to think straight and write clearly: we are mad at someone, sad about something, depressed about everything. Perhaps even inconveniently happy. "How can I think about this report when I'm so in love?" Freewriting is a quick outlet for these feelings so they don't get so much in your way when you are trying to write about something else. Sometimes your mind is marvelously clear after ten minutes of telling someone on paper everything you need to tell him. (In fact, if your feelings often keep you from functioning well in other areas of your life frequent freewriting can help: not only by providing a good arena for those feelings, but also by helping you understand them better and see them in perspective by seeing them on paper.)

Freewriting helps you to think of topics to write about. Just keep writing, follow threads where they lead and you will get to ideas, experiences, feelings, or people that are just asking to be written about.

Finally, and perhaps most important, freewriting improves your writing. It doesn't always produce powerful writing itself, but it leads to powerful writing. The process by which it does so is a mysterious underground one. When people talk about the Zen of this or that I think they are referring to the peculiar increase in power and insight that comes from focusing your energy while at the same time putting aside your conscious controlling self. Freewriting gives practice in this special mode of focusing-but-not-trying; it helps you stand out of the way and let words be chosen by the sequence of the words themselves or the thought, not by the conscious self. In this way freewriting gradually puts a deeper resonance or voice into your writing.

But freewriting also brings a surface coherence to your writing and it does so immediately. You cannot write *really* incoherently if you write quickly. You may violate the rules of correctness, you may make mistakes in reasoning, you may write foolishness, you may change directions before you have said anything significant. That is, you may produce something like "Me and her we went down and saw the folks but wait that reminds me of the thing I was thinking about yester oh dam what am I really trying to say." But you won't produce syntactic chaos: language that is so jumbled that when you read it over you are frightened there is something the matter with you.

However, you wouldn't be frightened if you looked more closely at how you actually produced that verbal soup. If you had movies of yourself you would see yourself starting four or five times and throwing each start away and thereby getting more and more jumbled in your mind; finally starting; stopping part way through the sentence to wonder if you are on the wrong track and thereby losing your syntactic thread. You would see yourself start writing again on a slightly different piece of syntax from the one you started with, then notice something really wrong and fix it and lose the thread again; so when you finally conclude your sentence, you are actually writing the conclusion of a different sentence from the ones you had been writing. Thus, the resulting sentence—whether incorrect or just impossibly awkward—is really fragments of three different syntactic impulses or sentences-in-the-head tied together with baling wire. When you write quickly, however, as in freewriting, your syntactic units hang together. Even if you change your mind in mid-sentence, as above, you produce a clear break. You don't try to plaster over two or three syntactic units as one, as you so often do in painstaking writing. Freewriting produces syntactic coherence and verbal energy which gradually transfer to your more careful writing.

What To Do with Freewriting

If you can view freewriting as an exercise to help you to grow in the long run rather than give you good writing in the short run, then you can use some of the good pieces that freewriting some-times produces. But if you slip into freewriting for the sake of producing good pieces of writing, then you put a kind of short-run utilitarian pressure on the process and hinder yourself from getting all the other benefits.

I suspect there is some added benefit if you read freewriting over after you have written it (better yet out loud) and if you let someone else read it. I think it may help you integrate better into your conscious controlling mind the energies that are available to your innards. But don't get criticism or comment of any sort.

If reading over your freewriting or giving it to someone else gets in the way of future freewriting, as it may well do, then it's better just to throw it away or stash it somewhere unread. Reading it over may make you too self-conscious or make you feel "YEEEcchh, what garbage this is," or "Oh, dear, there must be something the matter with me to be so obsessed." This may start you censoring yourself as you engage in more freewriting. Don't read over your freewriting unless you can do so in a spirit of benign self-welcom-ing. I used to be fascinated with my freewritings and save them and read them periodically. Now I just throw them away.

A Hunch about Resistance

I remember agonizing over a particular section of something I hoped I would be able to publish. It seemed forever that I strug-gled and still couldn't get my thought right. I was knotted and in-coherent. Finally I broke through into fluency. What a relief. For two days I hadn't been able to say what I wanted; then I could say it. But when I read the whole thing over a day or two later I no-ticed that the passage was particularly dead. It was limp, it was like a firehose after someone turns off the water.

This illustrates a kind of a myth I have come to believe without quite knowing how to integrate it into the rest of my beliefs about writing. To write is to overcome a certain resistance: you are trying to wrestle a steer to the ground, to wrestle a snake into a bottle, to overcome a demon that sits in your head. To succeed in writing or making sense is to overpower that steer, that snake, that demon.

But if, in your struggles to write, you actually break its back, you are in trouble. Yes, now you have power over it, you can say what you need to say, but in transforming that resistant force into a limp noodle, somehow you turn your words into limp noodles, too. Somehow the force that is fighting you is also the force that gives life to your words. You must overpower that steer or snake or demon. But not kill it.

This myth explains why some people who write fluently and perhaps even clearly—they say just what they mean in adequate, errorless words—are really hopelessly boring to read. There is no resistance in their words; you cannot feel any force-being-over-come, any orneriness. No surprises. The language is too abjectly obedient. When writing is really good, on the other hand, the words themselves lend some of their own energy to the writer. The writer is controlling words which he can't turn his back on without danger of being scratched or bitten.

This explains why it is sometimes easier for a blocked and inco-herent writer to break into powerful language than for someone who is fluent and verbal and can always write just what he wants. Picture the two of them: one has uneven, scrunched handwriting with pointy angles, the other has round, soft, even handwriting. When I make these two people freewrite, the incoherent scrunched one is often catapulted immediately into vivid, forceful language. The soft handwriting, on the other hand, just continues to yield what it has always yielded: language that is clear and per-fectly obedient to the intentions of the writer, but lifeless. It will take this obedient writer much longer to get power. It will take the scrunched writer longer to get control.

The reason the scrunched writer is so incoherent and hates writ-ing is that he is ruled by the steer, the snake, the demon. He is unable to take charge as he writes and make all those tiny deci-sions you must make second by second as you write. When I force him to do a freewriting exercise—or he forces himself to do one—he finally gets words on the page but of course he is still not completely in charge. He is not instantly transformed into someone who can make all the micro-decisions needed for writing. He gets words down on the page, but a lot of the decisions are still being made by the words themselves. Thus he has frequent bursts of power in his writing but little control.

The rounded fluent writer on the other hand is so good at making the quick decisions involved in writing—at steering, at being in charge—that even though he writes fast without stopping, his writing still lacks the vitality that comes from exploiting the resistant force.

The goal of freewriting, then, is not absolutely limpid fluency. If you are a blocked writer, freewriting will help you overcome resistance and move you gradually in the direction of more fluency and control (though your path will probably involve lots of writing where you feel totally out of control). But if you are a very controlled writer who can write anything you want, but without power—if you have killed the demon—freewriting will gradually bring it back to life. Forcing yourself to write regularly without stopping for ten minutes will put more *resistance* back into your language. The clay will fight you a bit in your hands as you try to work it into a bowl, but that bowl will end up more alive and powerful.

Sharing

Dialogue in my head

"Give it."
"No."
"You have to give it if you want to write."
"I don't want to give it.
I'll loan it
or disguise it
or sell it even.
I'll give it to certain people
if they promise to like it
—or if they promise to suffer.
But I won't just give it away."

Dialogue with a student

ME: That's good writing. You really looked it in the eye—
what you were writing about.

STUDENT: I didn't used to respect writers. I thought they were
just people who wrote things down easily. I didn't realize that writing took courage, took so much out of you.
I don't like to give.

The essential human act at the heart of writing is the act of *giving*.
There's something implacable and irreducible about it: handing
something to someone because you want her to have it; not asking
for anything in return; and if it is a gift of yourself—as writing
always is—risking that she won't like it or even accept it. Yet
though giving can sound rare and special if you rhapsodize about
it, it is of course just a natural and spontaneous human impulse.

This central act of giving is curiously neglected in most writing instruction. Otherwise people would have shared their writing— just given it to another human being for the sake of mutual plea- sure—as often as they gave it to a teacher for evaluation and ad- vice. For most people, however, the experience of just sharing what they have written is rare.

I'm embarrassed that it took me so long not just to understand the importance of sharing, but even to see it—to realize that there was something else useful you could do with a piece of writing be- sides getting feedback on it, namely just to give it: for your plea- sure in giving and for their pleasure in reading. The reason it took me so long, I suspect, is that I am primarily an English teacher, and the reason I am beginning to notice sharing is that I am beginning to be a writer. Writers are more apt to understand writ- ing as giving: "Here. Take it. Enjoy it. Thank me. (Pay me, if pos- sible.) But I'm not interested right now in evaluation or criticism." English teachers, on the other hand, usually can't think of any- thing to do with a set of words except to formulate criticism of one sort or another—high criticism for works of great literature, low criticism for works of student writing. I suspect this is why English teachers so seldom write.

Before I could see the importance of just giving writing, I had to satisfy two earlier itches: the itch for more *safety* in writing; that is, to find more ways to write without giving it to any reader at all; and the itch for more *empiricism* in writing; that is, to find more ways to learn what really happens in real readers, not just get eval- uation and advice from only one authority. With these itches satis- fied, I could finally feel that deeper itch just to share.

Many pieces of weak writing suffer more from the writer's not having really consented, deep down, to *give* her meaning than from whatever lack of skill she may have. That same person can write with considerable power and skill when she doesn't hold back at all, when she isn't ambivalent about yielding, handing it over for free. When I think back over much of my writing— especially in college and graduate school—I can understand what was going on much more clearly now in terms of giving. At the time I simply experienced myself struggling to write well—and mostly not succeeding. Teachers could see that I tried hard—"ty- ing yourself in knots" was how one teacher put it—and they could see that I had interesting insights I was trying to communicate, but

neither they nor I could figure out why it always came out so unclear. I remember one teacher who said, "Why do you have to complicate it? Why not write it down the way you first thought of it?" But it didn't seem to me that I was complicating things at all. Now, however, I can see—indeed I can go back and almost feel it—that my writing really was the product of a kind of complexifying process: a tug of war between my aboveboard eagerness to be a good student and my belowboard reluctance to *put out*—to give it to them. This ambivalence made a terrible wringer for my poor words and thoughts to go through before they got on paper. My writing didn't begin to escape from this maze till I finally tried to write a couple of articles for publication. I was no longer reluctant to give to my audience; in fact, I was driven by a considerable desire to make them take it whether they wanted to or not.

There are many ways to share. But unless you have an arena designated for it (or can easily publish what you write, for sharing is really a way to publish), sharing takes courage and assertiveness. It means going up to someone and saying, "Can I read you something I've written? I don't want feedback. I just want you to hear it." Sometimes that's not easy, no matter how good the friendship is. Perhaps you forgot to include it in the marriage vows: "To love, honor, and faithfully listen to all writing." Sharing is easiest if you can meet regularly with a group of three or more others for the purpose. It's a kind of celebration. You will find it a great relief, when you get used to it, not to worry about their reactions or think about feedback. Of course, you will get a few stray spontaneous reactions, as at a poetry reading or performance: a chuckle at one passage, hushed silence at another, yawns when your writing is opaque for too long. But the reactions aren't the point. The point is that you are heard. It opens up a door for you and somehow helps you think of more things to write.

Sharing also means sending off copies to friends who live far away, but there's a special power that comes from meeting face to face and reading out loud what you have written. You may find the reading out loud frightening, but it is crucial. For there is a deep and essential relationship between writing and the speaking voice. It's complex and mysterious, but one thing is clear: to write with clarity and power requires an essential act of taking full responsibility for your words—not hedging, holding back, being ambivalent. Reading your words out loud is a vivid outward act that

amplifies your sensation of responsibility for your words. That's why oaths and promises must be spoken out loud to work best. "Repeat after me. . . ." When you only make marks silently on paper and don't make noises with your throat, it is possible to withhold some piece of your self, to keep your fingers crossed behind your back.

Reading your words out loud is scary, and many people invariably mumble or read too softly or too fast. We shrink from such blatant showing of our wares. But that is just what helps most. Therefore when you share your writing, you need to give your listeners permission to interrupt and tell you if they cannot comfortably hear and understand your words—permission to make you *give* your words. Reading your words out loud is push-ups for the specific muscle used in taking responsibility for your words.

Here are some additional benefits of sharing. It's an easy way to learn about writing. When you hear someone read a piece every week or two, someone no better than you, and you see her come up with a passage that is terrific—but she's using the same old ingredients that she and you have been struggling with week after week—sometimes you learn more about how to improve your writing than you learn from clear explanations of what is wrong with it or good advice about how to fix it, or inspiring lectures on the seven essentials of good writing. And you don't have to talk about it. You are just listening and learning by ear. Matters of tone and voice are particularly hard to talk about or teach. They are best learned through hearing what you like and imitating it, and hearing what you don't like and getting rid of it.

Sometimes the sense of feasibility you get from sharing does more good than anything else. For what's been holding you back most is a deep sense that you couldn't possibly write something that actually *affected* someone. But then along comes that really good passage written by someone like you. It's not unbelievably good, indeed what's special is its believability: it's mixed in with other passages that are quite ordinary; it even has some obvious weaknesses. But it is so good that it makes you positively hungry to hear more, makes you wish you had written it, and then, finally, makes you realize that you *could* have written it. I love the bluntness with which I once heard this feeling privately expressed: "If that *nerd* can write something like that, so can I!"

Finally, sharing is perfect practice for giving and getting feedback. One of the main reasons readers find it difficult to give good feedback is that they worry too much about what feedback to give. They can't really hear or concentrate on the words. But sharing gives readers painless practice in just listening and enjoying what they hear and learning gradually to be confident of their reactions.

One of the main reasons writers find it difficult to benefit from feedback is that they are so nervous about giving to readers that they can't really hear or accept the feedback they get. But sharing helps them to learn to give their writing—scarey enough in itself—without the added burden of dealing with feedback. (I suspect that the fear you experience in reading your words out loud hinders your writing even when you are writing alone in a room and not feeling any fear.)

But if I talk too solemnly about fear, learning, and taking responsibility for your words, I will overshadow the main thing about sharing: that it is essentially social and enjoyable. It functions as a relief from the solitariness and effort of writing. People get to know each other and their ways of writing.

"Oh dear," you may say, "perhaps listeners in a sharing group will *like* something that's not good writing." If that worries you, you better watch out because it does happen. But I think about my two-year-old son Benjy who says "seep" for *sleep* and "pill" for *spill* and other such forms that make him unintelligible to most listeners. We understand him because we hear him constantly and therefore we hear *through* the externals of his language to the meanings and intentions that lie behind. Surely it is a help and not a hindrance in his learning to communicate better that he has one audience, anyway, where his words work.

For improving your writing you need at least some readers to be allies, persons who wholly *cooperate* in the communicative transaction. When you pass them the potatoes they don't just sit there and look at you holding the bowl with a look that says, "If I had wanted the potatoes I would have *asked* you for them." They take the bowl and thank you for it.

This chapter and the previous one on freewriting are two of this book's shorter chapters. They are short because the procedures they describe are so simple. But I believe you will improve your writing more through freewriting and sharing than through any other activities described in this book.

Dialogue in My Head

"Do you want your reader to have to struggle to figure out what you are saying?"

"Damn right! I had to struggle to figure it out. Why shouldn't he? Besides, if it's too easy for him, he won't appreciate it."

4

The Direct Writing Process for Getting Words on Paper

The direct writing process is most useful if you don't have much time or if you have plenty to say about your topic. It's a kind of let's-get-this-thing-over-with writing process. I think of it for tasks like memos, reports, somewhat difficult letters, or essays where I don't want to engage in much new thinking. It's also a good approach if you are inexperienced or nervous about writing because it is simple and doesn't make as much of a mess as the other ways of getting words on paper I describe in Section II.

Unfortunately, its most common use will be for those situations that aren't supposed to happen but do: when you have to write something you *don't* yet understand, but you also don't have much time. The direct writing process may not always lead to a satisfactory piece of writing when you are in this fix, but it's the best approach I know.

The process is very simple. Just divide your available time in half. The first half is for fast writing without worrying about organization, language, correctness, or precision. The second half is for revising.

Start off by thinking carefully about the audience (if there is one) and the purpose for this piece of writing. Doing so may help you figure out exactly what you need to say. But if it doesn't, then let yourself put them out of mind. You may find that you get the most benefit from ignoring your audience and purpose at this early stage of the writing process. (See Section IV for more about dealing with your audience.)

In any event spend the first half of your time making yourself write down everything you can think of that might belong or pertain to your writing task: incidents that come to mind for your story, images for your poem, ideas and facts for your essay or report. Write fast. Don't waste any time or energy on how to organize it, what to start with, paragraphing, wording, spelling, grammar, or any other matters of presentation. Just get things down helter-skelter. If you can't find the right word just leave a blank. If you can't say it the way you want to say it, say it the wrong way. (If it makes you feel better, put a wavy line under those wrong bits to remind you to fix them.)*

I'm not saying you must never pause in this writing. No need to make this a frantic process. Sometimes it is very fruitful to pause and return in your mind to some productive feeling or idea that you've lost. But don't stop to worry or criticize or correct what you've already written.

While doing this helter-skelter writing, don't allow too much digression. Follow your pencil where it leads, but when you suddenly realize, "Hey, this has nothing to do with what I want to write about," just stop, drop the whole thing, skip a line or two, and get yourself back onto some aspect of the topic or theme.

Similarly, don't allow too much repetition. As you write quickly, you may sometimes find yourself coming back to something you've already treated. Perhaps you are saying it better or in a better context the second or third time. But once you realize you've done it before, stop and go on to something else.

When you are trying to put down everything quickly, it often happens that a new or tangentially related thought comes to mind while you are just in the middle of some train of thought. Sometimes two or three new thoughts crowd in on you. This can be confusing: you don't want to interrupt what you are on, but you fear you'll forget the intruding thoughts if you don't write them down. I've found it helpful to note them without spending much time on them. I stop right at the moment they arrive—wherever I am in my writing—and jot down a couple of words or phrases to remind me of them, and then I continue on with what I am writing. Some-

---

* An excerpt from a letter giving me feedback on an earlier draft: "I tried the direct writing process. Though it sounds simple enough, I . . . see now that in the past I've often interrupted the flow of writing by spending disproportionate time on spelling, punctuation, etc. I can spend hours on an opening paragraph stroking the words to death; then, if there's a deadline, have to rush through the remainder." (Joanne Turpin, 7/24/78.)

times I jot the reminder on a separate piece of paper. When I write at the typewriter I often just put the reminder in caps inside double parentheses ((LIKE THIS)) in the middle of my sentence. Or I simply start a new line

LIKE THIS

and then start another new line to continue my old train of thought. But sometimes the intruding idea seems so important or fragile that I really want to go to work on it right away so I don't lose it. If so, I drop what I'm engaged in and start working on the new item. I know I can later recapture the original thought because I've already written part of it. The important point here is that what you produce during this first half of the writing cycle can be very fragmented and incoherent without any damage at all.

There is a small detail about the physical process of writing down words that I have found important. Gradually I have learned not to stop and cross out something I've just written when I change my mind. I just leave it there and write my new word or phrase on a new line. So my page is likely to have lots of passages that look like

Many of my pages

Still I don't mean that you should stop and rewrite every passage till you are happy with it.

This kind of appearance.

What is involved here is developing an increased tolerance for letting mistakes show. If you find yourself crumpling up your sheet of paper and throwing it away and starting with a new one every time you change your mind, you are really saying, "I must destroy all evidence of mistakes." Not quite so extreme is the person who scribbles over every mistake so avidly that not even the tail of the "y" is visible. Stopping to cross out mistakes doesn't just waste psychic energy, it distracts you from full concentration on what you are trying to say.

What's more, I've found that leaving mistakes uncrossed out somehow makes it easier for me to revise. When I cross out all my mistakes I end up with *a draft*. And a draft is hard to revise because it is a complete whole. But when I leave my first choices there littering my page along with some second and third choices, I don't have a draft, I just have a succession of ingredients. Often it is easier to whip that succession of ingredients into something usuable than, as it were, to *undo* that completed draft and turn it

into a better draft. It turns out I can just trundle through that pile of ingredients, slash out some words and sections, rearrange some bits, and end up with something quite usable. And quite often I discover in retrospect that my original "mistaken phrase" is really better than what I replaced it with: more lively or closer to what I end up saying.

• • •

If you only have half an hour to write a memo, you have now forced yourself in fifteen minutes to cram down every hunch, insight, and train of thought that you think might belong in it. If you have only this evening to write a substantial report or paper, it is now 10:30 P.M., you have used up two or two and a half hours putting down as much as you can, and you only have two more hours to give to this thing. You must stop your raw writing now, even if you feel frustrated at not having written enough or figured out yet exactly what you mean to say. If you started out with no real understanding of your topic, you certainly won't feel satisfied with what is probably a complete mess at this point. You'll just have to accept the fact that of course you will do a poor job compared to what you could have done if you'd started yesterday. But what's more to the point now is to recognize that you'll do an even crummier job if you steal any of your revising time for more raw writing. Besides, you will have an opportunity during the revising process to figure out what you want to say—what all these ingredients add up to—and to add a few missing pieces. It's important to note that when I talk about revising in this book I mean something much more substantial than just tidying up your sentences.

So if your total time is half gone, stop now no matter how frustrated you are and change to the revising process. That means changing gears into an entirely different consciousness. You must transform yourself from a fast-and-loose-thinking person who is open to every whim and feeling into a ruthless, toughminded, rigorously logical editor. Since you are working under time pressure, you will probably use quick revising or cut-and-paste revising. (See the next chapter and Chapter 14.)

• • •

Direct writing and quick revising are probably good processes to start with if you have an especially hard time writing. They help you prove to yourself that you *can* get things written quickly and acceptably. The results may not be the very best you can do, but they work, they get you by. Once you've proved you can get the job done you will be more willing to use other processes for getting words down on paper and for revising—processes that make greater demands on your time and energy and emotions. And if writing is usually a great struggle, you have probably been thrown off balance many times by getting into too much chaos. The direct writing process is a way to allow a limited amount of chaos to occur in a very controlled fashion.

It's easiest to explain the direct writing process in terms of pragmatic writing: you are in a hurry, you know most of what you want to say, you aren't trying for much creativity or brilliance. But I also want to stress that the direct writing process can work well for very important pieces of writing and ones where you haven't yet worked out your thinking at all. But one condition is crucial: you must be confident that you'll have no trouble finding lots to say once you start writing. (Otherwise, use the open-ended or loop writing processes described in Section II.)

As I wrote many parts of this book, for example, I didn't have my thinking clear or worked out by any means, I couldn't have made an outline at gunpoint, and I cared deeply about the results. But I knew that there was lots of *stuff* there swirling around in my head ready to go down on paper. I used the direct process. I just wrote down everything that came to mind and went on to revise.

But if you want to use the direct writing process for important pieces of writing, you need plenty of time. You probably won't be able to get them the way you want them with just quick revising. You'll need thorough revising or revising with feedback (see Section III). For important writing I invariably spend more time revising than I do getting my thoughts down on paper the first time.

Main Steps in the Direct Writing Process

• If you have a deadline, divide your total available time: half for raw writing, half for revising.

• Bring to mind your audience and purpose in writing but then go on to ignore them if that helps your raw writing.

• Write down as quickly as you can everything you can think of that pertains to your topic or theme.

• Don't let yourself repeat or digress or get lost, but don't worry about the order of what you write, the wording, or about crossing out what you decide is wrong.

• Make sure you stop when your time is half gone and change to revising, even if you are not done.

• The direct writing process is most helpful when you don't have difficulty coming up with material or when you are working under a tight deadline.

Quick Revising

5

The point of quick revising is to turn out a clean, clear, professional final draft without taking as much time as you would need for major rethinking and reorganizing. It is a clean-and-polish operation, not a growing-and-transforming one. You specifically refrain from meddling with any deeper problems of organization or reconceptualization.

The best time to use quick revising is when the results don't matter too much. Perhaps you are not preparing a final, finished product but rather a draft for friends. It has to be clear, easy to read—if possible even a pleasure to read. But it needn't be your best work or your final thinking. Perhaps it's a draft for discussion or perhaps just a chance for people to learn your thinking about some matter as though you were writing a letter to them. Or perhaps you are just writing for yourself but you want to clean up your draft so that it will be easier and more productive to read when you come back to it.

But there is another situation when you can use quick revising and unfortunately it is the one when you are most likely to use it: an occasion that is *very* important when the writing *has* to work for an important audience, but you lack time. You can't afford to resee, re-think, and re-write completely your raw writing in the amount of time you have left. Maybe it was your fault and now you are kicking yourself; maybe it was unavoidable. But either way you are stuck. It is 10:30 P.M. now and you have only ten pages of helter-skelter thinking on paper, you need an excellent, polished, full report by tomorrow morning, and you care very much how the reader reacts to it. In such situations you have to contend with anxiety as well as lack of time. You need the discipline of the quick revising process. I will describe it here as though you are preparing a substantial piece of writing for tomorrow morning for an important audience because I want to stress the experience of battle conditions with live ammunition. (If it is a small job such as writing that memo in thirty minutes, you probably won't go through all the separate steps I describe below. You'll probably just stand up and stretch now after your fifteen minutes of raw writing, and use your remaining time to look with fresh eyes through what you've written, figure out what you really want to say, and just write out your final draft—perhaps using substantial portions of your raw writing unchanged.)

Quick revising is simple and minimal. A lot depends on having the right spirit: businesslike and detached. A certain ruthlessness is best of all. Not desperate-ruthless, "Oh God, this is *awful*, I've *got* to change *everything*," but breezy-ruthless, "Yes, this certainly does have some problems. I wish I could start over and get the whole thing right, but not this time. I guess I'll just have to put the best face on things." If you are too worried about what you wrote or too involved with it, you'll have to work overtime to get the right spirit. You need to stand outside yourself and be someone else.

First, if this piece is for an audience, think about who that audience is and what your purpose is in writing to it. You had the luxury of putting aside all thoughts of audience and purpose during the producing stage (if that helped you think and write better), but now you must keep them in mind as you make critical decisions in revising. Try to see your audience before you as you revise. It's no good ending up with a piece of writing that's good-in-general—whatever that means. You need something that is good for your purpose with your audience. (See Section IV, in particular Chapter 18, for more about audience in this regard.)

Next, read through all your raw writing and find the good pieces. When I do it, I just mark them with a line in the margin. Don't worry about the criteria for choosing them. It's fine to be intuitive. If the sentence or passage feels good for this purpose or seems important for this audience, mark it.

Next, figure out your single main point and arrange your best bits in the best order. It's easiest if you can figure out your main point first. That gives you leverage for figuring and what order to put things in. But sometimes your main point refuses to reveal itself—the one thing you are really trying to *say* here, the point that sums up everything else. All your writing may be circling around or leading up to a main idea that you can't quite figure out yet. In such a dilemma, move on to the job of working out the best order for your good passages. That ordering process—that search for sequence and priorities—will often flush your main point out of hiding.

You can just put numbers in the margin next to the good bits to indicate the right order if your piece is short and comfortable for you. But if it is long or difficult you need to make an outline before you can really work out the best order. It helps most to make an outline consist of complete assertions with verbs—*thoughts*, not just *areas*.

And of course as you work out this order or outline you will think of things you left out—ideas or issues that belong in your final draft that weren't in your raw writing. You can now indicate each of them with a sentence.

If after all this—after getting, as it were, *all* your points and getting them in the right order—you still lack the most important idea or assertion that ties them all together into a unity; if you have connected all this stuff but you cannot find the single thought that pulls it all together, and of course this sometimes happens, you simply have to move on. You have a deadline. There is a good chance that your main idea or center of gravity will emerge later, and even if it doesn't you have other options.

The next step is to write out a clean-but-not-quite-final draft of the whole piece—excluding the very beginning. That is, don't write your first paragraph or section now unless it comes to you easily. Wait till you have a draft of the main body before deciding how to lead up to it—or whether it *needs* leading up to. How can you clearly or comfortably introduce something before you know precisely what it is you are introducing? So just begin this draft with your first definite point. Out of the blue. Start even with your second or third point if the first one raises confusing clouds of "how-do-I-get-started."

Perhaps you can use the good passages almost as they are—copy them or use scissors—and only write transitional elements to get you from one to another. Or perhaps you need to write out most of it fresh. But you can go fast because you have all your points in mind and in order, and probably you have a clearly stated, single main idea holding it all together.

If you don't yet know your single main point, there is a very good chance that it will come to you as you are writing this draft. The process of writing the real thing to the real audience will often drive you to say, "What I'm really trying to make clear to you is . . ." and *there* is your main point. This is especially likely to happen toward the end of your piece as you are trying to sum things up or say why all this is important or makes sense. When your main point emerges late in this way, you may have to go back and fiddle a bit with your structure. It is very common that the last paragraph you write, when you finally say exactly what you mean in the fewest words, is just what you need (with perhaps a minor adjustment) for your first paragraph.

On rare occasions you still won't be able to find your main point. You know this is a coherent train of thought, and you know you are saying something, but you cannot sum it up in one sentence. You are stuck and you now have to make some choices. You can open or close your piece with a clear admission that you haven't focused it yet. This is usually the most helpful strategy when you are writing for yourself. (Sometimes, in fact, stating your dilemma—as dilemma—as accurately as you can, serves to produce the solution.) Or you can just present your train of thought without any statement at all of a single main idea. Or you can try to trick the reader into a feeling of unity with a vague, waffling pseudo-summary. But this is dangerous. If a reader sees you waffling he is liable to be mad or contemptuous, and even if he is not conscious of what you are doing he is liable to be irritated. If it is important—for this audience and situation—to end up with a piece of writing that is genuinely unified and focused, there is nothing for it but radical surgery. Settle for the best idea you *can* find in your writing and make that your main point. Organize what goes with it and throw away everything else. This usually hurts because it means throwing away some of your best bits.

So now you have a draft and a clear statement of your main idea. Finally you can write what you need for an introductory paragraph or section. Almost certainly you need something that gives the reader a clear sense of your main point—where you are going. If you have been writing under the pressure of a tight deadline your final draft will probably have some problems, and so this is no time for tricky strategies or leaving the reader in the dark. Subtlety is for when you can get everything just right.

This is also the time to make sure you have a satisfactory conclusion: a final passage that sums up everything you have said with the precision and complexity that is only possible now that the reader has read and understood all the details. For example you have to begin an essay for most readers with a general statement that is easy to understand, such as "I want to explain how atomic bombs work," but at the end you can sum up your point more quickly and precisely: "In short, $E = mc^2$."

Now you have a draft of the whole thing that probably comes close to what you'll end up with. The next step is to change from writer-consciousness to reader-consciousness. For in writing that draft you were, obviously enough, functioning as a writer: a person trying to put down on paper what you had finally gotten clear in your own mind. Now you should read through this draft *as a reader*. The best way to do this is to read your draft *out loud:* you won't have to search for places that are unclear or awkward or lacking in life, you will *hear* them. If you are in an office or a library or some other place unsuitable for declaiming, you can get almost as much benefit by silently mouthing or whispering your draft as though you were speaking. If you put your fingers in your ears at the same time, you will actually hear your words good and loud. It is the *hearing* of your own words that serves to get you out of the writer-consciousness and into the audience-consciousness.

Finally, get rid of mistakes in grammar and usage. (For more about that process, see Chapter 15.)

Certain people on certain occasions can afford to collapse some of these steps together and type out their final, clean copy after they have settled on their main idea and numbered or outlined their best bits. But this means paying attention to spelling, grammar, and usage while you are engaged in trying to write clear language: focusing simultaneously on the pane of glass and on the scene beyond it. It's not a wise or efficient thing to do unless you are an exceptionally fluent and polished writer. Most people—and that includes myself—save time by waiting to the very end before worrying about mistakes in grammar and usage.

Even if you are writing informally for friends you must take care to get rid of these mistakes. Your friends may say, "Oh, who cares about trivial details of correctness," but in fact most people are prejudiced, even if unconsciously, against writing flawed in this way. They are more apt to patronize your writing or take it less seriously or hold back from experiencing what you are saying if there are mistakes in mechanics.

• • •

In thinking about the whole process of quick revising, you should realize that the essential act is *cutting*. Learn to leave out everything that isn't already good or easily made good. Learn the pleasures of the knife. Learn to retreat, to cut your losses, to be chicken. Learn to say, "Yes, I *care* more about this passage than about any other, I'm involved in it, but for that very reason, I can't make it work right. Out it goes!" Of course you don't need to be so ruthless about cutting if you are writing something to share informally among friends or to save for yourself. You can retain sections that feel important but don't quite work or don't quite fit. You can let your piece be an interesting muddle organizationally or conceptually—*so long as it's not muddled in wording or sentences.* Friends are willing to ponder your not-quite-digested thinking so long as your sentences and paragraphs are clear and easy to understand.

When you have *lots* of time for revising you tend to finish with something longer than you had expected. The thing cooks and grows on its own and you have time to integrate that growth. But quick revising usually produces something shorter than you had expected. The reader should probably finish a bit startled: "Done already? This seems a bit skimpy. Still, everything here is well done. Actually, it's not too bad." Better to give your reader mild disappointment at a certain tight skimpiness than to bog him down in a mess so that he stops paying attention or even stops reading.

In the last analysis, the main thing for quick revising is to get into the right spirit. Be your brisk, kindly, British aunt who is also a nurse: "Yes. Not to worry. I know it's a mess. But we'll clean it up and make it presentable in no time. It won't be a work of art, ducks, but it'll do just fine."

Main Steps in Quick Revising

• Try to step outside yourself and get into a spirit of pragmatic detachment. Emphasize cutting.

• Keep your audience and purpose clearly in mind.

• Mark the good passages.

• Figure out the main point.

• Put the good passages in order. Perhaps make an outline.

• Add pieces that are missing.

• Write out a draft—excluding the beginning.

• Write the beginning; make sure you have a suitable conclusion.

• Tighten and clarify by cutting. Reading your draft outloud will help you experience it from a reader's point of view.

• Get rid of mistakes in grammar and usage.

The Dangerous Method:
Trying To Write It Right
the First Time

There are obvious attractions to a writing process where you avoid the complications of the last two chapters and try to get your piece right the first time. You don't have to make such a mess with raw writing, you don't have to write in the dark without knowing where you are going, you don't have to engage in extensive revising—just a little tidying up, perhaps, at the end. No wonder most people instinctively try to write this way. Why keep on writing when you know something is wrong and will have to be changed? It feels obvious that you should stop and cross it out now and not go on to the next bit till you get this bit right.

If you want to use this one-step writing process, the main thing you must learn to do is what writers have traditionally been advised to do: get your meaning clear in your head *before* you start writing. (In effect you are stuck with two steps again: figure out your meaning, then write.)

There are lots of methods people use for figuring out their meaning before they write. Making an outline is probably the most common and versatile method. An outline, by its nature, almost forces you to figure out what you really mean. And because of its compressed visual form, it permits you to see your whole train of thought or narrative in one glance and thereby detect problems you miss when you go through your writing more slowly. (Remember that you are always moving more slowly through your writing than your reader will move: if you aren't actually writing you are constantly pausing to change or fix things.)

Outlining is most effective when you already know many of the ideas or incidents or images you want to use in your writing and you are trying to clarify and organize them. If you don't yet know much of what you want to say you may find outlining of no use at all. Who hasn't had the dismal experience (as you to follow the teacher's orders ansd start with an outline) of sitting there trying to transform one uninteresting thought into an architecture of Roman numerals, capital letters, arabic numerals, and small letters.

The most exotic way of working things out in your head is exemplified by A. E. Housman's practice. He would (according to his account, anyway) put in mind his general idea or ingredients for a poem, then have a heavy ale for lunch, and then take a long sleepy walk. By the end of the walk his highly polished poem would be completely worked out in his head. Evidently he didn't have to think actively or manipulate his ingredients, he could just let the poem steam itself done in his warm beery consciousness. I have heard of a number of mathematicians and designers who employ a similar method: they put in mind all the elements they are struggling with and then take a nap, and when they wake up they often have the answer or the approach they need.

The point is that a deeper level of thinking can go on when you relinquish your conscious grip on your material. A kind of letting go is necessary for this deep cooking. Having a beer, taking a walk or a bus ride, taking a nap or a shower—these all serve some people as ways of letting go.

A more common form of getting your meaning clear before writing is simply to put off writing till you have had a chance to mull and ponder and chew on your topic for at least a few days—longer if possible. Many competent experienced writers never actually *start* writing about anything without first giving themselves plenty of time for this early simmering process.

Another way to get your meaning clear before you write is to have a conversation or discussion about the topic—better yet, perhaps, an argument. This permits you to try out various ideas, approaches, formulations. Thoughts mature, crucial distinctions emerge, precise terms come clear.

Yet another way to figure out what you mean before you write is to think as hard and as clearly as you can about the audience (if any) for whom this piece is intended and the effect you want your words to have on it. Bring your readers into your presence by seeing them clearly in your mind. And as for purpose, don't settle for "I want my words to work." Visualize specifically *what* you want the words to do: Make the readers see something? Make them feel certain emotions? Perform certain actions? Change their minds? This clear grasp of your audience and purpose may focus your thinking in such a way that you immediately realize just what you need to say and how you need to say it.

You can also focus your thinking quickly by simply increasing the pressure on yourself. Pressure cookers permit higher temperatures, quicker cooking. That is, one of the things that keeps us from figuring out what we really mean is having too many interesting choices of things we *could* mean. We can't make up our mind. Blocked writers suffer from too many ideas more often than from too few. But if you are standing up on a stage and have already been introduced and the audience is sitting there waiting for you to speak, you simply have to decide on something to say. It may not be the right decision, but it's a decision and you are off.

It turns out that you can easily produce this same pressure on yourself in writing, too. Just put off all work till 9 o'clock the night before the piece is required. After an hour of pondering, the pressure will be great enough that you finally have to decide what you are going to say and start. "Oh, hell, it's ten o'clock, I guess I'll choose this conclusion to build my report on. I don't like it. I'm not sure I even believe it. But I've got to write something." (When you start writing something way before the deadline, sometimes the lack of pressure allows the consequences of making the wrong decisions to feel worse than the consequences of not writing at all and so you don't write at all.)

You can also give yourself this pressure by not letting yourself revise at all. Just as you cannot revise when you are standing up giving a talk to an audience—this is it!—so, too, you cannot revise if you type onto the official application form or paint right onto expensive stretched canvas without any sketching. I think of my late colleague Willi Unsoeld. Where the rest of us wrote our official evaluations of students in draft form so we could make changes or corrections before giving them to secretaries to be typed (for these are photographed as part of the student's permanent transcript), Willi would roll the official form into his typewriter and type without error his one- or two-page evaluation of each student. He was a mountain climber and believed in the importance of risk and performance under duress. He used the pressure of the audience and the moment to force his meaning clear and to transform an onerous task into a performance.

•   •   •

With this hymn to writing things right the first time, can I really go on to write a book which celebrates the opposite process? The fact is, I'm not going on to write the rest of the book. I've already written most of it now as I figure out this chapter. Having done so is what gives me the security to feel the virtues in what is nevertheless a dangerous method.

When the method works magically—that is, when you tap your deepest powers and cook everything completely before you write anything down—sometimes there is a finer integration and connectedness than you can achieve by revising. And even when it works only adequately—that is, when you merely settle on something that happens to be on the surface of your mind and then write it out—you may be able to write your piece more quickly and with less uncertainty than if you used two steps.

But it is a dangerous method because it puts more pressure on you and depends for its success on everything's running smoothly. If you are out of practice or insecure or just a bit off your form, you can take longer trying to get something right the first time than you would have needed for writing roughly and then revising. Indeed, the method often fails outright. That is, you can sit there and think and stare into space, try to make an outline, perhaps try beer and naps and walks, and still not figure out what you want to say—or even *anything* good to say. That need to get it right prevents the ingredients in your head from cooking, developing, progressing. You are at G, you are looking for Z, but your eagerness for Z prevents P, Q, and R from occurring to you since they are so different from Z.

By this time you have wasted most of the time you had available for writing this thing, you feel there is something the matter with you ("Everyone *else* can figure out what to say by making an outline!"), and so you either settle on something obvious and uninteresting or you fumble your way through the whole piece of writing without ever really deciding what you mean.

Even when you do manage to decide on your meaning before you start writing and you feel satisfied with it ("Yes, that's what I want to say"), sticking with that meaning as you write stops all creativity and the generation of new ideas. You have settled for what you already know and understand. You have locked yourself into duller thinking than you are capable of; indeed, you have virtually ruled out your best thinking. When you see a piece of really vacuous writing, you can be almost certain that it was the result of someone's feeling she had to figure out her thesis before starting to write and then stick to it at all costs. It's only sensible to try to write things right the first time if you know you already have terrific insights.

There's one more danger. Trying to write things right usually means writing very slowly and carefully. Long pauses between sentences and paragraphs to make sure of your bearings. This often leads to overwriting and overintricacy. You have too much time to work up clever turns of phrase and cunning complexities. Writing slowly and carefully, you also invest too much love and effort into that draft—after all, those intricacies *are* clever—so it becomes too hard to throw those cute gems into the garbage. Thus, odd as it may sound, trying to write it right the first time not only increases the danger of dull writing, it also increases the danger of writing that is cloyingly precious.

But if you let yourself write things *wrong* the first time— perhaps even the second or third time too—something wonderful happens: when you feel a story or an idea in mind but can't quite get a hold of it, you discover that by just starting to write and forcing yourself to keep on, you eventually find what you are looking for. And you didn't even know what you were looking for. You discover you can write almost anything you want to write. You get braver. Trying to get it right the first time, on the other hand, often makes people timid—less willing even to *try* writing things— because it often leads them to the experience of struggling and getting stuck and finally giving up with nothing to show for their efforts. The need to get things right the first time, I suspect, is often the culprit in the case of people who want to write but don't do so or stop doing so. I certainly wouldn't have gone through two years of total inability to write if I hadn't been trapped by the dangerous method.

Advice

• At *some* point before you finish revising any piece of writing, you should figure out and state clearly for yourself exactly what you are trying to say. In one sentence. (In the case of poetry or fiction it may not be your meaning or message that you must make clear to yourself—perhaps your piece does not have a meaning or message—but rather your plan or what your piece is about or what effect you are trying to have.) If you want to make your writing as good as possible—to tap your full range of insights and perceptions—it's usually better not to *start* with this exact conception of your meaning or goal but instead to let it emerge as you are writing or force it to emerge as you revise. If, however, your main goal is to save time and simplify the writing process, it may help to crystalize your meaning before you start writing. What's important to remember is that getting your meaning clear in advance is a simplification that only simplifies when you can do it quickly and well. Otherwise it complicates your efforts.

• Therefore it is probably worthwhile practicing methods for getting your meaning clear in advance. Outlining, thinking about your audience, and putting yourself under pressure are good methods when you already have a lot of ingredients in mind. If you are still pretty blank, a nap, mulling it over, or a discussion is probably more effective.

• One good way of learning to work out your meaning in advance is just go give it a quick try whenever you have to write anything. But don't insist on success or use up too much time on the effort.

• But when you are writing small pieces that aren't too important (as in the case of some memos, letters, reports, and abstracts) try *forcing* yourself to get your meaning clear before you start. These are just the kinds of writing where speed and ease of writing are more important than achieving the highest quality. You will be grateful if you can learn to write memos and reports and letters by just closing your eyes for a moment or jotting down a quick outline and then whipping them off pretty much as they belong. You have no choice but to master the dangerous method if you have to write essay exams or write letters by dictation.

• The best way to make an outline for nonfiction writing has two stages. First write down all the ideas you can think of in whatever sequence they occur to you. (If your piece calls for careful or complex thinking, force yourself to write each idea in the form of a full sentence with a verb. A mere word or phrase—"outlines" or "importance of outlines"—doesn't clarify your thinking as much as a sentence: "Outlines are important." You can clarify your thinking even more by insisting on an *action* verb: "Outlines *organize* your thinking.") Second, look through all these sentences and figure out your main idea—what you really want to say. Then arrange the sentences so they form a clear sequence—so they "tell a story." You may have to add a couple of points to make your sequence complete; and throw a couple away to get rid of some kinks in your sequence. Now you know just what you are saying and your order for saying it.

• When you try to write something right the first time, don't try to get it *absolutely* right. You can get the job done quicker and also avoid preciousness and overwriting if you give yourself some leeway about how to begin and about wording and phrasing throughout. That is, don't try to write your opening sentence or paragraph unless it comes to you immediately just right. You can waste an enormous amount of time trying to find a good opening, and it will probably need to be changed by the time you are done. Just skip some space at the beginning and start right in with the main body of what you are writing so you can come back later and write your opening when it will be much easier. And as you write, allow yourself to fumble a bit in your wording, try one phrase and then another, and don't insist that it's right before you put it down. You'll write more quickly and naturally if you are not always struggling for the exact word or phrase. When you finish you will be able to polish your piece very quickly by just going back through it once and crossing out the wrong words and occasionally writing in a new one. Your final language will be more lively and direct and you will have saved time.

• You can probably sense if you are one of those people who have a knack—or a potential knack—for the more magical kinds of cooking in their heads. If you are such a person you should work to develop and exploit your gift so you can use it even on creative and important pieces of writing.

• You might think that figuring out your meaning before you write would be especially helpful for inexperienced or unskilled writers since it gives so much security and confidence to have that outline in hand as you start to write. But really, only experienced pros can use this approach reliably. Only pros can count on getting life and creativity into those outlines or naps or sleepy walks. When you see a pro sitting there at the desk staring into space not writing a word, you can probably trust that she is engaged in creative, productive and efficient work. But if you see any of the rest of us sitting there like that, you'd be doing us a favor if you tapped us on the shoulder and said, "Get your pencil moving, Mac."

II

MORE WAYS OF GETTING WORDS ON PAPER

INTRODUCTION

Perhaps my general point would be clearer if I called this section "More Ways of Producing a First Draft," but I want to emphasize the fact that first-stage writing need not take the form of a draft. That is, it need not be a single connected piece of writing. There is no good reason why you must try to produce something in your first cycle of writing that resembles the form of what you want to end up with. Of course, if you *have* a vision of how your piece ought to be structured, yes, by all means do your raw writing in the form of a draft. But if you only have the hint of a hunch or some initial thoughts or incidents or images and you can't see how they should be shaped, it's usually best to go ahead all the same and plunge into what I call raw writing. Instead of a draft you will be producing a pile of rough ingredients. The fact is that you usually get more and better visions for how to shape these ingredients by starting to write them out however they happen to come off the pencil than by waiting till you get the so-called "right" structure. Any structure that you dream up before actually getting your hands dirty in the writing itself is apt to be like a plan you work out for travel in an unfamiliar country: it usually has to be changed once you get there and see how things really work.

The secret of success in getting words down on paper is learning to adopt a crucial attitude that is new for most people: a sense of trust that when you have the germ of an idea or even just the hankering for one, you will be led sooner or later to the words you are looking for if you just start in writing. You need to learn to avoid that commoner response to the itch of an idea: waiting and not writing till you see things clearly and have the words you want already in your head.

I have already in Section I described three ways of getting words on paper:

• Freewriting is an exercise for making the quickest and deepest improvements in how you write. The goal is in the process, not the product.

• The dangerous method, trying to write something right the first time, is useful to most people on certain occasions. Only a few people can use it efficiently and creatively as their normal procedure.

• The direct writing process is the simplest and most practical way of getting words on paper when you are writing something in a hurry or when you know you'll have no trouble finding material. It is a way of inviting relatively little chaos and keeping it within limited bounds. You don't try to get things right or in the right order as you write, but you do keep your goal in mind at all times—avoid digressions and getting lost.

"The Open-Ended Writing Process" begins this section and it is at the opposite extreme from the direct writing process. It courts the most intuition, it invites the most chaos, it takes the most time, and it requires you to let the writing determine entirely its own goals.

Next, Chapter 8, "The Loop Writing Process," tries for the best of both extremes. It helps you make good use of what might be called "almost-freewriting" for any topic you happen to be writing about, even if the topic seems very foreign to you. You will find the loop writing process especially helpful if your topic bores you or you can't think of much to say about it. This process is the most powerful way to bring creative imagination into nonfiction or expository writing.

Next, Chapter 9, "Metaphors for Priming the Pump," contains metaphorical push-ups for helping you see more about any topic and think more creatively.

In "Working on Writing While Not Thinking about Writing," I suggest some common occasions in life when you might not think to use writing but it will prove useful—occasions, however, when the writing itself doesn't matter and so you don't worry or even think about it. This kind of writing is peculiarly helpful in making your other, more formal writing more comfortable for you and more natural and lively for readers.

Finally, "Poetry as No Big Deal" describes a way of writing poetry where the emphasis is on modest goals and pleasure.

The eight ways of getting words on paper described in these first two sections are, in effect, different strategies for bringing out creativity. You can also think of them as different strategies for managing chaos. It has seemed to some readers of my earlier book as though I only celebrate chaos. It is true that I believe most people need to learn to exploit chaos better in their writing: it helps break down preconceptions and old frameworks and permits growth and new ideas. You can use chaos to blast open what you are stuck on. But once I persuade you to use chaos, I am eager to turn around and admit that there are many situations where you should keep chaos to a minimum (as in the dangerous method and the direct writing process). Chaos increases anxiety and may make the job take longer. There are many times when I cannot think at all till I have some firm structure to work from. I have to make an outline that is simple and neat—plodding even—before my mind will take the tiniest flight. On such occasions I may theoretically be limiting myself by starting with a rigid cage to keep out chaos, but practically speaking I would limit myself much more if I tried to deal with more chaos than I could handle. (Sometimes an outline serves best as a cage to break out of: it makes you think of ideas that won't fit inside but which otherwise wouldn't occur to you. This is an argument for not spending too long making perfect outlines.)

By settling on eight specific processes for getting words on paper and describing some of them in a very definite step-by-step fashion, I am not trying to suggest that these are eight pure essences made in heaven. I'm simply trying to lay out an admittedly artificial spectrum of processes which you can easily learn to use—perhaps even to vary and add to. By doing so you will finally free yourself from that common human condition of falling into a single and unvarying gear for trying to write whenever you sit down to write something. You don't see options and indeed you don't even see clearly your own process—you are "just writing." Some people have learned a good gear. Many are stuck with a terrible one. But no gear is efficient or creative for all writing tasks.

The Open-ended Writing Process

The open-ended writing process is at the opposite extreme from the direct writing process. It is a way to bring to birth an unknown, unthought-of piece of writing—a piece of writing that is not yet in you. It is a technique for thinking, seeing, and feeling new things. This process invites maximum chaos and disorientation. You have to be willing to nurse something through many stages over a long period of time and to put up with not knowing where you are going. Thus it is a process that can change you, not just your words.

As the most creative and unmethodical writing process, I associate it with poems or stories or novels. But it will also lead you to essays. It has led me to parts of this and my previous book about writing (in particular to the long essay in *Writing Without Teachers* on the doubting and believing games and to the voice chapters—25 and 26—in this book).

Ideally you should not choose in advance what you are going to end up with. Perhaps you start out thinking and hoping for a poem, but you may well end up with a story in prose, a letter to someone, an essay that works out one of your perplexities. The open-ended writing process goes on and on till the potential piece of writing is fully cooked and grown. Sometimes this happens quickly, sometimes you nurse it through decades (though I will suggest some ways to hasten the process a bit).

I think of the open-ended writing process as a voyage in two stages: a sea voyage and a coming to new land. For the sea voyage you are trying to lose sight of land—the place you began. Getting lost is the best source of new material. In coming to new land you develop a new conception of what you are writing about—a new idea or vision—and then you gradually reshape your material to fit this new vision. The sea voyage is a process of divergence, branching, proliferation, and confusion; the coming to land is a process of convergence, pruning, centralizing, and clarifying.

• • •

To begin the sea voyage, do a nonstop freewriting that starts from wherever you happen to be. Most often you just start with a thought or a feeling or a memory that seems for some reason important to you. But perhaps you have something in mind for a possible piece of writing: perhaps you have some ideas for an essay; or certain images stick in mind as belonging in a poem; or certain characters or events are getting ready to make a story. You can also start by describing what you wish you could end up with. Realize of course that you probably won't. Just start writing.

The open-ended writing process is ideal for the situation where you sense you have something to write but you don't quite know what. Just start writing about anything at all. If you have special trouble with that first moment of writing—that confrontation with a blank page—ask yourself what you *don't* want to write about and start writing about it before you have a chance to resist. First thoughts. They are very likely to lead you to what you are needing to write.

Keep writing for at least ten or twenty or thirty minutes, depending on how much material and energy you come up with. You have to write long enough to get tired and get past what's on the top of your mind. But not so long that you start pausing in the midst of your writing.

Then stop, sit back, be quiet, and bring all that writing to a point. That is, by reading back or just thinking back over it, find the center or focus or point of those words and write it down in a sentence. This may mean different things: you can find the main idea that is there; or the new idea that is trying to be there; or the imaginative focus or center of gravity—an image or object or feeling; or perhaps some brand new thing occurs to you now as very important—it may even seem unrelated to what you wrote, but it comes to you now as a result of having done that burst of writing. Try to stand out of the way and let the center or focus itself decide to come forward. In any event, don't worry about it. Choose or invent something for your focus and then go on. The only requirement is that it be a single thing. Skip a few lines and write it down. Underline it or put a box around it so you can easily find it later. (Some people find it helpful to let themselves write down two or three focusing sentences.)

If this center of gravity is a feeling or an image, perhaps a mere phrase will do: "a feeling that something good will happen" or "mervyn the stuffed monkey slumped under the dining room table." But a complete sentence or assertion is better, especially if the focus is an idea or thought or insight. Try, that is, to get more than "economics" or "economic dimension"—since those words just vaguely point in a general direction—and try for something like "there must be an economic reason for these events."

You have now gone through a cycle that consists of nonstop writing and then sitting back to probe for the center. You have used two kinds of consciousness: immersion, where you have your head down and are scurrying along a trail of words in the underbrush; and perspective, where you stand back and look down on things from a height and get a sense of shape and outline.

Now repeat this cycle. Use the focus you just wrote down as the springboard for a new piece of nonstop writing. There are various ways in which you can let it bounce you into new writing. Perhaps you just take it and write more about it. Or perhaps that doesn't seem right because what you already wrote has finished an idea and the focusing sentence has put the lid on it. If you wrote more about it, you would just be repeating yourself. In this case, start now with what comes next: the next step, the following thing, the reply, the answering salvo. Perhaps "what comes next" is what follows logically. Perhaps the next thing is what comes next in your mind even though it involves a jump in logic. Perhaps the next thing is a questioning or denial of what you have already written: arguments against it, writing in an opposite mood, or writing in a different mode (from prose to poetry). Stand out of the way and see what happens.

Whatever kind of jump it is, jump into a second burst of nonstop writing for however long you can keep it up. Long enough to get tired and lose track of where you started; not so long that you keep pausing and lose momentum. And then, again, stop and come out from the underbrush of your immersion in words, attain some calm and perspective, and find the summing up or focus or center of gravity for this second piece of writing.

The sea voyage consists of repeating this cycle over and over again. Keep up one session of writing long enough to get loosened up and tired—long enough in fact to make a bit of a voyage and probably to pass beyond what happened to be in mind and in mood. But usually a piece of open-ended writing takes several or even many long sittings. One of the major ingredients in the open-ended process is time and the attendant changes of mood and outlook.

As you change modes from writing to focusing and back to writing and back to focusing, practice letting the process itself decide what happens next—decide, for example, whether your focusing sentence springboards you into a new treatment of the same material, into a response to that material or into some other new topic or mode that "wants" to come next. If it sounds a bit mystical to say "Let it decide," I don't mean to rule out hard conscious thinking. "Letting it decide" will often mean realizing you should be rigorously logical at this point in the writing cycle. As you practice the open-ended writing process, you will get better at feeling what kind of step needs to be taken at any given point. The main thing is not to worry about doing it right. Just do it a lot.

As you engage in this sea voyage, invite yourself to lose sight of what you had in mind at the beginning, invite digressions, new ideas, seeds falling from unexpected sources, changes of mind. You are trying to nurse your thoughts, perceptions and feelings through a process of continual transformation—cooking and growing. (For a fuller treatment of the cooking and growing processes, see Chapters 2 and 3 of *Writing Without Teachers*.)

The sea voyage is most obviously finished when you sight new land—when you get a trustworthy vision of your final piece of writing. You see that it's an argument and where it is going; or you see it is a poem and feel the general shape of it.

To come to land you need to get this vision clearer and more complete. Perhaps your first glimpse showed you what is central: now you need to write out that central event or idea more fully. If what is emerging is primarily conceptual, such as an essay, you may well need to make an outline. You won't be able to see your structure clearly until you go through all you have written to find the points that feel important, write each one into a complete sentence, and then put these sentences into the most logical or easily understood order. Even for a long story or poem, you may need some kind of schematic representation of the whole so you can see it all in one glance.

But perhaps it is too early for any outline or overview. Perhaps you cannot really get this final vision clear and right except by plunging into a new draft in your present fame of mind—starting the first scene of the story or novel, the first line of the poem, the introductory thought for your essay—and just plowing along. Perhaps *doing it* is more helpful at this point than any method of planning or outlining.

What if you keep writing and writing and you sense that the sea voyage is really done, but you lack any glimpse of land. You feel you have gotten down everything you can get down, you are beginning to repeat yourself, there is no more divergence. You've succeeded in getting productively lost, but now this unknown territory starts to get depressingly familiar.

You can try to hasten the convergent process of coming to land. Go back over all the centers or focuses you have written down in the course of the sea voyage. Ponder them for a while. Then engage in some nonstop writing on the basis of them. Start writing "I don't yet know what all this writing is really about, but here's what the important elements seem to be: . . ." Of course you can't put them in the right or logical order—that's just what you don't know. You are trying to bring them together into the same burst of energy and attention. You might write something like this:

There's writing that sounds like the writer talking, there's writing that somehow just resonates in some mysterious way, there's radio announcer speech with great energy and liveliness but sounding completely fake, there's———, and there's———. How can I make sense of it all.

You are trying to get the important elements to bounce against each other in a tight place.

Keep up this burst of writing—this attempt to figure out what your writing is about—as long as you can. Perhaps a center will emerge. If not, go on to the step of standing back and looking for a center. If that isn't the final center, then go on to another wave of writing. Keep this up for a while. Keep up, that is, the same process you used for the sea voyage, but instead of using it for divergence and getting lost, use it for convergence and getting found. If this doesn't work, you may simply have to stop and rest. Give your writing more time in a drawer unlooked at. Anything that takes this long simply to emerge is probably important. Some complicated and important reordering of things is trying to take place inside you.

• • •

Now that I've suggested some of the different ways that nonstop writing can lead to focusing sentences, and that focusing sentences can lead to new bursts of nonstop writing, I would like to suggest some of the larger patterns of unfolding you might encounter in the whole cycle of the open-ended process.

• The writing may change moods and modes: from prose to poetry; from experiential to conceptual; from logical to associational; from first person to second or third person; from talk aimed at one person to talk aimed at someone entirely different or aimed at no one at all.

• Perhaps all the writing throughout the open-ended writing process hovers over the same territory. You are gnawing on a single tough bone. You are circling around and around like a plane zeroing in on an airport. Your writing yields successive photographs of the same general scene till you finally get the right perspective and focus. For example, you start writing about a particular afternoon that seems important in your life; your writing leads you to different views of that afternoon, successive versions of what happened, successive attempts to say what it means. Or perhaps you start writing about a particular fight and that's what all your writing continues to be about, but first you find yourself describing what actually happened, then how it felt from your point of view, then what the other person must have felt, and then a fantasy version. In the end you produce a piece of thinking that explains what the fight was really about; or perhaps you end up with a fictional version of a similar fight.

• But on the other hand, perhaps the open-ended writing process carries you not on a circling path over the same territory but on a traversing journey depositing you far from where you started: each stage is, as it were, a sketch of an entirely *new* scene, a treatment of new subject matter. Perhaps, for example, you start with that same fight, but you are led to a portrait of the other person, then to another person from the distant past, and finally to an important event from your childhood that is unrelated to that original fight. (Of course these pieces of writing may only appear unrelated: the childhood event may actually unlock the meaning of the fight.)

• The open-ended writing process may lead to successive versions of a short piece of writing as it goes through various stages or transformations: you end up keeping what is in effect the "last version" and throwing away all the previous ones—that is, throwing away 95 percent of what you have written.

• But on the other hand, perhaps you will find you have been engaged almost all the time in writing what is more or less one draft of a single, very long work. The periodic focusings are merely pauses in the slow unwinding of a single long thread. Perhaps it is a novel; perhaps it is a long letter where the focusings are pauses for the voice to say, "Let me pause to sum up what I seem to be saying to you." Or perhaps it is a long record of what has been going on with you: even though it goes through a lot of changes of mood or form, everything you've written seems to *belong*.

There is some danger that I have made the open-ended writing process sound too complicated. I could describe it more simply as follows: just start writing, keep writing, don't stop writing except for eating, sleeping, and living, and keep the process going till you have figured out what you are writing, and when you have done that, keep writing still until you get it right. This is the heart of the process and if it is what you do and it works, terrific. But I am trying to emphasize two additional elements that may well be part of your process without your paying much attention to them: first, let yourself start without knowing where you are going and even get more lost as you proceed; and second, alternate between nonstop writing and pausing to focus what you've written. As long as your nonstop writing is going well there is no need, of course, to stop and focus. But if you are writing and writing without getting anywhere, it will help to move deliberately back and forth between immersion and perspective. Doing so will help each wave of writing carry you farther and make each pause not just a rest but an occasion for progress.

• • •

• Here are two accounts of readers trying out the open-ended writing process. They are excerpts from feedback to me on an earlier draft of this chapter.

The open-ended approach surprised me. Perhaps not the process itself, but what I found its result to be. Like everyone else, I had something in my mind wanting to be written, but it really worried me. So I attacked it, diving in right at the point where it didn't want to be put in words. After four retries I found, to my surprise, that I had gotten a hold on the main idea and, though this may not be unusual in your experience, I found that the original somewhat slippery concept I was struggling with was not actually at the center of my subject. But by putting it down in writing and discussing it with myself I found out where everything was pointing (I hope). I ended up with a very broad but, I think, useful general outline that gives me a direction to head into. I suppose the process doesn't always work like this, but I was pleased to find that things surfaced as quickly as they did this time.

GLORIA CAMPBELL, 8/23/78

Following your suggestion, I began some nonstop writing. Feeling totally lost—and with absolutely no control over my writing for the first time in memory—I wrote: "I'm not sure why this piece of writing fights against my wanting to set everything down in a logical order, such as a compact magazine article would be. The subject of pilgrimage should fit neatly into categories describing history, how it's common to all faiths, etc."

From there I went on to record all the images flashing through my mind. Utter chaos. I'd done a good deal of research as well as a little travel in Palestine. In the jumble was Egeria, a 4th century traveling nun, Egyptians (during Herodotus' time) floating in a barge up the Nile to visit the shrine of a cat goddess, and a group of Arab teenagers sitting in the back of a camper, shouting and waving, "Hallo, American," as I trudged the long dusty road between the highway bus stop and the Mount of Beatitudes. There's much more, but you get the idea. I could begin to laugh at myself and write now with enthusiasm. What difference did it make, after all, where I was headed—I was having a terrific time going there. And then quite suddenly I reached a center, threw down my pencil, stared at the sentence, and the light dawned. I could finally understand what you meant about finding a center, "letting the writing make the choice."

I still have a long way to go on pilgrimage—finding new centers—

for eventually I hope to turn the subject into a different kind of travel book about the Middle East when I'm able to take another trip. Trying to explain what happened to writing friends, I described the process as the complete opposite of the traditional way of doing a piece; that is, standing back far enough to get an objective look at the material. In Open-Ended Writing, when I arrived at that first center, it was like standing in the middle of a circle, looking out and not being able to see the whole thing, but feeling quite excited about what I might see next if I turned just a bit more. What a different way to look at a subject. It's a bit scary too. Must be how a sculptor feels when he first starts to chip away.

JOANNE TURPIN, 7/24/78

• • •

After you have your vision of your final piece and after you have worked out that vision in a new draft—perhaps starting with an outline—you need of course to revise and polish your way to your final draft. Sometimes the open-ended writing process yields a draft that needs little revising, sometimes lots. (See Section III for options in revising.)

Main Steps in the Open-ended Writing Process

• Write for fifteen or twenty minutes without stopping. Start with whatever comes first to mind or perhaps with some particular topic you've been wanting to write about. But make sure to let the writing go wherever it wants to go.

• Pause and find the center or focus or main point in what you wrote. Write it down in a sentence.

• Use that focusing sentence for a new burst of nonstop writing. Again, let the writing go wherever it wants to go. Invite yourself gradually or suddenly to lose sight of whatever you started with.

• Again, pause and focus and write down the focusing sentence.

• Keep up this alternating cycle till you get to the piece of writing that is in you that wants to get written.

• Find a way to write it: perhaps you already have; perhaps you need to start in with a fresh draft; perhaps you need to make an outline or plan before you start a draft.

• The open-ended writing process is most useful if you sense you have something to write but don't quite know what it is; and if you are willing to allow for time and chaos while it develops.

The Loop Writing Process

I've described the two ends of the spectrum of writing processes. One extreme is the dangerous method of painstaking writing where you figure out your meaning entirely before you start and thereby maintain complete control while you write. (Not quite so far in that direction is the direct writing process where, by and large, you maintain control of where you are going.) The other extreme is the open-ended process where you let the writing steer itself and let yourself be ignorant of where you might end up. The dangerous method may save you time and perplexity but it often gets you in trouble or leads to dull thinking. Open-ended writing maximizes growth in yourself and new thinking on paper but you pay the obvious price in time, energy, and uncertainty.

The loop writing process is a way to get the best of both worlds: both control and creativity. On the one hand it lets you steer where you are going. Perhaps, for example, you have to write an essay on the causes of the French Revolution and the teacher won't accept a novel or love letter instead. But on the other hand it expands your point of view—sometimes even more than the open-ended process does; it generates copious new thinking; and it is a way to *focus* that creativity on goals other than the ones you happen to carry around inside you. Thus it is especially useful if you can't think of much to write or are stuck with a topic that bores you. The loop writing process will take you longer than the direct writing process, but not so long as open ended writing. (I will write as though your task were an essay or some other kind of nonfiction writing. It will be obvious how to apply the loop writing process to poems, stories, or plays.)

I call this process a loop because it takes you on an elliptical orbiting voyage. For the first half, *the voyage out,* you do pieces of almost-freewriting during which you allow yourself to curve out into space—allow yourself, that is, to ignore or even forget exactly what your topic is. For the second half, *the voyage home,* you bend your efforts back into the gravitational field of your original topic as you select, organize, and revise parts of what you produced during the voyage out. Where open-ended writing is a voyage of discovery to a new land, the loop process takes a circling route so you can return to the original topic—but now with a fresh view of it. Where open-ended writing is only suitable if you have free choice over the topic and form, loop writing is useful if you have *no choice*—and especially if you hate it or feel bored by it.

The loop writing process is really my response to something many people told me about *Writing Without Teachers:* that what I said about, "well, growing and cooking" was all very well for creative writing but it didn't help them to write an essay on the causes of the French Revolution for Monday morning. At first this response made me mad. "Yes, it *does* help," I wanted to say. "Everything you need is right there. I was thinking very much about just such a task." But after hearing the response often enough I finally had to admit I hadn't given as many directions as I could have for using fast and free writing on required essays, memos, or reports that you may not be interested in. When I finally gave in and set about trying to write what these people were asking for, the process led me to new ideas. I tell this story as a lesson in feedback. So often when readers complain that something is missing in a piece of your writing, you *know* they are wrong. But if you can finally manage to see it through their eyes, to have some of their experience, you don't just get new perceptions of your writing, you usually get completely new ideas that please you.

The creative element in the loop writing process comes from letting your topic slide half out of mind and doing some initial bursts of directed raw writing. This gets more of your *experience* linked to your thinking. Some teachers have objected, "Why encourage unskilled writers to put *more* into their essays when they can't even handle the little that is there?" But I have found that people produce their best writing when they finally have ideas that are powerful and exciting to them. When they try to weave an essay out of ideas that are watery and uninteresting to them, their language often disintegrates into incoherence: they are trying to make something solid out of what they know isn't really worth the effort. How can you reason well and produce strong language if you aren't connected to the topic and don't have any ideas that excite you? After you have that connection and after you have produced lots of writing that interests you, then you will be willing to summon the cold, hard discipline needed for the voyage home—for building an organized and focused piece of writing.

The Voyage Out

For the voyage out I suggest thirteen procedures for loop writing: directed freewriting. I will explain and discuss them before going on to describe the voyage home. You won't need all of them for any one piece of writing. Usually a few are enough. But if you practice them all you will have them all available and know which will be most suitable for any given writing task you face.

1. *First thoughts.* This is a good one to start with. Do it even before you have done any reading, research, planning, or new thinking about your topic. Just put down as fast as you can all the thoughts and feelings you happen to have about the topic. You will discover much more material than you expected. And not just feelings and memories either: there are probably solid facts and ideas you forgot you had.

Writing down first thoughts is more or less what you did during the first half of the direct writing process, and for some topics you will turn up enough material with first thoughts for your whole piece of writing. If so, go on to revising. Your ideas won't be as numerous or interesting as they would have been if you used some of the techniques I describe below, but you will have saved a lot of time and effort.

If it seems to you that you don't have any first thoughts, you are mistaken. It is because you aren't listening or accepting them. That is, I'm not calling for *good* thoughts or *true* thoughts—just *first* thoughts. If you have trouble, adopt the frame of mind of a scientist and simply record the reactions and thoughts that pass through consciousness as you struggle with the topic. More often you will have too many rather than too few first thoughts. Take the ones that appeal most.

If you are writing some kind of analysis or description—perhaps an evaluation of a person or a program, a write-up of a case, an abstract of a long article—first thoughts will often consist of certain details or incidents simply jumping out from your memory. You may not know why. They may seem senseless or random but they are not. These first tiny details and quick impressions often hold the key to important insights that you would miss if you proceeded straight to careful analytic thinking.

If you are having a particularly hard time making up your mind between two or three opinions—perhaps you are writing a report on two competing proposals, an essay on conflicting theories, a piece of personal writing to help you decide whether to break up with someone—first thoughts are particularly valuable. "What do you *think* you should do? Give an instant answer." "Which plan do you suspect you'll endorse in the end? First thoughts." Because these are naked hunches that lack any clear justification or support, you often feel shy about taking them seriously, much less writing them down. But you should. It's not that you can trust these hunches to be right (though surprisingly often they are: your instantaneous-computer-mind has taken everything into account and cranked out a judicious answer). But the slower, careful thinking you need for *deciding* if your hunch is right will go much better because you wrote it down blatantly: "Jung's account feels better than Freud's. Jung's feels . . . while Freud's feels. . . ." Of course your hunch may be wrong but if so, it turns out that writing it down bluntly somehow helps you to abandon it more easily than if you leave it lurking in the back of your mind.

Spend at least fifteen minutes of nonstop writing on first thoughts even if the process seems a waste of time. Take longer of course if the material seems good. But don't spend any time at this early stage trying to get your thoughts correctly ordered or reconciled with each other. Just get them all down as quickly as you can.

2. *Prejudices*. This, too, is a good one to start with—even before reading, thinking, or researching your topic. What are your biases in the area of your topic. With the example of the Jung/Freud first thoughts above, I was obviously illustrating prejudices too. What kind of explanation of the French Revolution would be most *satis-*

fying to you? Do you suspect that monarchy is an inherently unjust form of government? That royalty was really the root cause of the revolution? Do you feel that mobs always do the wrong thing? Or that "the people" are always right in the end? That intellectuals are trouble-makers? If you are writing to persuade someone or a committee to adopt a certain policy, write out your naked prejudices and preferences before you do any careful thinking. It will help you see the difference between your biases and your genuine arguments—something you need to see if you want to persuade effectively.

If it isn't clear to you what your prejudices or preferences are, do first thoughts and then—in a somewhat detached and clinical spirit—look through what you've written to see what point of view or assumptions or biases are revealed there. But then jump with both feet *into* that point of view and write in as prejudiced a way as you can. You aren't trying to think carefully, you're trying to let your own prejudices run rampant without any censorship so you can see more clearly what they are. If it is hard to stop censoring, pretend to be *someone else* who is an extremist. Write his views.

Even if your topic seems more a matter of facts than of opinion—perhaps you are writing an environmental impact statement—it is still helpful to write prejudices. Prejudice and point of view are even more slippery in issues of fact. Perhaps you can't find a prejudice in yourself to exaggerate if you are writing, for example, about the effects of widening a road on the adjoining area of the county. But even if you do lack overt prejudices, you still have a whole web of assumptions and preconceptions of which you are probably unaware but which you can learn about if you write as though you *were* someone who is very prejudiced on the issue— perhaps someone who lives on the road and feels strongly against the widening. By taking a point of view as different as possible from your own, and really trying to enter into it as seriously as you can, you will begin to notice your own unconscious assumptions as they begin to be violated. You do best of all, perhaps, if you take two or three different points of view—one of them your own "objective" view—and write an argument among them. (See Number 4, *Dialogues*, below.)

Writing down your prejudices also helps you generate new ideas and insights. It's only by being obsessed with an idea, taking it as far as you can and seeing it everywhere, that you will notice all the arguments and evidence that support it. Copernicus wouldn't have found the evidence for the heliocentric model of the planets if he hadn't been obsessed with the importance of the sun and given some scope to his obsession. In addition, when you give more scope to your prejudice you will be led to notice more ideas that run *counter* to it that you wouldn't otherwise have seen. That is, you will start to pay attention to what an opponent would say. This helps you think of better arguments for your own point of view.

3. *Instant Version.* It would be a miracle to turn out a final version of any extensive writing task in half an hour. But it's worthwhile pretending to pull off this miracle. Simply deny the need for research, thinking, planning and turn out a kind of sketch of your final piece—an instant projected version. You'll have to pretend you know things you don't know, act as though you have made up your mind where you're uncertain, make up facts and ideas, and leave out large chunks (perhaps symbolizing these omissions with little boxes). But by doing so you can *will* yourself into producing a quickly written final version.

Some people are paralyzed by the process of extensive research for a major report or paper. The more research you do, the more impossible it is to start writing. You already have so much material—whether it is in your head or in your notes—that you can't find a place to start, you can't find a beginning to grab hold of in that tangled ball of string. You can write more notes but you can't start. Besides, you never feel you have finished your research: there are a couple more books or articles to get a hold of; they sound promising; better not write anything yet because they probably have some very important material that will change the whole picture. This is the path to panicked 3 A.M. writing the night before the due date. (Or the night after.) Writing first thoughts or prejudices or an instant version keeps you from falling into this research paralysis. Have the sense to realize that it's easier to write now when you know less. You can use subsequent research to check your thinking and to revise your writing to any level of sophistication that you wish.

If you do write first thoughts or prejudices or an instant version—and especially if you use a couple of these techniques—you will be able to get much more out of any reading and research you have to do for your paper. The more boring or difficult the research, the more helpful these early pieces of writing. They will make dull research interesting because you will already be an "authority" on the topic: you will already have lots of thoughts and a point of view. You will find yourself interested and alert as you read to see when the other authorities are smart enough to agree with your prejudices and when they get off track. When they come up with data or thinking that is new to you, it will be interesting and energizing. In short, your mind will already have a "set" or receptive net which will help you absorb all this otherwise dull information. You won't be in that demoralizingly passive position of doing research with your mouth hanging open and trying to take in *everything*. You'll remember more with fewer notes.

You will also discover, by the way, how close you often come to valid conclusions and sound arguments *before* you have consulted the data and arguments of others. You end up feeling much more powerful. It gets you out of that helpless position where you feel you cannot write anything unless you find out what all the "authorities" have said—a frame of mind that seduces you into one of the major forms of poor writing: writing that merely summarizes what "they" say. First thoughts, prejudices, and instant versions catapult you into a position of initiative and control so that you use reading and research to check and revise your thinking actively, not passively just to find something to think.

Even if your research is purely quantitative, these early-writing procedures will help a lot. Perhaps you are writing about levels of pollution of various chemicals in Puget Sound; or about government expenditures for various kinds of armaments and "defense." Write an instant version by making up your own numbers (based either on intuition or fantasy) and reaching your own conclusions. Afterward you'll do a much better job of seeing, remembering, and understanding the real numbers when you turn to the dull research.

These three early-writing procedures have another benefit that is especially important when the paper is difficult for you. Even experienced and professional writers often waste a lot of energy with old and sometimes unconscious fears of "This one's too hard, I won't be able to think of anything to say this time, I'll be a failure." After you have written first thoughts or prejudices or an instant version, these old feelings can't trouble you so much because you don't, in a sense, have to "write a paper," you just have to "revise a paper": change some numbers, add some sections, reverse some conclusions, perhaps even adjust the whole organization. That's all. Even though you may start with a short, sketchy, disorganized paper consisting entirely of fantasy thoughts and information, it is still a sort of paper. And more often than not, there are strong parts that you will keep in your final version. You have already performed the essential inner miracle that makes all writing mysterious and difficult: you have created something out of nothing.

4. *Dialogues.* If you discover that instead of having one clear prejudice you have two or three conflicting feelings, you are in a perfect position to write a dialogue. Give each of the feelings a voice and start them talking to each other. Keep your pencil moving and stand out of the way and these voices will have a lot to say that is important for your piece. You will probably discover somewhere along the way *who* these people are: perhaps one is your head and the other is your heart or guts; perhaps one is your mother who always saw things in terms of individuals, and the other is your father who always saw things in terms of their public consequences. Perhaps one voice is someone especially wise or perceptive who once gave you a glimpse of how things could be. It will probably help your dialogue writing to give these voices their right names and actually be these people as you write in each voice. But don't get side-tracked into wondering what these people would actually say: just keep them talking. If the effort to be these people slows down your writing, go back to the nameless dialogue you started with.

But I'm not recommending that you always do dialogues before you have engaged in research or thought about your topic. They are also especially valuable afterward. They help you to digest and understand all that thinking, research, and early writing and help you to come up with conclusions. After you have read about Louis XVI and Voltaire, get them talking and arguing with each other about the causes of the French Revolution. Let others join the conversation: a peasant, a courtier, one or two of the authors you have read on the topic, yourself, whoever might have something to say. Or get that homeowner who objects to having the road widened talking to a land developer—but not just off the tops of their heads this time: pretend they know all this specific data you've turned up in your research on environmental impact and watch them help you interpret it as they argue.

The main principle of dialogue writing is that you don't have to know ahead of time what a person is going to say. Just pick the speakers, get them talking, and see what they do say. They will often surprise you by saying things you've never thought of. For though you may know everything that two old friends of yours might say on some topic if you just wrote solitary monologues for each of them, you don't know all they will say if you start them interacting with each other. Arguments are especially fertile ground for new insights.

It's sometimes helpful to pick people whose opinions are not completely obvious to you. If, for example, you have the feeling that you already know everything Louis XVI will say about the French Revolution, don't pick him, pick some courtier whose opinions will be related but slightly unpredictable. But don't worry about this issue: even if you think you already know what Louis XVI or your mother will say, they will come up with new and surprising things under the circumstances of a real dialogue. Think of a dialogue as an invitation to the unexpected and spontaneous.

Part of the power of dialogues comes from using the language of *speech* and *talking* and getting away from "essay language" which is usually more cumbersome and artificial and farther away from your felt perceptions. Therefore, make sure you *talk on paper*. It is important to sit inside each person's head in turn and actually write down the words that come out of that person's mouth. This means you'll probably write down lots of little words and phrases that occur in speech which don't contain much substantive meaning—phrases like "Well, um, maybe," or "You have a point there," or "I don't know, let me think about that," and so on. These are the phrases that occur when a person is in the middle of a conversation but isn't quite sure for a moment exactly what he thinks. That's exactly the position you should be in as you write your dialogue. Unless you write down what the people *say*, you won't actually get yourself into their heads and get the benefit of their thinking and points of view. Their "speech" is what they are, and since you need them to get the benefit of their thinking, you need their speech. Besides it's more fun just to let a real conversation unfold than to look for ideas or arguments. (And it helps all your writing to keep it in contact with the rhythms and textures of speech.)

Dialogues are especially useful if you have trouble writing analytically (which means you probably have trouble writing essays and reports). Writing a dialogue produces reasoning, but produces it spontaneously out of your feelings and perceptions. Get two people arguing with each other on paper—or give your opponent a voice so he can argue with you on paper—and you will naturally produce arguments: assertions, supporting reasons, and evidence. Since you are producing them in the heat of battle with your opponent interrupting you and perhaps changing arguments in midstream, they may be disordered or flawed, but you will nevertheless already have written most of the ingredients you need for an intelligent and muscular train of reasoning.*

5. *Narrative Thinking.* If your topic is confusing to you—if for example you find your mind shifting from one thought to another or from one point of view to another without any sense of which thought or point of view makes more sense—then simply write the *story of your thinking.* "I thought this, then I thought that," and so on. This process can help untangle bad snarls in your mind. It is especially useful if you are having trouble writing about something very complicated. If, for example, you are trying to analyze a tangled movie plot or a confusing legal case, move into the strict narrative mode and tell what happened and how you reacted; for example, "She described what happened to her and why she deserved to be repaid and I thought she was right, but when he answered I agreed with him, but then I began to change my mind again when I thought of. . . ." Needless to say you may not want your final version in this narrative mode—it's very slow—but this early narrative writing can help you finally see the issue clearly enough so you can write something very tight and to the point. In particular it often helps you notice unconscious assumptions that have trapped you.

6. *Stories.* The best way to write a letter of recommendation or a job analysis or an evaluation of a person or project is to start by letting stories and incidents come to mind and jotting them down very briefly: good stories and bad ones, typical stories and unusual ones, funny stories and, best of all, stories that somehow stick in your mind for reasons you cannot pin down. This will spare you

---

* Part of the reason why inexperienced essay writers benefit so little from the corrections of teachers on their essays is because the teacher is usually trying to correct *flaws* in an argument, while the student hasn't yet learned simply to *engage* in sustained argument by himself on paper. The student experiences the feedback as a double-bind: "You ask me to engage in sustained, abstract solitary reasoning—something that is difficult for me—and when I do it you punish my behavior."

from that awful dullness so characteristic of evaluations and re-ports: empty generalizations and dead lists of qualities or adjec-tives. Each story will have a lively insight for you and most of those insights—especially the ones that grow out of the perplexing stories—will be far more useful than what you come up with when you just try to *think* about the person or the project or the job. In addition you can include some scraps of these stories in your final version to make it more clear and alive. Letters of recommen-dation are most useful if they include examples of actual incidents.

As you think through your reading about the French Revolution, what stories or incidents come to mind? Some will be obviously important and illustrative. But stand out of the way and let others simply occur to you. They won't all be from your reading. Perhaps the plight of the royalty or the peasantry reminds you of situations you were in. Perhaps the behavior of the urban poor reminds you of something you once did. Write these associations down. Try, in addition, to think of stories and incidents related to theoretical or structural elements in the topic. For example, what stories strike you about *causes:* occasions when one thing caused another but it seemed different from what you usually think of as a cause; per-plexing arguments you've had about whether or not you caused something; cases where something had no cause or too many causes?

Write down these stories and events briefly and in a thumbnail way. You are trying to record as many as you can as quickly as you can. If there is a long and complex story, run through it in your head and write down a summary version in a long paragraph. You can use strings of phrases instead of whole sentences, but do in-clude details. The effectiveness of this loop writing procedure stems from dredging up lots of rich concrete detail from your memory. You want to get your mind working on the narrative and experiential level, and away from saying, "What are my *thoughts* about the causes of the French Revolution?" The previous loop writing procedures will give you thoughts. Now you want your mind asking, "What are my *memories* and *experiences* that some-how relate to the French Revolution?" There is plenty of precious knowledge locked away in your narrative and experiential memory that you can't get to by thinking. Many wise people do their best thinking by telling stories.

Learn to trust yourself. Learn that the stories and events that intrigue you in connection with your topic will end up useful to you later. Practice this technique so you can end up with at least three or four pages containing at least fifteen or twenty stories or events briefly told. Sometimes the material you come up with is so obviously important that you know you should devote more time to get it all.

7. *Scenes.* Stop the flow of time and take still photographs. Focus on individual moments. What places, moments, sounds, or moods come to mind in connection with the French Revolution? Not only from your reading, but also from your own experience. Assume that they will be important if they come to mind, especially if they stick in mind.

If you are trying to decide on a career or choose between two people or life situations, jot down as many scenes as you can think of from your past when things were going well or you were functioning well. Then note just as many bad ones. Afterwards read through these scenes and you will be able to reach some really trustworthy judgments about your skills and strengths and what you need to function at your best; and your weaknesses and what you should try to avoid.*

It is particularly valuable to use scenes if you are writing some kind of analysis of a novel, story, poem, or movie. What moments, sights, and sounds stick in your mind from the work? This will give you insights about where some of the centers of gravity are. What structure emerges when you look at all these snapshots together? Add scenes from the rest of your experience that come to mind. These will lead you to important insights about the work under analysis and about your own preconceptions and point of view.

8. *Portraits.* Think about your topic and see what people come to mind. Give thumbnail portraits of them: again not necessarily with full syntax; just phrases will do. Tell the qualities or characteristics of these people that stick in mind, such as their physical appearance, odd movements or posture or gait, intriguing qualities, things they said or did. Some portraits will have obvious relevance to your analysis. But see who else comes to mind as you muse about your topic: people from other areas of your experience who pop up in your train of reflection. Have faith that there is something useful in the fact that your third grade teacher comes to

---

*I first learned this useful tactic from Gail Martin.

mind as you think about the causes of the French Revolution. Tell what particular things you remember about this teacher and later on you will probably reap an insight.

If you are trying to evaluate an organization or analyze a novel, portraits will often lead you immediately to your best insights. If you are trying to make a hard personal decision, portraits of important people in your life will help you see what matters most to you and separate it from what's merely attractive or tempting.

9. *Vary the audience.* Write about your topic to someone very different from the real audience of your paper. If your audience is sophisticated, try writing to someone very unsophisticated, perhaps to a young child. If the audience is someone you don't know, write to a close friend. If the audience has a definite point of view about the topic, write to someone with the opposite view. If you are having trouble writing a letter of recommendation for a friend who is applying for a job, put aside for a while the question of what you want to say to the employer and do a freewriting letter to your friend telling him bluntly everything you feel about him.

If you have difficulty varying the audience, try actually visualizing these alternate audiences you are writing to; address them by name periodically in your writing as though you were actually talking to them. If you are one of the many people who tend in general to forget about their audience and write to sort-of-nobody-in-particular, your writing probably tends to be dead. Practice visualizing your audience as you write—your real audience and some of these alternate audiences.

The act of writing to a different audience doesn't just clarify your thinking. It also leads you to new insights. If you have to write a job description for a very bureaucratic audience, but you start by writing it to your children or your parents or to a close friend who has no connection with your workplace, you will find yourself noticing important aspects of the job you are trying to analyze that you never would have noticed if you just wrote to the official audience. Write about the causes of the French Revolution as though you were Mao Tse-tung giving advice to revolutionaries or as though you were Kissinger writing a memo to the rest of the government about how to prevent revolution. You will have new insights.

10. *Vary the writer.* As you vary the audience, you often naturally vary the writer. Each device has its own power to generate

new insights. Write as though you were someone whose view on the topic is very different from your own. Or write as though you lived in a different culture. If you are analyzing a particular policy, pretend to be someone affected by it. If you are writing about a particular person—perhaps an essay about a historical character or an evaluation of a client or colleague—it is enormously fruitful to *be* that person and write a *self*-portrait or *self*-analysis. Again you will learn things you didn't know. If you are writing about a novel or poem or movie, *be* one of the people in it and see what he or she has to say. Or be the author and give your understanding of your own creation.

11. *Vary the time.* Write as though you were living in the past or the future. Write, for example, about the French Revolution as though you were living at the time or as though it hadn't happened yet but you had an intuition of its possibility. Write as though the *topic* were in a different time: if you are writing about civil disobedience or the relationship between the sexes, write about the topic in the distant past or future. Similarly, try writing to an *audience* in the past or the future.

Varying the audience and the writer and the time is particularly fruitful if you can't think of anything to say about your topic, or if everything you think of seems ordinary and obvious and uninteresting.

12. *Errors.* Write down things that are almost true or trying to be true; things that you are tempted to think or that others think but you know are false; dangerous mistakes. "People only take care of things they own." "John is essentially lazy." "Revolutions are always part of progress." Writing these down lessens the static in your head. The process corrals your thinking bit by bit into a narrower and narrower space so that a sprawling, confusing issue slowly becomes clearer and more manageable.

13. *Lies.* Write down quickly all the odd or crazy things you can come up with. For example: "The French Revolution wasn't started by the Wobblies in Seattle, or by Lenin, or by Marx, or by the Marx brothers. It wasn't part of the women's movement. It didn't last forty days and nights, it isn't in the Bible, they didn't just get the enemy drunk and slide them into the sea." If you let the nonsense roll effortlessly for ten or fifteen minutes—spelling out some of the individual fantasies at more length, too—you can discover some ideas that will help your thinking even if they are

not true. (And they may be true. Could the French Revolution have been part of the women's movement?)

Writing down as many lies as you can as quickly as you can gives you glimpses of your unconscious mind. You will discover some important preoccupations and assumptions that relate to the topic. Many, of course, will be irrelevant, but if you are more aware of them you can think better about the topic. In addition, even if you cannot draw any conclusions from reading back over the nonsense you have written, the process of writing it all down serves to clear some of the fog in your mind that was confusing or slowing down your thinking. You often end up with renewed energy.

Applying These Looping Techniques

In most cases three or four of these techniques are enough to help you generate lots of good thinking on your topic. Occasionally, for hard cases, you'll need more. First thoughts, prejudices, and instant versions are good ways to get warmed up and creative at a very early stage in your writing. Perhaps errors, too. Dialogues, stories, scenes, and portraits are useful later, after you have done some of the research and thinking and early writing. Varying the audience, the time, and the writer is helpful at any stage in the writing. It is particularly useful for enlarging your point of view or getting yourself more personally invested in your topic.

Writing down your prejudices is particularly valuable if you are writing about an issue where opinion plays a major role such as politics or ethics—a topic like abortion. In your final paper you want to be *careful* in all the applications of that word: careful to look at the evidence, to argue well, to document your conclusions—careful, in short, not to let your prejudices fool you or blind you. Here you want to do the opposite. Sometimes it's only by relinquishing all care and seeing what spills out that you can really get a glimpse of your own assumptions and point of view from the outside. Only by doing so—by understanding your own frame of reference—can you deal well with difficult issues, whether your goal is to analyze objectively or to persuade subtly.

Dialogues are particularly helpful if you are having trouble finding a real issue, something to quarrel about or get involved in—if you seem to have nothing but a whole bundle of thoughts that are true but uninteresting. A dialogue generates tension and energy. A dialogue is also ideal if you have to do some kind of compare-and-contrast analysis: you can get the two proposals or candidates or poems or modes of government to talk to each other and fight about their differences.

If you have to analyze a novel or work of art of some sort, stories, scenes, and portraits help you notice hidden structures or centers of energy behind the surface of the work. Errors are useful for a topic you find so confusing that your head spins. Vary the audience, the writer, and the time when you are trying to digest and make sense out of what you know. These techniques also help in revising, when you are trying to bring focus or organization to something that persists in sprawling all over the place.

But you may end up choosing among these techniques not on the basis of the kind of writing task you are engaged in but rather on the basis of your own temperament and skills. Some people, for example, are more comfortable and skilled when they write from experiences than when they write from thinking. They are better at writing stories, telling what they feel, describing specific sights, sounds, feels, and smells than they are at abstract reasoning, analysis, argument, and building trains of thought. If you are such a person you probably sound much duller when you write essays and reports than you actually are. But you will be able to get real perceptiveness and intelligence into conceptual writing if you use the experiential loop writing techniques: stories, scenes, and portraits. When you read over what you produce with these techniques, you will see that almost every piece contains a good insight which you can now easily put into the conceptual mode: "Oh, now I see what those two stories are telling me. I can trust John to do energetic, conscientious work when I give him a certain kind of direction, but when I don't, he just goofs off." Or "This poem keeps reminding me of a bittersweet memory of my own that seems very different from anything in the poem. I never would have called the poem melancholy, but pondering this memory and the poem together, I can finally see a faint undertone of melancholy in some of the images—faint, but important in explaining why the poem is powerful."

If you have the opposite temperament and love to reason and argue on paper, your essays or reports will benefit in a different way from using stories, scenes, and portraits. You will get more life into your arguments. Indeed your very taste and skill for reasoning may *undermine* your power to persuade readers if your arguments are too abstract—too little grounded in human experience. You may get out-argued, as it were, by people with poorer arguments. Stories, scenes, and portraits will give your arguments more of the experiential texture they need to work on flesh and blood readers. In addition, these loop techniques will simply give you *more* ideas than you usually get, even though you love reasoning. Reasoning itself is deductive. It only tells you more about what you already know. But writing stories, scenes, and portraits is a very inductive process and will lead you to new insights and new points of view you couldn't reach by reasoning alone.

The important thing is to try out all these devices. You will learn which ones work best for you in various circumstances. And you will probably develop variations and brand new devices that are particularly suited to your needs.

The Voyage Home

Many new insights and understandings will come to you as you engage in this writing on the voyage out, but don't demand them or struggle for them. If you want to end up with new insights, you have to allow yourself to *lose sight* of your topic during much of the voyage out. You are letting goals, meanings, and end-products slip partly out of mind in order to allow for restructurings of your mind and new points of view that would be impossible if you kept your eye on the goal all the time.

But the voyage home is a process of bending the curve back toward the original goal. Return, then, to full consciousness of what your goal is: think as precisely and consciously as you can about your topic and audience. If there was an assignment or guidelines, think about exactly how they were phrased. And think about exactly what you want to do to your audience, about what they expect, and about their relationship to you. Then go back over all that writing you did during the voyage out and look for useful ideas and insights.

For in the voyage home, obviously enough, you are engaged in the process of revising. You have used your creative mentality to generate lots of examples and ideas and the makings of ideas, and now you need to use your critical mentality to shape a coherent draft out of this raw writing. You can choose among various methods for revising: I have already described quick revising in Chapter 5 and other ways are in Section III, "More Ways To Revise."

I usually start by just reading it all through without doing any writing at all—just to immerse myself in one jump in all the writing I have done from so many different points of view and in so many different modes and moods. Perhaps I mark the margin of what feel like especially good or important bits, or even jot down some notes when the reading makes me think of something new I'm afraid I'll forget. But this first read-through gives me the lay of the land. Sometimes by simply reading through everything you have written, you will see very clearly what you want for your main point and what all the other points are. But sometimes you won't see yet how to turn it into a draft.

For it is probably fair to say that the loop writing process, especially if you use it for a piece of expository or conceptual writing, makes more of a mess than the other writing processes. With the dangerous method and the direct writing process you keep your eye on the goal at all times. With the open-ended process you probably arrive gradually at your final piece of writing. With the loop writing process you may have to struggle harder for order.

For one thing you probably have to throw more away. A generative process as creative as this one will inevitably turn up more insights than you can logically or comfortably fit in one piece of work. You will have to develop the strength to throw away some good material. And when you figure out your final train of thought, you will probably find some gaps you need to fill in.

In addition you may have to work harder to clarify some of the insights it has produced. That is, even though some of the insights will be sitting right there on the surface of your raw writing, some will only be potentially there. While you were writing some particular story or portrait that somehow seemed intriguing, you weren't in the best position to see the insight into the causes of the French Revolution. But now that you are thinking carefully about your topic and applying all these varied pieces of writing to it, you will usually see the insight.

A few pieces will persist in being obscure. You have a dialogue where the two speakers are at loggerheads and their disagreement yields you nothing but perplexity. What does it tell you about the suitability of this candidate for the job? About the trustworthiness of your research on the environmental impact? You don't know. What is that story or portrait telling you about the causes of the French Revolution? Is it telling you to think about the influence of a certain person? Is it telling you to think about a certain meaning of the word *cause?* Some passages won't yield up their secrets. Get the ones you can and let the others go. Assume each has a meaning and think hard about what it might be, but after a while don't waste any more effort on it. Perhaps the meaning will pop up later as part of some other train of thought.

The loop writing process lends itself to a form of writing I call the collage which I describe in Chapter 14. I include there two collage essays which illustrate the use of ingredients produced by the loop writing process.

Summary of Loop Writing Procedures

- First thoughts.
- Prejudices.
- Instant version.
- Dialogues.
- Narrative thinking.
- Stories.
- Scenes.
- Portraits.
- Vary the audience.
- Vary the writer.
- Vary the time.
- Errors.
- Lies.
- The loop writing process is generally helpful in bringing life to conceptual writing and it is especially helpful if you feel bored or unconnected to your topic.

9

Metaphors for
Priming the Pump[*]

This chapter contains metaphorical questions that will help you produce more ideas, perceptions, and feelings about a topic. These questions will help you see more aspects of what you want to write about and also see the limits or blind spots in your accustomed point of view.

Suppose, for example, you are preparing to write a case study or report or essay about someone you have known or worked with. "Describe ——— as *two* people and tell how these two people work together (or don't work together)." "What would never happen to ———? If it did, what would be the result?" "Describe ——— as a bad person." "Tell the three or four most important sounds that come to mind in connection with ———." If you try quickly answering these questions about someone you know, you will figure out things you didn't know or only half knew before.

Your new impressions need not all be accurate, however, to be useful. When you let yourself describe people as bad, you may discover for example that the vague disapproval you've always felt toward them is really part of a deep but only partly conscious prejudice in you that comes from old feelings or attitudes. Or that you've never forgiven them for not inviting you to that party ages ago. The free writing helps you see around such impediments and thus see more accurately.

* I am indebted to the help I received from Dwight Paine in devising an earlier version of some of these questions. For more about the theory of metaphor making and thinking that underlies these exercises, see "Real Learning and Nondisciplinary Courses," Peter Elbow, *Journal of General Education*, vol. 23, no. 2, 1971.

These questions are generally most useful when you first begin your thinking and writing for some writing task. You need not write down long answers to all the questions. Often a phrase will do. Some items, however, such as perhaps "Describe ——— as bad," will set you off on an important piece of writing. The main thing is to make sure that after you have answered a set of questions you plunge immediately into as much fast raw writing as you can manage to do. Answering the questions puts you in a condition where you have more ideas and insights than usual.

These are also exercises in metaphorical thinking. If you use them regularly you will gradually increase your creative and imaginative capacity. (Aristotle was right when he said that metaphorical ability is a mark of intelligence but wrong, I think, when he said it could not be learned.)

Every metaphor is a force-fit, a mistake, a putting together of things that don't normally or literally belong together. A good metaphor in poetry or any kind of writing is also somehow graceful and just right. (William Carlos Williams starts a poem: "Your thighs are apple trees/whose blossoms touch the sky.") But the questions here and the answers you give needn't be graceful or just right. They should in fact wrench and violate your accustomed way of thinking about your topic.

Perhaps, for example, you are analyzing an organization, say Acme Packaging or the C.I.A. The question asks: "If, in addition to French-kissing, there were Acme Packaging kissing (or C.I.A. kissing), what would that kissing be like?" Perhaps Acme Packaging kissing is kissing a sheet of paper and sending it through inter-office mail. Would C.I.A. kissing consist of quick hard hugs once every two months, making sure not to look at each other? Your answer may seem immediately useful, it may seem meaningless, it may suggest something you already knew perfectly well, or it may make you notice a half-conscious perception and then go on to find words for it.

Perhaps you are writing about why Shakespeare begins *Hamlet* with the ghost-on-the-battlements scene, and the exercise says "Pretend the pump needs priming." "How then," you must say to yourself, "is pouring water in a pump to make it draw like starting a play with this scene?" Various answers will come to mind. The first one that occurs to me is that Shakespeare puts us off balance in the opening scene (you can't tell what's happening the first time you read or see it) to get us ready to experience uncertainty as one of the main underlying feelings and themes of the play. I find it a play which refuses to settle down or be clear.

But the main usefulness of these questions won't come from just one of them, no matter how lucky the insight you get from it, but from a whole succession of them: twisting and stretching what you are trying to write about by mapping it against a variety of terrains—seeing a variety of possibilities in it.

The next item for *Hamlet*, then, would be "Imagine the problem of the opening scene as a problem of defective materials." What comes to my mind first is to wonder whether there might be a problem of availability of actors. Is it something about having to start with Bernardo, Francisco, Marcello, and the ghost because of some complication growing out of actors taking two or more parts? Or were these actors needed to do things backstage next scene? It doesn't seem to make much sense, but it's fine to settle for far-fetched or ridiculous answers to these questions. And don't be held back by lack of data. You are mind stretching, not trying to be sure.

But then in the midst of these fumblings another more immediately fruitful thought strikes me. The *audience* is defective material. Some members of the audience are probably still coming in when the play starts. Others would not yet have shifted full attention to the play from the business of their day or from their conversation with companions. This scene has a certain amount of power to capture audience attention—its mystery and drama—but more important, probably, is the fact that the scene is a bit expendable. If it takes half the scene for some viewers to get around to paying good attention, they are not penalized, they don't miss something they need for comprehending or enjoying the play. That seems a useful thought.

Next item: "Too many cooks." Too many actors? I tend to be confused by the people running around in the beginning of the play. Too many writers? Could others have collaborated in writing this scene? Was it a suggestion from one of the other actor-shareholders that Shakespeare could not turn down? Could it have been a popular ghost scene from one of the earlier versions of *Hamlet* or some other play? The metaphorical questions often don't *give* you answers, but rather make you ready to look at more kinds of answers.

The trick in answering one of these questions is to force yourself to come up with something without spending too long. And then go on to the next one. That means making things up and sometimes producing nonsense: cartwheels of the mind. If it takes you more than a minute or two, go on to the next one anyway. Not to worry. You may find it impossible to answer all the questions in a set. But you do need to bring to these questions a spirit of entering in, pretending, playing. (If that work of art you want to write about were your body, where would you find its head, hands, feet, heart? If it were a car, where would you find the motor, the muffler?) If you can't enter into the spirit of these questions, it is probably not worth struggling. But before you conclude that the questions are too silly, think about the fact that you engage in the same kind of far-fetched metaphorical thinking every night when you dream (even if you don't remember). Your ability to make rich and creative metaphorical connections is there ready to be brought under more conscious control.

Sometimes you will notice the significance of an answer right after it comes to you. ("Hmm. Freedom is round. Does that mean I take it for granted that freedom is perfect?") But often it's better not to seek interpretation as you are answering the questions. It can make you too self-conscious, too interpretation-hungry so that when you are asked to think of your organization as a method of poisoning you can only follow a path of conceptual translation: "Let's see, what opinion do I have of my organization? Now what mode of poisoning does my opinion remind me of?" That misses the leverage in these questions. Best if you can let a poison float to mind without having to think about it. Perhaps the poison that comes to mind seems totally irrelevant in itself, but when you think of it in conjunction with some other seemingly ridiculous answers, you find a new and valuable insight about the organization. Indeed your answers will fertilize your raw writing even if you never work out their implications consciously.

• • •

I have divided these questions up into sets and phrased them to fit particular writing tasks as follows:

a. Questions to help you write about someone you have known or worked with.

b. Questions to help you write about someone you have studied or read about.
c. Questions to help you write about someone's life as a whole.
d. Questions to help you write a self-evaluation.
e. Questions to help you write about a place.
f. Questions to help you write about an object.
g. Questions to help you write about a work of art.
h. Questions to help you write about an organization or group.
i. Questions to help you write about a problem or dilemma.
j. Questions to help you write about an abstract concept.

Many of the questions in one set can well be applied to a different writing task. My groupings are sometimes arbitrary. You will find that some questions particularly suit your imagination and are especially fruitful for you on almost any enterprise. You will also find it helpful to start inventing your own questions.

a. Questions to help you write about someone you have known or worked with (for example, you have to write an evaluation or a letter of recommendation or a case report, or perhaps you simply want to understand someone better).

1. What would ———'s face tell if you knew nothing else?
2. What would ———'s body tell if you knew nothing else?
3. What would ———'s posture and gait tell you if you knew nothing else?
4. What would ———'s manner or style tell if you knew nothing else?
5. ———'s name is the name of a color. What color?
6. ——— is an animal. What animal?
7. ——— is a food. What food?
8. Who would play ——— in a movie about her?
9. ———'s brains are not in the head, heart not in the chest, guts not in the belly. Tell where they really are.
10. ——— is two people. Describe them and how they work together or don't work together.
11. ——— is really a spy. For whom? What assignment?
12. If you were going to spend a year in close contact with ———, where would you prefer it to be and under what circumstances? What would be the worst place and circumstances?

13. Imagine that you believe all character and behavior comes from imitating significant "role models" when young. Who and what sorts of people do you suppose ——— imitated?

14. Imagine you are a kind of Platonist/Pythagorean/Buddhist who believes souls are reincarnated over and over again as they work their way gradually from being a vegetable to being a pure spirit. Where is ——— in this cycle? What previously? What next? (You slip backwards for bad behavior.)

15. Imagine you are an extreme Freudian who believes that all important behavior grows out of unconscious feelings—usually sexual or aggressive. Give a quick interpretation of ———'s behavior and functioning.

16. If you were writing the history of the *sounds* you've heard while being with ——— (excluding words), what would be the three or four most important sounds in that history?

17. Imagine you think ——— is a very good person. Now describe ———.

18. Imagine you think ——— is a very bad person. Now describe ———.

19. What is something that would never happen to ———? Imagine it happening? What would be the outcome?

20. Imagine an important situation when you were with ———. Close your eyes and try to bring the experience back. Now pretend to be ——— and describe that situation.

21. What weather does ——— bring into the room?

b. Questions to help you write about someone you have studied or read about (for example, a politician or historical character or person in a work of art).

1. Describe ——— as an ordinary person.

2. Describe ——— as a unique and special person.

3. Imagine ——— were the opposite sex. Describe the life that ——— would have lived.

4. Describe the life ——— would have lived in a very different era.

5. Make up or guess the most important childhood event in ———'s life.

6. Describe ———'s life if that event hadn't occurred or something entirely different had occurred.

7. Tell a science fiction story with ——— in it.
8. Tell a soap opera plot with ——— in it.
9. What does ——— most need to cry about?
10. Imagine you are very angry and strike ———. How and where do you strike?
11. What is the caress that ——— most needs to get?
12. Give ——— an accurate compliment that ——— probably never hears.
13. Imagine ———'s hair were entirely different from how it is or was. What would it bring out that you hadn't noticed before?
14. What's a secret about ——— that ——— hasn't told anyone?
15. What's something about ——— that even ——— doesn't know?
16. How would ———'s mother or father describe ———?
17. How would ———'s child describe ———?
18. Describe ——— as a good president of the U.S.A. A bad president. What would be the important policies or decisions in both cases?
19. Tell a recurring dream that ——— has.

c. *Questions to help you write about someone's life as a whole.*

1. Describe ———'s life and character as essentially unchanging. What may look like changes are really just ways of staying essentially the same.
2. Describe ———'s life and character as essentially determined by important changes or turning points (even if it looks to most people as though no such changes or turning points occurred).
3. Imagine you believe people are truly free: they somehow choose or cause everything that happens to them. Describe ———'s life or character.
4. Imagine you have the opposite point of view: people are not free, they are determined by events they cannot control. Describe ———'s life or character.
5. Find as many rhythms as you can in ———'s life: events that repeat or recur whether the scale is in moments or years.
6. What events in ———'s life only occurred once?
7. Describe ——— as primarily a product of national, cultural, and ethnic influences.

8. Describe ——— as primarily a product of personal and family influences.
9. Describe ——— as primarily a product of economic and class influences.
10. Describe ——— as essentially the product of conditioning. What behavior was rewarded and what was punished?
11. Describe ———'s character as a solution to past problems.
12. Describe ———'s character as carrying the seeds of future problems.
13. Think of two or three very unlikely professions or occupations for ———. Describe ——— in those professions. (For example, describe Napoleon as a poet.)

d. Questions to help you write a self-evaluation (for some job or enterprise or life period).

1. Who will play you in the movie about this period or enterprise?
2. What was the predominant weather for this whole time? Or what changes occurred in the weather?
3. Think of yourself as having done a wonderful job. What do you notice?
4. Think of yourself as having done a terrible job. What do you notice?
5. Take responsibility for everything that went wrong. You did it all on purpose or because you didn't give a damn or because you were mad. Explain the events.
6. Tell the three most important moments in this period.
7. What did you learn from each of those moments?
8. What qualities in you did this period bring out?
9. What qualities in you remained hidden or unused?
10. Imagine this period as a journey. Where did it take you? Where did it start?
11. Imagine it is only a half journey, you are only halfway there. Where? What is the second half of the journey?
12. Imagine this period as an interruption or detour or setback in some larger journey. What is that larger journey and how does this function as a time-out?
13. If this enterprise was *work*, describe it as play. Or vice versa.

14. Imagine this enterprise turns out to have very different goals from the ones you expected. Imagine some of these surprising goals.
15. Invent a dream you might have about yourself in this enterprise. Just use what first comes to mind. It doesn't have to make sense.
16. Imagine this whole enterprise *was* a dream. What is it a dream about? What will you wake up to?

e. Questions to help you write about a place. Go to this place in your imagination. Pick a particular time of the year and of the day. See it, feel the weather, hear the sounds. Make contact for a few quiet moments.

1. How is your mood affected by being there?
2. Imagine being there for a whole year. How would that make you better? How worse?
3. Imagine you have just seen, in only five minutes, the whole history of this place since the beginning of the world. Briefly tell this history.
4. Imagine your body is the whole world. Where on your body is ———?
5. If someone said "It's a ——— day," what kind of a day would it be?
6. Imagine you have always been blind. Describe your place briefly.
7. Let the place describe you.
8. Your place is an animal. What animal is it?
9. Your place is a person. Who?
10. Name a story, a song, and a movie your place reminds you of.
11. What is the first thing that comes to mind which your place would never remind you of?
12. What other place does your place make you think of?
13. In what weather is your place most itself?
14. Some places have a proper name all to themselves—like "Chicago." Other places only have a general name they must share with similar places—like "bathroom." Give your place the opposite kind of name from the one it has.
15. How does this new name change things. (For example, how

would your feelings be different? What things would you notice now? What would you *not* notice now? Would things happen differently there now?)

16. Find as many of your place's rhythms as you can. (For example, find things that happen there at regular intervals—whether they happen every second, every month, or every thousand years. Or any other sorts of rhythms you notice.)

17. Name as many things as you can that only happen there once. Are there any rhythms among any of them?

18. Think of your place as if it were old and near death. Now tell what place it was when it was only a child.

19. Think of your place as if it were a young child or young animal. Now tell what place it will grow up to be.

20. If "———" stands for the regular name of your place, what does the following sentence mean: "If you do that again, I'm going to ——— you"?

21. Imagine your place was the whole universe and you had always lived there. Tell how you and your neighbors explain the beginning of the universe. How do you folks think the universe is going to end?

22. Think of your place as if it is carefully planned in every detail. Now describe it briefly from this point of view.

23. Think of your place as if everything just happened by accident, chance, and luck. Describe it from this point of view.

24. Think of your place as if it is haunted. Tell about it (for example, how it became haunted; what it does to people it doesn't like).

25. Imagine an anti-universe where everything is opposite or backwards from the way we know it. Describe your anti-place in this anti-universe.

f. Questions to help you write about an object.

1. Think of a particular moment in which this object was meaningful or important to you. Close your eyes and take yourself back into that moment. Bring back the reality of the object and the scene for a few moments. The time of day. The time of year. The air. The smells. Your feelings.

2. If you had never seen the object before, what would you notice when you first looked at it?

3. If you knew it fairly well, what would you notice when you looked at it?
4. If you knew it better and longer than anyone else—if you knew it closely for a whole lifetime—what would you see when you looked at it?
5. Tell two or three different ways you might take it apart.
6. Tell what it's like to take it apart and then to take apart the parts till you get down to its basic ingredients. (Go fast. Don't worry.)
7. Imagine a different world in which this object was made of completely different ingredients. What would they be? Tell the advantages and disadvantages of this new arrangement.
8. Tell how this *particular* object came to exist. (Not this *kind* of object. That is, if you are talking about a pencil, don't tell how *pencils in general* came to exist. Tell how this particular pencil came to exist: where it was made; where the wood, lead, and rubber came from; how they came to be put together.)
9. Pretend it came to exist in a different way and tell what it was like.
10. Tell the history of this particular object since it first existed.
11. Tell its history for the last five minutes.
12. Tell how this *kind* of object came to exist (for example, pencils in general).
13. Tell another story of how this kind of object came to exist, but this time make the story a kind of a love story too.
14. Think of as many ways as possible of grouping a whole bunch of these objects. (In the case of pencils, for example, by length, by color, chewed/unchewed, free/paid for, by color of lead, etc., etc.)
15. Think of a lot of different ways it is actually used.
16. Tell three ways it *might* be used, but isn't.
17. Tell a mystery story of how it came to be used in one of those ways.
18. Tell three ways it could not possibly be used.
19. Tell a science fiction story of how the world changes in such a way that it *is* used in one of the ways you just called impossible.
20. If this object were an animal, what animal would it be?
21. If it were a person, who would it be?

22. If it could speak, what would it tell you about yourself that you weren't aware of?
23. Tell three things it might *stand for* or remind you of. (For example, a pencil might stand for a tree, school, or writing.)
24. Imagine you are much richer than you are and think of something it might stand for. Imagine you are much poorer than you are and think of something it might stand for.
25. What might it stand for if you were much older than you are? Much younger?

g. *Questions to help you write about a work of art.*

1. Pretend you made it. Something important was going on in your life and you poured strong feelings into it. What was going on? What were those feelings?
2. Pretend you made it, but nothing special was going on in your life and you had no strong feelings. Describe what you liked about this thing you created.
3. Pretend you made it and are very dissatisfied. Why are you dissatisfied with it?
4. You made it as a gift for someone you know (a real person in your life). Who? How did she feel about your gift?
5. Imagine this work of art as medicine. What is the disease? What are the symptoms? How does this medicine cure it?
6. Imagine this work of art as poison. It destroys whoever experiences it. Describe the effects of this poison, the course of deterioration.
7. Imagine that everyone on the globe owned this work of art or all infants were repeatedly exposed to it. What would be the effects?
8. What is someone most apt to notice the first time she encounters this work of art?
9. What would you notice about this work of art if you had never encountered *any* other works in its medium (any other novels, movies, ballets, or whatever)?
10. What tiny detail in this work says more about it than any other?
11. Is this work male or female?
12. What other work of art would it marry?

13. What works of art do they have for children?
14. Imagine this work of art as part of an evolutionary process. What work did it evolve from? What work will it evolve into?
15. This work is the only human artifact transported to Mars, the only evidence they have about humans. What guesses or conclusions would they reach about humans on the basis of this work?
16. Imagine your work of art as evolving into different media (poetry, novels, movies, paintings, music, ballet, etc., etc.). Describe two or three of these new works of art. See what these evolutions tell you about the original work.
17. High art/low art: describe ———— as though it were in the opposite category from the one it usually occupies. (For example, describe *Paradise Lost* as a soap opera.)
18. Anonymous folk art/signed art made by individual artist: describe ———— as though it were in the opposite category from the one it usually occupies. (For example, describe a tribal chant as though it were a Beethoven symphony.)

h. Questions to help you write about an organization or group of people.

1. What animal is ————?
2. What are the rhythms in the history of ————? Events or cycles that recur, whether on a scale of decades or days?
3. What are some of the things that have only happened once to ————?
4. What are the three most important moments in the history of ————?
5. ———— is alive, chooses, acts. Describe its behavior as completely conscious, willed, deliberate.
6. ———— has feelings. What does it feel now? What is the history of its feelings?
7. If there were two of ————, where would the second one be? How would they interact?
8. Imagine ———— is a machine, like a car or a pinball machine. Describe how it works. (For example, where is the motor? the flipper?)
9. What is the most important part of the machine? Which part breaks down most?

10. Map ——— onto your body: where are the head, feet, hands, ears, eyes?

11. Imagine all organizations had the same structure or mode of operating that ——— has. What would be the effect on the world?

12. What human qualities does it bring out in members? Which ones does it suppress or fail to use?

13. If in addition to French-kissing there were ——— kissing, what would that kind of kissing be like?

14. Describe ——— as a poison; its effects; its antidote.

15. Describe ——— as a weapon. How do you make it go off? What does it do? Who invented it?

16. Think of ——— in the scheme of evolution. What did it evolve from? What is it evolving toward?

17. What physical shape is ———? Imagine that shape in locomotion: how does it move?

18. Think about ——— as part of an ecological system: What does it depend on? What depends on it? What does it eat? What does it emit? What eats it? What emits it?

i. Suggestions to help you write about a problem or dilemma.

1. The pump needs priming.

2. Defective materials.

3. Too many cooks: a committee designed or executed it.

4. A bribe will do the trick. Bribe whom? With what?

5. The problem is that God is angry. At whom? Why? What did that person do to make God angry?

6. It's a problem of addiction. Who is addicted to what?

7. The problem has been stated wrong. Find two or three ways of stating it differently.

8. The problem comes from bad data. Guess what data are wrong and why?

9. It's a Gordian knot: stop trying to untie it, cut through it with a sword.

10. The problem is a car that won't start in the winter. What are the things you would do.

11. It's a problem of logic; for example, a is to b as c is to d (A:B :: C:D).

12. It looks like a problem, but really everything is fine if you only take the right point of view.

13. Assume the problem has no solution. What is the sensible course of action or strategy that follows from this conclusion?

14. It's a problem in numbers. Try performing the following operations on it: addition, subtraction, division, multiplication, percentages, moving a decimal place.

15. It's just something wrong with digestion: someone ate the wrong thing or has diarrhea, constipation, vomiting.

16. It's a problem of people: incompatible temperaments; struggling for dominance; loving each other but unable to admit it; feeling scared but not admitting it.

17. Outdated design.

18. It's problem of too little money; or rather too much money.

19. It's sabotage.

20. It's a matter of physical sickness. Need for (a) special drug; (b) long recuperation with not much medicine; (c) helping the patient deal with the impossibility of cure.

21. It's mental illness. Needs: (a) shock treatment; (b) talking therapy; (c) group therapy; (d) conditioning therapy; (e) help and support in going through craziness and coming out on the other side; (f) recognition that society is crazy and patient is sane.

j. Questions to help you write about an abstract concept (such as freedom, democracy, altruism, sexuality, justice; topics like these benefit particularly from the experiential techniques of the loop writing process, such as prejudices, stories, dialogues, moments, and portraits).

1. What color is ————?

2. What shape?

3. Imagine that shape moving around: what is its mode of locomotion?

4. Give the worst, most biased, distorted definitions of ———— you can give.

5. Imagine this word or phrase did not exist. (Imagine a people with no word for it in their language.)

6. What would be different because the word did not exist?

7. Imagine ———— is a place. Describe it.

8. What animal would make a good insignia for ———?
9. What persons are connected in your mind with ———?
10. If ——— fell in love with something else, what would that something else be? What would they have for children?
11. Design a flag for ———.
12. Think of three or four abstractions that are bigger than ——— or can beat it up; and three or four which are smaller or can be beaten up by ———.
13. Think of ——— as part of an ecological system: What does it depend on? What depends on it? What does it eat? What does it emit? What eats it? What emits it?
14. What are the most memorable sounds associated with ———? Smells?

10

Working on Writing While
Not Thinking about Writing

> The door opens. In comes Abby, crying.
> "Wah meeg blah egg rogg wee rogg."
> "What happened?"
> "Wah meeg blah egg rogg wee rogg."
> "What happened? I can't understand you."
> "Wah meeg blah egg rogg wee rogg."
> "Benjy threw a rock at you?"
> "Wah meeg blah egg rogg wee rogg."
> "You ate a rock?"
> "Uh huh."

While Abby fails to communicate, I examine her language with all my attention. As soon as minimal communication occurs, I ignore her language and all my attention slides through it, past it, to the meaning, to the nonlinguistic reality, to the question of whether to call the hospital. When the glass is fogged up, we look at the glass. The glass is all we can see. As soon as it gets unfogged, we ignore it and see through it to the scene outside.

You will help your writing if you can find occasions when the job you are doing matters a lot but the quality of the writing doesn't matter at all—occasions when you pay no attention to the glass and look only at the scene beyond it. A good example is if you are trying to make up your mind about which of two jobs to take and after sitting and stewing and not getting anywhere for a few days, you finally decide to spend a couple of hours writing out all your thoughts and feelings. You don't try to make an orderly presentation or argument, you just write and write until your thoughts and feelings are on paper. The process gets you unstuck. At first, you lean in your writing toward one job and start to get excited about it, then toward the other. But it isn't mere vacillation as it was when you were just thinking. Writing somehow makes it into a *working through* process so there is development, growth, progress.

It's a great relief to write seriously and usefully, without thinking about your writing. And it helps the rest of your writing. It makes you more comfortable putting words on paper and it makes those words more natural and lively. In this brief chapter, I will suggest a few more occasions when you can work on your writing while you are getting other jobs done.

• If you are facing a difficult dilemma as in the example above, write out your thoughts and feelings as quickly but as fully as they occur to you. Don't just make lists of reasons for and against (except perhaps at the end). Follow threads of thought and feeling where they lead.

• If you want to digest and remember what you are reading, try writing about it instead of taking notes. Stop periodically—at the end of each chapter or when something important strikes you—and simply write about what you have read and your reactions to it. This procedure may make you nervous at first because you can't "cover" as many points or make something as neatly organized as when you take notes. But you will remember more. Perfectly organized notes that cover everything are beautiful, but they live on paper, not in your mind. The same procedure is helpful for lectures. You will learn more if you take no notes at all and instead put all your attention into listening; then at the end sit and write for ten or fifteen minutes about what you have heard and what it means to you.

• If you have to give a talk or speech, work out what you want to say by writing out trains of thought instead of sitting there trying to work it out inside your head and just writing down mere words or phrases for your notes. You'll think better and get your thoughts clearer in your head. After you write you may still want some notes to speak from, but you can make them quickly and they will be briefer because they are just small notations to remind you of what you've figured out. The process of writing and of using shorter notes will probably enable you to talk in a more relaxed way and make better contact with your audience.

• Keep a journal. Explore different ways of doing so: not just what happened, but thoughts, feelings, portraits, snatches of conversation, quotations; not just by writing at the end of the day or week, but intermittently at odd times of the day. Try, for example, taking a moment at the beginning of the day (as you sit down to your desk or after breakfast or on the bus) and write about what you want to accomplish that day or about the spirit or attitude you want to maintain. One particularly illuminating way to keep a journal—to explore not just the present but the shape of your whole life—has been developed by Ira Progoff. (See *At a Journal Workshop*, New York, 1975.)

Some people find it a treat to write in an elegantly bound journal with fine paper—a sensual event. But for many others this adds the pressure to write nicely, to make it memorable, even to think about readers and this makes writing more of an ordeal. If you make your journal a folder rather than a book, you can write on whatever paper comes to hand at odd moments in the day when a thought strikes you.

• Write informal notes to people when a thought strikes you. "Dear Byron, I appreciated the way you ran that meeting. It helped a lot that you told that story about yourself. I was grateful that you got us back on the agenda when we were all sidetracked. The troops seemed restless today. I think you are doing a terrific job." Even when you see someone frequently, sometimes it's easier to get something across on paper than by talking. When it's appreciation you want to express, sometimes the other person is too self-conscious and blots out what you say with protests. ("Oh no, actually I've screwed up about this and that.") And when you've finally decided to tell someone how he is frustrating or hurting you, sometimes he blots you out with arguments or excuses. If your goal, in short, is to make someone *hear* what you are saying, often you do better writing words on paper than trying to have a conversation. Even nonstop uncareful writing.

• Write informal letters. Of course it seems easier to call; or to wait till next month when you will see the person. But in addition to the good practice in writing, letters work better in certain ways than conversations. Often it takes the leisure, privacy, and reflectiveness of writing to permit you to tell him what's important: perhaps deep feelings you have about him or a delicate, tentative train of thought. And often you give your reader much more of the texture of your life in writing than you give on the phone or even in talking. You describe better that day in the woods or what struck you as you were walking to work. The uninterrupted monologue of writing permits you to tell what it was really like, to say what you really felt, to finish the whole story, instead of so often being sidetracked by the give and take of conversation.

• • •

There are certain times in the natural cycle of any enterprise—a job, a trip, a relationship, a course of study, a writing task—when it is useful to stop and write out some of your thoughts and feelings.

• At the start. When you are starting a new job or course of study, for example, you will do much better if you sit down and write out your hopes and expectations and fears about what it's going to be like. If you write fast and freely you will discover important assumptions and feelings. "I wonder when this one will end." "If it's the right job for me, I'll love every minute." "School learning can't be useful and it's got to be boring."

The process of writing out your *goals* helps you in particular to come closer actually to achieving some of them, instead of being vaguely hopeful for a while and then vaguely disappointed. Writing helps you see which goals are actually attainable and which are unrealistic traps. You can see which ones conflict with which others. Try to zero in on a few important goals and force yourself to specify the first concrete steps. "I have to find so and so's phone number." "I have to get a pair of waterproof boots."

• Stuck points. When you are stuck at any task, you can often get going again by writing down everything that is going on. When did things start to go wrong? How would you describe the problem from where you now sit? Tell the sequence of events inside you; outside you. Even if this writing doesn't solve the problem, it heightens your awareness of this kind of problem so that next time you'll notice it sooner and deal with it better.

• Breakthroughs. It's such a relief to get out of a jam that you just want to forge ahead. But if you use some of that relief to fuel a short writing-break to tell yourself what you did right or what the necessary ingredients seemed to be—while it's fresh in your mind—you will be more in charge next time and not just have to trust luck.

• Final reflections. At the end of a job or a series of meetings or a day, try writing briefly about what you did well and what you could have done better. This kind of conscious reflective writing can mean the difference between growing and just continuing to function at the same level. Much good learning I see here at The Evergreen State College comes from students having to write a reflection on what they have learned and how they learned it at the end of each quarter of study.

• • •

Use writing to aid group process.

• At the start of a taskforce or series of meetings, it helps people to work together if you can get everyone to take a couple of moments to write about what they hope, think, and fear will happen, and then either to share these pieces of very informal writing or to speak briefly on the basis of them. Of course, people will disagree. "I'm looking forward to a close-knit comfortable friendly time." "I'm looking forward to some good knockdown dragout arguments." But it's a great benefit if these can be public right at the start. Some disagreements can actually be negotiated. Others can at least be accepted with realism. A few people may realize they've come to the wrong place and leave. When expectations are left unexpressed and the conflicts come as a surprise, it leads to that familiar pattern in group functioning where people have high hopes at the start and then gradually withdraw their involvement as they get disappointed—sometimes even sabotaging the enterprise as they pull out.

• If, in the middle of a meeting or seminar, a particularly hard question comes up, it is helpful to have everyone just write in an exploratory way for five or ten minutes. People will have better ideas. Like brainstorming, writing provides safety for exploring, but it doesn't take so much time. And if some people are habitually quiet so that you lose the benefit of their thinking and their point of view, it's probable that they want more time and privacy to reflect a moment on their first thoughts and check that they are not silly or obvious. Trying to talk and think at the same time is the bane of most meetings: some people love to do it and speak badly and too much; others are reluctant to do it, so the group loses their contribution. (If those who work with you don't want to interrupt a meeting for reflective freewriting you can just tune out and do it yourself.)

• When a meeting ends, especially if the group will continue to meet in the future, it's useful to take just a few moments for everyone to write down a couple of perceptions about what was helpful and not so helpful about the process (for example, the agenda was well planned; someone was particularly good at formulating an issue; someone else kept interrupting). These perceptions can be quickly shared either on paper or in brief comments. No need necessarily to discuss them. Matters usually improve gradually by themselves through the airing of these perceptions. The goal is not to figure out the absolute truth, but to learn how people experienced things.

Obviously these writing tasks I propose for meetings could be performed by speaking rather than writing, and it is easy to assume that speaking is always more authentic, immediate, and genuine than writing. But if, for example, you decide to end a meeting with a few minutes of *spoken* feedback from everyone about the process, you will find that people often blather and don't really say what is on their mind. "I enjoyed the meeting. I think it would help a lot if we all tried to stick to the subject a bit more." If the person who said that had five minutes to write his thoughts down first, he would be much more likely to come out and say, "Larry, I think you are making it harder for us to get our work done because you keep interrupting people before they are finished, and when you talk you make long speeches. Please stop doing that."

The reason for the difference is interesting. If someone asks you to *speak* your perceptions in a group, you have to do three jobs at once: figure out what you think; figure out how to say it so others will understand; and also figure out whether you *want* to say it (especially if it is controversial or personal). Trying to do all three at once in front of an audience is difficult, and so you often solve the difficulty by deciding not to say anything at all. When you have the privacy to collect your thoughts in writing, however, you often find the courage to share a thought which, while you were writing it out, you assumed you could not share. Seeing your thought on paper somehow helps you see that it's not such a hard thing to say, not such a big deal—makes it easier to say to yourself, "I don't need to beat around the bush. It's time someone was blunt with Larry about his behavior in meetings."

• • •

People usually assume that writing is always meant to communicate with others. When you use it that way you must think very carefully about it *as writing*. "Will these words really mean to the reader what they mean to me? Will they have the effect I assume they will have?" But writing is also very useful as a way to work out your thoughts and feelings for yourself alone. When you use it in this way as a process of exploration and discovery, you don't have to think carefully about it as writing (however carefully you may think about the matter you are exploring). Oddly enough, writing as exploration usually helps your writing as communication.

Poetry as No Big Deal

I remember Jeremy, a little English boy whose mother had to tell him that his music lessons were ending. His music teacher had decided he wasn't musical. He looked crestfallen and said to his mother, "But I *feel* musical."

Many people *feel* poetic. Capable of poetry. Sometimes they feel that way even though they have no particular idea or image or feeling they want to write about. Just a feeling that they would like to write a poem and that they could write a good one. It's a feeling that inhabits the midparts of the body anywhere between the gut and the breast.

Most of us* sadly learn to put those feelings away. They lead only to disappointment. We search for what to write a poem *about,* and either we don't come up with anything or, worse yet, we do—in which case we produce a piece of writing that is poetic in all the worst senses of the word: sticky, mawkish, embarrassing.

But it turns out that this is the worst possible approach to writing poetry—searching for what to write a poem about—particularly if we are inexperienced. It turns out that there is a completely different approach, and that is to ignore almost entirely the whole question of what to write about. Assume simply (and correctly) that you have plenty to write poems about and that your job is to keep

---

*I write here as a non-poet, that is, someone who enjoyed trying to write profound poems as an adolescent, got over it when introduced to sophistication, and then restricted himself to writing a birthday poem to a loved one about every seven years. But in the last couple of years I have enjoyed writing poems much more frequently in the fashion described in this chapter.

from mucking it up by paying too much attention to it. (Not that you ignore what's *in* the poem, only what the poem's *about*.) Somehow you have to let it emerge by itself so it isn't too falsely poetic or fake or manipulated. You need to keep your mind on what I suspect many poets have their minds on: the formal problem of the poem.

Robert Frost said that writing poetry without rhyme is like playing tennis without a net. And that having to rhyme helped him think of words and even ideas. Try writing a poem by keeping your mind only on the net and how to hit the ball over it. Consider the writing of a poem as the playing of a game, getting the ball through a hoop, a technical problem to be solved. It may seem very unpoetic but it leads to better luck with poems.

What you need for writing poems then is some interesting games to play, that is, some interesting rules you must obey. Allen Tate once described a poet as someone "willing to come under the bondage of limitations—if he can find them." In this chapter I will suggest a whole variety of mostly simple games, rules, or limitations. Gradually you can make up your own.

"The meter must be regular and the lines must rhyme" is the first rule that comes to mind when we think of poetry, but for various reasons it's not a good rule to use for a long time. It leads most of us to stilted language and inauthentic feeling—greeting-card poems. Most other rules, however, will have the opposite effect.

A good rule to start with is an easy one: "Write a long string of lines without stopping, and begin each one with 'I wish.' "* This rule for generating words is a good way to warm up. It permits you to write without stopping; indeed, that initial phrase is a kind of syntactic trampoline. It makes each sentence start itself with a bit of momentum so that more words just arrive without having to be sought. It helps you stand out of the way. This rule is also good to start with because it doesn't call for poems that are necessarily unified or organized—just strings of lines, some of which will have

---

*Homage to Kenneth Koch. Much of what I present here is derived from his books: *Wishes, Lies, and Dreams: Teaching Children To Write Poetry* (New York, 1970); *Rose, Where Did You Get That Red: Teaching Great Poetry to Children* (New York, 1974); *I Never Told Anybody . . . : Teaching Poetry in a Nursing Home* (New York, 1977). Readers particularly interested in this chapter should consult Koch's books.

genuine merit, many of which will give pleasure to you and even to readers or listeners.

In the first few pieces you write (and the first one or two of any particular writing session) don't try for good lines, just try to keep on writing, as in freewriting, and see what comes. Loosen up. Repetition, nonsense, even cliché, or deadness is fine, just as long as you keep on writing. The process will usually lead you to some good poem-ingredients, and even if it doesn't, it warms you up. I wrote the following at the start of a writing session.

> I wish it were April Fool's Day but it's Sadie Hawkins Day.
> I wish I were done with this quarter and my book.
> I wish my father wouldn't die.
> I wish I were with him now.
> I wish I wish I wish.
> I wish things would happen.
> I wish—do I wish anything? Maybe everything is fine.
> I wish I didn't itch, but my life is built on itching.
> I wish I didn't itch, but my life is built on itching.
> I wish it were April 15.
> I wish—I don't like writing I wish—it reinforces my habit of
>   conditionalizing the moment. I refuse, therefore, to write
> I wish. There. See. I won't do it any more.
> "I wish." Stop. Shut up. No more.
> "I wish." Enough I won't hear any more.
> "I wish." If you don't stop saying
> I wish, I'll scream.

I had trouble getting started—I think I didn't really want to write—but by gradually accepting and writing about my resistance I drifted into playing with the rule itself. That play produced some verbal energy and pleasure for me and finally a sense of closure. It served to warm me up. After writing it I wanted to go on and write more.

Another one-line rule is to begin each line with "Once." What follows is a more unified piece.

> Once Ma had a cookie jar shaped like a peach, only
> once I thought it was an apple cause
> once I said, Hey why a yellow apple and
> once I had said it Ma said No.

> Once you look at it for 10 years,
> once you grow accustomed to it, at
> once it begins to resemble a peach until you think how
>   strange
> once to have thought it was an apple.
>
> SUZANNE RESS

The following piece represents someone using the rule "Begin each line with *now*." The rule served to give some concentration and order to a frightening time:

> Now in the paling of her face,
> now I can see there's a sickness there that hurts her.
> Now, and still later. . . .
> Now she cries out,
> now calm, I worry, bringing water and smiles,
> now forgetting how, cause
> now she sweats so seriously I'm scared.
> Now she sleeps, silent,
> now, moaning, crying, calling out.
> Now sweet and still, we seek distraction in Gorky,
>   or Pasternak or Cummings or. . . .
> Now she twists her face into an alien design of pain and
> Now I pray.
>
> KIM KAUFMAN

There are innumerable ways of starting lines to give yourself a recurring pulse of syntactic energy. Begin each line with "yes," or "no," or "and," or with the name of someone you know. But remember you aren't trying for shaped complete poems, just warm-ups and perhaps some good ingredients. For a good way to search out memories from the past (and to give them some concentration and keep them from being too stilted in language), begin each line with "I remember."*

*You can use this structural principle not only for generating poem-ingredients, but also for generating ideas or perceptions or memories for any piece of writing. It aids invention. If you have to write about someone, try freewriting where you begin each sentence with the person's first name and you address your words *to* her and you don't permit yourself to stop writing no matter what words come out. Or begin each sentence with "I remember. . . ." You can use the same technique for writing reports about an organization, project, or period of time. You may get better ideas more quickly this way than by any other method. Some sentences get long—even develop into short paragraphs. But don't forget to keep coming back to beginning

Koch suggests two-line sequences, too:

Once . . . ,
Now. . . .

Or "I seem . . . ,/but really . . . ," "If . . . ,/then . . . ,"
Question/Statement, "Morning . . ./Noon . . ./Night . . ." "8
o'clock . . ./9 o'clock . . ./10 o'clock . . ." and so forth.

Koch suggests some one-line formulas that are nearly as easy
and useful for warming up, but which don't provide you with the
opening word and hence don't have that repetition. For example,
make each line a lie.

> I feel great.
> The sun shines on beautiful tanned bodies.
> Time is honey slow and people smile inwardly and love their
>   government.
> The dogs run free and so do we.
> I hate this course, it produces nothing.
> But I like to be lazy and vegetate.
> I'm never attracted to people, women or men.
> They never like me either, too bad.
> Fluorescent lights are great, they make you look so healthy.
> Boats are really boring, they make me groan and weak.
>
> SIMON ANSELL

It was just a warm up but it yielded the following:

> The sun shines on beautiful tanned bodies.
> Time is honey slow and people
> Smile inwardly and love their government.
> The dogs run free.

Other formulas: each line must mention a color; a word in Spanish;
a part of the body.

What seems important to me about this sort of initial easy rule
for writing strings of poem-ingredients is not just that they warm
you up, but that they warm you up in a particular way. They help

---

new sentences with the germ formula. Keep using this syntactic pump till your
source is dry. This continual looking your subject in the eye and addressing your
words *to* it—or this recurrent "I remember" which drags your mind back to events
without giving you a chance to think analytically—these gimmicks somehow force
you to blurt out what is important.

you generate words you didn't plan, words that surprise you or come from a part of you not easily available. They help you stand out of the way. Once you are warmed up, you can keep that capacity, that openness to the unexpected, and go on to write things more like poems: writing where you allow yourself some time for deliberation and reflection and second thoughts as you write.

But as you go on to attempt more shaped pieces in a more deliberate way, be sure to keep the two crucial elements in the process: have a rule you must obey and don't dawdle.

Having a rule doesn't just give you a technical problem to occupy your attention, it also takes a tiny element of authority off your shoulders. "I can't think of anything to write a poem about. But if *she* is going to make me write a haiku* about breakfast, I guess I can work something out. It may not be any good, but it was her idea not mine." The trick is that *you* can be that *she*—that person who says, "Hmmm, let's see, haiku: breakfast." Not because you have any preference or need for a haiku or any particular memory or feeling in mind about breakfast. It's probably best if you don't. (You can even give all responsibility to chance by putting rules on cards and shuffling them.)

And don't dawdle. Some reflection, yes, second or third thoughts now and then as you go along—this isn't freewriting as in "I wish"—but don't let fifteen or twenty minutes go by without at least a short poem to show for your efforts. You simply have to force yourself to accept some unsatisfactory sections, some unsatisfactory whole poems and just say what the hell. It's only raw writing after all. You can revise later or simply throw it away. You'll have lots of poems to choose from.

You can use a phrase to generate stanzas, not just single lines. Rule: write a poem about childhood (about your father, mother, favorite car, whatever) of three rough stanzas, each one beginning with "I remember." Even though you are not setting up a rhyme scheme or metrical demands, the formal repetition of "I remember" and the fact that you are calling this a poem helps you give your words the concentration characteristic of poetry.

---

*Haiku, a traditional Japanese form in which you are restricted to seventeen syllables. Purists say the lines should go 5, 7, 5. For example:

　Small bare feet, cold floor.
"Me want a breakable bowl."
　Waddler in diapers.

But you can give more concentration by tightening the rule a bit: start three four-line stanzas with "I remember." Get some form of the word remember (for example, memory, remembering) in each fourth line. Repeat some word or phrase in lines one and two or in lines two and three.

Write a short poem about an object you can see that begins "The (object) (verb). . . ." Within a line or two say "It makes me. . . ." Somewhere include a question.

> The electric outlet flashes, it sizzles, and
> Peering into the socket I see a tunnel,
> Irridescent blue sparks flying back through the inside of time.
> It makes me wonder how far my hate really goes.
> To the wire? the station? the turbine? the water?
> The dam? the rain? the sun? the night? the doorway?
> The fire? the iron? the harp? the weaver?
> The pasture? the challenge? the whisper? the word?
> The silence-singing crystalline air dissolves
> And there is no more.*
>
> WILLIAM L. MCNAUGHTEN

This formula could be expanded: describe a room or a place by writing three stanzas which follow the preceding rules. However, the last stanza should not have a question.

A favorite of mine is to insist that the poem start off with a short bit of actual speech, unfinished perhaps. Spoken words seem to inject life.

> "But on the other . . ."
> He paused,
> Looking down at his right hand,

---

* A note about revising. Sometimes it's hard to resist over-clarifying or over-stating your meaning when you revise. Or at least that's what I feel McNaughten did when he revised as follows:

> The wall outlet flashes and sizzles threateningly before me. Peering into the socket I see a tunnel, irridescent blue sparks flying backwards through time.
> . . . It makes me wonder just how far my hate really goes. . . .
> to the wire? station? turbine? dam?
> to the river? rain? sun? sea?
> Straining, I see stellar fragments; cosmic clash,
> then, only silence.

I believe he could enhance the strength of his original by making no changes at all in wording and only cutting some items from the end of his long list. If you can cut away what isn't needed, but leave the best original words with juice, that is often the best way to revise.

his hand with all five fingers curled to a point
around the little chalk-end
which pointed toward his face;
his hand that he didn't even see because his eyes were glazed over;
his hand that was the word he forgot to say.

One student nervously looked around with her eyes,
holding her head absolutely stationary.
She'd never been to his class before.
The others, scattered round the windowless room
listened appreciatively to the air conditioning
and gave themselves up to the
pleasure of smelling chalk dust.

PETER ELBOW

I made myself the rule without any phrase in mind. "But on the other [hand]" was simply the first thing I thought of after I decided on the rule, and being stuck with that I *had* to proceed and simply see what came next. Being boxed in and having to work from there—and write *something*—had the effect of dredging an image from me that was totally unplanned (and unremembered as far as I could tell). The process helped me to invent in a way I seldom can. It was such a pleasure not feeling the poem has to be about anything, just to fulfill a rule and sort of go along till it seems to end itself. I didn't force my pen to keep moving at all times but if a pause or stuckness lasted a whole minute or two I forced myself to put down something—like forcing myself to settle for "it" in Scrabble when my time runs out. I edited the results right afterwards, in a couple of minutes, leaving out a couple of lines and a handful of words and phrases.

Write a short poem that begins with a swear word.

Dammit!
You're always complaining,
Bitching at me.
Nothing I ever did was right.
But that's just too bad.
You're dead now.
So leave me alone.

KAREN GREENE

Write a poem that begins with pronouncing a curse or spell on someone.

A form that I know from Richard Hugo's use of it: make a poem by writing it as a real letter to a real person. Here is Karen Greene again:

> Dear Sharon
>
> I've been trying to find the time
> To write to you.
> I got your last letter
> such a long time ago.
>
> Elizabeth can crawl now.
> When she smiles
> There are two teeth.
>
> Michael's O.K.
> We don't live together
> any more.
> I don't love him.
>
> I have a one bedroom apartment,
> upstairs with a balcony,
> green shag on the floor.
>
> KAREN GREENE

A favorite germ for me involves using (instead of just fighting) the demon who tries to stop you from writing. This time I said make the demon talk to you.

> Whitney,
> You know the sound of that typewriter
> only gets me horny.
>
> Listen,
> Such an Om . . .
> Click, click, click.
> Godamn inhuman machinery.
> You know, Whitney,
> If you were out in the sunshine
> then a sunny metaphor would
> inform and transform
> this page.
> It would not so reek
> of metal and electricity.

Turn off the typewriter, Whitney.
Ouch, your ears.
Why, art cannot come from such pain
transforming and deforming
Deflowering and overpowering.

Can't you see that it's feeding me, Whitney?
It's making me stronger.

WHITNEY BLAUVELT

Sometimes the very structural principle that you used to generate the poem in the first place can be omitted when you are done.
Paula Aldrich found she could take down the scaffolding ("begin
each line with the name of a person you care about") and end up
with a structure that stood better by itself.

Dad, you're gone.
Dad, you're dead. Cremated.
Dad, I miss you.
Dad, I cry when I miss you.
Dad, *why* do I have to cry?
Dad, why must I feel alone without you?
Dad, why did you have to die?
Dad, it's been two years, why can't I adjust.
Dad, it's spring coming.
Dad, it's planting time.
Dad, the snow is melting.
Dad, fields are waiting for your tractor—for your hand in sow-
    ing the crops.
Dad, is it spring where you are?
Dad, are you planting there?

. . .

Dad, you're gone.
You're dead. Cremated.
I cry when I miss you.
It's been two years, why can't I adjust?
It's planting time,
the snow is melting.
Fields are waiting for your tractor,
for your hand in sowing the crops.
Dad, are you planting there?

PAULA ALDRICH

Poets have traditionally built on elements or structural principles they found in other poems. Kenneth Koch read Blake's "Tyger, Tyger," and asked children to write a poem in which they spoke to an animal.* We were reading *Hamlet* in a class and, almost as a lark, I made the rule "Begin a poem with a phrase and a negation of it (as in 'to be or not to be')." I ended up with this.

Hamlet at the Beach

Going in or coming out.
That's all they seem to do.
Water drips off them as they come out.
The women pull up their stupid tops.
The men glance down at their crotches, pretending not to
  look.
They shake their head and make little drips fly out in all di-
  rections.
Some bang their heads against their stationary hands.
The idiots.
Going in they are either sleep walkers or crazy mechanical
  dolls.
And greasy from the oil.
A problem in geometry: where would the sun have to be so
  that I see not one gleam from a perfectly oiled body?
Behind a cloud. Behind the earth.
Up their ass.

Going in or coming out.
Let them do it.
Why should I care.
They do nothing once in. They do nothing once out.
They only need to change.
They need me to look at them.
We all have our job.

Again the central element in the process was forcing myself to *take* the first or second phrase-and-negation that came to me in response to the arbitrary rule ("going in or coming out"—along with an image of swimmers on a hot beach). And then forcing myself to

---

* In *Rose, Where Did You Get That Red: Teaching Great Poetry to Children* (New York, 1974), he stresses how the procedure can be seen as a way to read existing poems, not just write new ones.

proceed from there even though I had no plan. The title came afterwards. What feels to me important about the process is the way
it helps me stand out of the way and still concentrate my attention.

Write a poem that looks at or talks about the same thing over
and over again as in Wallace Stevens's "13 Ways of Looking at a
Blackbird." I wrote:

> Before we moved
> I broke the rotten section off
> the cherry tree behind the house on Percival Street
> even though there were still some blossoms on it.
>
> When we used to look out our bedroom window
> we saw the cherry tree.
>
> The cherry tree helped
> when I had need of looking out the bedroom window.
>
> The cherry tree did not take sides
> in our arguments.
>
> To smell a blossom I had to stand so close
> that I couldn't focus on it. Simple justice.
>
> Decisions, decisions: every cherry has to come
> either alone or in pairs or trios.
>
> Is every leaf really the same?
> It depends what you mean by the same.
>
> Let us suppose that for every cherry there is a bird.
> Would that make life simple?
> Would we get no pie?

I see now that it is about missing the house on Percival Street
where we used to live. Perhaps it needs a final stanza to put things
back in the past tense, and it would point up the theme a bit more.
But there lies the danger. If I had tried to write a poem about
missing that house, it probably would have been terrible. Being
stuck with having to write tiny stanzas about the cherry tree did it
for me.

But of course there is a price to pay. It wouldn't be a bad poem
(by some sort of kindly amateur standard) if it wasn't so obviously
an imitation. But if I'm willing to pay that price, I get in return the
ability to write something better than I could write without help.

Long before Kenneth Koch started using simple rules with chil-

dren and others inexperienced in writing poetry, Theodore
Roethke was using complex rules with serious poetry students.

Roethke's solution to this problem involved, in part, using a number
of exercises in form, exercises so monstrously arbitrary and not of the
student's choosing that the arguments against false emotion or the
dreads of vanity can hardly appear. Richard Hugo describes one such
exercise in "Stray Thoughts on Roethke and Teaching" (*American Poetry Review*, 3, No. 1, 1974):

Nouns	*Verbs*	*Adjectives*
tamarack	to kiss	blue
throat	to curve	hot
belief	to swing	soft
rock	to ruin	tough
dog	to bite	important
frog	to cut	wavering
slag	to surprise	sharp
eye	to bruise	cool
cloud	to hug	red
mud	to say	leather

Use five nouns, verbs, and adjectives from the above lists and write a
poem as follows:
1. Four beats to the line (can vary).
2. Six lines to the stanza.
3. Three stanzas.
4. At least two internal and one external slant rhyme per stanza. (Full
   rhymes acceptable but not encouraged).
5. Maximum of two end stops per stanza.
6. Clear English grammatical sentences. (No tricks.) All sentences
   must make sense.

After reading Hugo's piece, I tried the exercise with a class and
found that, if I presented it as a game, students were willing to play.
What could they lose? It wasn't their poem, but a game at which one
can only win. The exercise is marvelous in its resource of always giving back to the students a little more than they put in. Gifted students, apparently, will turn the exercise into their own piece, for the
poems below are remarkably individual. The less gifted, at least
learn, *firsthand*, important things about diction, rhyme, and rhythm.
As Roethke says, "even to 'hear' a good poem carries us far beyond
the ordinary in education. And to write a verse, or even a piece of
verse, however awkward and crude, that bears some mark, something
characteristic of the author's true nature—that is . . . a considerable
human achievement."

Pliny at Stabiae

South of Pompeii the helmsman balked,
refused to go further. He cursed his gods
and watched the flame column burst up
curve, branch like a pine. Waves pitched
our sloop while molten lava swallowed
whole vineyards on the eastern slope.

Mud slaked down from a dense blue cloud.
In the wavering hot air, dogs howled
in fear. Sharp rocks and pumice pieces
were raining, bruising men who ran
for shelter through the rubbled streets,
hugging pillows over their heads.

At length came a sort of calm. Ash fell
thick and silent as snow. I asked for
water to cool my burning throat,
and slept a bit. When I awoke
I found the others were gone. The sun
Swung wildly in the red streaked sky.

MARGARET WHALEY

[Two other poems are omitted here.]

Since using the exercise I have developed others which also encourage students to tinker and to remake and which free students
from the usual personal obstacles. I ask them, for instance, to translate a poem from a foreign language and to explain what was lost or
gained in the process; I give them a handful of poems which I have
rewritten as prose and I ask them to restore them as verse (including,
usually, William Carlos Williams at his prosiest, and a ringer: a piece
of prose that scans and perhaps rhymes, as do some sections of Vladi-
mir Nabokov's short story, "First Love"). Sometimes we take a handbook such as Lewis Turco's *Book of Forms* and use it like the *I Ching*
or the *sortes Virgilianae*. . . . Close your eyes, flip the pages; whatever form your finger stops on is your momentary fate: a rondelet, a
Welsh cyhydedd, etc.*

Translating poems is another way to give yourself constraints—
nets to hit the ball over. You can even translate from a language
you don't know if you find a version with a literal translation in-

*From the article "South of Pompeii the Helmsman Balked," by John Balaban,
College English, vol. 39, no. 4, December, 1977.

cluded. (Best if you can hear it out loud in the original. Much poetry is recorded. The Penguin books of poetry in foreign languages
have literal translations of each poem at the bottom of the page.)
Or take an old poem and make it new. Or simply take a poem and
twist it somehow. "Amateurs borrow, professionals steal," said T.
S. Eliot. I have been trying to illustrate in this chapter how amateurs can write pleasing poetry in an amateur spirit, but now I
want to illustrate that even a serious professional poet writing a
serious poem can still attain this spirit of somehow not making too
big a deal out of poetry:

Psalm 81 *

All all come before you
Big wigs and small
The down and out
The up and coming
The boisterous   the preposterous
Left fielders   right wingers
The motley   the mortified
Flag wavers   free loaders

What a procession!

Every one cut down
The scythe ranging wide and far
(those bony implacable arms
Those harvester's hands!)

Like the newborn fawn's
Legs sheared off in the long grass

Bundled in
Guts and spring wheat
Eyes
Half opened in birth
Half closed
In death

Harvest and planting
The hunter
Stuffs his sack and strides on

Have mercy on us
Have mercy
DANIEL BERRIGAN, translator

*Printed in *The Catholic Worker*, January, 1980.

Many of the poems I've quoted were written in a class or a group. Often I, as teacher, suggested the rule to obey. In a certain sense that was an aid to the others: my authority took some of the onus off them and helped get them going. I didn't have any special authority over myself of course, yet a willingness to follow my own rule was usually extremely helpful to me, too. If you have a small group of people who want to try this approach, it is fun to share the responsibility for setting the rules. Five people could each bring one rule for an evening's writing.

However you arrange it, other people somehow help. Their presence writing with you, the fact that you have to get on with it and write *something* even if it is terrible, and the chance to read some of your pieces out loud and hear what the others have written: these things usually help you get words down on paper, energize you, and focus your attention. Particularly if you are inexperienced. Writing in a group can get you going and later you can use the same approach on your own.

Writing group-poems can be a good way of pooling imagination. There's the familiar party-game approach where each person writes just one line. (You can have each person write knowing all the previous lines, or else have each person know only the preceding line, or else play with everyone blind to *all* other lines.) These games often provide a kind of loosening up, randomness, even hilarity. They usually increase everyone's verbal and imagistic resources. More substantial than pooling single lines, however, is something like a group childhood poem: each person writes a short stanza beginning with "I remember." You may or may not want other restraints (for example, each person is assigned a toy, implement, room of the house, time of day, whatever). There are many ways to build a shaped group poem. We were reading Shakespeare and seven of us decided to write "The Seven Ages of Woman."

Infant

Having moved from womb to breast
the lack of warmth bewilders me.
No longer am I safe and protected.
So much awaits me I have yet to comprehend.
Fists clenched, legs kicking
helpless, I cry
without thought.

Only feelings and instinct
tell me I am hungry and alone.

Schoolgirl

I chased Bobby today.
He ran. Ran from my cooties.
Boys are stupid sometimes.
I stopped when I got tired
laughing at the springtime air.
Laughing at Bobby glancing behind himself nervously.
Boys are stupid most all the time.

Lover

Fire flames reflecting colors off of your back,
rippling light as you move into a curling wave
of our self-created moisture.
I let you touch me and feel our rhythms
beat within the movement
leaping into blues and greens
coloring me from moves within your wave.

Housewife

Musky smells penetrate the night air.
Paper shuffles, cans collide like
a waterfall. Sounds carry to
depths below with a thundering
crash.
The plastic trash can leaves an angry hand,
hitting pavement with a bound.
Next time he can do it for once.

Mother

   My belly soft
  from too many children
  too often
  too soon.
My eyes are tired.
  I have seen—
  And I have known—
  The painful world
  that my babies
  Must learn to live in.

But
   I want to
   keep them safe from it.
I know
   that they think I
   don't know anything.
That Mom
   is just an old-stick-in-the-mud.
But honestly,
   I just want to
   keep my babies
   safe with me.

Grandma

I dole out the treats
and receive my thanks
from their glowing eyes
and gooey grins.
The sticky fingers
will remain behind
for me to wipe away
with a contented sigh
tomorrow.

Aged

"Turn off that news!
Put it back to Hollywood Squares.
Just because you can still walk around
doesn't mean you get to choose the program."
I've been here longer than any of them.
People used to visit me too.
I've seen 'em peter out.
I'll see their honey-sweet relatives stop coming too.
"You won't be so smart alecky then!"
Oh no, the door bell.
My hair isn't ready.
I wonder if I'll let him muss it up
after the dance.
Oh mommy, I don't want to go to school today.
Please let me stay home and cook with you.
They're mean to me,
   they pull my hair.
"Don't you touch that dial.

My eyes weren't closed.
I was just thinking."
PAM CORWIN, BRUCE CLIFTON, LAUREN PHILBRICK, BING
  BRISTOL, KAREN KLOCKE, GINA KANEVSKY, PETER ELBOW

In short, by not making too big a deal of poetry—letting it be
play-within-rules, letting it be about what it turns out to be
about—you can write poems which please but don't try too hard.
You will sometimes get a poem that is terrific or could be made so.
This is a bonus. And if you decide to cross over that dangerous line
and start making a big deal out of poetry, you probably won't do it
till you have learned to make up rules for yourself, to cut away
what's weak and not feel stuck with your original scaffolding, to
find authentic language by choice rather than just by accident, and
most of all to develop an ear for when poetry is too pretentious.

MORE WAYS
TO REVISE

INTRODUCTION

The creativity needed for getting good words on paper is available to everyone (though some people find it difficult to let themselves use it). But revising requires wisdom, judgment, and maturity. There is no way to get these qualities except through practice and experience. The most inexperienced writer can sometimes produce brilliantly but only scarred old pros revise brilliantly.

But I don't want to emphasize this dismal view too much. Yes, revising is the hardest task of all—most difficult and most unpleasant—but if you manage yourself right you won't have to revise until you have produced enough so there is plenty to throw away. Revising is only killing when you do it in a fruitless way—and an unfortunately common way: revising as you write and thus judging and correcting and trying to throw away every sentence while you are in the act of writing it; or trying to fix a pinched and scrawny draft that you know with a sinking heart has nothing solid in it.

As you improve your ability to put down words on paper—to put down more and worry less—you will find yourself naturally developing the critical consciousness that leads to good revising. Not just brute negativity: the ability to detach yourself from your own words so you can throw away what's bad or inappropriate. But also an imaginative critical-mindedness: the ability to look *through* your words as they are and see which parts *could* be good and see how the good parts *could* be shaped.

I have sometimes been accused of ignoring revision or denying its importance or being uninterested in it. As a result I have watched myself for a number of years with a particular eye to revising. I have learned some interesting things. In spite of my fine preaching about the importance of free, unworried writing— and in spite of my progress in finally learning how to practice what I preach—I discovered that I spent far more time revising than I did producing. But I didn't *think* about revising. I just put my head down and did it. That's why I tended not to notice it and, more important, why I tended to do it inefficiently. But as I watched my revising behavior I began to realize that I didn't only have lots of practice at it, I also had a small spectrum of approaches that I could improve and then develop into a set of options —options that I could then learn to apply more consciously to different writing occasions.

I also reflected on the question of *why* I spend so much of my time revising. One reason, not surprisingly, is my temperament: I am a worrier and always think of how readers will object or disagree. This was the temperament that led to my being totally blocked and unable to write for a couple of years. But even after I got myself writing again I continued to devote enormous time to the revising process and this time it wasn't just because I was a worrier. The reason I finally got myself writing again was my belief that I had something important to say and my decision, in effect, to force the world to listen to me. I didn't just want to get things written for my own pleasure; I didn't just want to hand something in that would satisfy or even dazzle some examiner or judge; I wanted lots of people to believe what I was saying, to change their minds, and, damn it, to change their behavior.

I would suggest, then, that the most trustworthy motive for revising is the desire to make things work on readers. The spirit of worry had led me only to compulsive fiddling. I didn't get to productive revising till I insisted on being heard.

It's helpful to realize that there isn't just one way to revise. You have different needs depending upon the kind of writing you are engaged in, the circumstances, and your temperament. If you practice quick revising (Chapter 5) and the revising methods below, you will have a wide array of techniques at your command for a wide array of situations. I won't try to summarize or describe these chapters here because the titles are for the most part self-explanatory:

Practice Revising on Other People's Writing

What makes revising hard is not so much the actual skills you must use. I will describe them in the following chapters. These skills are demanding, but we could learn them steadily and easily if we didn't have to learn them on our own writing. Surgeons don't learn cutting skills by turning the knife on themselves. It feels like cutting your own flesh to take your own writing apart, rearrange it, and throw away large chunks.

Use the knife on other people's writing and you will learn quicker not only the outward techniques of good revising, but also the essential inner reaction that will lead you to those techniques: an intolerance for something that doesn't work and a willingness to make changes even if it means discarding wonderful stuff. Once you get comfortable wielding the knife and seeing blood on the floor, it turns out to be easier to wield it on yourself.

It is easy to get together with a few others and practice revising by revising each other's drafts. In addition each writer will get three or four rewrites of his draft. This is good feedback—if sometimes painful: a re-drafting is a re-seeing of what you've written. What's really hard about revising is to believe that what you have written can undergo major cutting and changing and still say what you mean. When someone shows you how to say it more simply and in less space—whether by cutting and rearranging your words or by rewriting it afresh in his own words—it makes you more willing to practice cutting and recasting your own words.

But even if for some reason you don't want to work with others in this way, there is writing all around you that needs revising. Choose the kind of writing you want to work on. Revise articles, reports, or memos that come across your desk. Translate poems. Newspapers and magazines are full of writing that needs revision: stories, arguments, letters, essays, how-to-do-its. Most of it was written and revised in a rush. Because these things are set so neatly in print and don't for the most part have mistakes in spelling and grammar, they often feel as though they *belong* just the way they are. It's hard to undress them in your mind and see how they could look—how they could be organized or conceptualized differently. But that's exactly the skill you need for revising. Your own writing is similarly hard to undress and reconceptualize—not because it's neatly printed without errors, but because it is yours.

If you revise published writing, you may fear you will make it worse rather than better. You probably won't, but even if you do, you get the essential practice of cutting, reconceiving, and reordering.

Revising someone else's words gives you an especially good opportunity to find out how words work on readers. Since beginnings are so crucial in determining whether a reader fights the words or goes along with them, it is especially useful to test different beginnings for the same piece: a quick overview for business-like perspective; an informal or even chatty statement directly to the reader; an anecdote that introduces the topic; an example that somehow symbolizes it.

Since it is easier to fool around with the writing of others, you can fairly quickly turn out alternate versions of an entire piece. Try different tones: chatty, authoritative, ironic. Try different ways of organizing: starting with the conclusion, building up to it last. Persuade with reasoning, with anecdote. Hide the weak arguments, admit them openly. Try to write it in half the length. Try different formats on the page such as lists or pictures or diagrams. Of course you can do the same thing with stories, essays, poems. You can make these controlled experiments with your own writing, too—and this practice will lead you to do so—but it's much easier to start with someone else's writing.

By the way, when you revise someone else's writing you are, in effect, collaborating. If you try it you will notice an interesting method for *collaborative writing*. Three people might proceed as follows: A writes a rough think-piece or discussion-piece (perhaps they had a preliminary discussion, but not necessarily, and they didn't have to try to agree with each other); everyone reads it and discusses the issues (not the quality of A's writing); B takes notes on the discussion and then writes his own fresh draft—not trying, however, to get everything right since things are still in process; everyone discusses B's draft in order to advance the group's thinking and to decide where the draft reflects their agreement and where it doesn't; C takes notes and then writes a near-to-final draft; all give feedback and someone does final editing. This method is especially useful if the collaboration must be conducted by mail: everyone can mail their thoughts and reactions to the next writer.

This method usually achieves more genuine collaboration than other methods (where one person really does all the writing and gives his imprint to the piece; or where the authors each write one segment and the resulting piece lacks integration and smooth joints). Most important, it leads to the best sort of thinking-and-writing: new ideas emerge in mid-course that all agree on—that feel like "just what we wanted to say"—but that are original. The process may sound like much more work, but often it is not because it involves such unpressured writing. People churn out their drafts quickly and get good practice in writing because no draft has to be "just right" till it's obvious what "just right" is.

No Revising

Learn when not to revise. It's because I take revising so seriously that I say this. For if you try to revise everything you write you will use up too much time that you could spend on new writing. After all, you can write thirteen new pages in the time it takes to revise three pages well. And you will get so duty-bound and bored about revising that you will begin to settle for a perfunctory job of it—instead of really re-seeing. Make sure, then, that you devote enough of your time to rough exploratory writing you don't revise, so you are sure to produce *some* writing that really pleases you. Your desire to get others to read it will ensure that you revise it. This will solve the biggest problem in revising: motivation and energy to do it enthusiastically.

Of course anything must be revised if you really want it to work for an audience, so what I am really saying here is to make sure you do other kinds of writing. Write for yourself: use freewriting, explore a train of thought, figure out a decision, write yourself out of a depression. You can even dash off pieces for certain audiences on certain occasions when you don't care how they react. You aren't giving them a finished product, you are just letting them look around in your messy studio at some of your work in progress. You'll discover you can produce all these kinds of unrevised writing almost as quickly as you have ideas. You will end up writing lots because it's not such a big production. (See Chapter 10 on the use of writing for other tasks.)

Best of all, write things you can throw away. For the central act in revising is throwing things away. All the subtler transforming and rearranging skills in revising depend upon a willingness to chop. For some reason people have found it easy to adopt a throw-away mentality with respect to the world's natural resources. "What the hell, there's plenty more where that came from." Yet there *isn't* plenty more where that came from. It's curious that people often find it difficult to learn a throw-away mentality with respect to our own mental resources. When it comes to words, ideas, feelings, and insights, there *is* plenty more where that came from. The more you use and throw away, the more you have available. You will find, then, that your ability to revise quickly and without too much pain will be tied to your ability to produce copiously and creatively.

Besides, if you always try for quality and always try to make your writing work for an audience, you inhibit certain kinds of growth and development in your writing. It would be as though you only played a musical instrument in performance—you never practiced or fooled around. When you always revise for an audience there is always pressure on you to be prudent. But for growth you need to take chances. Certain kinds of slow underground development won't happen unless you write in quantity and let yourself try out new approaches, new ideas, and wild experiments.

• • •

But there is another kind of no-revising. This is when you are writing along freely without worry—perhaps freewriting, perhaps writing a draft of something—and all of a sudden you find yourself writing it just right. You are saying exactly what you want to say, exactly the way you want to say it. You cooked it perfectly in your head. No need for revising at all.

It's hard to try to *make* this happen, but it will happen. Everyone is visited by the muse under certain conditions (excitement? sanctity? trust in self?). But even when it happens, you must still revise. That is, you must re-see, look again at your writing with your critical, doubting, revising consciousness to make sure it really is as good as you thought. For sometimes it seemed like divine inspiration last night as you were writing, but now this morning you discover it was only hot air.

The fact remains, however: if you want to take revising seriously and make good use of the methods for revising that I describe in the following chapters—especially thorough revising and revising with feedback—you need to write plenty that you don't revise.

12

Thorough Revising

Where the leverage in quick revising comes from stepping out of your skin and being someone else, the leverage in thorough revising comes from time. Not just work time, but putting-it-away-and-forgetting-about-it time. What you can accomplish in three hours of wrestling with your draft can be accomplished in one hour—and a much less frustrating hour, too—if you first set it aside for a day or two. Indeed, there are some improvements you can never achieve through wrestling alone, such as a fresh conception of your material. Often you can only find a new shape for your piece if you take a vacation—a time for forgetting, for preconscious work, for letting it get bumped out of shape by an experience from an entirely different part of your life. So make sure that at least on two occasions during the thorough revising process you put your writing aside long enough to forget about it—a couple of days or better yet a couple of weeks: once during the first half when you are hammering out and organizing the thing as a whole and once during the second half when you are cleaning up and polishing and paying more attention to details of language.

Shaping Your Meaning

First step in thorough revising: if this piece is intended for an audience, *get your readers and purpose clearly in mind*. Just as with quick revising or any revising, you must now keep your audience and purpose clearly in mind, especially if you allowed yourself to ignore them while you were getting words on paper. There is no such thing as good-writing-in-general. You must make it good for this purpose with this audience.

Next, *read over what you've written and mark the important bits* (just as in quick revising).

Next, *find your main point or center of gravity*. This is the same step as in quick revising, but this time you don't take No for an answer as you sometimes had to do when you were revising in a hurry. Sometimes, of course, you knew precisely what your main point or focus was even before you started writing: the whole reason for sitting down to write in the first place was to focus on exactly that one thing which you had already formulated in your head. (But don't hold too tenaciously to it. The process of writing will often lead you to better things.)

But if you haven't found your main point during the writing process, now you must demand it. This is often a crucial, delicate, frustrating process. You have lots of good stuff, but as you turn it over and over, you can't find the center, the main point, the one thing that sums it all up. You are trying to wrestle a powerful snake into a bottle. It writhes and writhes and you can't get control over it. You have two main options, putting it aside and wrestling some more.

Putting it aside for a couple of days is easiest and best. The main point will often come perfectly clear to you all by itself, as you are walking around doing something entirely different or else when you sit down again after your vacation. Your mind will chew on the problem by itself while you are supposedly ignoring it. But if that doesn't work, you'll just have to wrestle some more with that snake. Indeed, you probably get the most benefit from a vacation if you wrestle a bit first to get the problem fully permeated into your mind for your unconscious to work on it.

Here are the ways of wrestling that I have found most useful.

• Arrange the good bits in the order that makes most sense. That helps you see where they are coming from or trying to go.

• Think some more about who will read these words. You're not looking for some main point in general but the best emphasis for getting through to those readers.

• Summarize each of the good bits in one sentence (or in two or three sentences if there are two or three separate points in one passage). By making each point *assert* something in a full sentence with a verb, you clarify half-thought ideas. If you put these sentences then into a logical order you will almost invariably find your main point.

• Do more raw writing. Abandon the detached consciousness of critical revising and plunge back into uncritical, involved writing. This new burst of unworried words, after you have been wrestling, helps you find that main idea.

• Last resort. If you still can't find the main point, make a "false" main point. Distort or oversimplify what you are saying and force as many of your points as possible into a slightly wrong focus that is easier to find than the right one you are seeking. Or adopt the opposite point of view and quickly make up an outline of assertions in support of it. Summing things up into this simpler or distorted or dead-wrong point of view will often produce the idea you have been looking for.

• And of course another vacation is always a good idea if wrestling doesn't go well.

Next, *put your parts in order on the basis of your main idea*. If the pieces don't fall easily into an obvious order you must make an outline that consists of full-sentence assertions: find each idea in your best bits of raw writing, force yourself to summarize it in a sentence that asserts something, then put those sentences into the order that tells the most coherent story. (Of course there are likely to be gaps you must fill in to make a coherent story.)

Next, *make a draft*. Using your outline as a blueprint, write out a rough draft of the whole thing. You may be able to use large chunks of your original writing. Scissors and a paste can carry you a long way (if you were smart enough to write on only one side of the paper). But often you must write lots out new. The goal, however, isn't perfect, clear, graceful language. I, at least, fare better if I just try to get my thoughts *said* and don't worry too much about awkwardness, repetition, roundaboutness—even imprecision—at this stage. There are all these decisions I must make as I write a draft: can I use this favorite word again here? does this distinction belong here or later? which of two similar words is the right one? These decisions are always easier to make *after* I have written out a draft of the whole thing. (The general principle here is to bring the whole piece along gradually: don't polish any particular section very much *more* than any other, since *final* decisions here always depend on final decisions there. It feels like keeping lots of balls in the air at once, but it's easier in the long run.)

Possible detour: deal with a mess. This is a stage in revising when you have to be ready for a mess. Perhaps just a minor mess. For example, as you write out sentences they tug against the structure you have carefully worked out. Perhaps you are writing out the third idea in your list of assertions, but it keeps grabbing the reins out of your hands and leading to the seventh assertion instead of the fourth one. Three-to-four seems so logical in an outline, but three-to-seven feels unavoidable as the words themselves flow into sentences. The question is whether the writing-out has led you to a better order or whether you should resist that tug and force the sentences to follow the original organization. To make up your mind you need perspective and taking a break is probably the best way to get it. Often, in fact, it doesn't much matter which way to go, but you need new perspective to see that clearly.

But sometimes it's a major mess, or at least it threatens to be one: not just a possible minor shifting of points but a major coming apart. Perhaps you have to change your mind about what you thought you were saying.

Here's how it's apt to happen. You know your main point and your organizing shape and you are writing out a draft, but now in mid-stride, as you are explaining some small detail or bringing in some small illustration you hadn't thought of before, suddenly that detail turns into a land mine and blows up your whole draft in your hands. You've stumbled onto a specific case that seems to deny or disprove your main idea. Or perhaps as you are arguing some point you try to think of what an opponent might say—as you should—and suddenly you think of an opposing argument that you cannot answer. This is the most discouraging moment in expository or conceptual writing. It helps to realize not only that this kind of thing is common in writing, but that, despite how you feel right now, something *good* just happened to you.

For this is how new and better ideas arrive. They don't come out of the blue. They come from noticing difficulties with what you believed, small details or particular cases that don't fit what otherwise feels right. The mark of the person who can actually make *progress* in thinking—who can sit down at 8:30 with one set of ideas and stand up at 11 with better ideas—is a willingness to notice and listen to these inconvenient little details, these annoying loose ends, these embarrassments or puzzles, instead of impatiently sweeping them under the rug. A good new idea looks obvious and inevitable *after* it is all worked out and the dust has settled, but in the beginning it just feels annoying and the wrong old idea feels persuasively correct.

So when you first stumble onto this difficulty as you are engaged in writing out a draft, you don't know whether it is just an unimportant exception or whether it is trying to lead you to a new better view of things. You've struggled to work out your thinking and your organization and now this pesky detail calls it into question but gives you nothing to replace it with. You have nothing but a doubt, a difficulty, and some bent edges where you tried to force this puzzle piece into the only available opening.

It's at this point you have to make a decision. If you don't have the time or willingness to let things really come apart, then you'd better retreat and save this interesting dilemma till later. Since you can't make the puzzle piece fit your structure, you must somehow sweep it under the rug or put it in your pocket and hope no one notices. Distract your reader away from the unfilled hole to other issues. You can hope that your original idea and structure are in fact right and that this (now pocketed) detail only *looks* like an exception.

But if you are willing to follow this unravelling thread where it leads, you have to put aside everything you have already done. The most useful tactic at this point is usually to plunge into new, open, unworried writing: to think on paper and let this difficulty or seed of doubt grow. Follow new thoughts where they lead; plunge deeper into the forest of confusion. Here, in my experience, are the outcomes you can expect:

• Your new exploration may lead you quickly to a happy ending. You discover how to explain this apparent contradiction, and happily your main idea and original structure remain solid—indeed strengthened. The apparent contradiction may be unimportant and not worth mentioning or it may be very helpful to you as a vivid detail to illustrate your main idea.

• But sometimes this exception or anomaly, when you really let yourself explore it in a burst of new writing, leads you to a genuinely new idea or new way of looking at everything you have been saying. Perhaps your old idea is all wrong and must be scrapped altogether.

• Sometimes you go through an interesting change. First you see your new idea as right and your old idea as wrong, and you immerse yourself in all the implications of the new idea. But then gradually you come around to see how the old "wrong" idea is nevertheless right *in a sense* or *in certain cases*. For now you see it through new eyes and you can explain it more fruitfully as a sub-case of your new idea.*

• The most frustrating outcome is when you pursue your contradiction farther and farther into the woods and you just get more and more lost. You are left entirely stuck. You have lost your faith in your original idea, but you haven't figured out anything coherent or complete to replace it with. In the long run this is a happy state of affairs: you are likely to be on to something important, you are charting new territory, this is the best kind of thinking—the kind that makes you smart and creative. But for the moment, you are stuck.

The most effective way to deal with this frustrating case is of course to take a break. Put your writing away and forget about it for more than a day or two. You should be doing this periodically throughout revising. But there is another tactic that also helps: stop trying to solve the dilemma and simply *accept* it and *describe* it. Stop beating your head against the wall, stop pushing so hard against an immovable object, take the pressure off your shoulders. Pretend that things are just fine as they stand now, in their state of contradiction or confusion, and *describe* the conflicting details or ideas as accurately and happily as you can. This will often lead to new perspective and a solution.

Of course you don't always have to take this detour through a mess. Most of the time you just write out your new draft as planned. I could make my story simpler by ignoring this occasional problem. But when the mess lands on you, you badly need assurance and help. And I suggest you be tolerant or even welcoming toward this whole process of things coming apart in your hands after you thought you had them all organized. It is the most trust-

---

* I went through this process numerous times, but I wasn't able to see clearly what was happening to me—it felt simply like fumbling—till I read Thomas Kuhn's interesting book on how the scientific community moves from one explanation of things to a new one, *The Structure of Scientific Revolutions* (Chicago, 1970). The classic case is Einstein discovering that Newtonian mechanics are all wrong—strictly speaking and from the largest perspective—but that in fact the Newtonian model still works for most events of human scale. In a sense, Einstein leaves all of Newtonian mechanics still standing validly in place, but forces scientists to understand it in a different light—as a special limited case of the larger principles of relativity.

worthy way to create new ideas. If these messes never happen to you, perhaps you are not listening sympathetically enough for pesky examples and contrary arguments.

At the end of this messy detour you *may* have to begin the revising process over again: mark the good bits, find your main point, make an outline, and write it out. But usually, once you have really thought through your reconceptualization, you can make adjustments to your draft without too much discomfort.

These detours reflect the fact that in any serious or difficult piece of writing you must sometimes move back and forth between getting words on paper and revising. Sometimes the producing process is given some focus by standing back and trying to revise and shape and make sense of things; and sometimes the revising process is perked up by a new immersion into the creative process of writing quickly—perhaps even writing off into an unknown direction. (See pp. 349–51, Chapter 28, for a fuller account of my own experience with this kind of alternation.)

Strengthening Your Language

Next, *tighten and clean up your language*. The hardest work is done now. You have a newly written draft that says what you want to say in the right order. Nevertheless it is liable to be imprecise, wordy, and awkward. You need to stop being the writer and read over your draft with the fresh eyes of a reader. The best way is to put it aside for a while and then to read it over out loud.

In cleaning up your language you have two goals: precision and energy. The more you zero in on the precise meaning you have in mind, the more you can strip away unnecessary words and thereby energize your language. The key activity is crossing out words and sentences. Your new draft may have large chunks from your raw first-draft writing, rearranged with scissors and staples. These sections may need extensive cutting. When you wrote them during the producing process you were permitting yourself to write without necessarily making up your mind what you were saying. You were hurrying and allowing for ambiguity and ambivalence—driving a small crowd of horses down the road without making up your mind which one to ride on. It's natural to end up with too many meanings, too many words, too many strands—sometimes in one sentence. But now you have forced yourself to choose among strands and decide exactly what you mean; you must ruthlessly throw away all the words that were part of abandoned strands. Some may feel very precious to you.

And even your new writing probably needs cutting. Although you were engaged in saying, as it were, only *one* thing instead of allowing for multiple possibilities, you probably didn't say it as clearly and economically as you can now when you look back as a *reader* instead of as a writer.

Remember that every word you throw away means another unit of energy preserved, another reader who may hang in there a bit longer before giving up. The psychological transaction that helps most in cutting is to read your words out loud. Look for places where you stumble or get lost in the middle of a sentence. These are obvious awkwardnesses that need fixing. Look for places where you get distracted or even bored—where you cannot concentrate. These are places where you probably lost focus or concentration in your writing. Cut through the extra words or vagueness or digression; get back to the energy. Listen even for the tiniest jerk or stumble in your reading, the tiniest lessening of your energy or focus or concentration as you say the words. Can you remember listening to someone read a story out loud and how you could tell when the reader got the tiniest bit bored or distracted and stopped giving full attention to the words? Listen for that when you read your own words. Listen for places where the words themselves seem to stop paying full attention to their own meaning.

These are all places where you need to increase the precision and energy in your language. You don't have to know what the problem is. No need for sophisticated diagnosis. It doesn't matter whether it is a modifier or a conjunction that is acting up. Just grab yourself by the shoulders, shake yourself, and insist that you mean business: "*Stop* beating around the bush. Just tell me what you mean to say. Stop *explaining* things or talking in 'essay' or translating what you have on your mind into 'writing' language: just *say* it!" Pretend someone is being this firm with you because he cares about you and wants to know what's on your mind.

A sentence should be alive. Does it sag in the middle or trail off at the end? Is it fog or mush? Sentences need energy to make the meaning jump off the page into the reader's head. As writer you must embed that energy in the sentence—coil the spring, set the trap. The meanings should spring up when the reader steps on the first word. If you just leave your meanings lying around on the ground, readers will have to stoop over to pick them up. You won't have many readers except those who are doing you a favor or already want to know what you have to say—and even those readers won't get experiences from your words, only meanings.

The best sentence is the kind that comes out during the best moments of raw first-draft writing. You are warmed up, writing fast, excited, but not worried. You are fully involved in your meaning, not conscious of anything else. The sentence flows out alive and loud so the reader hears it. Obviously much of your raw writing won't be that way, and it's harder still to achieve that kind of language as you revise—when you are using language slowly, carefully, and consciously. Revising is like constructing a difficult mathematical equation: continually you must stop in the middle of sentences to ponder the right word, to search your memory for alternatives, to wonder whether this sentence fits what came before and comes after. Instead of the producing consciousness where you bend all your efforts singlemindedly toward making contact with what you are writing about—toward full participation with your meaning—in revising you must necessarily be thinking about the reader, about the structure of the whole, about whether your words are true. In good raw writing you *give birth* to sentences, in revising you have to construct them.

Ideal revising, perhaps, would consist only of crossing out and rearranging live words born in the producing process so that every word in the final draft has psychic energy invested in it. (I am exaggerating the value of your raw writing. Not all is alive. Much of it, rightly enough, is produced by slogging onwards when the spirit is dead. One of the main reasons for learning freewriting is so that you can keep on writing even when you are not in the mood.)

But if your raw writing doesn't contain the sentences you need ready-made or uncoverable, there's nothing for it but to *construct* the best sentences you can. Here are a few suggestions:

• After you have constructed the meaning that is right, force yourself to *say* the sentence out loud. It must sound strong and energetic.

• Think in terms of energy. If it's not there, make changes till it is. There is something important about clenching—clenching your jaws or your arms or hitting your hands against something hard.

Cut away unnecessary words and grunt energy into your constructions. Notice, for example, how I can turn an impossible sentence into one that is at least feasible by simply rearranging things as I clench for energy:

(Original):   Intelligence, universalistic standards of evaluation, autonomy, flexibility, and rationally oriented legitimate achievements are features of this extended socialization.

(Revised):   The extended socialization has these features: intelligence, autonomy, flexibility, universalistic standards of evaluation, and rationally oriented legitimate achievement.

It is an extreme example (it turns out to have been written by a noted sociologist) and I don't do anything to improve the worst problem of the sentence: the string of arrogant abstractions. But I want to illustrate how even these horrible inert lumps need not stop the flow of energetic syntax if we exaggerate the germ of energy. When the lumps of deadness come at the beginning they snuff out that fragile spark of life.

• Simplify. In your best moments during the producing process—when you are warmed up and writing with intensity and involvement, you can produce long and complex sentences, even gnarled or involuted ones, that nevertheless have energy and life. But when you are having to construct sentences as you revise, it's much harder to breathe life into something long. Clench your jaw. Break that long sentence into three short ones. You may not be able to get genuine life into your sentences as you revise, but you can at least make verbs active and lively, leave out extra words, and keep sentences from dribbling out to a flabby end, like this one does, so it drains energy from the reader.

• Use active verbs, avoid the passive voice and too much of the verb "to be." The previous section, for example, begins with the one-word sentence "simplify." Originally I had written "Be simple," and then "Use simplicity," but I realized in revising that I could slightly increase the life by using a plain active verb—which is pure energy—instead of an adjective or noun ("simple" and "simplicity") which are pieces of used up energy.

• Almost everything in *The Elements of Style* by Strunk and White is good advice for this stage of revising. It's small and usable and a pleasure.

Final step in thorough revising: *get rid of mistakes in grammar and usage.* (See Chapter 15.)

Summary

The main weapon in thorough revising is time—especially for breaks and vacations. Here are the main steps.
- Fix readers and purpose in mind.
- Read over raw writing and mark important bits.
- Find your main point.
- Put the parts in order on the basis of your main idea.
- Make a draft.
- Possible detour: deal with a breakdown.
- Tighten and clean up your language. Reading out loud helps.
- Remove mistakes in grammar and usage.

13

Revising with Feedback

Revising with feedback is the most powerful way to revise, and happily enough it is also the most interesting and enjoyable technique. No-revising relies on a magical polishing process inside you—using luck and your unconscious. Quick revising relies on a detached critical consciousness: you step out of your involvement with your writing and clean it up with dispassionate pragmatic eyes; you can make quick harsh decisions because you haven't got time to vacillate, you must cut your losses. Thorough revising relies most of all upon time—more time for careful wrestling and more time in addition for setting your writing aside, which gives you newer, fresher eyes than you could get by mere will power or any vow to be dispassionate. Cut-and-paste revising (next chapter) relies on aesthetic intuition. When you revise with feedback you are of course trying to use all these faculties, but in addition you are using the most powerful tool of all: the eyes of others.

How Much Feedback and When

You can bring feedback into the revising process either early or late. If you bring it in early you are in effect using the reactions of others as part of the very process of making up your own mind. If you bring it in late, you are reaching all your conclusions alone but using the reactions of others to help you make those conclusions *work* better on readers.

You will want to hold off on feedback till the end if you are in a hurry or if you know you don't want to make any changes in your thinking or if you are nervous about using feedback. In these situations you get feedback only once and you use it only for making minor or cosmetic changes. But bring feedback in early if you want the most powerful and interesting process and have time. It means getting feedback on two or more drafts and inviting others to be part of a slower and more organic process as you work out your thinking.

Here's how this longer process might look. You start by producing a draft. It's probably something you've long wanted to work on, something important to you, not something you have to force yourself to write for a deadline. You revise it enough to make it interesting and readable, but you aren't trying to make it your best work. You don't spend much time revising it and it probably doesn't represent your final thinking. (Cut-and-paste revising is especially useful here.) It probably has serious problems of structure and consistency. But it must be readable.

You get two friends to read it and then you sit down with them. You are more interested in their thoughts on the whole matter than their criticisms of your writing. Why try to fix weaknesses when you will probably take a whole new approach on your next draft? The conversation with them helps you see the whole thing in better perspective, gives you new ideas, and helps you make up your own mind what you think. Your draft was really just a letter to friends exploring your thinking.

On the basis of this first step of informal feedback you can "re-see" the whole thing and write a brand new draft—not just strengthen that first draft.* On this draft, too, your main priority is not to try to get it right, perfect, make up your mind once and for all (unless you are in a hurry and know you have to stop with this draft). You are trying to let the whole thing develop slowly through your interaction with others. Wait patiently for things to jell. Again, you get readers to give you feedback on this draft: perhaps the same readers, perhaps new ones. And here, too, you are interested in all their thinking on the topic, not just their reactions to your writing. At this point things may click and it may be very clear to you how you want your final draft to go; but perhaps not.

---

*Occasionally, of course, you find that you stumbled onto the right idea and the right structure the first time and so now you are just improving that first draft rather than writing a completely new one.

You may take it through this process once or even twice again depending on your time and on how much you care.

Indeed, other people's feedback can lead you to a whole new understanding of the writing process so you develop a much longer time frame. That is, perhaps the feedback you get on this second round is very confusing: each reader has entirely different reactions, feelings, suggestions. You know your piece of writing isn't right yet, isn't done, but you are unclear about what changes to make. Perhaps you realize it could evolve in two very different directions but you don't know which you prefer. But you also know it's already good. Good enough, if you just polish it slightly, that others will want to read it; good enough perhaps even to publish. You are not done in the long run, but you know you have carried it as far as you want for now. You need to give it time to settle, give yourself time to have new thoughts and experiences and grow into a slightly different person. Then months or even years later you come back to it. You revise it and finally get it right.

I have let my story of a typical case of revising with feedback stretch into an extreme case. But the point I want to make is that when you revise with feedback, you develop a looser and more conditional sense of what it means to be *"done."* Instead of a clear one-step change from *rough draft* to *final draft*—from raw to cooked in one transaction—you are allowing a gradual evolution through time and through successive audiences. At each stage you can call your draft "done" or "not done" depending on how you want to use it. On the one hand you start using the word "done" early: you learn to polish slightly and re-type even your earliest drafts so that they are useful for others to read. But on the other hand, you learn to think of things as "undone" on into late drafts since you know that hearing the reactions of others can trigger continued growth even when you thought your mind was made up.

Enormous benefits flow from this odd flexibility about when to call something done. You aren't always struggling for perfection, worrying "Do I really know enough yet?" Instead of wrestling to get it right on the first try, you experiment without anxiety on different approaches and *wait* for the right way to pop into your mind. It will. There's a wonderful deep thud you feel when your meaning finally drops into place—just what you wanted to say— which is hard to achieve without trying out a draft or two on real readers and feeling how they understand your words.

Perhaps it seems as though this approach allows for too much indecision. I hear a tough person saying, "There's something wrong with all this tentativeness. Damn it, you can't write unless you learn to make up your mind." Which is true. Writing *is* a process of making up your mind, and much bad writing is bad because the writer didn't have the guts to do so—or because he made up his mind but still had inner doubts which fog up his writing and prevent him from asserting his conclusion crisply. The point is, though, that most people make up their minds better if they do so gradually without being under too much pressure.

This method of successive drafts not only helps you be more decisive in your final draft, it also helps you write more decisively on earlier drafts. You aren't committed to what you write on early drafts, so you don't have to hedge and be cautious. You find it easier to use bold strokes and definite language—to avoid the mumbling qualifications and maybe's that destroy strong writing. And sometimes you discover that an interesting hunch is true only because you permitted yourself to overstate it, go with it, and thereby discover arguments and evidence you never would have thought of if you had remained judicious.

Once you start enjoying the power of this slower interactive way of revising, you will learn to use it for other writing, not just pieces you want to write for yourself at a relaxed pace. You will learn to handle deadlines differently. If you have a month, you will be eager to use this new leverage of feedback and get yourself to produce an exploratory draft in a week so there are three more weeks for feedback and more drafts. Even if you only have a week, you will discover that you can dash off a draft tonight—since the pressure is off—and get at least one round of feedback and discussion before you have to figure out what you really think.

Your decision about when to bring in feedback, then, turns out in the end not to depend so much on *time* as on how much you want of that creative mess in which you let the thinking of others get all mixed up with your own. Here is a schematic summary of your options:

1. Minimal feedback. You should *always* use feedback to help you eliminate errors in grammar and usage from any final draft that needs to be polished—no matter what kind of revising you engage in. But don't let them talk about what you are saying or how you say it—just spelling, grammar, and usage.

2. Little feedback. You don't have much time or you don't like feedback or for some reason you want to keep others largely out of your writing process. You get one round of feedback only at the end, and you know you will stick with your conclusions no matter what they say. But you can still get enormous benefits from their reactions. Even if they happen to think you are dead wrong in one of your major ideas, their objection will help you make improvements in how you present that idea. For example:

- explain the idea entirely differently,
- insert a needed clarification or defense,
- remove a troublesome example or detail,
- put the idea in a different place in your whole structure.

And their reactions will help you make other small but important changes:

- remove bits that don't work,
- untangle some snarls in language or logic,
- change an annoying tone of voice here and there,
- insert some little introductions or transitions or clarifications that may make all the difference in the world to a reader's staying with you or not.

"Please find mistakes in spelling, grammar, and usage; and any awkward or unclear sentences. Don't tell me if you dislike or disagree with my thinking. I haven't got the time or strength for any major rewriting. But please point out places where you think I make an absolute fool of myself." This is a feedback request I sometimes make of my wife—usually at the last minute.

3. Medium feedback. Your mind is made up about your main message. You aren't willing to give yourself the grief of rethinking your position entirely, but you are willing to engage in *major* revisions of structure and strategy. Perhaps you argued your case through abstract reasoning, but feedback convinces you it's worth trying to do it almost entirely through example or anecdote. Perhaps feedback convinces you that you have to turn your whole structure upside down. Usually your revisions are less drastic. Once you understand what is confusing or bothering a reader, it is usually not too difficult to find a way to deal with the problem.

4. Lots of feedback. Everything is up for grabs from the beginning. You share drafts from the start—before you know your thinking. You let the interaction carry you on a voyage of discovery.

The crucial thing is to decide how much of the feedback process you want. As I finish typing on this sheet of paper and take it out of the typewriter and put it face down on the pile to my right, I am reminded of how sometimes I don't want much. For I notice on the back (I usually write on the back of already-used paper); it says "Draft III, FSU, DR, p. 17." This is the third draft of a chapter David Riesman wrote about a competence-based program at Florida State University and circulated to readers for feedback. And yet I am on at least the third draft of this chapter now and haven't let anyone see what I've written. (I will get some feedback before I finish with it.) Sometimes, in short, I just want to work out my ideas myself. "I can do it my *own self*," says Abby, age three, as I start to help her with something difficult and she pushes my hands roughly away.

But Abby's phrase is ominous too. For sometimes after she has pushed me away, she must come back sheepishly and ask for help. And so have I numerous times had to put a draft through a major change later on after I thought it was settled but late feedback shows me I'm wrong. I fight the change harder when I've already invested so much work and made up my mind. It would have been easier if I had been willing to bring in feedback earlier. On other pieces of writing—where I feel more secure or unpossessive—I'm comfortable with bringing in feedback from the start.

You may be surprised by a powerful side effect of using feedback for revising—especially if you bring in feedback early. You may find that after years and years of strenuous but unsuccessful efforts to make your writing clear for *real* readers—teachers, employers, editors, strangers—all of a sudden you can write much more clearly now that you are just cleaning up a rough draft for a friend to read and respond to. You aren't even trying to make it your best writing yet your language turns out clearer, simpler, more direct. Once you realize that your reader is a friend and helper, sometimes you cut right through that abstractness or complicatedness or fog that has plagued you for so long. The important point psychologically is that when we write for "real audiences" like teachers and employers, the stakes are very high and we get too clenched. What's more we are liable, without realizing it, to feel the reader as *enemy*. After all, they *are* the enemy: they've hurt us deeply time and again in the past, the dirty bastards. When, on the other hand, we feel the reader as genuine friend and ally, suddenly words flow more easily and humanly. This effortless change of audience can do more than all your strenuous wrestling in the past.

Your main task in getting feedback is to listen and see if you can experience what your reader is experiencing. If you succeed in doing so you will be able to see whether there's really something there to fix and if so how to fix it. Try being totally silent after you ask a few questions. Avoid the temptation to keep talking about what *you* had in mind; try discovering what you got into *their* minds. Try *believing* your readers: not so you are stuck with their view forever, but so you can see your writing through their eyes. You are not yet trying to make up your mind about anything, you are trying to enlarge your mind. You probably made up your mind as you wrote your draft so in a sense you are trying to unmake your mind. For more about how to get feedback see Section V.

The essential skill in all revising is the ability to look at your own writing and see potentialities: see what is almost there or sort of there or even to see what is not there at all but ought to be. It is like the ability to look at a room and see how it *could* look with different furniture differently arranged. More specifically you need:
- to see what the words don't yet say but want to say,
- to see a potential shape that's not yet there but which would make everything click,
- to see a simple way to say something that's now roundabout,
- to see bits you can leave out, even though you love them.

Time, intuition, and a detached critical consciousness are obviously helpful tools if you want to look at your writing and see what could be there. But nothing is so powerful as a chance to see your words through the eyes of others.

Cut-and-Paste Revising
and the Collage

14

One of the great advantages of an approach to writing where you make a mess during the first half is that you have to clean up that mess before you are done. You can't let yourself slip into half-hearted, soft-minded revising where you just tidy things up and call it a day. Making a mess means that your revising tool is not a touch-up brush, to start with anyway, but a chain saw. It means that you can't possibly revise without stopping and thinking hard about what you really mean, about what you are trying to accomplish—even if you think you already made those decisions. The main message about revising in this book is that it is a lot of work.

But there is an easy way to revise—not simple but relatively quick and effortless: cut-and-paste revising. It's especially useful if you are in a hurry or don't care too much, but it can also lead to very good final drafts. Better, sometimes, than you achieve with other methods of revising.

For one of the most frequent problems in writing, especially creative writing, is making things worse instead of better when you revise. You start out with raw writing that you know has good things in it, or perhaps you've even worked out a coherent draft and you are pleased with its strengths, its life. But obviously it needs revising. So you revise. But when you finish you discover you've snuffed the life out of your piece. You've removed the problems you were trying to get rid of but somehow you've also destroyed or crippled what was good. (See note, p. 107, for a case of this problem.)

Cutting and pasting is a minimal revising process that helps you get rid of what's weak without undermining what's strong. You let your good passages speak for themselves but you don't add the flat-footed writing that sometimes comes later as you try to make sure that all your ideas get through clearly—or in the case of poems, stories, and plays, the soggy writing that often comes when you start "clarifying" and interpreting your own imaginative vision.

The essential process is obvious. *Cut-and-paste* virtually says it all. In effect you throw away your pen or pencil and revise with nothing but scissors and paste. You will be like a stone sculptor who never adds anything—only removes. Or like one of those painters who first applies a number of layers of pigment on the canvas and then creates a painting solely by scraping with a knife. There is an act of discipline and faith here. You must insist on find-ing the ingredients you need in what you've already put on paper. And you must insist on creating the coherence you need by rearranging, not rewriting. Thus this method only works well when you've achieved some richness in your raw writing.

The steps are as follows.

• Find the good passages and cut them away from their sur-roundings—even if you need to cut in mid-sentence. And cross out the words and phrases that can be removed even from these good passages. Unnecessary words.

• By looking over these good passages and playing with different sequences for them, and by thinking back over the rest of your raw writing, try to figure out what essential thread or shape or meaning is trying to emerge from it all. (This is different from other revising processes where you might look through your raw writing and see that it more or less says X, but then realize—perhaps by seeing it on paper—that Y is really what you want to say: such revising per-mits you to change your mind. But with cut-and-paste revising you must find the best thread in your material and go with it. You aren't so much deciding *what you want to say*, as you are sensing *what is good* and seeing what it points to.) You may need to make some kind of outline or visual plan at this point if your piece is at all complicated.

• Next put your pieces in their best order. It can be intriguing to make a game of it and see if you can actually finish the job with this step and produce a final coherent draft with no new writing at all. But this purist puzzle-solving approach will probably use up any time you might otherwise save with the cut-and-paste method.

• Now that all your pieces are in the right order, do what little writing is necessary to connect them and make a complete and coherent whole. There may be some places where you need to add something entirely lacking in your raw writing. There may be some places where you can't get your fragments to connect with each other except by adding a sentence or two. And you may feel the need for a freshly written introduction or conclusion. But be sure to experiment with passages you already have. Often what looks like an unlikely passage will click into place when you actually try it out in that beginning or ending slot.

• You will probably be able to tighten and clarify a bit as you copy it over and remove mistakes in grammar and usage.

The cut-and-paste method, especially if you are trying to save time and effort, should result in a stripped-down kind of final draft. The weaknesses will consist primarily of omissions, but omissions often do less harm than passages that don't work. Indeed if you get skilled with this method, you can begin to achieve effects—as in those bare Picasso line drawings—where the minimalism is a strength and not a weakness.

The Collage

A collage consists not of a single perfectly connected train of explicit thinking or narrative but rather of *fragments:* arranged how shall we say?—poetically? intuitively? randomly? Without transitions or connectives. (On rare occasions the joints can be invisible.) When it works it is terrific. Indeed, there is often a deeper impact on readers because the collage invites them to create actively out of their own consciousness the vision which organizes those fragments—the sparks which cross those gaps. But when a collage doesn't work it seems merely opaque or annoying—a lazy cop-out.

Simple collage stories or poems or plays don't feel very odd to many readers now. Perhaps we get a glimpse of the main character in the subway in the morning; then a picture of his daydream as he takes part in a meeting at an oval table; then a dialogue with his wife over the dinner coffee; then an evocation of him brushing his teeth; then a piece of childhood experience as he is falling asleep. Much poetry and some fiction go farther. They don't just leave gaps in chronology, they abandon it. They arrange scenes, images, scraps of dialogue or meditation in an intuitive or associative order rather than logically or chronologically. Many writers and readers seem to have agreed that the goals which are served by clearly explained conventional narratives—perhaps to convey a complex experience, a vision of the world, a sense of a person's life—can also be achieved with fragments or pieces arranged differently. T. S. Eliot's "The Wasteland," to name a cultural landmark, is a collage. So too, obviously, is much modern poetry.

Collage writing can be produced by careful planning from the start, but there's a much simpler way which is not out of place since the organization of a collage seems by its nature to invite intuition. First, do lots of raw writing; then look through it all to find the good bits; tighten and polish them to make them even better; and, finally, lay them out on the table or floor where you can see them all at once and find the best order for them.

The heart of the matter is that instead of emphasizing unity and coherence and singleness as your principle of revising, your only rule is this: get rid of everything dead, keep everything alive.

It's a great relief to stop trying for coherence and connectedness. So often you have these *good* pieces of writing and somehow they trick you into bad writing: you need a way to lead up to one of them, then ways to get from one to another, and finally a way to end the whole thing, and before you know it your whole piece of writing is weak and soggy. Some professional writers have learned to finesse this problem. Just stick with what is already good. Period. No faltering beginnings or sagging ends, no dead spots where you keep trying to make something work but it doesn't. It's a good way to write a biography, autobiography, or novel: a succession of live moments. It's surprising how much can be left out, how much need not be said.

If your final piece has nothing in it but strong writing, much organizational weakness can be forgiven. But the odd thing is that when you stop trying for unity and connectedness and put all your effort into just getting rid of what doesn't work, you often discover a surprising coherence lurking in your pile of good pieces. Many of the worst problems of organization really come from trying to organize pieces when some are weak. Hasn't it often happened to you that you struggle and struggle unsuccessfully to get from P to Q and then suddenly realize you can junk Q and end up with a lovely transition from P to R? And Q wasn't that good to start with.

Collage Essays

Once you start working with this odd but liberating principle—
throw away everything that doesn't work and shake up the good
bits to see how they want to arrange themselves—it turns out that
you can apply it to expository writing: essays, reports, profiles.
Essays are a traditionally loose form: the essay, when it was invented, was an "assay," that is, a "try," a "go at" something. Some
of the best essays have been informal, chatty, and associative in
structure. But whereas essays have traditionally had a strong con-
versational thread, here you don't worry about a thread at all, you
just look for quality. You get an *implied thread* to assert itself by
arranging the good bits in the right order. I remember a recent
New Yorker profile of a college professor (volume 55, number 43,
February 18, 1980) which was really a string of paragraphs or
groups of paragraphs, each one tending to begin with "——— at
the office," or "——— talking to students," or "——— taking a
walk." Lazy and simple, but it worked. And there was an implied
thread. The object of a transition is to get you from A to B. If you
can do it without the transition, why waste the reader's time?

The loop writing process is an ideal way to produce material for
a collage essay: something that fulfills the function of an essay but
is made up almost entirely of passages in which you try to give
your reader an experience of what you are saying rather than an
explanation of it.

Sometimes one of your good bits will explain clearly and directly
what you are trying to say in the whole piece (or what you discover
those good pieces of writing are trying to say). Such a passage will
probably go well at the beginning or the end of your collage. If
there is no such piece in your original writing, you must figure out
what your essay is driving at as you contemplate and arrange your
good fragments, and on that basis write an introduction or conclusion.

Many feature stories in daily and especially Sunday newspapers
drift into the collage form—for example, a neighborhood in Brook-
lyn written up in a series of bits that present rather than explain:
portraits of people and of terrain, street corner scenes, mini-narra-
tives, dialogues, and reminiscent monologues.

I'm struck with the way many regular news stories now jettison
the traditional who-what-when-where opening—or rather delay

it—in order to begin with a bit of collage: a piece of presentation-without-explanation. Here is the beginning of a story about a policy change at city hall—a story from the first section of *The New York Times*—but notice how it begins with a little piece of particularized drama:

> *Under New Mayor, Philadelphia Police Shift Tactics*
> By LESLIE BENNETTS (Special to *The New York Times*)
>
> PHILADELPHIA, April 11 [1980]—A couple of weeks ago, Marlene Nimmo strolled up to a woman in a midtown bar and asked her if she had any nickle bags. The woman reached into her brassiere and pulled out two bags of marijuana—whereupon Mrs. Nimmo showed her police identification and said, "You're under arrest."
>
> "Her eyes bugged out, her jaw dropped open, and she was in a complete state of shock," Mrs. Nimmo recounted. She said, "When did this happen? This isn't supposed to be!" Mrs. Nimmo laughed. "I fool the daylights out of them; I make the buy and I make the bust. They'll sell to a woman because they don't know any women are narcs."
>
> Until recently, drug dealers were correct in their belief . . .

and so on into a conventional news story about changes in policy in the mayor's office and reasons for these changes.

Jane Howard's book *Families* (New York, 1978) is really a collage in which she presents portraits of all sorts of families and family arrangements. She spells out her message or conclusion in the introduction and the final chapter. Ken Macrorie's *Uptaught* (Rochelle Park, N.J., 1970) is a memoir of experiences and an argument about teaching. He makes it a collage in which experiential fragments such as narratives and portraits are intermingled with conceptual passages explaining his argument. Martin Duberman, in writing a careful history of Black Mountain College, includes fragments from his own diary and imaginary dialogues between himself and some of these characters he never met (*Black Mountain: An Exploration in Community*, Garden City, N.Y., 1973).

You might make a collage essay on the causes of the French Revolution that consists entirely of stories, portraits, and scenes. You would have to choose and arrange your fragments in such a way that they tell why the French Revolution happened as it did. Or you might have one that consists entirely of dialogues: between nobles, peasants, middle-class city dwellers, and thinkers of the period; between people who came before and those who came afterwards. Of course you may have to revise and polish some of these fragments to make them as good as possible—perhaps even write some more bits to give at least a minimal coherence.

You could write a collage essay that explores the meaning of a poem or another work of art by juxtaposing brief passages from the poem with incidents from your own experience or from history or other works of literature. An essay about a work of art or scholarship could consist of an interview between you and the author or between the author and one or two of the characters who figure in it.

Options in the Collage Form

Perhaps an essay—strictly defined—must spell out its conclusions explicitly. But you can take the collage principle a bit further and write an effective collage which fulfills many of an essay's functions but doesn't *say* what it is saying. It only presents ingredients. Studs Terkel's *Working* (New York, 1972), for example, is a book-length collage which nowhere explicitly concludes anything from all those monologues, scenes, and portraits of people's experiences of work. The question is whether we understand what Terkel wanted to say. When you just present ingredients, different readers draw different conclusions.

But if you do it just right, readers *will* understand what you are saying, and your message will go deeper for the very reason that readers create it themselves, they don't read it. You've used a purely inductive method. But it's easy to miss. And readers can be understandably suspicious that perhaps you were just too lazy to think your way through your material to a conclusion. They'll think you're just borrowing the style of bad TV documentaries: blip/blip/blip vividness-with-no-thinking.

On some occasions you may not even care whether your readers reach your conclusion or indeed whether they bother to reach any conclusion at all. Your goal is only to get these incidents and issues and facts and dilemmas into their consciousness. In certain circumstances you increase your chances of success if you don't even give your own conclusions so that readers don't get distracted by the question of whether they agree or disagree with you. You trust your material itself, sooner or later, to have the effect on readers that you want.

And on some occasions, finally, you haven't even reached any conclusions yourself and are not trying to pretend that you have. You are working on something important and you need a few more days or months of living with your material before you can figure out your conclusion and work out a final structure. But you need a finished draft now. Or you want a draft to give others to help you with your simmering. In such a circumstance you can still produce a powerful piece of writing in the collage form.

Thus the collage essay provides you with a continuum of choices about how explicit to be. At one end is a piece whose meaning is totally implicit consisting of associatively arranged ingredients: virtually an evocation or even a poem rather than what most people call an essay. At the other end is an orthodox essay (a completely connected explicit argument) which you interrupt only intermittently with blips of scene, portrait, dialogue, or narrative in order to make your meanings more alive.*

Summary

• The essential process in cut-and-paste revising: try to avoid all rewriting; make do with clever excerpting, ruthless pruning, and imaginative rearranging. Cut-and-paste revising is most useful if you are in a hurry or if you have a tendency to squelch all the life out of your raw writing as you revise.

• The essential process in the collage: choose what is alive and discard what is dead; polish the good pieces and figure out how they want to arrange themselves.

• The essential process in the collage essay: don't just explain your meaning (or don't explain it at all); convey your meaning with passages which evoke it or recreate it or present it, such as scenes, portraits, tiny narratives, dialogues, or internal musings. Make your argument or conceptual meaning somehow give birth to itself inside your reader's head.

• It would probably be a mistake to give up orthodox essays al-

*This is what I was trying for in my chapter on competence-based teaching in *On Competence: A Critical Analysis of Competence-based Reforms in Higher Education*, Gerald Grant *et al.* (San Francisco, 1979).

together. You need to master that form because it is so often called
for. In certain circumstances you will put some readers off merely
by adding a few blips of experiential writing to an essay which is
otherwise fully explicit, reasoned, and connected. ("You can't trust
his thinking. He's a creative writer. He's too emotional.") And you
can get lazy because the collage form requires so much less work.
You can get in the habit of not quite figuring out any conclusions
from your material. An orthodox essay may not always provide you
with the best way to *have* ideas or even to convey ideas to readers,
but it usually provides the best way to clarify, evaluate, and develop further the ideas you have already figured out.

Two Collage Essays

Collage essays may sound odd, unfamiliar, and difficult to imagine.
For that reason I conclude with two examples written by students in
two of my classes. I led these classes in the use of the loop writing
process for producing raw writing. I don't know whether the sum-
ming-up or explaining passages in the following essays were written as part of the original raw writing or were written later during
the cutting and pasting process.

   The first piece was in response to an assignment entitled "What
am I doing Teaching?" that I gave to a class of primary and secondary school teachers. Though the title may suggest something
theoretical, I made it clear I was asking for a concrete and practical
piece of work. I said, in effect, "you will sometimes lose sight of
what you are really doing and why; in the midst of day to day
struggle you may lose the focus or foundation of your teaching that
you most need for keeping it up and doing a good job. In this
paper, therefore, figure out your priorities so that if you get confused or have to retreat under pressure you will be able to hold
fast to the main thing." (I am indebted to Lester Krupp for the
idea of this assignment as an aid to survival.)

What Am I Doing Teaching?
by CATHY ELLIS

   I want a purpose and teaching gives it to me. All the inequality,
unfairness in the world—I can make a stab at it in teaching, I can
even it out a little.

   I remember being placed in a reading group in first grade. My
group was group two. We sat at an ordinary wooden table with ordi-

nary wooden chairs. Group one sat at a pastel yellow table with pastel yellow chairs. They read better than we. They were treated better than we. They were given the special picture of Santa Claus to color at Christmas time while the rest of us read. I didn't like them very much and yet I terribly wanted to sit at that yellow table. I asked the teacher once why none of the rest of us got to sit at the yellow table or got to play games like they did or color special pictures. It's funny but I remember thinking she was embarrassed. She looked like I did when I'd been caught doing something wrong. When she answered she sounded as if she were angry with me. She said that they worked harder. They earned their privileges. I didn't understand. I thought I worked hard, but I was afraid to ask any more.

In later years, during high school, I and a group of friends were turned away from a high school dance because we arrived late. We stood back and watched while another group, a couple of cheer-leaders and their friends, were admitted after we were turned away. That night I wrote a letter to the editor of our local newspaper com-plaining of favoritism in our schools. I made a couple of copies, and friends and I passed them around school to obtain signatures. At the end of the day we had over one hundred signatures and the threat that if we returned to school with the letter the following day, it would be confiscated and we would be sent home. The principal wanted each of those signing the letter sent to the office in the way of a warning. There was some talk of suspending the instigators from school. The school board instructed the administration to leave us all alone. And yet I wonder if we would have been dealt with the same if my father had not been the editor of the paper.

Dear Trevor, Richard, and Pacer,

The reason I decided to teach, the reason I continue to teach is for children like you. Children who never seem to have a fair break, for whom school is just one more put down, while the other children continue to get the awards, the honors. I want to even up the score—for you and for my whole childhood which was not nearly so devastat-ing as yours (however, at times I felt it was).

I think at least a moment of childhood should be grand for everyone—and learning should be the most exciting part. I want the learning to be that moment for you. Because maybe then you'll be able to make that moment last forever—or at least recall it whenever in need. If that happens, then maybe I've compensated just a little for the unfairness of childhood, the inequalities of life.

Sincerely,

Mrs. Ellis

A portrait of Trevor: when he received his first award for completing his work for the week. A look of surprise, followed by a shy smile. Pug nose looking more in place rather than an out-of-place feature on an adult face. Sauntering up to pick out his prize. Trying not to lose all of his Mr. Cool.

A portrait of Pacer: when he completed his math page correctly and independently, his whole face was a smile, no longer trying to give an impression of Mr. Tough Guy; totally unaware; a candid photograph.

An important moment. The classroom in the morning before the bell. Children waiting for me at the door. Smiles. Rush of words prefaced by "Teacher!" The door opens—a room that begins only to exist at this moment each day—warm little bodies file in. Desks open and shut. Security settles in. All's the same. More remarks to teacher. I'm busy. Children follow me. I hang up yesterday's pictures, writing. Children madly search to find theirs. "That's mine teacher. See?" Friends. A good feeling. The whistle blows from outside. Stragglers come in. Order presents itself. All in their seats. Lunch count. It's begun.

A bad moment. A writing assignment for my 6th grade English class. I explain, "It's not much I'm asking of you, just a paragraph or story paragraph, so to speak. Tell me about a good moment you've had. Everyone has had some good moments. Try to include some color and sound words. Make me see the moment."

"Does it have to be something good?"

"Surely you can think of one good moment."

"No, nothing good ever happens to me." Subdued laughter from the class. Several other voices join in:

"Nothing good ever happens to us."

"All right then, pick a bad moment, but write something." I feel myself fighting the desperation in my voice. I hear a chorus of "Do we have to?" Defiant faces, turning around, talking to each other. I'm hurt, I'm angry.

"All right, I'll give you a choice. You can write the paragraph I suggested or copy from a dictionary. Which has more meaning for you?"

Half a dozen children or more move out of their desks, smirks on their faces, and shuffle over to the shelves for dictionaries. Good God, they're even drawing the illustrations. One shows me hers for my approval. Wants to know if she can do more dictionary work for extra credit. She's serious. I don't believe it.

Last night I dreamed I hit one of them. The solid feel of flesh smacking flesh. It felt good. It scares me. I've got to get out of here.

So after a year of attempting to reach the twelve to thirteen year olds, I returned to my first grade classroom. It was like another good moment—going home.

A first grade language assignment. Sun shines in through our windows, lighting up the playing fields, reflecting on the bars and jungle gym, drying up yesterday's mud puddles.

"Let's write about what you like to do in the sun." A blizzard of hands in the air.

"I got one teacher, I got one." Decisions. I choose a hand, a face:

"I like to lay in the sun." I write it down on the chart. Giggles in the background as I draw a little stick figure of Donny lying under the sun.

More hands. More choices. A bombardment of words, ideas. Soon the chart is covered with sentences, pictures, holding a special meaning for each child. A scramble for pencils, crayons, paper. A vying for position—each child looking for his story or his friend's.

It seems I've no sooner sat down than papers are waving in my face.

"Look, teacher, look at mine."

"Read it teacher." Or better yet, "I can read it teacher. Listen. I watch the clouds. See, that's me and there's the clouds." Such a smile. He just grasped a tiny part of the world.

Dialogue.

Vickie: "Sure they all love you. But little kids drive me crazy. At least fourth graders can take care of themselves."

Me: "So can first graders, and they have much more potential. It hasn't been squelched by previous education. They're moldable and full of creativity."

Vickie: "And running noses and colds. You can have them."

Me: "Thanks. I'll take them."

Portrait of me by a colleague.

Cathy is a very idealistic person. She thinks she might save the world from the classroom. The first grade classroom at that. She feels she has a sensitivity maintained by the very few that allows her to understand and reach children in a way others couldn't. And because of this ability of hers she feels she will reach her children in such a way that they might literally save the world.

Basically, Cathy lacks realism. She forgets her children grow up, they change. Trevor, Pacer, and Richard might make some headway in the first grade, but they will revert to their basic natures by adolescence. They need firmness a great deal more than they need Cathy's pampering. But she'll continue with her idealistic ways because that is the only way she can teach and the only reason that she does teach.

Finally I reach the point where I must answer the question, "What am I doing teaching?" My first thought was to share this title with my fellow teachers. Somehow I knew we could all have a chuckle over it. Why? Because the title says so much and so little. What am I doing teaching? How often does a teacher ask herself that? I'm trying to find a purpose—satisfaction—make my life worthwhile.

So I chose teaching. I wanted to contribute. First I wanted older children—old enough to be intellectually stimulating, but young enough to be innovative. Middle school age. I found the primary children were a little more of both—at least for me and for my personality.

I don't like discipline. I resented being on the receiving end as a child and I detest being on the giving end as an adult. But with the younger children, even though they may require discipline, I find I needn't distort my personality to work with them. I can be myself. I need that to find satisfaction.

But satisfaction isn't altogether purpose. Purpose comes from achieving a lasting impression, one that makes you a bit immortal.

First grade reeks with purpose. In nine months' time the printed word gains meaning. Non-readers become readers. Children unable to express themselves on paper without adult assistance transform into mini-authors. Numbers have gained meaning and their world has become more comprehensible. The children feel a little better about themselves because of me. They know someone cares for them—their first grade teacher—and they remember. Over the years they come back to visit—and a piece of my spirit travels in each of them.

Pre-writing and first grade are much the same: a creative flow, a build up of the creative process, a period of productivity when confidences are built and ideas planted. Only after this period of time has been exhausted in thought and activity is the writer ready to evaluate and revise his work. And only after a full year in first grade is the child ready and able to handle criticism. Only after a beginning successful year is he able to say, "OK, that was wrong. There is more where that came from." All the more reason to stress the beginning years—to emphasize the positive, the creative. First grade builds a well to draw from and success demands that it be full. That's the essence of a first grade teacher: she opens the first doors of the mind. My reason for teaching: I want to open that door for *all* my children, and maybe just a little wider for those children forgotten in the foreground.

• • •

The second collage essay was on a topic of the student's choice though I had required that there be an essay as a culmination of some independent thinking, writing, and research into his own learning.

Science Is a Verb Not a Noun
by BILL MCNAUGHTEN

When I was younger, still going to grade school, I had the good fortune to spend 4 years at a junior high school where the "doing" of science was given equal footing and emphasis with the "knowing" of science. The scientific inquiry process of Problem, Hypothesis, Experiment, Data, Conclusions, provided a logical framework within which we explored a vast number of physical phenomena.

I've built this pendulum down in my basement, you see. I built it to see if the earth really does turn underneath it like it's supposed to. I've made it from a 500-gram brass weight, some old fishing line, and a piece of bent wire which hangs as a pointer on the bottom. It's not very big, and the air slows it down pretty fast after I start it swinging. But, in twenty minutes it'll move 5 degrees on the circle; I usually go upstairs and eat dinner when I wait that long. Then, when I come back I measure it to see how much it's changed since I started it.

Three nights ago I tried to figure out which way the pendulum was supposed to be moving based on the positioning of my house. I'm not sure what happened, but I came to the distinct conclusion that either the earth was "turning backwards," or something was very wrong with what I had been reading about pendulums. Both prospects seemed highly unlikely, and I tried orienting myself again and again. . . . "OK, that's east and that's north, now the sun rises in the east so therefore I'm moving towards it from the west. Therefore, the earth should turn under the pendulum *that* way . . . but it's not, it's going the other way!"

Conclusion: No need to worry though, I finally figured out that I had been visually imagining the earth as rotating the wrong way. So, at least for the time being, pendulums and the earth still move the way the textbooks say that they do, but it was fun for a while half-seriously thinking that I had discovered an inconsistency in the physics they were teaching us in school.

I now own several gray lab notebooks full of questions, possible answers, details of testing those possibilities: pictures, graphs, descriptions of procedure, and finally, the implications of what we had found; those books are a reminder to me of how learning science can be, delightful and fascinating. Later on though, things were different:

Subject: Chemistry exam—endless pages of information: electron orbitals, valences, radical ion transformations, pH, redox reactions, carbon bending, polarity, etc., etc.

Problem: Why is studying this stuff simultaneously fascinating and boring, science used to be so easy for me?

Hypothesis: Facts, Formalism, Theory; *Reading* about *other* people's ideas and experiments. This is all science "knowing," with no science "doing."

Experiment: Watch what's happening.

Data: Phil, Jack, and I had been studying for the Chemistry exam all day. We had gone over our notes again and again looking for pieces of information not yet memorized. If there was one thing I had learned about Machemer's Chem exams it was that you simply had to know every word he ever said in class. Phil and I had started taping class lectures and then transcribing them back at the beginning of the semester; we were now glad we had. It was the only way you could survive in that class.

Into the night we quizzed each other until we could spout forth information on any subject; mental knee-jerking. Finally, we, Prof. Machemer, and the exams arrived in Lab Science 203, Saturday, December 18, 9 a.m. Silence; nervous pencils, calculators, and slide rules dance and skitter across the desktops.

Two hours later; we emerge, some comparing answers, some staring into space and moving silently off, probably to another exam at noon or three. I consciously pull the flush handle on my mind and drain away all thought of Chemistry from it; I have an English and Philosophy exams on Monday, French on Tuesday, and Calculus on Wednesday morning. I suppress the urge to reward myself for yesterday's hard work; there is too much yet to memorize, and too little time.

Later on, while studying I hear through my window: "Science is the root of all evil. It has destroyed our land, poisoned our streams and wildlife, polluted our air, and threatened our very existence on the planet. We must cease our dependence on this menace to our lives and return to a natural state such as our ancestors knew." As I listened to her speak, I noticed the small pink scar of a smallpox vaccination on her arm, I guess she'd forgotten that it was there.

Conclusion: Two worlds have grown up where there once was
just one,
Two worlds co-existing in space.
There peoples divide, then turning walk away,
Only to wind up face to face.

The polarization between science and the rest of human study has
many roots, not the least of which are the post-Sputnik math/science
push in education, and the technological utilization of the results of
scientific inquiry for destructive and inhuman purposes. With technology tooting science as its parent, it is easy for those who see the
destruction resulting from the misuse of technology to point at
science as being innately amoral or evil. And yet, I have experienced
science as a joyful and beautiful thing. Is there something different
(wrong) with me? Is there something about science that makes it easier for some people than others? What's wrong here?

Problem: What is science?

Hypothesis: Exploring, observing change, suggesting reasons for
change (and testing them).

Experiment: Looking under a rock; watching the night sky; leaning out the air/fuel mixture on a car getting poor mileage.

Data: The process takes asking, takes time, takes patience, takes
encouragment, takes taking time to find the right to ask.

Conclusion: Science is the way that we think:
  Problem: What's in (under, behind) this?
  What will happen if I change this?
  What needs to happen to make this better?
  Hypothesis: Let's try this and see what happens.
  Experiment: "making changes."
  Data: getting feedback, experiencing what happens.
  Conclusion: what was there, what caused what.

Problem: What to do next?

Hypothesis: How about this. . . . ? . . . etc.

Problem: Is this true? How do we think and learn in "the arts"
(which tend to reject science as rigid and uncreative)?

Hypothesis: Science and the arts both involve two directions of
study:
  1. Outside to Inside—technique, theory, training, discipline;
  dealing with thought, ideas, and logic; intellectual.

2. Inside to Outside—self-awareness, creative, intuitive, unconscious: dealing with feelings, images, and *doing;* expressive.

Experiment: Observe the "Expressive Arts."

Data: Movement Class: Contact Improv—Starting slow, starting
still, unsure partners. Hands held out, fingers almost . . . and
then touch; Contact: a single finger tip. Eyes closed, touching
only allowed. Neither leading nor led, swaying starts, contact
remains: one finger, . . . two, . . . three, . . . one again.
One hand swaying, no-see mirror; deep swinging slows at
height of reaches then hands fall fluttering. Arms touch and
turn, both hands now match each other in motion. Fingers
sliding; contact remains, shifting: arm to arm, arm to shoulder,
shoulder to back, to hip, to leg, and return. Now back to back,
lean and hold; extend and be held; pushing, giving way. No
thought, just sensing the contact making itself move or not
move; we follow it. Sliding past and around now, maximum
contact, interweaving flow, body touch body, waves of motion
tumbling across one another, and finally . . . subsiding, slowing, gentle touch of sitting close, only hands moving: together,
almost still. One finger touching: Contact.

Concert Choir: "Learn it until you don't need the music anymore, then we'll sing it together." First, we all sing alone
reading each note, one by one, trying to "get" the bass (alto,
soprano, tenor) lines from the piano into our heads. Stopping
repeatedly, individual parts being played, difficult transitions
being repeated and emphasized. Now, sing it together; stop:
"Altos, measure 24 to the end, bases, top of page 3." Again,
together; David wants us to look at him, we want to look at the
music; we feel too unsure yet to give up looking at the notes.

Rehearsal again, new music, old music. "Oh, not that one
again!" Once through with the music; surprisingly, we do
alright with it, well balanced, most notes right. Checking in
with David: "We don't know that measure, how does it go?
. . . Standing, heads up, no music this time; I begin to listen
and hear the others around me. We are "coming together."
David marks the pace, but we make the music. Listening to
each other we are simultaneously performers and audience,
correcting pitch, tone, and rhythm, and reaching for how *this*
song should feel. And when we sing for others we don't stop
listening to one another, but there is a difference. We become
no longer a group of individuals singing together, but a choir,
an instrument that plays itself. In that moment, if we have

learned it well, we cease to sing the song, for the song has begun to sing us.

Writing: I didn't plan it, in fact I didn't know the concluding idea and final brilliant point of the paper until I wrote those last two sentences which simply sprang from my hand. I had gotten involved in the writing; I wrote and knew that the writing was going somewhere but I didn't know where. I was spinning a web but I couldn't really see it all until I anchored that last corner and then stepped back to take a look.

Skating class, private instruction:

Kathy Wainhouse, skating instructor: "OK, that's enough time to warm up, now let's see your flip jump."

Me: "Well, let me just practice the beginning a few times so I can remember it and get the sense of it."

KW: "OK, one's enough, now do it this time."

Me: "Well, OK. . . ." (Shaky takeoff, arms flailing, bad landing; I fall and slide on the ice.)

KW: "Your arms were all over the place. Do another one."

Me: "Let me just practice the arms for a second. . ."

KW: "No, just go ahead, you can do it."

Me: ". . . all right (mumbled) . . ." Thoughts racing, ". . . stroke, arm change, turn, down, poke, arms in, head up, then land, arms out, leg back." (Again, shaky, rigid takeoff and fall.)

KW: "Do another one, you're trying too hard and its making you stuck."

Me: To myself, "OK, OK." Few thoughts this time; anger at being pushed . . . turn . . . jump . . . land.

KW: "That was better, you were higher and the takeoff was good. Remember your arms; bring them around."

Me: To myself, "Allright, lets do it, 1, 2, 3, . . . arms in! out! . . . whaaaa! (falling)."

KW: "Bill, You're thinking about it too much, your arms were so strong that you overrotated and fell. Do it again and try to remember how the good one felt. Relax, you'll get it!"

Me: Talking to myself while skating around the rink a few times, ". . . I can do this, and even if I fall it's OK. Whatever happens is just fine; I'm doing this because I want to." One more lap around the rink, not too fast, then turn, poke, jump, land. Without a pause, I skate around for another one: turn, poke, jump, land.

KW: "Good, do another."

Me: No thoughts, . . . feeling the rhythm: swing leg, turn;
        down, swing, poke; up, spin, land; arms out, leg back.

KW: "Do one more and bring your arms in more this time."

Me: Lapping the rink, images running in my mind I see
        myself jumping: . . . "arms in" . . . and then turn,
        poke, arms in, arms out, land.

KW: "Good, keep working on it, don't stop to think about it."

Later—People whizzing everywhere, doing spins, flying camels,
lutzes, axels, flips, double flips and loops, and an occasional double
lutz or double axel. This is the club practice session for competitive
junior skaters. I, 23, self-consciously practice my loop and flip, trying,
sometimes unsuccessfully, to stay out of the way of these younger
people flashing around me. I do a loop: mohawk, down, spring up,
around, land, . . . fall. A skater I had smiled at earlier when she fell
laughs and calls to me encouragingly, "I've seen you do those better
than that!" I accept her challenge and throw out my self-consciousness. Music comes on, I skate. "Hop, hop, flip," Hmmmm, good.
"Hop, hop, flip" . . . better! "Hop, hop, flip" . . . alright! Again and
again I jump, no longer isolate, but in concert with those around me,
reveling in flight over ice.

Conclusion: Creative expression requires a degree of both ex-
                ternal training and internal awareness. Too much
                emphasis on training results in great flexibility
                within the limits of a stylized form; too much em-
                phasis on internal processes results in chaotic or
                simplistic effort with no defining framework.

Essentially, then, scientific exploration is artistic exploration; both are
creative. Both say, "Look what's here (inside me or out there); let's
look at it; see what it is, does, and feels like; how it acts, moves,
responds, and changes. Both need logic, both need intuition (intuition is usually quite logical anyway, even if we cannot immediately
see the logic we can usually sense it and how accurate it is). Creativity, as I have come to find, is a very conscious, but only partly intellectual process. To create we need both sides of the brain working
because creativity is the melding of details (intellectual) and overall
concepts (expressive) to form a specific, accurate, and uniquely
human response to the environment.

Problem: What does the writer, dancer, sculptor, musician, art-
             ist seek? What does the scientist seek?

Hypothesis: The greatest art begins within human consciousness and is a response to the universe saying, "*this* is the order, truth, beauty, simplicity that I see underlying all human and natural existence."

The greatest science begins within human consciousness as a response to the universe saying, "this is the order, truth, beauty, and simplicity that I see underlying all human and natural existence."

Experiment: Part #1 Ask questions, observe, draw conclusions, question your conclusions and ask more questions. Observe, make changes, observe some more.

Part #2 Find something that you feel needs changing; change it, see what happened, change it again. Stop, go away; come back in a minute, a day, a year, a life time and see how it looks (feels, sounds, is still working) then. Change it again if you want.

Part #3 Take a thought, image, idea and write it, play it, paint it, make a picture of it, build it, dance it, try it, but *do* it. Don't worry, just *do* it! Better yet, *do* it first without knowing what you're doing it about. Now, *do* it again; keep it the same, organize it, scramble it, move it, reverse it, change it, rearrange it. Then, *do* it again. Quit when you're bored or tired and come back to it later; or push ahead past the boredom and see what happens.

Data: Part #1 This is scientific inquiry.

Part #2 This is how people live their lives.

Part #3 This is how "self-expression" works.

Conclusion: Human beings are creative and think creatively regardless of whether they are involved in doing art, science, or cleaning the bathroom; the process is the same. The ability to do abstract/intellectual creative thinking, and the ability to do expressive creative thinking are not mutually exclusive. They both involve questioning, exploring, testing, observing, making a response, and coming to a conclusion.

For many people, science as they have experienced it in school and in their lives has failed to live up to its creative potential. We have stressed the techniques developed for scientific exploration over the exploration itself. As any dancer knows, too much technique without putting in time to finding out how your body *wants* to move frustrates and stifles the joy of movement. Creativity *is* the nature of our thinking. Let us acknowledge it in ourselves and rejoice in our schools and in our lives at the power of our minds to think, create, respond, and love.

• • •

Because I saw an earlier version in the form of a conventional expository essay with no blips of experiential writing, I think I can see some particular benefits that resulted when he adopted the collage form. The presence of experiential writing seemed to improve his conceptual or "essay" prose here. His language was much more abstract and dead in the earlier draft. And the collage form also seemed to improve his thinking. In the earlier draft he had succumbed to the temptation of almost denying any differences between science and the arts in his eagerness to press home his point about creativity inhering in both of them. Here, the experienced blips, even though a vehicle for his main point about creativity-in-both, nevertheless forced him to do justice to the differences.

15

The Last Step: Getting Rid of Mistakes in Grammar

I suppose I shouldn't talk about "getting rid of mistakes in grammar" because I'm not just talking about grammar strictly defined but also about punctuation, spelling, and mechanics; and because these things are really conventions of usage rather than matters of absolute correctness or error. Whether a given usage is a "mistake" or not often depends on the audience and the situation. But I would rather talk crudely about *grammar* and *right and wrong* since that is the way most of us experience this whole business and that is the way we are going to have to come to terms with it.

Like it or not, there is a deep psychic importance to that whole set of rules and conventions for writing which we tend to sum up loosely as grammar. Grammar is glamour. They are the same word. Like *channel/canal* or *guard/ward* or *porridge/pottage*, the two words just started out as two pronunciations of the same word—a mere matter of regional accent. For grammar *was* glamour. If you knew grammar you were special. You had prestige, power, access to magic; you understood a mystery; you were like a nuclear physicist. But now, with respect to grammar, you are only special if you lack it. Writing without errors doesn't make you anything, but writing with errors—if you give it to other people —makes you a hick, a boob, a bumpkin. Grammar school used to be a special gateway into privilege for a select few. Now grammar school is the lowest, simplest, least special school there is.

The result, oddly enough, is that now grammar often preoccupies people *more* than when it was glamour. People who don't know grammar are liable to think about it all the time when they are writing. They have only to pick up a pencil and their attention is almost entirely occupied with the question of whether things are right or wrong. They are even liable to feel nervous when they speak—at least if they are speaking to strangers. In addition, lots of people who *do* know grammar well cannot see a mistake in their reading without being completely distracted from the meaning of the words. And it's not just people who know grammar well: everyone gets distracted. The only thing that's different about people who know grammar well is that they find *more* mistakes. (English teachers may be hawk-eyed about mistakes, but actually they are better than most people at paying attention to the meaning of words while still noticing mistakes in grammar.) Grammar is writing's surface. When you meet strangers, you can hardly keep from noticing their clothing before you notice their personality. The only way to keep someone from noticing a surface is to make it "disappear," as when someone wears the clothes you most expect her to wear. The only way to make grammar disappear—to keep the surface of your writing from distracting readers away from your message—is to make it right.

So what follows from this peculiar power of grammar to monopolize people's attention? from the nasty fact that grammar, like sex and money, can only be ignored when it's fine?

Perhaps the most obvious thing that follows is the desirability of learning grammar if you don't know it. (Not the theory of grammar, though that is an interesting subject, but how to write right.) Learning grammar well would free some people from a gnawing if sometimes unconscious insecurity and enable them to hold their heads up in some arenas where they now feel they can't. Happily, it's not hard to find good instruction in grammar. There are lots of courses for people of all ages and lots of good programmed textbooks from which you can learn it by yourself in six months of diligent slogging. For many people, a class brings up intolerable feelings of "Oh, I don't know grammar, I'm an idiot." But a class is probably the best method for ensuring that you keep going. If you take a class, try to shop around to see if you can find a teacher who suits you.

But you can't learn grammar overnight. If you want your words to be taken seriously you have to find some other way to remove the mistakes from your final draft. Mistakes in grammar lead readers to notice other weaknesses. And most readers cannot keep from assuming, even if unconsciously, that you are stupid if they find mistakes in your grammar. If you weren't brought up to speak and write standard, middle-class, white English, you'll probably be twice penalized for any mistakes in standard written English you make—and not just with white middle-class readers either. Removing errors may well be the most "cost effective" of all revising activities.

You can learn lots of grammar in six months, but it would take two or three times that long to learn everything you need. I, for example, even though I have a pretty good knowledge of grammar, cannot remove enough errors from my final draft to make readers take me as seriously as I want to be taken. I get a friend or two to help me by proofreading. You can't see your own mistakes. Learning grammar is a formidable task that takes crucial energy away from working on your writing, and worse yet, the process of learning grammar interferes with writing: it heightens your preoccupation with mistakes as you write out each word and phrase, and makes it almost impossible to achieve that undistracted attention to your *thoughts* and *experiences* as you write that is so crucial for strong writing (and sanity). For most people, nothing helps their writing so much as learning to ignore grammar as they write.

Short-Range Goal: Getting Rid of Mistakes

I know no other way than to get the help of a proofreader or two for any piece of writing that you want taken seriously. It is best, of course, if you can find someone who is good at finding mistakes. But if none of your close friends has that skill, you can use acquaintances or even find a competent person you don't know. You need to pay back whoever helps you. It won't take long for someone to get rid of mistakes in your final draft—*if* you get rid of all the ones you can find, *if* you provide a clean copy, and *if* you make it clear you don't want feedback on style or content, only correction of grammatical mistakes. (If you pay to have something typed, you can usually find a typist who will also fix mistakes at the same time.) And three careful friends, even if they are shaky in grammar, can get rid of *most* mistakes if you give them a neatly typed copy and use a good handbook for difficult cases. (There are many such books on the market that are designed for easy reference. They are usually called "writers' guides" or "writers' handbooks" or "writers' indexes." I like one that is put out for secretaries: *Reference Manual for Stenographers and Typists*, Ruth Gavin and William Sabin, 4th ed., New York, 1970.)

Here are the steps that make most sense to me:

• Try as hard as you can to put off till the end of the revising process any attention to grammar. It may take you months to learn to put aside your grammar itch as you write, but it's worth the effort.

• If you have difficulty getting things correct, make sure you write out a fresh copy of your piece at this point. It's much harder to find mistakes if you work with your battle-scarred draft with its crossings-out, tiny words cramped in tinier spaces, and arrows lassoing words back from the margins.

• Take a break so you can come back to this clean copy with fresh eyes. Morning is a good time for fresh eyes and proofreading. Reading it out loud will also help you find mistakes.

• Type your final version or write it out neatly on good paper. Don't use both sides of the paper unless there is some special reason. Avoid thin onion-skin typing paper: it makes reading much more difficult. Your goal is to make your writing easy to read. The physical appearance of your writing has a big effect on how people experience your words.

• Proofread for errors. This is essential, even though you may be sick to death of this piece. Mistakes in copying and typographical errors are almost inevitable. And you will notice some mistakes in mechanics as a result of seeing the words set out neatly in a new placement on the page. Use a friend or two to help find errors. Corrections should be made neatly, but they needn't be absolutely invisible except in the case of very formal or legal documents. Most readers will be pleased, not bothered, to see evidence that you worked right to the end to remove distracting errors.

Long-Range Goal: Learning Grammar

Unless you have an expert secretary always at your disposal or an infinitely patient friend who proofreads well you will probably want to learn grammar. It will not remove the need for proofreaders altogether since it's so hard to find your own mistakes. But you don't have to feel so dependent since their task will be minimal.

Don't make an all-out assault on learning grammar unless you are already very secure in your writing; or unless you have decided for some reason to take a rest from working on your writing. Or unless you are so bothered by your problems in grammar that you can't stop yourself from thinking about them all the while you write, no matter how hard you try to concentrate on your meaning.

But to learn grammar you don't have to make an all-out assault. Lou Kelley* suggests a useful way to learn grammar slowly in a fashion that will not be too distracting. It is, in effect, a way to sneak up on grammar. I have slightly simplified her procedure as follows:

Each time you revise a piece of writing and get help in removing mistakes, pick a few of those mistakes that were most trouble-some—especially ones you repeated. Just pick four or five. Don't try to learn everything at once.

For those few errors, try to understand why you made them and what the rule is for getting them right. Your handbook should help you with the rule. Perhaps it is a misspelling that results from the way you tend to hear and pronounce the word. Perhaps it's a grammatical usage that's all right in talking, but not for correct writing (such as "ok" or "everyone got their reward"). Perhaps it is a mistake in punctuation, such as with commas, where there's not a clear rule and you simply need to *feel* what's right. Record these mistakes in a notebook or file, along with the correction, your theory of why you make this mistake, and your best understanding of the rule.

When you next correct a piece of writing, pull out your file or notebook and refresh your memory on the mistakes you are likely to make. This will help you to find them as you correct. But as this list of errors grows, don't look at more than the most recent ten or fifteen. You can't hope to remember everything. You are simply trying for a list of *recent and correctable* mistakes so your mind can be chewing them over—both consciously and unconsciously. You can even throw away old pages after a while since you're not trying for some huge complete catalogue of errors. Your handbook provides that. Your file or notebook should be like a muddy pond with

---

*See her helpful book on writing, *From Dialogue to Discourse* (Glenview, Ill., 1972).

water coming in one end and spilling out at the other—but getting clearer and clearer over the months and years.

If you are interested in a readable study of the mistakes most often made by people with difficulties in grammar, and an analysis of why they are made, see Mina Shaughnessy, *Errors and Expectations: A Guide for the Teacher of Basic Writing*, New York, 1977.

16

Nausea

Revising is when it may hit you. Revulsion. The feeling that all this stuff you have written is stupid, ugly, worthless—and cannot be fixed. Disgust.

Nausea hits some people at the beginning of the revising process. They have successfully produced pages and pages of words, fast and furiously, or perhaps (unaffected by my preaching) they pondered every word and continually corrected as they went along. But either way, when they turn back to revise, they find *nothing* of value in all they have written.

Nausea doesn't usually hit me at the beginning of revising. I seem to be cheered and reassured just by having managed to produce a pile of writing at all. Besides, I haven't yet put lots of work into the words. Nausea hits me most at the end. I have taken a piece of writing through the entire writing cycle—days and days, perhaps weeks or months. I have revised with great care: gotten into messes, gotten out, cleaned things up, made new changes, and again cleaned up the mess. Finally I am done and I am making a few final corrections or else typing it over when now, after all that work, I find myself completely revolted by my piece of writing. It seems wrong, stupid, trivial—and irredeemable. Especially after all that work. It almost seems as though the more I have invested in it, the more likely that these feelings will hit me.

But I have finally learned that nausea need not ruin everything. If you are a victim you can learn to fight it in various ways. First of all, recognize it for what it is: a stupid game you play with yourself, a sneak attack by demons, a bad habit. Gradually you will learn to see the pattern in it, a trick your feelings play on you as they try to keep you from being effective. First the demons try to stop you from writing at all. If they fail, then they try to stop you from making some passages strong. If they fail again, then as a last ditch effort they try to trick you into *thinking* that what you have is garbage. They try to trick you either into throwing it away in disgust or else into taking the whole thing apart again and thereby luring you back into the swamp where you will finally give up in exhaustion.

Once you come to understand the pattern of this recurring nausea, you can deal with the feelings: do a freewriting in which you let go and tell how disgusted you are by everything you've written and how worthless it all is. When you give the feelings full rein, it's easier to see them for what they are. Or you can scream or cry the feelings out to a friend or a mirror or a closet. And it may help to turn back to some already completed writing of yours that you know is good—to reassure yourself of your powers.

Finally, learn to be prudent about what you *do* to your writing during these attacks. Acknowledge that when these feelings are upon you, you are in an intellectually and emotionally weakened condition. Don't let yourself engage in taking the whole thing apart again for major revising even though your feelings say, "This thing must be *completely* done over, it's worthless."

That way lies the swamp. Settle for cut-and-paste revising or quick revising. Get done. Don't make any major changes. Get rid of what's absolutely impossible, sweep the extra pieces under the rug, touch up the blemishes, and wipe up the blood and be done with it. Have the courage—the wisdom, really—to settle for something less than terrific, perhaps even something second rate. If you insist that everything you write be your best work, that tells the demons they can shut you down whenever they feel like it.

Besides, suppose it really is as terrible as your feelings say. It's still a mistake to use thorough revising when you are beset by nausea. To go back and unleash the chaos of major overhauling would make sense only if you have lots of time and a deep commitment to the piece. Yet if you have time and commitment there's no point in revising now. You'll do much better to put it all in a drawer and forget about it for a week or three. When you come back to it you may discover it doesn't need thorough revising, or if it does, you will have the fresh view and energy you need.

Now when your mind is clear you can make a simple rule to cling to later when your mind is clouded: never do major revising when nauseated by your writing.

AUDIENCE

INTRODUCTION

Not paying enough attention to your audience is a problem inherent in the nature of writing itself. After all, in speaking we have our audience right there, hearing each word as we speak it. We can scarcely forget its needs. But writing is solitary. The readers aren't with us as we put the words on paper so we are liable to use only our own frame of reference and ignore theirs. By the same token, of course, readers are solitary, too. They don't have us with them as they read and they lack all those cues they would get from watching our movements and hearing our tone of voice and emphasis. In writing we must get the words on the page so clear that there's no need for audio-visual aids. Thus, readers in their solitariness need more of the very thing that writers in their solitariness are most likely to omit. The moral of the story is obvious: pay lots of attention as you write to your audience and its needs.

But there's another story. For some of the best writing comes from writers not really worrying so much about audience—even letting readers flounder a bit—while they pour all their attention into what they are saying. Look, for example, at the opening of Virginia Wolf's *Mrs. Dalloway:*

> Mrs. Dalloway said she would buy the flowers herself.
> For Lucy had her work cut out for her. The doors would be taken off their hinges; Rumpelmayer's men were coming. And then, thought Clarissa Dalloway, what a morning—fresh as if issued to children on a beach.
> What a lark! What a plunge! For so it had always seemed to her,

when, with a little squeak of the hinges, which she could hear now, she had burst open the French windows and plunged at Bourton into the open air. How fresh, how calm, stiller than this of course, the air was in the early morning; like the flap of a wave; the kiss of a wave; chill and sharp and yet (for a girl of eighteen as she then was) solemn, feeling as she did, standing there at the open window, that something awful was about to happen; looking at the flowers, at the trees with the smoke winding off them and the rooks rising and falling; standing and looking until Peter Walsh said . . . [and so on].

As readers we get little help in knowing what is happening—we are just plunged into the middle of we're not sure what. More striking still, we get little help in realizing that the beginning of that third paragraph is a flashback (on the sound of door hinges) to thirty years earlier. She is willing for us to flounder for a while and only gradually realize that the location and point of view were changed without warning—and even more gradually figure out what these new locations and points of view are. She couldn't have been saying to herself, "Let's see, how can I begin this novel so that the poor reader is not lost or perplexed?" *If* she was thinking consciously about the needs of her audience during this opening paragraph she must have been saying something more like, "How can I start this novel with words so real that readers don't care a hoot about their own needs and are happy to be disoriented."

"Beware of Virginia Woolf," you may say. "Only people who are already experts should ever dream of taking her for a model." Perhaps. But probably not. At any rate some of the best writing by beginners comes when they just plunge in with full attention to what they are seeing and saying so that they ignore considerations of audience and point of view. And some of their worst writing— both jumbled and flat—comes from worrying too much about audience all the time. Blindingly full attention to your meaning is what often gets the audience with you. And yet of course it is also true that the most frequent *weakness* in the writing of beginners— especially in expository or nonfiction writing—is too little attention to the needs of the reader. It's so easy to take too much for granted and assume that readers will understand you as they usually do in face-to-face speaking situations.

The conclusions then are not obvious about how to think about audience and deal with its needs. Perhaps indeed the theme of this section is paradox.

• Writing is usually a communication with others. And yet the essential transaction seems to be with oneself, a speaking to one's best self.

• Sometimes you can't figure out what you want to say and how to say it till you get into the presence of your audience (or think intensely about it). Yet sometimes it's only by getting *away* from your audience that you can figure out your meaning and how to convey it clearly: your real audience can distract or inhibit you.

• You can't get an audience to listen and hear you till you have something to say and can say it well. Yet I think the process by which people actually learn to speak and write well is often the other way around: first they get an audience that listens and hears them (parents first, then supportive teachers, then a circle of friends or fellow writers, and finally a larger audience). Having an audience helps them find more to say and find better ways to say it.

By taking account of the complexity involved in matters of audience instead of trying to oversimplify things, I think we can work our way through to some clear conclusions. In each of the following chapters I explore one aspect of audience and I conclude each with concrete practical advice.

• In Chapter 17, "Other People" I expore how other people are sometimes a "safe" audience which makes it easier for your to communicate well and sometimes a "dangerous" audience which makes it harder.

• In Chapter 18, "Audience as Focusing Force," I explore the tendency of audiences to suck your words into their point of view. This tendency sometimes is helpful and sometimes must be fought.

• In Chapter 19, "Three Tricky Audience Situations," I explore the special difficulties of persuasive writing, compulsory writing, and uninvited writing, and then suggest ways to deal with these difficulties.

• Chapter 20 could have been called "The Trickiest Audience of All," but I called it "Writing for Teachers."

• • •

Just as it often feels as though schools and colleges would work much more smoothly if it weren't for students, so it often feels as though writing would go better without audiences to worry about.

Yet it may well be (especially if you have already worked hard on your writing) that the one thing your writing needs most is readers. And if you want to give the best gift possible to a writer—and you can—give an audience.

Other People

17

The question is this. Do other people help you or hinder you in your writing? The answer, not surprisingly, is mixed: sometimes they help and sometimes they hinder. But it's worth working out the answer in some detail because it turns out you can do something about it when an audience hinders your writing.

Four Images

1. A mother with her toddler chats with a friend in the parking lot outside Safeway. The child wanders back and forth as far as he can without letting go his grasp of his mother's middle finger, sometimes babbling to himself and sometimes even to his mother and her friend. But he knows they aren't listening, he doesn't expect an answer. He also takes a kind of pleasure in half listening to their talk even though he doesn't understand lots of what they say. Sometimes he comes closer and stares up at the friend's face. In short, the child and the friend could be said to be paying half attention to each other. Then the friend squats down and pays full attention to the child: "How are you? Did you get a cookie in the store?" and the child slides around and hides his face behind his mother's leg. This is not a scary or unknown person. The child has often played with him and will do so again. But his first reaction to full attention is to hide.

2. It is a grey late November Northwest day. I am giving a lecture to a large class—a hundred or so students. I have worked in seminar with some of them. Most of them I know only slightly. I

can't seem to create any coherent speech even though I have clear notes and I got quite excited last night preparing them. I mumble, stammer, bumble. It's not that I don't make any sense at all. I do. I'm saying what's in my notes—after a fashion. But it's halting and cramped and not very clear. It's as though my notes and ideas have left-handed threads and the language in my mouth has right-handed threads. I mumble more than usual, especially at the ends of sentences. A couple of hands go up in the back, they can't hear me, will I please speak louder. I do so, but after a moment or two I lose volume again and a couple of hands go up with the same message. When it happens a third time I'm annoyed. I come from behind the podium to the front of the stage and stand on the very edge—as close to them as I can get. Holding my notes in my hands I start talking again. I feel more exposed without the podium but in a way I don't care because I'm sort of mad. It's as though I'm pushing against them with my chest or my whole trunk. "Damn it, if that's the way you're going to be, then I'll bulldoze right through you with my words." And, suddenly, I can talk coherently. It's not just that they can hear me now because I'm closer and keep my voice up. In addition, the threads of my ideas and speech finally seem to mesh with each other. And I can push those words out and make contact with listeners, make a dent. I can tell I'm being heard. Which helps me find more words. I'm a bit *more* nervous now, nakeder, but I'm able to turn that into some kind of forcefulness or even aggression that had been lacking before.

3. I remember a time in my 20's when I was particularly troubled, scared, having difficulty hanging on. I'd never felt that way before. At moments when I was most frightened of coming apart I would call up one of my friends and ask if I could visit. When I arrived I didn't pour out all my troubles or bad feelings. That's not what I wanted. I wanted to feel regular—like the old me: whole and rational and in one piece. And that's precisely what the presence of a friend automatically permitted me to feel. We would do the regular things and talk in the regular way. Things would snap into perspective. Without even noticing it, I felt reserves of strength and solidity. I no longer felt watery-frightened.

4. But during this same period, being with a particularly close friend or family member occasionally had the opposite effect on me. Instead of helping me be my old regular self—hold on better—the presence of that person somehow drew the threaten-

ing feelings closer to the surface. That made me feel scared of coming apart. I didn't want to utter any of those words that were beginning to appear in my head. I would get the urge to go away and often did: "Well, I guess I have to go now. See you."

The Effects of Other People on Our Words

How, then, do other people affect the way we put out words? I mean to suggest by the four preceding images—all images of getting attention from other people—that the answer is complicated. But also that we can arrive at an answer if we work our way through the complexity.

Sometimes what strikes me first is that other people make it *harder* for us to put out words. The larger the audience, the more nervous we are apt to be. Imagine, for example, that you are talking to someone and having no particular difficulty finding words or saying what you mean. But then your listener, for some reason you can't fathom, bends forward and looks at you more closely and listens more intensely. That's liable to make you examine your words more carefully. Then someone else comes into the room and starts listening, too. Then others, some of whom you don't know. In this progression of increased attention, most people get increasingly nervous. The more we have people listening to us—unless we have complete assurance of their support—the more we are liable to wonder how they will see us and whether they might find us wrong, foolish, unlikable. The child hides behind his mother's leg when given a burst of full attention. It is a natural response.

But this very example of the child reminds us that of course it can work the other way. After you give the child some time to feel safer with the increased attention, he will begin to pour forth a stream of words. More attention will call up a limitless fund of things he wants to tell you: "Do you know what? . . . Do you know what? . . . Do you know what? . . ."

And the other story about getting more and more attention as you talk can be retold to show how increased attention helps you put out words. Perhaps, for example, you start to tell about your vacation and the other person listens with merely polite attention. Your account is a bit perfunctory. But, then, as you start to tell about how your child got hurt, the other person, a parent too, leans forward and gets involved in the story and this leads you to tell more about how you felt, perhaps even to feel again some of the upset feelings from the accident. When listeners really want to hear what we have to say, they seem to suck more words out of us. When listeners are bored or distracted, it is hard to talk clearly and well.

And even though larger audiences may seem inherently scary, they sometimes serve to give more support and make talking easier. Most of us have had the experience of three or four friends listening intently to us in such a way that we end up finding more words and being more eloquent than usual. People such as speakers, actors, or teachers who address groups know the peculiar power that can come when an audience is really with you. It gives a kind of excitement-plus-support that is exhilarating and leads you to find unexpected words and power. Thus most good, experienced performers are not calm and unruffled before performances. They let themselves feel excitement and even anxiety because they know what to do with these emotions. They don't blot out awareness of the audience; indeed, they probably have more awareness of the audience than a terrified beginner. They come to meet the audience and get the audience to come to meet them, and out of this transaction they build a performance they could not otherwise achieve. By the same token, if you are physically tired or else bored with a topic, an audience can get you *up* so you can concentrate again and invest yourself in it.

In fact, though the attention of other people can make us more anxious, we wouldn't speak at all without that attention. We need other people not just to teach us language but also to listen to us and reply. The wild child brought up only by animals in the woods does not speak at all. Any "back to basics" movement in the teaching of writing needs to start by ensuring each child the most basic thing of all: a real audience for his written words—an audience that really listens and takes the interchange seriously.

We can better understand, then, the effects of other people on our writing if we distinguish between a *dangerous audience* and a *safe audience*. Whether an audience is one or the other is partly an objective matter: are your readers a bunch of hostile critics just itching for you to make a mistake, or are they a crowd of friends or fans who look forward to enjoying what you have to say and won't hold anything against you even if you have difficulties?

But safety and danger are partly subjective matters, too. Some people are terrified no matter how friendly the audience is, while others are not intimidated even by sharks. Either way, however, you can almost always tell whether an audience is functioning as a safe one or a dangerous one for you at a given moment. You can tell whether the audience is helping or hindering you in your efforts to put out words. (Occasionally it takes you a little while to wake up to the effects of an audience: "Hey, I've been struggling to write this memo for three hours now and hardly gotten anywhere. I thought it would be easy. Oh, yes, that's why I'm stuck. I have to send a copy to————and he's been bothering me for the last six months.")

Most of us have had a teacher or reader who made us want to write—and unfortunately, also, the opposite kind. The safe reader gave us a kind of attention that somehow made us feel respected, taken seriously, and supported, and, as a result, we usually ended up having more and better things to say than we had expected. Because I call him safe I don't mean to say such a reader is always gentle and soft. Some safe readers are tough and demanding but they listen hard, they respect us, they want to hear what we have to say, and in this way they bring out our best skills in writing. The unsafe reader makes us feel that we don't count or that our words are irrelevant and makes it harder than usual for us not only to think of things to write, but also to put down on paper what we already have in mind.

Audiences, then, are the source of the attention we need if we are to be social animals at all, but they are also the source of danger. By paying attention to us, they can help us to find more to say, but that very same attention holds out the possibility that they'll find our words wrong, dumb, boring, or laughable. (The special power of the one-to-one relationship—the *tête-à-tête*—is that it is probably the easiest way to maximize attention and minimize danger. Two listeners have more attention and support to give, but one person's wholehearted attention is easier to get and to hold.)

Sometimes fear of an audience is great enough that we would happily sacrifice attention altogether just to get rid of danger. And that is exactly what it is possible to do in writing if not in the rest of life. Freewriting gives us relief from the danger of readers and attention. When people first do freewriting they usually experience an immediate release from pressure. It doesn't matter what words come out. In the absence of danger they find new words, thoughts, feelings, and tones of voice they didn't know they had. Most of all, they discover that the process of writing doesn't have to be an ordeal.

• • •

The basic idea, then, is a simple one: when an audience is safe you put out words more easily, when it is dangerous you find it harder. But this simple idea fits the complexities of actual writing experiences better if I add two slight complications.

First, a dangerous audience can inhibit not only the quantity of your words but also their quality. That is, if you are trying to talk to a dangerous audience, instead of finding yourself mixed up or tongue-tied or unable to think of anything to say, you may find yourself chattering away nervously, unable to stop but also unable to say anything important. If, for example, I have to speak to a person or group that I find difficult, I might adopt a voice that hides my real voice and speak with, say, a tinny jolliness or an inauthentic pompousness. If, by contrast, I am with someone I trust, I may say less than usual but talk from my depths—sometimes even revealing more than I wish I had revealed. And so it can occasionally happen that we *feel* an audience is safe that invites us to keep on chattering happily in a gear that is habitual and protective. And we occasionally feel scared or threatened by an audience that invites words from the center. Thus, in the third and fourth images at the start of this chapter, I felt safer in the presence of fairly close friends who snapped me back into my habitual, protected self and helped me to forget about the scary inner feelings, and I felt threatened by the attention of really close friends who seemed to suck difficult words and feelings to the surface.

Second, we must distinguish between real audience and audience in the head. That is, no matter who the *actual* people are for whom we intend these particular words, we are usually influenced by people we carry around inside our heads. We have a habitual way of relating to readers-in-general, and we have some particular memories of past audiences in our heads which can get triggered by present circumstances. (For example, some people always "talk down" no matter whom they are talking to; and some people, whenever they deal with an authority figure, revert to the tone they used toward the junior high school assistant principal who kept them after school.)

When you are writing it is usually easier to notice the effect of the actual audience than the effect of the audience in your head. For example, you will quickly notice if a particular report is unusually hard to write because the reader is someone who is currently giving you a hard time. Or perhaps a story or poem is a joy to write because you are writing it as a gift for someone you love.

Because the audience in your head is invisible yet always there, you may be unaware of it and of its subtle effects. If you are scared of speaking or writing to most audiences even when they are supportive and caring, you are probably responding to a dangerous audience you carry around in your head all the time (a dangerous audience that probably derives from some real audiences in the past that were dangerous for you). If there's one particular person who flusters you as audience even though you know he is supportive and caring—perhaps a particular administrator or teacher—you can assume that he must somehow trigger your reaction to a dangerous audience in your head.

The audience in our head usually affects us more when we write than when we speak. When we speak, the real audience is right there dominating our attention and drowning out other audiences. When we write, however, all audiences are in the head, even the real audience. In the dark of the brain a real audience is easily trampled by an insistent past audience.

To summarize, we can get a pretty good understanding of how other people affect our writing if we look at these three factors: Is the audience safe or dangerous? Does it affect quantity or quality of words? How much are we being affected by the real audience for these words and how much by some other audience we carry around in our heads?

Dangerous Audience. When you experience an audience as dangerous: (a) it may make you so anxious that you actually cannot write at all; or (b) it may make you merely nervous, preoccupied with mistakes you might make, unable to find words naturally and smoothly, and, hence, unable to concentrate easily on your thoughts; or (c) it may not inhibit words or thoughts at all, but lead you into a protective voice which makes you feel safer, but drains your language of power.

Safe Audience. When, on the other hand, you experience an audience as safe or eliciting, it opens you out: you think of more ideas, feelings and images; words come more easily. But on a few occasions a safe audience can threaten you by making you feel things inside you that you'd rather not feel.

Safe Nonaudience. When you write for no one—for the wastebasket, for yourself, for the process itself—words often come pouring out of you. You find new voices, sounds, and tones.

Dangerous Nonaudience. But when you feel you have no real audience at all—no one who cares what is on your mind either immediately or in the future—you are likely to drift into dull muteness: to feel as though you have nothing to say, nothing on your mind, no thoughts to share.

Advice

• If you are having a harder than usual time writing something, it may well be because the audience is dangerous for you or is triggering a reaction to a dangerous audience inside you. You can usually improve the situation by changing your audience for your early writing. Either ignore audience altogether and do lots of fast freewriting (as in the loop writing process). Or do your early writing to some very different audience that brings out your best. For example you can address a draft of your technical report to your loved one—even permitting yourself some of the fun and games your make-believe audience inspires. You will have more to say— even on the technical subject—you will get more life into the words, and you will produce your draft more quickly than if you had written to the difficult audience. You'll then find it's not hard quickly to revise your peculiar first draft to fit the real audience— getting rid of what's inappropriate, but saving the good ideas and the juice.

Since the pervasive effects of audience in the head are trickier (and more common in writing than speaking) the remaining pieces of advice are aimed at dealing with them.

• Are you almost always frozen or blocked in your writing? Fear of audience-in-general is probably holding you back. Even if your actual audience is sweet and loving, you are probably still reacting in your head to past audiences who were not. Do lots of freewriting for no audience at all and experiment with a safe audience.

• Do you get the writing done but find yourself always self-conscious, always worrying about whether your writing is good enough, always worrying about mistakes? This, too, probably comes from fear of a dangerous audience you carry around in your head. Lots of freewriting without an audience will help here too—and experiments with a safe audience.

• Do you find yourself trapped in a voice that you sense is somehow fake or unreal? Perhaps stiff or too cute or fake-sincere? Freewriting will help—that is, the use of a safe *non*-audience. The safety encourages real voice. But it may not help as much as sharing your writing with an actual audience that is safe. For if you already write fluently, but your voice lacks power, you may freewrite hour after hour—weeks and even months—in a gear that is, in the last analysis, defensive. Your safe, habitual, and fluent writing is the path of least resistance. And, in a sense, your writing works just fine: it's easy for you to get your ideas onto paper. But your lack of voice makes it hard for you to get your ideas into readers.

A safe audience can help you break out of your protective but ineffective voice. Most people lack a safe audience or at least do not make use of one they could use; for example, a friend who simply likes to read and appreciates what you have written. But if you look you can find one or more people who want to provide this support for each other. (See Chapter 3, "Sharing.") Even though the absence of audience removes objective danger, only the presence of live supportive readers gives you positive safety.

• Is your writing almost always too complicated and elaborate? Too many twists and turns in your train of thought, too many qualifications in your argument? This is a frequent problem for writers in the academic world—both students and teachers. It is probably because you are locked into some kind of combat with an audience. As you write you are wrestling with those critical readers—those piercing intelligences who are just waiting to pounce on a careless mistake or a naïve assumption. You are busy shooting down every possible objection before it gets a chance to take flight. As a result you can never permit yourself simply, calmly, and in a friendly way just to say what is on your mind.

Force yourself to write as if you were writing to friends. Explain what's on your mind as though your readers—is it possible?—are just itching for a chance to understand and enjoy what you are saying. Have the courage to stop wrestling with the foe and give gifts to allies. You will surprise yourself at how much easier it is to write—and how your argument often turns out more persuasive even to adversaries. And it needn't be make-believe: write early drafts to friends who really will read you this way.

• Are you wallowing in safety? Just words and words, pages and pages, but none with focus or electricity? You may need *more* real audience for your writing. Perhaps even a dangerous audience. It will help you get more *up* for your writing, help you make the writing process a bit more of a performance in the good sense of the word. Those feelings of excitement, anxiety, perhaps embarrassment: you can't have the attention of readers without them.

And if you must write to a difficult audience (in fact or in your head), don't forget about the possibilities of *confronting* them: forcing yourself to look them in the eye, to make contact with the enemy, instead of taking refuge in safety. You probably have to get mad, but you may thereby find an unexpected source of strong and coherent words. This is what happened to me on that occasion when I was having such a hard time lecturing.

• • •

A child cannot learn to speak unless he has other people around him (and it seems to work best if they are loving people). Yet after he has learned language he can speak and write in total solitude. There is a profound principle of learning here: we can learn to do alone what at first we could do only with others. From this principle I derive my final item of advice and sum up this whole matter of safe and dangerous audiences. We should use an audience—and especially the support of a loving audience—as much as we can and as long as it helps. But the goal should be to move toward the condition where we don't necessarily need it in order to speak or write well. Probably for a long time we will be hurt by people's disapproval, ridicule, or indifference to what we write. It is sensible to avoid dangerous audiences if they hold us back in the work of learning to improve our writing. But we need to learn to write what is true and what needs saying even if the whole world is scandalized. We need to learn eventually to find in *ourselves* the support which—perhaps for a long time—we must seek openly from others.

18

Audience as Focusing Force

I prepared my lecture carefully. I arrive and start in and suddenly realize I have the wrong approach. I thought carefully last night about what I was going to say and worked out a focus, but now that I see my audience I realize it's the wrong focus for them. The presence of the real audience gives a new orientation to the material in my head.

A teacher is asked a hard question in class. He thinks for a few seconds and then turns around and walks to the corner of the room, hunches over a bit, closes his eyes and scrunches up his face and thinks silently for a full minute—perhaps two. Then he comes back and cheerfully tells what he has figured out.

In this chapter I propose a slightly different image of the audience in order to emphasize a different way in which other people affect our writing. Instead of concentrating on other people as safe or dangerous—as creatures who either cheer us on or suck lemons as we try to play our trumpet—I will concentrate on audience as a kind of magnetic field which exerts an organizing or focusing force on our words. As we come closer to an audience, its field of force tends to pull our words into shapes or configurations determined by its needs or point of view. As we move farther away from the audience, our words are freer to rearrange themselves, to bubble and change and develop, to follow their own whims, without any interference from the needs or orientation of the audience. Even if an audience is safe, it still exerts this focusing force.

• • •

Different kinds of writing imply different distances from an audience. At the near extreme is audience-oriented writing. You are writing to a particular audience and the whole point is to produce a particular effect. Unless the words have that effect you won't get the money or the contract or the job, you won't get into college, no one will come to your meeting. This is get-the-results writing.

At the opposite extreme is get-it-right writing. You don't care whether readers like it or not. The only result that counts is the satisfaction that comes from getting it the way you want it. Perhaps you are writing a poem or story and you have decided you are the only judge that counts. Or you are writing to work out the truth about something important to you and you are trying to serve truth, not readers. Maybe the writing will in fact go to readers; maybe they'll like it; that's nice. But if they don't, that's their problem, not yours. (Of course you may *use* readers for get-it-right writing. Their reactions can help you enormously—but for getting it the way you want it, not the way they want it.)

Audience-oriented or get-the-results writing is pragmatic and it's usually only a part of some larger transaction with people. Memos, letters, reports, applications are typical examples. The writing is a means to an end. After you have gotten the results you can often happily throw the writing away. Get-it-right writing, on the other hand, is usually writing as an end in itself. No matter what nice things result from having written it, you won't want to throw it away. Because pragmatic writing is part of a larger action-in-the-world, it often involves deadlines and so you are often writing in a hurry. Get-it-right writing, on the other hand, since audience doesn't count so much, is often more leisurely.

If you know at the start that this is a very audience-oriented piece of writing, such as a memo or letter of application, try concentrating on your audience and your purpose right at the very beginning. As you start to write, or even before, picture your audience in your mind's eye and figure out just how you really want to affect them—and then write very much *to* them. If this strategy works, it will save you much time and effort. The presence of the audience in your head will give your words more focus, will help you thread your way among the many things you could say to what you should say. You won't have to waste your time with inappropriate approaches you will later discard. You won't have to try to write everything you know. The problem of how to reach this particular audience may even help you figure out something important you've never understood before.

When you establish in your head a good relationship with your audience, suddenly your writing runs strong and clear. You can find words and they are right. You are looking readers in the eye and directing your words right to the center of their brains, not staring at their shoes or mumbling distractedly as you stare at the ceiling. When this works, everything clicks.

If, for example, you are writing to the school board to protest a certain policy, you will avoid some of the commonest writing problems if you keep those readers vividly in mind. You will be less likely to get off onto a tangent about how smart and delightful your child is, or how terrible you feel because of the way you've been treated, or what bastards they are, or what the seven most important educational principles are that you learned in a certain book. Seeing school-board members in your mind's eye will help you keep to the main point, figure out your best argument, and help you realize when you are likely to bore them or anger them or make them condescend to you. Sometimes you can't even figure out what you need to tell people till you see them. That's what happened to me when I worked out my lecture alone and then tried to give it to the real audience and realized I had the wrong approach. I hadn't done enough to make contact with my audience in my mind the night before.

But of course sometimes this strategy doesn't work. Keeping the audience in mind may hinder your efforts to write. Instead of your language running strong and clear, it gums up or goes dead. Perhaps you know those members of the board and three of them intimidate you. Keeping them in mind makes you nervous, stilted, unable to think straight—just as you would be if you were standing there in front of them in the official meeting room with polished tables. Or perhaps you don't know them at all and that blocks you: sitting down and writing to these official names-without-faces suddenly brings back all the anxiety you have ever felt about mysterious authority figures.

But it's not just danger that can make an audience hinder you. What concerns me in this chapter is the focusing or organizing force they exert. Perhaps, for example, you are writing a background research paper for a friend who is running for political office. You are not at all intimidated by her but she sees everything polarized in terms of republican-or-democrat. Every time you try to write *to* her, you get sucked into that polarization—either giving in to it or spending all your energy just fighting it. Keeping your audience in mind prevents you from working out the truth and saying clearly what *you* need to say. You finally realize that you need to ignore her, get yourself out of her magnetic field, do lots of fast first-draft writing to help your thinking cook on its own. When you finally work out clearly what you have to say, then it is safer—indeed necessary—to move back into the field of force of your audience so it will help you shape your material to her concern with party division.

Or perhaps you are writing a story for a particular magazine, say a children's magazine. Again, you are not threatened, you have written others before. But every time you start to write to your child audience your writing slips into certain overworked or corny patterns. You feel the pull of certain audience expectations—or of certain habits or expectations you have with this audience—sucking you down paths you sense you should avoid. You finally realize you have to move out of the field of force exerted by that audience, write the story as *it* wants to be written—let it grow in the directions it is trying to grow in—no matter how inappropriate the result may be for this audience. When it is finished you can make some changes in it—perhaps even very radical changes. You can change inappropriate language, leave out whole episodes, entire characters, change the plot. That may sound like radical mutilation, but it can lead to a deeper "rightness"—verbal and textural integrity—than you can usually achieve by constantly fiddling and adjusting and adapting your story to your audience *as* you are trying to write it for the first time.

And what you usually discover is how little you need to change to fit it to the audience, even though you were ignoring its needs as you wrote. (See Auden's poem "The Truest Poetry Is the Most Feigning" for a wry treatment of this point.)

• • •

Again a paradox. When you attend to audience from the start and let your words grow out of your relationship with it, sometimes you come up with just what you need, and in addition your words have a wonderful integrity or fit with that audience. Everything is on target. But sometimes the effect is opposite. The audience hinders your writing by exerting too much pull on you (or intimidating you). And occasionally when you think too much about audience, your words are too heavy with audience-awareness. Your words feel too much like those of a salesman who is trying too hard to make "audience contact."

But it's not really so much a paradox as an occasion for exercising choice and staying in charge of your own writing process. That is, you can choose *when*, during the writing process, to enter into the magnetic field exerted by the audience. If your piece is audience-oriented and if you are in a hurry, you should try entering into it at the beginning and staying in it. You may be lucky and not have to do much revising. But if that keeps you from being as inventive or creative as you need to be, then stay out of reach of your audience and approach it later, during revising.

Your choice about when to enter the audience's field of force will also be affected by your own temperament. Some people are better at writing from within the circle of audience, others are better at writing from outside it. Some people, that is, are good at audience contact, at talking while they look their listener in the eye. They find it natural to speak and write in ways that fit particular audiences. They are good at feeling the listener's point of view and speaking appropriately. They are good at letting the audience sit inside their head and have a say in how the words come out.

I lack this skill. I'm bad at thinking while I look my audience in the eye. Sometimes I can't even figure out what I'm feeling till I look away or close my eyes. (I am not, however, the teacher I pictured at the start of the chapter who goes into the corner to think. I'd probably teach better if I dared do that.) It makes me mad that some people should be so good at something I find so difficult.

It has taken me a long time to realize that even though such audience-oriented writers have an enormous advantage over the rest of us, they are simply displaying *one kind* of verbal intelligence, and the rest of us have another kind. It sounds odd to say but we are good at *excluding* the audience from a place in our heads as we write. We non-audience-oriented temperaments are better at speculating, musing, flying high, or diving deep—letting words and thoughts lead us where they are going despite the pull of audience. When I can stop being jealous of the audience-oriented writers long enough, I can also be smug: those folks got good grades in writing all the time and can get their memos and reports written more quickly and fluently than I can, but they aren't so good at freeing themselves from audience needs and expectations and coming up with what is original and authentic.

Thus audience-oriented verbal intelligence is in a way more practical and realistic than the other kind, but it is important to realize that neither is superior. They simply represent two different linguistic muscles, two strategies for putting out words, two distances at which to sit from an audience as you think. If you have the first sort of temperament, you are probably better at getting things written quickly, clearly, and in a way that fits the audience. You have an enormous advantage for the kinds of writing required in school or business and the practical world. If you have the other kind of verbal intelligence you are probably better at getting-it-right writing: letting your own piece develop according to its own internal potentialities (and in your own interests) and not caring so much about the needs of audience.

Because the audience-oriented temperament is so much better for the quick execution of pragmatic writing tasks, many people with the other temperament simply conclude that they are congenitally bad at writing. And they are often branded as dumb or illiterate in school. They give up and don't learn to *use* their brand of verbal intelligence (which mostly means learning to revise enough to *harness* what they have figured out for an audience). They end up never writing. But still, some of the great works of speculative thought and imaginative literature are deficient in audience contact: the writers didn't give a damn about audience. They produced works that are difficult and obscure—organized in the worst possible way for someone who doesn't already understand the ideas or partly share the vision. Conversely, some writing that is especially clear to readers is, as it were, *too* clear. It succeeds too well in merely following the beaten paths that already exist in readers' heads. It lacks originality or authenticity in thought or language.

Once you realize that we are dealing here not with a matter of good and bad writers but rather with two complementary habits of relating to an audience, you can learn to exploit your strong side instead of just feeling bad about your weak side. The important thing is that you get to decide how far away from your audience to sit while you do most of your writing. If you are more like me you will find it better to ignore audience as you write and then during revising make a special effort to orient what you have to say to the audience. If you have the opposite temperament and skill, you may find you get things written best if you keep mental contact with your audience as you write. Indeed you may even want to use some of your revising efforts for trying to *break out* of audience orientation, instead of trying further to adapt your material to their needs.

But in addition to using your strength for tasks at hand you can gradually work on your weak side. I need to practice writing while I look my audience in the eye. It will help me be quicker in writing pragmatic audience-oriented pieces. Audience-oriented writers need to practice detaching themselves from the pull of audience and encouraging a drift of focus, an evolution of organization, bubbling.

The only thing to watch out for—especially if you have a non-audience-oriented temperament—is the feeling that says, "I'm a *writer* not a mere communicator. I don't care about pragmatic success with readers, I care about *quality*." The truth is that even if you are writing something that won't ever go to an audience, you often can't get it the way *you* want it till you spend some of your writing or revising time thinking of this piece in terms of a particular audience and situation. For I overstated earlier the advantages of staying away from an audience if you want creativity and cooking. Audience is not the only influence on your words that may prevent them from evolving into new and different orientations. This same kind of inhibition can come from yourself. Often you cannot get an essay out of its rut or find that central image your poem needs till you go up and sit almost in the lap of a powerful imaginary audience and do some more writing. Sometimes you need to overpower your *own* field of force in order to shake things up and produce new growth, and you can best do this by visualizing your audience so they are vividly present to you as you write, and directing your words to them. (It can help to work with a sharing group.)

Summary and Advice

• Beware the common advice that has blocked so many people over the years: that you must *always* keep your audience in mind from the beginning of any piece of writing. This is wrong just like that other common advice: that you must *always* figure out your meaning before you start. The point is that figuring out your meaning and keeping your audience in mind are both *focusing procedures*. If you already have plenty of good material in your mind, or too little time, you may want to focus your mind before you start writing. But if you want your best insights you are probably better off avoiding focus for a while. Here's a correct statement of the rule: *sometime* before you finish writing you must figure out your meaning and think about your audience; and then revise strenuously in terms of this focus.

• Get a feeling for what it's like to write from inside and from outside the magnetic field of your audience and for the temperament that usually goes with each. Figure out which is your strength and which your weakness so you can exploit the one and gradually strengthen the other.

• Learn, therefore, to take conscious control over when you bring to bear the focusing effect of audience on any writing project. For example:

If your piece is unfocused and wandering, continually bubbling, and you want to *end* the fission or chain reaction, bring your bubbling pot closer to the audience: that is, bring your audience more strongly to mind and write more *to* it.

If it won't bubble enough, if you can't find enough to say, if you feel stuck saying dull or obvious things, try ignoring your audience and following the words where they want to go or else writing to very different audiences (as in the loop writing process).

Don't forget, however, the possibility that your writing may be stuck because it's too much in *your own* magnetic field. Try concentrating *more* on audience and perhaps address yourself to other audiences. That could start the bubbling that you need.

19

Three Tricky Relationships
to an Audience

Perhaps you've noticed there are two distinct *kinds* of difficulty in writing. One kind feels as though you are straining to lift a heavy load of bricks onto your shoulder or struggling to carry something unwieldy across a stream with only slippery stepping-stones to walk on or trying to thread a needle whose eye is almost invisibly small. Taxing or scary or frustrating but also clean, hard work.

But there's that other kind. You are trying to fight your way out from under a huge deflated silk balloon—layers and layers of light gauzy material which you can bat away, but they always just flop back again and no movement or exertion gets you any closer to the open air. Or you are lost in a dense fog with no sense of direction—or rather just enough sense of direction to realize you are going in circles. Or you are sinking slowly into swamp mud and every effort to crawl or swim gets you in deeper. Or you are trying to saw through a thick plank and the harder you try the tighter your saw gets stuck in the cut. It's this kind of difficulty that makes you feel helpless and angry and finally stops you.

I have learned that when my writing feels difficult in the first way, it is a sign that I am indeed wrestling with the difficulties of writing itself: figuring out my thoughts, working out the logic, finding language for what is just barely emergent in my mind, or finding the right approach for a difficult audience. But when I experience that second kind of difficulty, it means I haven't yet managed to get my teeth into the writing task itself. There is some mix-up. Often it is because I am going about my work in a self-defeating way—perhaps trying to edit my words carefully while

I'm only just writing out my earliest tentative thinking. But often it's a mix-up about audience. This feeling of working at cross-purposes to my goal—this continual racing of the motor while the gears refuse to engage—often comes from being afraid of the audience or confused about who it is or mistaken about what I am trying to do to it.

I talked in the last chapters about the difficulties caused by dangerous audiences—inside and outside your head—and how to work on these difficulties. And about how to use or avoid the focusing or organizing force exerted by audience. But in addition there are certain relationships to an audience that are inherently tricky because at the same time that they make it hard to write well, they also keep you from realizing what is causing the difficulty. Here are the three that I have noticed as I watch myself and others struggle: writing when you are trying to persuade readers, when readers are compelling you to write, and when your writing is entirely uninvited.

A. Persuasion

"Can't you see how wrong you are?"

There is nothing tricky about those occasions when you can use what could be called *straightforward persuasion*. You can jump right in and give good information, argue with reason, and season the whole thing with good manners. For example:

• Your committee (company, neighborhood, school) has to choose between three plans. You have been appointed to study and recommend one. Your report will go to people in an audience who have not made up their minds yet. Indeed they are really asking you to help them make up their minds. They don't want tricky tactics or emotional appeals, they just want the best information and arguments. Your task is similar if you want to persuade them but are not yourself on the committee.

• You are writing a letter to the newspaper to persuade readers to vote for a certain candidate or measure, but you are trying primarily to sway the undecided readers, not the enemy. (Some studies show that more people read letters to the editor than any other section of most newspapers.)

• You are writing a job application or applying for a scholarship.

You know the reader has to give someone the job and is trying to find the best candidate and so will read your qualifications with interest. It's important in such pieces of writing not to be bashful, roundabout, defensive, or coy in telling your strengths. In a kind of neutral, disinterested, and succint way, you must frankly brag. (If the reader has a huge stack of applications to read; he will probably make a lot of 60-second eliminations in order to cut the number of applications down to manageable proportions before reading them carefully. Therefore, you must summarize your best material in your opening paragraph or cover sheet—don't include there anything questionable that could be used to eliminate you.)

What makes these occasions for straightforward persuasion is that your readers are open to your words either because they have not made up their minds or because you have some kind of authority on the topic or because they need to make a decision and are therefore open to new information or arguments. Your job is clear: to present the best information and arguments in the most reasonable and human way.

Before going on to tricky persuasion I suggest this one simple but deep strategy for straight-forward persuasion. Try hard to find good arguments for your position, but then try even harder to find arguments to refute yours. Then figure out how to answer those refutations. That is, the doubting game or the dialectical process turns out to be a powerful way to generate good persuasion. The strength of your argument depends more than anything else on your willingness to be a smart lawyer for the opposition. The only problem with this strategy is that you sometimes discover your original position is wrong. But that's useful information, too.

• • •

What concerns me in this chapter, however, are tricky audience situations and, in this case, I am thinking about the many times when you are trying to persuade someone in a straightforward way but actually you are wasting your time.

• You are writing a letter to the newspaper to persuade readers about a certain bill or candidate or situation, but this time your position is a minority one. Perhaps you want to argue for an end to all armaments—or income taxes or welfare. Or perhaps you are writing about a polarized issue like some of the recent bottle-deposit bills and you are not satisfied just to write to the relatively few middle of the roaders with open minds. If your bill is to win, you've got to *change* some of your opponents' minds.

• You are trying to dissuade someone from dropping out of college or hitchhiking around the country or divorcing you. Or trying to persuade your reader to accept your decision to do one of those things.

• You are writing an article or pamphlet or leaflet to persuade workers at a nuclear plant that nuclear power is a bad thing; or to persuade intellectual undergraduate women that abortions should be illegal.

What makes these attempts at persuasion tricky is that you are addressing your words to people who have a *stake* in what you are trying to refute. You are caught in a bind. The more you try to persuade them, the more their stake in their view causes them to dig in their heels. For you to win they must define themselves as losers. You can't argue without making your readers into your enemy, and enemies can't be persuaded—only beaten. But you can't beat people with words—or at least not if they don't consent to be beaten—because of that brute fact about reading: words only work if they are inflated with human breath and it's the reader who has to do the blowing.* Why should the enemy pedal if you are steering where he doesn't want to go? "Let me come up to your tower and show you that you are stupid for opposing deposits on bottles," but your reader has to haul you up in the hand-crank elevator. Why should he? "Let me show you movies to prove you are a murderer for condoning abortion," only the reader has to crank the generator to make electricity for your movies.

So what can you do? Trick them? Say "I have a wonderful trip I want to show you, you'll love it," and get them to pedal while you steer and then suddenly take a turn down the path they hate? Keep your destination secret? "Have you ever thought about the fact that all men are mortal? Odd, isn't it? And perhaps you haven't ever looked at it this way before, but, you know, Socrates is a man. HA HA! GOTCHA! Socrates is mortal!"

If your readers have a stake in what you are arguing against, you cannot take straightforward persuasion as your goal. You must resist your impulse to change their beliefs. You have to set your

---

*See the beginning of Chapter 27, "Breathing Experience into Words," for a fuller account of this aspect of the reading process.

sights much lower. The best you can hope for—and it is hoping for a great deal—is to get your readers just to *understand* your point of view even while not changing theirs in the slightest. If you can get readers actually to entertain or experience your position for just a moment, you have done a wonder, and your best chance of getting them to do so is not by asking them to believe or adopt your point of view at all.

In short, stop trying to persuade the enemy and settle for planting a seed. If you think about the way people actually do change their beliefs—which is rarely—it is usually a gradual process and depends on a seed lying dormant for awhile. Something has to get them to a position where they might say, "Imagine that. He actually believes that stuff and he's not crazy. I never could imagine a sane person thinking the country could get along without an army. I always thought it was some kind of emotional hang-up—something odd said by people who have a thing about uniforms or guns or something. I didn't realize that there really were coherent arguments. Of course they are all wrong, deeply misguided arguments, but now I can see why they appeal. It's interesting to know what it's like for a person to actually see things that way."

If you can get a reader to take your point of view for just that one conditional moment—to inflate your words with his breath—then future events will ocassionally remind him of the experience. Contrary views are inherently intriguing. And if your position has any merit, your reader will begin—very gradually of course—to notice things that actually support it. For the first time, for example, he will begin to notice specific incidents when armies or armaments increase danger to his country rather than decrease it. A seed is the best you can hope for.

So how do you plant a seed? You do it by getting the person actually to see through your eyes. There are many ways of doing this, but I think they all depend on one essential inner act by you: seeing through his eyes. And it's not enough just to do it as an act of shrewd strategic analysis: "Let's see what actually passes for thinking in the minds of those rednecks." For them to experience your point of view even for a moment, they must let down their guard. You can't get them to do so unless you let down yours, too: actually experience *their* point of view from the inside, not just analyze it. Though persuading can employ the doubting game, planting a seed calls for the believing game.

What does this mean in practice? If you relinquish your effort to make readers change their beliefs and settle instead for trying to get them merely to entertain yours for a moment, and if you start with an honest attempt to see things through their eyes, you will find a whole range of specific ways to write your letter, article, or report—depending on your skills and temperament. You can trust your instincts once you understand your goal: somehow to persuade readers to work *with* you rather than against you in the job of breathing life into your words. For example, if I were writing a short article or leaflet to readers with a stake in what I'm trying to refute, I wouldn't say, "Here's why *you* should believe nuclear power is bad." How can I get them to invest themselves in words which translate "Here's why you've been bad or stupid"? I would take an approach which said, "Here are the reasons and experiences that have made *me* believe nuclear power is bad. Please try to understand them for a moment."

There are various ways to try to get readers to work with you. Your best choice depends upon your temperament and the circumstances. But if you are trying to change deeply held beliefs, autobiography, biography, and fiction turn out to be among the most effective types of writing. After all, changing a belief requires having an experience, not just getting some information or logic, and it's not surprising if imaginative and experiential writing sometimes prove more effective than argument.*

It's no accident that people so often use arguments on the enemy that only work on allies. Most of the things that *feel* like good arguments only work on people who agree with you or are at least open-minded. It's all too easy, as you are writing along in your room, to start hammering home arguments which prove resoundingly that the enemy is *wrong!* These feel like good arguments because of a mix-up about audience. We have let ourselves forget the real audience and started to write a speech about the evils of nuclear power that is just perfect for people who already believe nuclear power is evil. It would bring down the house at an anti-nuclear rally. But unfortunately it will make no headway at all on someone who doesn't already agree.

*There is an interesting literary problem opening up: how can you write what could be called propaganda, but is honest and doesn't make the reader feel manipulated—in short, good literature? It no longer seems as self-evident to me as it once did that good literature and propaganda must be contradictory categories.

So what works on opponents? There is no simple answer. You need feedback to find out. Very few people get accurate honest feedback from an opponent as to how their arguments are working—feedback that says, "Here's what it felt like being your opponent and reading your words. Here are the places where you actually made a dent on me, made me listen, made me actually consider your words seriously, and here are the places where you just made me dig in my heels all the harder against you." The only occasion when we are likely to get sincere, thoughtful feedback from an opponent is when we write something for a teacher who happens to disagree. But teachers usually don't give you "here's-what-it-felt-like-to-be-your-enemy" feedback. Usually they try to extricate themselves from combat and give you more theoretical feedback about the quality of your reasoning and use of evidence—feedback on exactly those techniques of persuasion that won't work here because they only work on disinterested readers with no stake in the issue.

What you need then more than anything else is feedback from opponents. It's not easy to get, but it's possible. Find a friend who is an opponent on your issue and coax him to give you honest feedback. To get a helpful opponent you may have to ask a favor of a friend's friend. And if you can't make a friendly contact with someone who disagrees strongly with you on the issue you are writing about (shouldn't that be cause for concern?) you can practice on other topics where you and your friends actually disagree.

Summary and Advice

• For any persuasive writing, take time to think carefully about your relationship to your audience and what you are asking of it. Can you really hope to make those people *agree with you* or should you settle more realistically for just trying to get them to *listen to you?* Have they made up their minds yet? If so, how much stake do they have in the view you want them to abandon? Do they have any special reasons to listen to you? Is there some authority you have which they will accept? Is there some new decision or action they must perform that might make them willing to consider new information and arguments? In short, are you trying to persuade or to plant a seed?

• How much do *you* have at stake in the issue? If you are arguing for one of your important beliefs, you will probably have an almost irrepressible urge to make readers agree with you—an urge that may destroy any chance of success.

• Get accurate feedback—especially from the enemy. Find readers who will tell you honestly what their position was before they read your piece, what happened to them as they read, and what changes, if any, were finally produced in their views. It's often discouraging feedback because words seldom produce change of position, but if you are trying to persuade, perhaps the most useful thing you can learn is how seldom it is possible.

• There's one more strategy that does wonders whether you are trying to get someone to agree or just to listen: be right. If you're right you can sometimes succeed even though your writing has serious weaknesses. Reality helps you make your case. (It's not foolproof, of course, since sometimes being right makes you so insufferable that people are willing to stay wrong just for a chance to disagree with you.) It sometimes helps you to define your task of persuasion as part of a larger task of finding out the truth.

• Whether you are trying to persuade an open-minded reader to agree with what you are saying or trying to get an enemy reader simply to experience what you are saying, there is one essential thing you must learn: how to enter wholeheartedly into the skin of your readers and see or argue as they would.

B. Compulsory Writing

"I think I'll just hold this gun to your head till you finish."

Much of the writing we do is compulsory. It starts in school and continues on the job. Writing an important thank-you letter as an adult can feel just as compulsory as when your mother sat you down and forced you to write a letter to Grandma for a birthday present you didn't like. If you write at all as an adult, it's probably because you have learned to be stoical and resigned about compulsory writing. "I wish I didn't have to write this thing this weekend. I'd like to be outdoors. Still, that's the way it goes, this is always happening to me." But as you work on the writing, you have a particularly hard time. You take all weekend and don't finish till late Sunday night. And all the while you tend to say to yourself, "I'm so *bad* at writing. I wish I had *skill* in writing."

It is hard for you to see that you ruined your whole weekend needlessly. You could have gotten the job done in half the time, in fact you could have gotten it done at work before the weekend even started. You think your weekend was ruined by your difficulty in writing but what ruined it was your difficulty in dealing with compulsory tasks. You were so busy complaining about how bad a writer you are, you didn't remember the times when writing went much better. You may not have had *many* good writing experiences—but then you may not often write without a gun at your head.

Or perhaps you aren't so stoical. You get so furious that you fume and stamp your feet and bang your fist all weekend. And yet you may not realize how much that impedes your writing. That blankness in your mind when you try to think of ideas, that difficulty you have in just letting yourself write down sentences at all, that pressure in your head when you try to organize what little you have to say: you tend to experience these as lack of intelligence or lack of skill in writing when really they come from your inability to deal with compulsory tasks.

I don't mean to imply that this analysis makes things easy. Solving the problem of your reactions to compulsory tasks is probably harder than learning how to write well. But at least there is hope of progress if you can tell which one is holding you back—if you can feel the difference between trying to saw through a thick plank with an imperfect saw and trying to saw through that plank when your own efforts are binding the saw. If you persist in thinking your only problem is a writing problem, you block progress on both fronts.

If you have to do a piece of compulsory writing it helps to face the central issue squarely: are you going to consent or refuse? To consent is not necessarily to cave in. You don't have to like the task or the taskmaster, you don't have to grovel, but if you want the writing to go well, you have to invest yourself in the job wholeheartedly. If this is hard for you, it is probably because it *feels* like groveling or caving in. You may not be able to put your full strength into the job—to consent—unless you feel you *could* refuse. And this is a matter of power. It feels as though "they" have all the power. It is true that they have authority and therefore they probably have sanctions. They can fire you or flunk you. Or hate you. But the final power is yours. You are in charge of whether you consent or refuse. What feels compulsory is not compulsory. Even people "compelled" with actual guns have sometimes insisted on their power to refuse. I am thinking of the successful nonviolent resistance by Norwegian school teachers during World War II.*

Does it help, you may well ask, to portray your harrassed supervisor or your bumbling teacher as a sadistic TV Nazi pointing a gun at your head, when what you are trying to learn is to consent (when appropriate) to, compulsory tasks? But if you can feel, underneath your alleged difficulty in writing, your older feelings left over from the many times "they" twisted your ear or somehow compelled you to give in, you will have much better luck in stepping beyond those past feelings and getting this present job done quickly. (Those TV movies with Nazis wouldn't have such appeal if they weren't really about the universal childhood experience of being helpless before superior power.)

But you may not believe in your power to refuse unless you really use it—openly and with full responsibility (instead of fooling yourself into being sick or having an emergency or "trying as hard as you can" and somehow not succeeding). Perhaps refusing is not the ideal solution, but it's better than that familiar worst-of-both-worlds compromise: you don't get the fun of saying No or the satisfaction of doing the job quickly with investment. All you get is a ruined weekend and a sense of powerlessness.

Summary and Advice

• Figure out whether the writing is compulsory. Is someone else *really* demanding it? If not, it's not compulsory. If so, it's not still compulsory: you can refuse.

• Are you sure the price of refusal is too high? Will you really be fired? Are you sure you want that job? Will they hate you for life? Are you sure you care? It is easy to assume the world will come to an end if you say no.

• If you finally decide to consent—if you decide it's not worth whatever the price is just to get out of doing this piece of writing— then *consent!* Do the job wholeheartedly without fighting it. You

*See "Nonviolent Resistance and the Nazis: The Case of Norway" in *The Quiet Battle*, Mulford Sibley, editor (Boston, 1963). Also the second section of Part III of *Conflict Regulation* by Paul Wehr (Boulder, Colorado, 1979).

don't have to love the job just to invest your best efforts in getting it done quickly and getting some pleasure from it.

• If angry resentful feelings hold back your writing, stop, recognize those feelings for what they are, scream them out or write them down for ten minutes, and then get back to your job. Insist on your power to write efficiently.

• But don't forget the advantages of compulsory writing. Sometimes you learn things because people "make" you. Children seem to be aided in learning self-control by internalizing the control exercised over them by others. When you sign up for a writing course, what you may well be doing is simply paying someone to make you write every week. You realize you cannot yet get yourself to write every week, but you are willing to pretend the teacher can make you do it. There's nothing wrong with putting that make-believe gun into his hand if it will help you learn faster. But, remember, it's make-believe.

C. Uninvited Writing

"Pssst! Hey Mack. You wanna buy my novel?"

What a relief, then, to write, not because someone is demanding it, but because you want to. Even if it is a tricky letter, even if it is a piece of persuasion that will be hard for you because you lack the professional training you need, or even if it is a novel you know will keep you in the woods for years; still it gives enormous satisfaction to feel that *you* have made the decision to expend your time and effort this way. You know you will have frustrations, but you want to write this thing and so you find it easy, comparatively speaking, to put up with them. The main psychological fact about uninvited writing is that you naturally invest yourself in the writing task.

Or do you? For if uninvited writing always goes so well, how come everyone doesn't do it? Part of the problem may be that most people are introduced to writing in school where it is compulsory. "Who would ever write if they didn't have to?" But, in addition, uninvited writing has a built in difficulty of its own. It takes arrogance, *chutzpah*, *hubris*. "Uninvited writing" is just another way of saying "no audience." You have to walk up to strangers on the street and tap them on the shoulder and say, "Excuse me, would you please stop what you are doing and listen to me for a few hours? I have something I'd awfully much like to tell you." You know the reply you will get.

Why engage in uninvited writing if you have to put up with that? And so most of us don't. Which would be fine except for one small fact: we *do* have things we want to tell people even if they haven't invited us to do so. But there is another fact. We are all capable of stopping people on the street and fixing them with our eye and getting them to listen and making them glad they did. We are, that is, capable of writing things which make readers want to read and glad they did. We just have to *do* it, and probably put up with a lot of rude refusals for a while. But we can insist on being heard.

Insisting on being heard. I remember the particular moment when I saw clearly how essential that feeling is for all writing, but especially for uninvited writing. I hadn't yet, I think, published anything—and no one had asked me to write this piece I was struggling with, but I was trying to say some things in it that were very important to me about teaching and learning. I had already managed to get down on paper in one form or another a lot of what I wanted to say. (In other words, my fear of tapping strangers on the shoulder wasn't so overwhelming that I pretended I had *nothing* to tell the world.) But the writing was going terribly. The whole thing was a mess, and no matter how hard I tried I couldn't seem to get things clear. And then finally things went better. I stopped to reflect on what had happened, and I wrote a note to myself (shortened and cleaned up here):

6/11/71. I'm correcting a near-to-final draft. Finally I'm making it much clearer and better. I'm rearranging sentences and points so they finally work. I had it all screwed up—my interpretation all mixed in with my information in an ineffective way—and my information unclear. Then a series of rearrangings make things fall into place with a click.

So what made this possible? It can't be any new knowledge about logic or sentence-arrangement or rhetoric. I was already trying as hard as I could to use all of that knowledge I had. I was struggling over and over again—writing and rewriting, arranging and rearranging—and it was still mud. It didn't work. All my best knowledge didn't help.

But finally I can see what did help. It was the feeling "Damn it,

I've got to be done with this thing and I know goddamn well most people won't really hear it and thus they won't accept what I'm saying—it will all roll off their backs—even if they read it, which they probably won't do because it is such a mess—but if they do they will think it's just a fuzzy harebrained scheme of Elbow's. I'm tired of that. I'm not willing for that to go on any longer." In short, what made the difference was a *decision* I made about my stance toward the reader. That inner act of readjusting my transaction with readers *caused* the words and ideas finally to come out in a different and better order.

It was like my readjustment to my lecture audience where I got mad at students saying they couldn't hear me and I moved from behind the podium to the front of the stage. A combination of frustration and anger made me finally insist on being heard and this made me suddenly able to do something with language I hadn't been able to do till then.

The essential question for writing, then, is this: how long are you willing to be unheard?

• • •

It would be impossible to avoid all compulsory writing and sad to run away from all uninvited writing. But having a gun at your head and having to go out and tap strangers on the shoulder are not your only ways of relating to the audience. Readers can *invite* you: call you up and say "Will you come out to dinner with me? I'll pay if you will tell me about your trip." Or "It's on me if you'll tell me your thinking about the project you did last year. I have one now just like it." What better way to make you enjoy communicating and to bring out the best thinking. An audience that invites your words but doesn't demand them acts like suction.

Ten years ago I had only a vague sense that I might write a book. It was sort of a fantasy that I didn't take seriously. But when a publisher's representative knocked on my office door to show me books for the courses I was teaching and asked at the end whether I had any writing projects in mind, and when he said that his editor might like to talk to me about my idea, and when after some negotiation the editor was willing to offer me a contract, suddenly I started to take the idea seriously. Because someone was willing to publish me, I started to have more ideas and, more important, I started to write them down like mad.

If you want to see the vivid effect of an inviting audience, think back to occasions when people wanted your thinking or advice about something you'd never thought about. At first you had nothing to say but the fact of their asking probably put things in your head.

Writing's greatest reward, for most of us anyway, is the sense of reaching an audience. Ideally the audience should love what we write, but in the last analysis, it's enough if we can feel them reading. The fisherman falls in love with fishing because of that unpredictable wiggle, that moving pressure on his hand, even if the fish gets away. At least you felt them tasting your bait, at least you made contact with someone on the other end of the line. This experience makes you want to pick up the pencil and try again. *This* time you'll hook them. But it is you who are hooked.

The usual way to get yourself invited to write something is by doing well under the two previous conditions: writing something uninvited or compulsory that's good enough to make them call you up and ask for something else. (A good reason to learn to deal with uninvited and compulsory writing.) It seems unfair. The rich get richer. The best racers get the best starting place. You don't get the delightful encouragement of an invitation till you have already had a success.

But you don't have to wait for the invitation. Without having to muster all the courage it takes to stop strangers on the street, you can nevertheless find friends or make acquaintances who will *want* to read your words. In effect, publish: find an inviting audience, even if you have to copy out your writing in two copies or ditto it or pay for xeroxing; even if you have to start with friends who read it partly because they like you and care about what's in your head. Invite them over to read or listen, even if part of the incentive is a nice dinner or good refreshments. And you can find others who will want to read your writing because they want someone to read theirs. However you get it, a willing audience does wonders. It causes you suddenly to write more easily, to think of more, and get more satisfaction from writing.

Many people sabotage their hunger for an audience by sending off their stuff to highly competitive magazines or publishers who will almost certainly reject it. Too many rejection slips can make you so discouraged that you give up. Don't attempt large unknown audiences till you have made full use of a small known group of willing readers: connected with it, gotten pleasure from it, gotten feedback and learned to improve your writing on the basis of it. Only then are you in a good position to decide what to send off into the unknown and how much rejection you are willing to put up with.

People also sometimes sabotage their instinct for finding a real audience by feeling they need to get permission from an expert before giving their writing to the real audience. If experts are the real audience for your writing, by all means give it first to them. But if, for example, you are writing up some important insights you've learned about how to be a better parent, you are likely to have the impulse to give your writing first to a psychologist or therapist or university professor in the field. You feel you need an expert to check out your words before they go to the real audience of parents. It's a natural impulse. I've certainly acted on it numerous times. We seek someone with authority to tell us if we are right or to give us suggestions. Most of all, we seek a midwife to usher our child into the world.

But watch out. Checking your writing with an expert often turns out to kill the whole project. First you have to find the right expert. That can be a problem. Then the expert may not respond. Experts are busy. Even if they respond positively, their response may actually stymie you: "This is very interesting. I think you should read Smith and Jones, oh yes, and Abernathy"—just three people to him but a year's reading or more for you—and if you do start reading, you are liable to conclude, "Oh dear, I have nothing really new to say," or "Oh dear, there's so much I don't know about this field, I can't write till I master it." And your project withers and dies even though you have already written a piece with lots of good insights—a piece that might in fact be more useful to real parents than Jones or Smith or Abernathy if only you get a little feedback from parents and do a little revising.

And, of course, the expert may discourage you in a much more straightforward manner. Once I sent off an essay about learning that I was excited about to an expert I thought would see the genius in it and give me some good suggestions. I got a reply which said nothing more than "I wish people wouldn't use the word 'concept' unless they really understood what it meant." But how could it be otherwise? The authority is tired of reading about child rearing. He's read too much already. He is not a willing audience for your words. At best he reads out of duty or as a favor. He will simply notice the differences between what you have written and what he believes to be the best writing in the world about the topic.

I paint a bleak picture. Of course it *can* work out well. The expert might give you just the encouragement you need—along with a few suggestions which are just right for helping you revise and give your writing to the audience. But I'm deeply suspicious of the impulse that makes so many people feel they must get clearance from readers for whom the words are *not* intended before giving them to readers for whom they *are* intended. Experts are experts because they know a lot, but the one thing they cannot tell you is what it is like to read your words as a non-expert—for example as a curious or baffled parent who has read very little about child-rearing.

"But what if my thinking is false," you may say, "and my advice about child care is wrong?" But if you were riding on a bus or talking to friends you would tell them what you have to say about child-rearing if they were curious to know. So why do you need permission now from an expert to do the same thing? To engage in the essential audience transaction in writing—directing words to people who are interested in what you are saying? Speaking would be a curious business if we felt we had to get permission from listeners who are not likely to want to hear our words before directing them to people who are likely to want to hear them.

You are in a good position to go to experts *after* you have road-tested your words—after you have seen what works in practice and what doesn't and then done some revising. At this point you will have a crucially different relationship to experts than if you sent it to them first. You won't be saying, "Please sir, may I have permission to let this thing out into the world?" (as though your writing were a new drug that might turn out to be thalidomide). You will feel more like a colleague saying, "Look, I've got something interesting here, something that works. I wonder if you would be willing to tell me where you agree and where you don't."

Summary and Advice

• Don't wait for an invitation. You probably have writing you want to give the world, even if the world hasn't gotten around to asking you yet. Write it and give it to the world uninvited. Insist on being heard.

• But work things out so you also get invitations. Find a willing audience of real people who are interested in what you are writing about and who will actually enjoy reading it. If you start by sending your writing to magazines or publishers who are unlikely to take it or by trying to get experts to stop what they are doing and take you in hand, you are likely to snuff out your instinct to be heard.

• After you are getting the help and nourishment that comes from having a real audience, then make use of experts and try to expand your audience by wider publication.

• Look for writing situations that are half-way between invited and uninvited. For example, write letters to newspapers and magazines. They didn't specifically ask *you* for *your* thinking—they won't necessarily publish your letter—but they did ask for people like you and thinking like yours.

Writing for Teachers

Teachers are one of the trickiest audiences of all, yet they also illustrate the paradox that audiences sometimes help you and sometimes get in your way. I think I got much of my original deep feeling for writing because of one of my high school teachers, Bob Fisher. He took me seriously. He wanted me to write. He asked me to write about things that were important to me. He opened me out. He assumed that I could write creatively in ways I never would have thought of, and I could. He assumed I would be deeply interested in topics I had never thought of, and I was. With him as a teacher I came to like writing, to look forward to it, to feel I was doing something important when I put words on paper.

Many people have had this kind of teacher. A good teacher can be a perfect audience. Not just because he likes us or praises our writing—though that may be necessary for adolescents who lack confidence in themselves (is there any other kind?). Sometimes that good teacher's caring takes the form of fierce rigor, but he manages it so we still want to write for him.*

---

*I think of C. S. Lewis's description of one of his beloved teachers:

I soon came to know the differing values of his three openings. The loud cry of "Stop!" was flung in to arrest a torrent of verbiage which could not be endured a moment longer; not because it fretted his patience (he never thought of that) but because it was wasting time, darkening counsel. The hastier and quieter "Excuse!" (*i.e.*, "Excuse me") ushered in a correction or distinction merely parenthetical and betokened that, thus set right, your remark might still, without absurdity, be allowed to reach completion. The most encouraging of all was, "I hear you." This meant that your remark was significant and only required refutation; it had risen to the dignity of error. Refutation (when we

With that good teacher, whether tender or tough, we feel we can go for broke, wrestle full out. We can write about truth, about God, about right and wrong, about Being, even about fear. With everyone else, it seems as though when we start to talk passionately about these issues or whatever else is burning a hole inside us, they look at us funny or change the subject or go blank. As adolescents, especially, we are subject to the tyranny of the crowd. Worse than being caught with your pants down is being caught caring deeply, being corny, vulnerable, pure. But a special teacher gives us permission to care about honor or Dostoyevsky or relativity or irony—not just gags or girls or cars. A good teacher seems to understand us. A good teacher can hear beyond our insecure hesitation or faddish slang to the authentic voice inside and reach in and help us use it.

I can't understand, now that I'm a teacher and know more about the conditions of work, especially for primary and secondary school English teachers, how those special people were able to be as good as they were. How could they listen so deeply and care for our pimply individual selves when we were one among the one hundred to one hundred fifty students they worked with each day? But they did it and do it. Most people have had a special teacher who was this good.

But other teachers later brought me to an anxiety and fear of writing that seemed just as deep as my original caring for it.* Writing became harder and harder till I finally reached the point in graduate school where I couldn't write anything no matter how hard I tried. (Being unable to write, I had to stop being a student and take a job as teacher.)

But I am not interested here in what is special about good or bad teachers. I am interested in the problematic relationship that

---

got so far) always followed the same lines. Had I read this? Had I studied that? Had I any statistical evidence? Had I any evidence in my own experience? And so to the almost inevitable conclusion, "Do you not see then that you had no right, etc."

Some boys would not have liked it; to me it was red beef and strong beer. [From *Surprised by Joy*, New York, 1956, p. 136.]

*I don't mean to put all responsibility on my teachers for my feelings and actions. Long before I ever met Bob Fisher I already had a deep love of words and ideas. And long before I ever met those other teachers I already had a deeply insecure tendency to depend almost entirely upon the judgment of others for my opinion of myself. But in those two tendencies, did I really differ from most other adolescents?

exists between the student writer and the teacher reader—even when the teacher is a decent person doing a conscientious job.

Look then at the teacher engaged in being an audience. He sits at his desk reading student papers. He is half done with a batch, the unread stack neatly piled to his left, each paper tightly folded longwise; the graded pile a bit helter-skelter to his right, a bit unfolded, a bit like discarded clam shells at the end of dinner. It is late and he stops for another cup of tea, annoyed he didn't start earlier in the evening. Sitting down and setting the cup among the ring-stains on his desk, two dictionaries nearby, he picks up the next paper, reads through it, writes a few comments here or there in the margin and then writes a grade and a general comment at the end.

The papers are all on the same topic, which he chose. Sometimes he gives free-choice assignments, but when he does, more of the papers seem fruitless journeys down dead-end streets and he suspects that the students learn less about writing—though a few students take off and write something splendid. But he knows he's got to give free choice now and again just for relief to the troops. (If he is a junior or senior high school teacher he probably has one hundred to one hundred fifty students; if he is a college writing teacher he has something like fifty to one hundred students. Many, however, teach writing for only part of their load.)

If he is a conscientious teacher he assigns a paper every week to every student he has. But he also kicks himself as he sits there sipping tea because he is acutely aware of how it is *he* who brought this job down on his own head. Every time he stands up in class and assigns a paper he sees in his mind's eye that stack of papers on the corner of his desk waiting for him to grade. If he isn't so conscientious he assigns writing every few weeks but he feels guilty because he knows this doesn't give his students enough practice and it means that his comment and advice on a student's paper this time will probably have no useful effect at all on what the student writes next time. Or maybe he is one of those teachers who have simply given up on writing and don't believe that anything they do by way of assignments or comments makes any difference at all. There are probably as many teachers in each category: conscientious, middling, cynical.

• • •

Really that brief image says it all. But I want to spell out more fully what kind of audience the teacher becomes by virtue of his role.

When you write for a teacher you are usually swimming against the stream of natural communication. The natural direction of communication is to explain what you understand to someone who doesn't understand it. But in writing an essay for a teacher your task is usually to explain what you are still engaged in trying to understand to someone who understands it better. You seldom feel you are writing because *you* want to tell someone something. More often you feel you are being examined as to whether you can say well what *he* wants you to say. Even if you are invited to write on a subject you know better than the teacher, the teacher's knowledge turns out to be the standard for judging whether you really do know it. There's nothing wrong with this as a testing or evaluative relationship, but it's peculiar as a communicative or audience relationship.

The result of this wrong-way communication is a pervasive weakness that infects much student writing—and persists in many people's writing for the rest of their lives: a faint aura of questioning which lurks behind assertions. The student writes "This is so and that is so," but somehow between the lines he is also saying "Is this so? Will you buy that?"

If it is a story or poem rather than an essay you are writing, it's hard to feel that you are doing what is most natural for someone writing a story or poem, that is, trying to give pleasure or enlightenment. It feels as though your task is to *satisfy* or *get criticism* from a teacher who must read from 25 to 50 such pieces in one sitting. Instead of *giving* the reader something with a definite gesture, hand thrust firmly outward, students usually hand in their stories or poems with a bent and hoping arm. Instead of a statement—"Here is something for you, here is a piece of me, take it"—the student often implies a question: "Is this ok? I hope I didn't do something wrong?" It's striking how often students actually say those words to you as they give you their papers: "I hope this is what you wanted?"

This subliminal question mark lurks in the writing even of some very skilled students, but skilled students more often risk a different infection. A student who wants to be a good student cannot be content just to satisfy teachers. He must write a paper that will wake the teacher up and give him some relief when he is groggy from reading those twenty-five to fifty papers on the same topic. Such students must do something different, striking, unique with the same old ingredients. The school setting has rewarded generation after generation of good students *not* for saying clearly what is important and what they want to convey, but for doing some kind of better cartwheel or handstand. Good students often write not to communicate but to impress. Over and over again I have seen good students knocked off balance when they get out of school and try to write for an audience other than teachers and discover how unsuccessful those shenanigans are which used to win good grades. Real readers are different from teachers.

·   ·   ·

But that's the point. Teachers are not the real audience. You don't write *to* teachers, you write for them. You can feel the difference vividly if you write a regular essay assigned by your teacher and then go on to write something directly *to* him: write him a letter asking him to change your grade or to contribute money to your political campaign. You will find these writing tasks refreshing and satisfying compared to regular assignments—even if harder. It's a relief to put words down on paper for the sake of *results*—not just for the sake of getting a *judgment*. "Getting an A is results," you may say, but see how you feel if you write your teacher for a contribution and get an "A" instead of a check. The grade or comment says "good persuasion," but you know your words failed if there is no check in the envelope.

As teachers we come closest, perhaps, to being the real audience when we ask you to write an essay that persuades us on some issue. But in most cases there is something make-believe about the task, given our conditions as readers. If as a teacher I am reading a stack of papers all on the same topic I know I can't use completely realistic standards and only give a good grade to papers that actually change my mind. That would be unfair—too hard—especially since I probably know more about the topic than the student. I give good grades and comments to papers which seem "well argued" but which don't happen to budge my position at all. (And some papers, of course, are trying to persuade me of what I already believe. How can I measure success there?) For the most part then my feedback is not really a measure of how much change the words actually produce in me but rather my guess about how much change they *would* produce on some (ill-defined) hypothetical reader. Occasionally a teacher says, "Your job is actually to change *my* mind," and really carries through—but more often he says, "Your job is to write as though you were trying to change my mind." Those two words, "as though," turn up often in writing assignments.

If you do write directly *to* your teacher on a persuasive or informative essay he will usually feel something wrong. If, for example, you write "I disagree with what you said last week in class about why Hamlet delays so long. Here are some difficulties with your readings of the play . . .," the teacher will probably say, "You are not supposed to write a letter to me, you are supposed to write an essay." In short there is usually something fictional about the transaction between reader and writer in most school writing—a mismatch between what's actually going on between student and teacher and what's allegedly going on between "the writer" and "the reader": the student pretends to explain something to someone who doesn't understand it; the teacher pretends to be this general reader reading for enlightenment.

(In most exams, by the way, the relationship between writer and reader more nearly matches the actual human transaction between parties. The teacher/reader is saying fairly openly, "Tell me what you know about the Incas—about why Hamlet delays—so I can see if you know what I think you should know," and the student/writer is saying just as openly, "I'm going to explain to you what you already know in order to show you that I know it, too.")

Pretending, in itself, is not a problem. All children are good at it and if a college student is not he needs to learn again. "Write to the Longshoremen's Union about manual versus desk labor," "Write to the third-grade student council about how to deal with bullies in the playground," "Write to Robert Redford about how he could best handle this scene from *Hamlet*." I doubt that there would be much problem with engaging in the fiction of writing to those audiences and then handing in your paper to an entirely different sort of reader, namely your teacher. Perhaps there's not enough pretending in school and college essay writing.

Or at least the problem lies in the slipperiness of a situation in which students must simultaneously pretend and not pretend when they write to the audience for most school and college writing: the general reader. This "general reader" is a tricky character. Teachers seldom define explicitly who he is, but common practice in the educational and academic world is based on the assumption that he is a creature blessed by intelligence, a certain amount of education ("general"), and an open mind. Someone much more reasonable and *general* than those longshoremen or third graders or even Robert Redford; someone, in short, much more like——guess who?—the teacher. Except this reader is general, not particular like the teacher, and is not meant to be an authority on the topic or someone in a position of authority over the writer.

In short, the audience situation is confusing because of the tricky combination of make believe and no make believe. The student is writing *for* a teacher and *to* a general reader. But this general reader does not exist. He is a construct. He is not a particular person like the teacher who reads the words. And yet one of the main things about him is that he reads in a peculiar way in which no one else but teachers read: not because he has a special interest or allegiance or commitment to the subject—not from a position of engagement in the world—but because he seeks a kind of disinterested enlightenment or disembodied pleasure. As a construct, the general reader is 100 percent audience, 0 percent person.

Yet none of these tricky audience issues tend to be raised for discussion. It's no wonder then that students have only a vague, fuzzy or shifting sense of their audience and write in a vague, fuzzy, or shifting voice. (That's also the kind of voice, by the way, that people often use when they write in a bureaucracy. The problem is the same: you are writing to an audience that seems unreal and ambiguous. School essays could serve as good practice for writing in bureaucracies if teachers spent more time talking about problems and solutions of dealing with "unreal audiences.")

Because of this slippery way in which the "general reader" is both like and unlike the teacher, teachers, too, are often unclear in their own minds as they comment on a student's paper whether they are saying "This doesn't work for *me*—given my knowledge of the topic, my position on it, and my situation in the world," or "I don't believe this would work for a general reader who doesn't already understand what you are trying to explain or doesn't already have his mind made up on the topic." It's hard to argue well or learn about argument when you are unsure who your audience is and what its position on the topic is likely to be.

• • •

And yet it could be an advantage rather than a problem that teachers are not the real audience. After all, what could be better than having a coach who is different from your real audience but whose job is to help you achieve success with that real audience? The problem is that most student writing never does go to a real audience. Writing for your teacher is like playing your violin for your violin teacher. It is a great help in learning to play the violin, but it is not the goal. The goal—and thus the reason for getting the teacher's help in the first place—is to play for yourself or for your friends or for a wider audience. Of course your violin teacher is, in a sense, a *good* audience. He listens carefully and thinks all the time about you and your technique. Your real audience doesn't do that because they are busy doing the one thing your teacher cannot do: they are listening for the enjoyment of hearing you and the music.

Writing for a teacher is like hitting the ball to your tennis coach. It should teach you a lot and it may be great fun, but it is practice or exercise rather than the real thing. It's a means toward improving your performance at the real thing—whether the real thing is success in professional competition or fun in casual tennis. But whereas very few play their musical instrument only for their teacher or hit balls only to their coach—or at least if they do they usually realize they are leaving out the goal for which the teaching is designed—most students in school and college write only for teachers and take the situation for granted.

It's true that teachers prepare their students for other teachers, but that is as though tennis coaches kept their students moving up the line, volleying with one coach after another, till everyone got so used to the process that finally no one ever bothered to ask the obvious question any more: "Hey coach, when do I actually get to play a game of tennis?"

When you write for a teacher he won't stay put on the other side of the net or across the dueling ground. When you make a really good shot and wipe the sweat from your forehead and look over to see him sprawled full length on the court unable to reach the ball—or when you put down your smoking pistol and walk over to see him flat on his back with a neat red hole in his brow—all of a sudden you hear someone say, "Nice shot," and there he is over on the sidelines, unharmed, unsweaty, unruffled. Next time you don't try so hard.

But students couldn't take it if teachers played for real instead of just practice. Students only dare get in the ring with their teachers because they know the teachers will pull their punches. Yet every now and then the student does get knocked flat on his back—even though the teacher didn't mean to. Students discover they get knocked down more when they try their hardest. All but the born fighters learn to hold back—to do less than their best—when they spar with teachers.

This odd state of affairs has serious consequences for learning to write. For one thing, it's hard to put your heart in your work when you never get the excitement and satisfaction of a real performance for a real audience. You may get *anxious* when you write for a teacher, but you don't get the satisfaction that goes with a real performance, the satisfaction of knowing that you can actually affect your reader with your words. Occasionally, of course, teachers *are* informed, persuaded, or entertained by student writing, but the conditions under which teachers read are the worst possible conditions for being informed, persuaded, or informed.

• • •

It is no bed of roses for teachers either. As a teacher I am a slave reader. I must read every piece to the end. I must say to every student those magic words that every writer wants to hear, "I couldn't put your writing down," only I say it through clenched teeth. Even if some of the writing is enjoyable, I can't really read for enjoyment when I'm not free to stop reading. I can't just sit back and be enlightened or entertained, I must look for weaknesses and mistakes.

Inevitably I improve. But students don't improve with me. That is, each year I get better at finding weaknesses and mistakes, but each new batch of students is just as unskilled as last year's batch. Thus, every year I find more mistakes and weaknesses per page. (How could I not believe that students get worse every year?) And yet I cannot do what every real reader can do, namely, say "The hell with you" or "That makes me furious, I want to punch you in the nose," and throw it in the trash. I must continue on to the end and then try to write a comment that will be helpful. And I mustn't express to the student the annoyance that I feel—sometimes the fury. Is it surprising if these feelings sometimes get through anyway? Or that I am not always as helpful and supportive as I ought to be toward these creatures who cause me weekly agony?

In short, teachers cannot easily give their real reactions to the writing of their students because their real reactions are usually too critical and sometimes unprintable. They know that their students cannot handle or benefit from a mirror which shows so devastatingly every single weakness and mistake. Therefore since teachers cannot communicate to students what it actually feels like to read these words, and since there is no one else who reads these words, the student *never* gets the experience of learning what actually happens to a real reader reading his words. He gets only the conclusions of a skilled cataloguer of weaknesses and (one hopes) strengths.

As a result of all this the student's job is both too easy and too hard. It's too easy in that the student knows his reader will keep on reading to the end, no matter how bad the writing is. The student never has that frustrating but healthy sense of a reader on the other end of the line making minute by minute decisions about whether to keep on reading or put it down. Nothing really gives you the strength you need for revising but that feeling of trying to keep a reader from hanging up on you; that feeling of having only one thin thread connecting you and the reader. Once that filament breaks, you have lost your reader for ever back to the wide sea—or at least until you manage to hook him again with some combination of luck and good bait.

And yet writing for teachers is at the same time too hard. For there is a price you must pay for having a reader who never stops reading your words. He never really takes your words seriously as messages intended genuinely for him.

In what is the trickiest audience situation of all, then, it is easiest not to think very much about audience—about whom your words are intended for and what you want those words to do. And not thinking about audience is one of the best ways to block improvement in writing. Most people keep up their school habit of not thinking enough about audience even after they leave school or college—unless they write a lot for real audiences and also get lots of accurate feedback from these audiences about what their words actually did. Most people just struggle along as they are writing something in an effort to make it "good writing in general" instead of thinking carefully or precisely about "good for what effect on what reader."

Teachers, too, drift into ignoring audience. It is unhelpful, for example, to give assignments—as most teachers do and indeed I realize I tend to do—without specifying clearly who the audience is and what effect the words are supposed to have on it. Are these words meant to inform? To inform whom? How much prior knowledge do they have? To persuade? To persuade whom? How much do we know about their position on the issue? To give pleasure? To whom? What kind of reading do they like?

It is also unhelpful to evaluate and give feedback to student writing about its quality *in general*. It is meaningless, really, to try to tell a student how successful his writing is in general without saying how successful it is at achieving a certain effect on a certain audience. The only way you can give feedback on "quality in general" is by doing what teachers have historically tended to do: concentrate mostly on the conventions of writing as a medium, namely, spelling, grammar, footnotes, and paragraphing, and ignoring the question of how well it would work on what kinds of readers. It's not that the conventions of writing as a medium are unimportant or easy to learn. Quite the contrary. They are *too* hard and onerous to learn if you try to learn them by themselves—as mere push-ups—without the incentive of actually trying to use them in real communication to real readers.

Advice

Advice for anybody—whether currently writing for teachers or not:
   • Check your writing for habits that may still undermine it even if you haven't written for a teacher in years:

Are you still writing like a nervous student? writing to your examiner? tentative, hesitant, beating around the bush? Is there an air of worry in your words as though you are talking to someone who makes you uncomfortable? Is your writing like the speech of people whose tone of voice always curls up into a mini-question mark at the end of every sentence?

Are you still writing like a timid student? always playing it safe? Is your writing always scrubbed behind the ears? Are you always hedging your bets, always saying "On the one hand ——, but on the other hand ——," always ending with a sweet, positive, noncommital sentiment ("And so we see that this is a difficult problem though some significant progress has been made"), never daring assert any of your real convictions? Does your writing still pursue those gold stars for clean finger-nails that you got (or didn't get) so many years ago?

Are you still, twenty years later, writing like that angry student who is covertly giving the finger to the reader who made you write when you didn't want to? Do your words, though perhaps civil on the surface, really carry a hidden message that says, "Dear reader, if you don't like this, screw you."

Are you still writing like that star student, working harder to impress the teacher—to show off, be fancy, or win points—than simply to get a message across? Does your writing try harder for an *A* than for communication with a human being? Are you turning off every reader except those few who are willing to relate to you as hot stuff?

These vestigial bad habits manifest themselves in infinitely subtle ways. You may be unaware of them. Even your readers may be unaware of them. A reader will complain about your argument or your organization—even your spelling—when really he is annoyed without realizing it by one of these half-buried ways of relating to your original school audience. But you can easily sniff them out if you just ask yourself and your readers "What is the relationship to a reader in these words? How do you feel that voice talking to you?" Even inexperienced readers will be able to detect those old and destructive tones of voice.

The best corrective for these old bad habits (in addition to getting feedback from readers about your tone of voice and stance toward readers—see Section V, "Feedback") is to make sure you engage in two opposite kinds of writing: very practical writing and very impractical writing. By practical writing I mean words designed to make something happen in the world—words you want to *work*, not be *judged nice*, for example, requesting a refund or a contribution, writing a resumé or a letter of recommendation, writing to a publisher with a prospectus or proposal. By impractical writing I mean words which in a sense don't matter at all: words for the wind or for the wastepaper basket, for example, freewriting or exploratory personal writing that is not trying to make anything happen (except perhaps for yourself).

These two writing experiences are opposite yet essential. In the first case everything matters. The words you put down determine whether you get that money or whether the publisher asks to see your MS. Writing as *action in the world* intensifies the relationship between you and the words you put down on paper. With impractical writing, on the other hand, you get the experience of total freedom. Nothing matters. This intensifies in a different way your relationship to the words you write. There are certain trains of thought and feeling, and certain voices, that you never discover except by writing freely when nothing matters—as well as discovering that writing itself can be easy and painless. The opposite activities of practical writing and freewriting help you counteract the harmful effects of writing only for teachers where you get the worst of both extremes: all the anxiety yet none of the satisfaction of practical writing; all the ineffectualness yet none of the freedom of freewriting. That is, when you write for teachers you can be hurt by their verdict but you have no hope of actually making a dent on your reader.

Advice If You Are Currently Writing for Teachers

It can be a great gift to have a writing teacher—to have the services of a coach watching you play, suggesting exercises, and giving you feedback and advice. But you will miss most of this benefit unless you learn to take a certain amount of control of your situation and use your teacher as a service, a helper, an ally—not fight him as an adversary or go limp. Here are some concrete suggestions for getting the most out of teachers.

• Don't just hit balls to your coach, find someone to play tennis with. Give your papers to a friend to read—first for sharing, later for feedback. Get together with a small sharing or feedback group. If you give your writing only to teachers you get into a terrible rut of caring too much about your writing in one way—as an ordeal—and not caring enough about it in another way—as a message that matters to real human beings.

Once you start giving your words to someone in addition to a teacher you will feel an immediate relief: new perspective, new energy. Even if you *hate* the assignment you now have an interesting challenge: taking your *friend* seriously enough to find something worth saying about that topic or to find a way of writing that gives pleasure. Both tasks, while difficult, turn out to be feasible and enormously rewarding.

• Work out alternative assignments with your teacher so that it will be easier and more natural to give your writing to others. If you make it clear to your teacher that you are really serious about your writing and if you accept the fact that he probably has a serious agenda of skills and techniques for his assignments, you can usually work out some alternatives:

Something quite close to the assignment. Simply ask if you can write about the topic exactly as given but in the form of a letter or personal essay to a friend, or a memo or article to some other audience you would enjoy addressing.

Significant variation. If you are supposed to write about some aspect of *Hamlet,* ask if you can write something you could submit to a literary magazine or to the arts section of a newspaper: something about *Hamlet* and some other play, novel, or movie that provides an interesting comparison—and promise to treat prominently that aspect of the play the teacher wanted you to treat. If you are supposed to write a history paper about a period in the relatively recent past, see if you can write it in terms of what it was like then for your ancestors and make it a piece of family history. If you are assigned a piece of persuasion on a topic of no concern to you, perhaps you could choose an entirely different topic where you have a real audience but where the *kind* of persuasion demanded is exactly the same as in the teacher's assignment. You may find the teacher more amenable if you ask him what skills or issues he is trying to emphasize in his assignment and then agree to emphasize them in your alternative assignment. For example, he may want you to document everything you say about *Hamlet* with quotations from the text; or to deal particularly with imagery; or to highlight economic conditions in the period of history you write about. You can do these things in your alternative assignments.

Something completely different. Something you need to write or want to write such as a short story, a memo, a letter of application, a political pamphlet, a letter to the editor. Emphasize the fact that you'll work at least as hard or even harder on it than you would on his assignment—and learn a lot about writing. Make sure, however, that you aren't just trying to do exactly the same kind of writing over and over again (for instance, nothing but science fiction stories about the future) since the teacher will probably feel, legitimately, that you won't be practicing the range of skills he's trying to stress.

• Ask teachers to specify clearly the audience and purpose for any writing assignment they give. It helps most if these audiences are actual people or groups even if the writing is not in fact delivered to them. And there is always a useful real audience available to whom writing can easily be delivered: other members of the class.

• Ask teachers to give some class time to discussing this issue of audience and if possible to bring in some outside readers—other teachers, magazine or newspaper editors, public relations officers of a business—to describe frankly their specific reactions to actual pieces of writing.

• You need to master the traditional genre of writing essays for that tricky general reader. But ask the teacher to explain more clearly who he thinks this general reader is and to sponsor some discussion of the matter. What level of knowledge should you assume a general reader has about the topic? What point of view should you assume this reader has about the issue? There is an easy way to remove this slippery issue from the realm of the hypothetical and that is to ask your teacher to specify for every essay assignment a particular magazine or journal in which it should be published. Then the readership and editorial policy of this publication can be discussed and people can look at some of the pieces that it actually publishes. (Remember of course that it may help you to do all your raw writing to a different, more comfortable audience, or no audience at all, and wait till revising to make your words fit the general reader or the readership of this publication.)

• Ask your teacher to assign pieces of writing where he is, indeed, the direct and real audience: pieces of writing designed to affect him in particular. If he is trying to persuade his own child to do something or trying to decide which brand of whatsis to buy, students could write genuine advice to him. Ask him to think of theoretical or political or practical issues where he cannot make up his mind. Also issues where he already feels strongly one way or the other. Since he is the real audience, he can give accurate feedback on how the writing worked and didn't work on him.

• Ask your teacher to grade and comment on your paper not just as to its quality in general but as to how he thinks it will work on the particular hypothetical audience. This change in feedback will come naturally if you have already persuaded him to specify audience and purpose more clearly—or worked out alternative assignments where you specify your own audience and purpose. And this change, interestingly, will usually lead him to do something else very helpful, namely to tell some of his own particular reactions—speaking as himself rather than as "representative reader." It will become easier for him to say things like "This would probably work on Robert Redford but it bothers me because . . ." or "I found this section particularly interesting but I don't think it will make sense to your third-grade readers."

• Almost all these suggestions involve asking for more and clearer feedback than your teacher usually gives. Find ways to make it easier for him to give it. For example, try attaching a sheet of paper to your writing with some questions on it that will permit him to say more in fewer words. On the next page is an example that can easily be varied.

If he didn't specify audience and purpose, you will have to say what your audience and purpose are on that sheet of paper.

See the next section on feedback for other questions to ask of a reader.

Offer a cassette (and cassette player) with your paper so he can speak his comment without writing. You'll get a much more human comment and learn more about how your writing affected him. (This is probably feasible only if he reads papers in his office. You can't ask him to carry a cassette player home.) Don't ask for conferences on every paper. That takes too much time.

• Ask your teachers to point out at least one thing you did well on each paper. If possible, one thing that's better than last time. (If they have too many students, however, you can't expect them to remember your last paper.) When teachers read huge stacks of papers they often drift into doing nothing but finding weaknesses. The goal of this request is not just to spare your feelings (though if you are too hurt you will learn poorly). Knowledge of what you did well is actually more potent in helping you improve your writing than knowledge of what you did poorly. If your teacher shows you what you did well, or even sort-of-well, you can do it again, more often, and even expand on it, because you already have the feeling

Please put a straight line alongside passages and underneath phrases that you like or that work for *you* as a reader; and a wiggly line alongside passages and underneath phrases that annoy or don't work for you.

Please write a brief comment here about the one matter that most affected your reading.

For the *intended audience*, which section(s) or aspect(s) of this piece do you think will work or be most successful? Why?

What do you think will fail or backfire on the intended audience? Why?

Here are some aspects of my writing that I especially want feedback on:

	strong	adequate	weak
• paragraphing	☐	☐	☐
• convincing argument	☐	☐	☐
• convincing evidence	☐	☐	☐
• liveliness of language or humanness of tone	☐	☐	☐
• punctuation	☐	☐	☐

What is the quickest simplest change I could make that would create the biggest improvement?

What one thing do you think I should try to work on or think about in my next piece of writing?

for how to do it. You need only improve a behavior you already possess and learn to use it in more contexts. And as you learn to get your strengths into more of your writing you naturally tend to get rid of some of the other weaknesses. But if your teacher only tells you what you did wrong you may not be able to fix it no matter how clearly he explains the problem: he's asking for behavior you've never produced before.

For example, if you have consistently terrible organization and occasional powerful sentences, you may well improve your organization more quickly by trying to expand that gift for strong sentences than by working on organization. For some reason you have a serious blind spot or lack of feeling for organization, and it seldom does much good in such cases for someone to shout at you "pay more attention to organization." *You* have to develop that feeling for organization, and often you can't do so until you improve enough *other* aspects of your writing that your imagination can finally work on organization.

• To get the most help from a teacher you need him as your ally and helper rather than as your enemy. You will go a long way toward that goal if you can get him to specify the audience for the writing assignments and then to grade them and give you feedback in terms of how he thinks your writing would succeed with that audience. This makes your teacher into a kind of coach helping you aim words at some third party. But there's a lot more you can do to overcome the structural features of school and college which make teachers into opponents and policemen (a role most teachers would like to get out of). Pretend, for instance, that in reacting and commenting on your paper, your teacher is a *friend* doing you a *favor*—not an employee doing a duty. (He certainly is doing you a favor if he does it well.) Think of the specific things you would do for your friend if you were asking a favor:

You would probably make your paper neat and easy to read. I get mad at students when their papers are messy. I begin to feel them as the enemy.

You would probably get your paper to him at a convenient time. I resent students who turn in papers late. It usually makes my life harder, and even when it doesn't, it makes me feel I have to be on guard against them.

You would probably proofread and correct carefully to get rid of all the mistakes you can. When I get a paper full of mistakes I know the student could have removed, I immediately feel like *not helping* him. I feel he's treating me as a servant who is supposed to pick his smelly socks off the floor when he could just as well do it himself.

You would probably make sure to stick to the assignment. When I come to a paper that avoids or drifts away from the assignment, I instinctively feel, "Uh oh, here's someone trying to get away with something. I'd better be on guard." I start relating to him as the enemy. (Usually, by the way, you *can* find a way to include almost anything that interests you, even if it seems quite distant, as long as you think carefully about how to make it *part* of something that does address the assignment squarely.) You can probably add to my list of suggestions for helping make your teacher into your ally rather than your adversary.

• None of those suggestions entails doing any *more* writing than what is already assigned to you by the teacher: merely giving that writing to other people and adjusting the transaction between you and the teacher. But the most powerful thing you can do to increase what you get from teachers is to write *more*. Not just because quantity helps—though that is probably the main fact about writing—but because you learn most from teachers if your writing for them is a *supplement* to other writing you are doing. Try to think of writing for teachers as sneaking off for a little help on the side, getting in some volleying with the coach between your real games of tennis. Writing more means working more, but the amount of writing your teachers ask for will suddenly seem small once you stop treating assignments as ordeals and scary performances for the enemy and start treating them like mere practice games or chances for feedback from an ally on a nearly final draft.

Once you can write more you can look to them for what they *can* give and look elsewhere for what they cannot. Teachers are good for giving criticism because they read papers in piles of 25 or 50. Take that criticism and use it. They are good at making you write when you don't feel like it, simply because they have authority. Instead of resenting this, try appreciating it and internalizing from it what may be the most important skill of all: the ability to write when you are in the wrong mood. They are *not* good at telling you what your writing feels like to a real human being, at taking your words seriously as messages directed to them, at praising you, or perhaps even at noticing you. Get these things elsewhere. They are easier to find than what a teacher has to offer.

V

FEEDBACK

INTRODUCTION

No matter how productively you managed to get words down on paper or how carefully you have revised, no matter how shrewdly you figured your audience and purpose and suited your words to them, there comes the time when you need feedback. Perhaps you need it for the sake of revising: you have a very important piece of writing and you need to find out which parts work and which parts don't so you can rewrite it carefully before giving it to the real audience. Or perhaps you have already given an important piece to the real audience—it's too late for any revising—but nevertheless you need to learn how your words worked on the reader. Or perhaps you've simply decided that you must start learning in general about the effectiveness of writing.

Some people don't need to be encouraged to seek feedback; indeed, they need to be restrained. To some of you, that is, I would like to say, "Stop worrying so much about how your words work, about how *good* they are; just keep your mind on your writing, have fun, get confident, write lots." In short, if you are a compulsive worrier and keep leaking your attention away from *what* you are doing to *how well* you are doing it, forget about feedback till you have done enough writing and sharing and feel more secure.

But some of you need to be encouraged to get feedback. Probably you have been burned in the past. Most people experience feedback as painful, however they get it. After all, getting feedback on an early draft usually means getting criticized before you've had a chance to make your piece as good as you can make it. But getting feedback on a final draft feels even worse because you are usually getting criticized for your very best work, and besides, you are so tired of working on it by now that you can't even bear to look at it any more. If you follow the suggestions I give in this section, however, getting feedback can be a useful and gratifying experience.

It's easy to know when you should start getting feedback. Just keep in mind what's, more important than what: writing is more important than sharing your writing with readers; and sharing your writing with readers is more important than getting feedback from them. That is, if sharing begins to stop you from writing, then don't share. And if getting feedback begins to stop you from writing or sharing, then stop getting feedback. Writing is what's most important. But when you can share and get feedback *without* hampering your writing, then you will benefit enormously from those two activities.

It may be that getting feedback has been hampering you more than it needs to. For if you use the approach suggested here you can avoid the most common problems in getting feedback: people beating around the bush and not telling you anything at all; or giving you a vague wholistic judgment such as "B-plus" or "I liked it"; or going into a negative gear and "critiquing" you by finding every single real and imaginable mistake there could be ("I hope I didn't discourage you or anything"); or else trying to imitate what they remember getting from their teachers and talking about nothing but "topic sentences"; or else grabbing it out of your hands and trying to rewrite the whole thing the way they think it ought to be; or else just telling you everything your writing reminds them of.

The four chapters of this section help you take charge of the feedback process by showing you the options you have and then providing you the tools you need.

• In Chapter 21, "Criterion-Based Feedback and Reader-Based Feedback," I explore the two kinds of feedback you can get and the particular strengths and weaknesses of each kind.

• Chapters 22 and 23 provide the tools you need for actually getting good feedback—specific questions to ask readers to help them find more useful and substantive things to tell you than "I liked it" or "I didn't like it." Chapter 22 is a catalogue of questions for getting criterion-based feedback, 23 a catalogue of questions for getting reader-based feedback. You may want to glance through these two chapters as you read this section but you can't really use these questions till you have a piece of your own writing in hand to which you want responses and a reader or two willing to give you feedback.

• In Chapter 24, "Options for Getting Feedback," I explain the many possible procedures you might use. At the end of the chapter, I describe one particular way that is especially valuable: getting feedback regularly in a writing support group.

21

Criterion-Based Feedback
and Reader-Based Feedback

Criterion-based feedback helps you find out how your writing measures up to certain criteria—in this case to those criteria most often used in judging expository or nonfiction writing. To get criterion-based feedback you ask readers four broad, fundamental questions:

a. What is the quality of the content of the writing: the ideas, the perceptions, the point of view?
b. How well is the writing organized?
c. How effective is the language?
d. Are there mistakes or inappropriate choices in usage?

But because these questions are so broad, you usually get better feedback if you ask much more specific questions such as these: Is the basic idea a good one? Is it supported with logical reasoning or valid argument? Are there too many abstractions and too few examples or concrete details? Is the whole thing unified rather than pulling in two or three conflicting directions? Are the sentences clear and readable? Chapter 22 contains twenty-four of these questions grouped under the four general questions listed above.

Reader-based feedback, on the other hand, instead of telling you how your writing measures up to preestablished criteria, tells you what your writing does to particular readers. To get reader-based feedback you ask readers three broad fundamental questions:

a. What was happening to you, moment by moment, as you were reading the piece of writing?
b. Summarize the writing: give your understanding of what it says or what happened in it.
c. Make up some images for the writing and the transaction it creates with you.

Here too you usually get better feedback by helping your reader out with more specific questions like these: Now that you have finished reading just the first one or two paragraphs or stanzas, are you an interested, cooperative reader or are you bored or resistant in some way? Point to the places where you had the most trouble and describe what kind of trouble it was for you. Summarize your understanding of the whole piece. What mood or voice do you hear in the words? What kind of people does the writer seem to be talking to: people in the know? nincompoops? interested amateurs? How is the writer giving it to you: willingly? slyly? grudgingly? hitting you over the head with it? The next-to-last chapter in this section, 23, contains forty-one of these specific questions grouped under the three general questions above.

• • •

Criterion-based feedback, then, tells you how your writing measures up, reader-based feedback tells you what it does to readers. What is its quality? vs. How does it work? But the distinction between the two can sometimes, in practice, seem fuzzy. That is, sometimes when a reader gives you a piece of criterion-based feedback (for example, "This piece isn't unified"), it may just be his way of saying what was happening inside him ("I felt a bit in the fog most of the time I was reading—I didn't know where I was going"). Or if a reader gives you a piece of reader-based feedback ("When I got here, I stopped short and said, No sir! I won't buy that for one minute!"), it may just be his way of saying "Your logic is faulty here." Indeed, a reader cannot possibly give you a piece of criterion-based feedback except on the basis of something having happened inside him; nor can a reader give you a piece of reader-based feedback without at least implying a criterion of judgment or perception.

But that interdependence between the two kinds of feedback does not diminish the important difference between them. It will make a practical difference to you whether you ask readers for one or the other.*

---

*This reminds me of arguments about the relationship between form and content. Some people want to say there is no meaningful distinction between form and content because each can, in the last analysis, be expressed in terms of the other. But though that may be theoretically true, the distinction is still a real one that has immense practical importance. If you look for form you will notice things you miss if you look for content, and vice versa.

Thus if a reader tells you "This piece lacks unity," you can surmise that something happened inside him, but you don't really know *what* happened. Perhaps he felt foggy and lost, as I interpreted above, but perhaps he knew perfectly well where the writing was going, but he saw extraneous matter in it that didn't belong. Did it annoy him or did it just violate his sense of unity? Did he feel mosquitoes continually distracting his attention or just notice with calm disapproval the toys scattered on the floor? His comment on your lack of unity tells you nothing of how he experienced your words.

Conversely, if a reader gives you reader-based feedback—for example, "I felt lost here," he's giving you information about his reaction but not much about the writing: Is he lost because of your logic? your wording? Or do you have so many details here that he can no longer follow the main point?

So if you want messages about the writing you should ask for criterion-based feedback, and if you want to know what happened in the reader you should ask for reader-based feedback. That would seem to indicate that you should always ask for criterion-based feedback since it is writing you are trying to work on, not psychology.

But the crucial question about any piece of writing intended for an audience is not "How does it measure up against certain criteria" such as good sentences, good logic, or good paragraphs, but *"How does it work on readers?"* The quality of the sentences, logic, or paragraphs is irrelevant if the writing does to readers what you want it to do.

So that tips the scales back again to reader-based feedback as more useful. But of course it's not that simple. For even if you know all about what's going on in readers, you also need messages about your writing if you want to fix it or change it in any way. Otherwise you'll be stuck telling your reader, "I *know* you are lost, you've given me a vivid description of your lostness, but what is it in my *writing* that makes you feel lost? Is it my wording? My paragraphing? My logic?"

And so of course you should try for both criterion-based and reader-based feedback. Indeed, each kind of feedback enhances the other. Every time you get some criterion-based feedback, you can encourage the reader to tell you about the reactions he had which gave rise to his statement about unity or paragraphs or spelling. And every time you get reader-based feedback you can encourage the reader to tell you what it was in the writing that caused these reactions in him—was it the logic, the use of evidence, the diction, or what? Nevertheless each kind of feedback has its own special virtues which make it particularly useful in certain situations.

Virtues of Criterion-based Feedback

• Criterion-based feedback is the kind of feedback most people are accustomed to—what they've usually gotten from teachers—and so it's the kind of feedback that comes most naturally to people's lips when you ask them for feedback. And because I provide such a long list of very specific questions, you can avoid one of the main problems of criterion-based feedback: people not knowing what qualities to look for in the writing or else commenting entirely on the basis of just a few favorite criteria.

• It's the more practical and easier to understand of the two kinds of feedback because it speaks more directly about your writing. You have an easier time figuring out how to improve your writing if someone tells you your piece is not clearly organized than if he tells you he felt vaguely uneasy the whole time he was reading. Thus, it is especially good for revising (rather than for general long-term learning about the effect of your words on audiences).

• Indeed, you can even use these questions to get feedback from *yourself* as you are revising—as a checklist for finding weaknesses in your draft. These questions help you see what you have just written through fresh "outside" eyes—through the grid of external criteria. Reader-based questions, on the other hand, would be hard to answer by yourself.

• Criterion-based feedback helps you isolate particularly troublesome aspects of your writing and then concentrate on them in revising and in future writing. For example, perhaps you have trouble getting rid of digressions or making clear transitions between sections. Once you learn this through criterion-based feedback, you can check each piece of writing yourself for these particular dangers. And you can ask readers specifically for feedback on these matters which they might otherwise neglect.

• Thus you can use criterion-based feedback more quickly if you want to: just zoom in and inquire about a couple of areas and stop. It's hard to get reader-based feedback quickly.

• If you have only one reader for feedback, criterion-based questions will help him pay attention to a broad range of qualities in the writing—noticing things he might neglect if he just reacted naturally. Perhaps he mostly reacts to the kind of person or tone of voice he feels in the writing and neglects organization and logic altogether. Or perhaps he reacts almost entirely to logic and evidence but ignores tone of voice.

• Criterion-based feedback is good for readers who are insensitive to nuances or who are reluctant to talk about their own reactions.

• Criterion-based feedback is more verifiable than reader-based feedback. If a reader says your logic or spelling is wrong you can verify his judgment. If a reader says your organization or paragraphing is weak, you cannot verify his judgment, of course, but if you get three or four intelligent readers to give you their judgments too—and give you their reasons and discuss the question among themselves—you probably can reach a trustworthy objective conclusion.

• Criterion-based feedback is good if you want to work on your conscious understanding of the criteria used in judging writing. It helps you have brief and instructive discussions on the order of "What makes a good introduction?" or "Well, what *does* make a paragraph hang together?" It leads to discussions of conscious craft in writing.

• Criterion-based feedback is useful for readers who must comment on *many* pieces of writing in one sitting or in a comparatively short period of time. That's why teachers tend to use it. It's nearly impossible to read a whole stack of papers in one sitting and react to each one fully, for itself, and on its own terms. It's much easier—and perhaps even fairer in the long run—to choose a manageable set of good criteria and apply them to each paper as you read it.

Thus if I must read and comment on a large stack of essays in one evening I will tend to read each one in terms of criteria such as unity, argument, clarity of language, mechanics, and how well they fit the audience/purpose. I will also try to include something about how it felt to read this essay, but if I am too tired or bored or worried about something else, I may not have any feelings other than the ones that are intruding on me from the rest of my life—boredom or irritation or impatience. Criterion-based feedback has the enormous virtue of permitting you to read with less than full attention and still—if you are practiced—give accurate feedback on specific criteria.

• If, in particular, your task is to *judge* or *rank* a set of writings—if, for example, you must choose among ten job applications or if you are on a committee to chose the best essay or poem for a competition—you can probably be more fair and accurate if you judge in terms of explicit criteria. Otherwise it's often a matter of judging apples against oranges—just a matter of each piece producing noncomparable reactions in readers. And if you *feel* one piece is clearly best, that feeling may be based entirely on one criterion that you especially value—for example clarity of language or the personal qualities that show through—and you may be neglecting seven other important criteria that are well achieved in some other piece of writing that happens to leave you cold.

• And so if you are writing something for a reader who will judge the writing according to criteria—perhaps for a teacher who will read and evaluate a large stack of essays in one sitting—criterion-based feedback may be especially helpful to you in revising your piece. You can try to find out what criteria he will use. Many requests or guidelines for writing tell you the criteria readers will use, for example, guidelines for a grant application or a letter of recommendation ("Applications will be judged on the basis of . . ."). It's worth asking a teacher to tell you about the criteria he uses in grading, even if he doesn't use them with complete consistency. But it's important to remember that people often judge on the basis of different criteria from the ones they think they are using.

Virtues of Reader-based Feedback

Despite all those strengths of criterion-based feedback, I find reader-based feedback even more useful. If you neglect reader-based feedback, you will miss many of the main advantages and pleasures of the whole feedback process.

• Reader-based feedback gives you the main thing you need to improve your writing: the experience of what it felt like for readers as they were reading your words. In the long run you get more out of taking a ride inside your reader's skin than you get from a precise diagnosis of the strengths and weaknesses of your writing. That precise diagnosis can be surprisingly useless in actually helping you to *change* the way you write. It may even paralyze you.

Besides, readers often hide their own reactions behind criterion-based judgments about, say, paragraphs, the digressions, the diction. They don't feel comfortable saying, "I was bored after the first couple of pages" or "Actually I sort of felt you were badgering me and talking down to me" or "Somehow I found myself disagreeing with you more at the end than I had at the beginning but I didn't know why.".

People are nervous about saying these things because they can't explain or justify them. Yet such felt reactions are often just what you need for improving your writing, especially if you can get the reader to tell you a bit more about where and why they arose.

• Reader-based feedback is the most trustworthy feedback because you are only asking for "raw data"—what they saw and what was happening to them as they read. With criterion-based feedback, on the other hand, you are asking them to *translate* those perceptions and reactions into a judgment about what is good or bad in the writing. That act of translation is tricky. It takes an experienced reader to translate his discomfort or annoyance into an accurate statement of what's wrong with your logic or diction. He may tell you "too many digressions," for example, or "too many generalizations," but perhaps the essential thing is that you didn't get him to be a cooperative reader. If you had, he wouldn't have complained about the digressions, indeed he would have seen them as integral to your argument. And even if you fix the digressions, he'll probably stay irritated and uncooperative and find something else to complain about. And all the while, you never learn the essential point: some tone or stance in your writing made him irritated and uncooperative. If, on the other hand, you can *enter into* his reactions and *feel* his irritation in those very words which you thought were perfectly straightforward and well-mannered—if you can learn to experience your words as he experiences them—you can usually find a way to translate all that into practical action: you can decide whether a change is needed (or whether his reaction was peculiar) and what kind of change will fix that irritation.

• Therefore, reader-based feedback has the advantage of keeping you more in charge of the whole feedback process. Readers get to tell you what they saw and what happened in them, but *you* take over from there. You do all the translating. You get to decide what their reactions mean and what changes if any you want to make. One of the main reasons so many people hate feedback or fail to learn from it is that it makes them feel so helpless. Getting feedback has always felt like putting themselves entirely into someone else's power. You don't do that if you use reader-based feedback. (Of course, there *are* times when you are busy and tired and have great faith in your reader, so you say, "Don't bother me with your reactions, just tell me what's wrong and how to fix it.")

• Reader-based feedback has the enormous virtue of being available from *anyone*. You don't need experts or experienced writers. Teachers and editors have no special headstart. You can even read pieces out loud to people who can't read, and you will be surprised at what excellent feedback you get. You can use friends, children, people you like to work with, whoever is available, people who know lots about the topic but nothing about writing. The quality of their feedback has nothing to do with their ideas or theories about writing. In short, it is much easier to give good reader-based feedback than to give good criterion-based feedback. And more fun.

• If you are writing an audience-oriented piece such as a memo or a tricky letter—writing that must *work* on your intended reader rather than be good in some timeless or abstract fashion—reader-based feedback will be more helpful to you. Not only will it tell you a lot about how your words work on a real person, you can go out and get feedback from readers *just like* your intended reader—even if they are inexperienced or uninterested in writing. If you are writing children's stories, you can't ask children about the unity or diction in what you read to them, but you can ask them lots of these reader-based questions about what happened to them. If you are writing advertisements meant to work on small business owners, you *could* ask them about diction or digressions, but that's not the point. The point is what happens to them.

• Because reader-based feedback emphasizes the practical question of what the words are doing rather than the theoretical question of how good they are, it is less evaluative and judgmental. It usually leads to more listening and learning, less arguing. Criterion-based feedback, on the other hand, is based entirely on ideals or perfect models and so every item of that feedback is likely to be a statement of how your words didn't quite measure up. It's hard not to be defensive and to argue against it: "Well, you may not *think* that's a proper introduction, but you just have a rigid, simpleminded notion of what an opening paragraph ought to be like." With reader-based feedback there is seldom anything to argue about. You can't say, "I disagree. You were *not* confused during that opening paragraph." And even if you think he was stupid to be confused, your act of simply listening and seeing it through his eyes will probably lead you to improve that first paragraph.

The main thing people feel when they first learn to get reader-based feedback is an enormous sense of relief that value judgments and "measuring-up" are not the focus of every statement. It's an exhilarating experience when, as sometimes happens, you get a rich set of reactions to a piece of your writing—you are getting good insights and taking notes like mad as you listen to this person tell you his reactions—and then it is all over and you start to listen to the next person give you feedback and suddenly it hits you: "Hey! I don't even know whether he *liked* it or not." Suddenly that tyrannical matter of liking and not-liking pales into its not-very-significant place.

Of course you often do get value judgments in reader-based feedback since liking or not liking is likely to be one of the events in the reader. But it's only one of the events and usually not the most important one. And it's easier to accept a value judgment and learn from it when it consists of a statement of how the reader is bothered or put off or made uncomfortable by your words than when it consists of a statement of how your writing doesn't measure up to some criterion.

• In this sense, then, reader-based feedback is the most *efficient* kind of feedback: it can lead to the fastest and most pervasive improvement. It is more apt to speak to the root causes of strength and weakness in your writing, not just the surface effects. That is, if you ask for reader-based feedback you are apt to hear things like this: "Damn it, stop beating around the bush and come out and say what's on your mind. Stop working so hard at fending off my possible disagreements. Just write what you have to say. Your constant defending is making it harder for me as a reader just to follow your thoughts comfortably, in fact it's making me angry." Think how much more useful it is to hear that than to hear someone say "It's too long and wordy, too many dependent clauses, try for simpler syntax and a clearer progression of logic." Once a reader helps you hear a note of insecure beating around the bush in your own writing voice, you can strengthen your writing much more quickly and pervasively than if he just told you to get rid of dependent clauses and use simpler diction and better logic.

Reader-based feedback gives you someone saying "I get annoyed and don't take your argument seriously because I always hear a kind of whine in your voice," instead of someone saying "too many passive verbs, adjectives, and adverbs. Not enough crisp verbs of action. Your diction isn't lively or energetic." (I'm not saying you can get rid of a habit of voice overnight once you hear it. Since it is a habit it will slip out again and again in speaking and freewriting. Indeed, now that you realize a whine is there you ought to invite it out as much as you can in freewriting—to exaggerate it, play with it, get a better feeling for it, and see what it is trying to tell you. This will improve your ability to *remove* it when you revise —and gradually to grow out of it.)

Reader-based feedback gives you someone saying, "I get mad at you when I read this because I feel you being arrogant and snotty. You just ski as fast as you can and you don't give a damn whether I fall down or not as I try to follow you. You never even look back." Most of the time that kind of reaction helps you more than "Too many abrupt changes, too few clear transitions, too many abstractions without illustration, and even when you do give illustrations they are not obvious ones." I'm not saying that the reader is always *correct* in his picture of you. Even though he is intimidated by you, you may not in fact be writing in an arrogant or snotty way, just having a good time enjoying your own powers—skiing fast because you have fun skiing fast. But you can often improve your writing more quickly and easily when you realize how it *feels* to a reader, even if that reader is making an incorrect judgment about you, than if you were given entirely correct statements about your syntax or paragraph transitions.

• Reader-based feedback is especially necessary for poetry, fiction, and other kinds of creative writing. There are so many different ways in which poems or stories can succeed—or fail—that it's impossible to spell out a list of specific criteria for them. Indeed I am nervous about having you depend too much on my list of criterion-based questions even for nonfiction or expository writing. It's a safe list. Most teachers would agree with most items. But many successful pieces of nonfiction *fail* to meet some of these criteria, for example, they digress or they are hard to read or they have peculiar paragraphing. And many unsuccessful pieces measure up well on most criteria, but fail to have that certain something that makes them succeed with readers.

Summary

I can summarize the complementary virtues of the two kinds of feedback by pointing out that criterion-based feedback forces criteria to be conscious and reader-based feedback allows criteria to remain unconscious. Conscious criteria help readers notice things they would miss if they just gave themselves over to natural or habitual reading. But these conscious criteria can also be a screen between readers and your words—a filter which keeps readers from contacting and experiencing your words directly—leading them instead just to compare your words to a model, hold them up against a template, check off categories on a list. Amateur readers, in particular, sometimes go into a peculiar gear when you ask them for criterion-based feedback. They don't just read the way they would normally read. They say to themselves, "Well, now I've got to give help on writing, let's see, I've got to be on the lookout for faults, now let's see what should I look for, good organization, spelling and grammar of course, that's important, paragraphing, yes, that's what my teachers stressed a lot. Tone. I had this terrific teacher who talked about tone all the time, but I never did figure out what he meant. And not too many adjectives; not too many long sentences." Readers can't tell you much about your writing when they have all that noise in their heads.

Reader-based feedback, on the other hand, by allowing criteria to remain unconscious, yields just the opposite virtues and defects. It allows readers just to relax and read your writing for enlightenment or pleasure, and to experience it on its own terms. It allows them to notice and react to more qualities in it than they could consciously analyze, and it allows them to be more sensitive to nuances—especially matters of tone and presentation of self that are difficult to categorize but often determine success or failure. Leaving criteria unconscious, however, can also permit narrow reading: reading that is a slave to one or two unconscious criteria—

for example, how a reader feels about the tone of voice or the "vibes."

In short, the two kinds of feedback encourage readers to take different roles. When you ask a reader to give you criterion-based feedback you encourage him to function like an expert, a coach, or a commentator, that is, to stand off to the side and watch you from the stage wings as you give your violin concert and not get too involved in your music. This helps him to tell you about your technique. When you ask your reader to give you reader-based feedback, on the other hand, you encourage him to function like an audience, that is, to sit right out there in front of you and experience your music. This helps him to tell you about what your music does to the audience.

The moral of the story, then, is to use both kinds of feedback. I present criterion-based feedback first here because it is more familiar and easier to understand, but generally you do better to ask for reader-based feedback first. That way readers can just read for pleasure or enlightenment and tell you about whatever happens to them when they read in their accustomed way—before you make them into more self-conscious and technique-oriented readers by asking them criterion-based questions.

22

A Catalogue of
Criterion-Based Questions

The twenty-odd questions in this chapter will help you find out about four basic qualities in a piece of writing.

a. What is the quality of the content of the writing: the ideas, the perceptions, the point of view?
b. How well is the writing organized?
c. How effective is the language?
d. Are there mistakes or inappropriate choices in usage?

These four criteria can be fruitfully applied to any kind of writing but most of the specific questions in this chapter are framed so that they fit expository or nonfiction writing better than poetry or fiction. The questions which follow are too many to ask any one reader on one occasion (although you could ask *yourself* all these questions if you were revising one of your own pieces as carefully as you could). As in the rest of the book, I am trying to help you take charge of things by giving you more recipes than you can use for one meal. Try out these questions on different pieces of your writing and on different readers so you gradually learn which ones are most useful for you and which ones will be most important under various circumstances.

• • •

a. What is the quality of the content of the writing: the ideas, the perceptions, the point of view?

1. Is the basic idea or insight a good one?
2. Is it supported by logical reasoning or valid argument?

3. Is it supported by evidence and examples?

4. Is it really saying something or is it just a collection of thoughts or observations (however unified and well written) sitting there limply? Did the writer communicate why this whole thing matters?

5. Is there too much abstraction or generalization? So few details, examples, and explanations that it ends up dull, empty, impossible to experience? or perhaps even impossible to understand?

6. Is there too *little* abstraction and too much clutter of detail? Too little standing back for perspective? Too little forest per tree?

7. Does it do what it says or implies it is going to do? Does it satisfy the issues it raises?

8. Is there a point of view or is the writing just disembodied statements from nowhere? And is that point of view unified and consistent?

9. Is the piece fitted to its audience? Has the writer understood their needs and point of view?

b. How well is the writing organized?

10. Is the whole thing unified? Is there one central idea to which everything pertains? Or is it pulling in two or three directions or full of loose ends and digressions?

11. Are the parts arranged in a coherent or logical sequence?

12. Is there a beginning? That is, does it start off in a way that allows you to get comfortably started? (The safest and most common way of doing this is to give an introduction—for example, a quick explanation of what's to come. But of course that's not the only way. Indeed plunging the reader into the middle of things without warning *can* function as a good beginning.)

13. Is there a middle? A body, some girth or solidity, some sense of meat and potatoes, sufficiency? Or does it turn around and say good-bye almost as soon as it is finished saying hello?

14. Is there an ending? Does it give you a sense of closure or completion? (The safest and most common method of doing this is to end with a conclusion—not just repeating what went before but figuring out what everything means or adds up to. But again, that's not the only good way to end a piece.)

15. Were the paragraphs really paragraphs? Could you tell what each one was saying? Did they function as helpful and comfortable

units of thought: not too much to carry in your arms, but not so little that it feels like a wasted trip?

c. How effective is the language?

16. Are the sentences clear and readable?
17. Are the words used correctly?
18. Is it succinct enough for the purpose and audience? Not too long, repetitious, dull?
19. Is it full enough? Or does the writer squeeze out so much of the juice of human communication, the oil of actual spoken discourse, that the language, even if correct, is indigestible?
20. Does the diction, mood, or level of formality fit the audience and occasion?
21. Is the language alive, human, interesting? Either because of interesting metaphors or turns of phrase; or because of a voice or presence in the words—a sense of someone's actually being there?

d. Are there mistakes or inappropriate choices of usage?

22. Are there mistakes in grammar, usage, spelling and typing?
23. Are there mistakes in footnotes, graphs, or other special effects?
24. Is it neat and easy to read on the page?

23

A Catalogue of Reader-Based Questions

The forty-one questions in this chapter are just specific practical ways to ask your reader three broad questions about how your words affected him:

a. What was happening to you, moment by moment, as you were reading the piece of writing?

b. Summarize the writing: give your understanding of what it says or what happened in it.

c. make some images for the writing and the transaction it creates with readers.

Sometimes a reader can tell us without difficulty or hesitation exactly what was going on in him as he read our words—either because he was surprised by his reactions or because he was in a particularly meditative, self-reflective mood. But often it is difficult for readers to tell in any detail what was happening to them as they read. Nor is this necessarily a fault. One of the marks of good reading is wholehearted investment in the words and meanings and no attention to the self. If a reader can remember nothing at all about what was happening as he read your words that may be a sign of total success.

But as writers we need to know what was going on in our readers. It would pay us, if we could, to hook up little cameras in all the corners of readers' innards so we could see all the thoughts, images, feelings, and impulses that occur as they read our writing. I like to call reader-based feedback *movies of a reader's mind*.

Get a reader to answer enough of the following questions and you will get those movies. Being inside his skin as he reads your words is the most valuable experience you can get as a writer. It is valuable for readers, too. They not only discover more than they knew about this particular piece of writing, they also learn to be much more perceptive readers.

Remember, however, that these questions—and I give a formidable number of them—are nothing but ways to help readers tell you how they experience your writing. Some readers will give you good feedback without your asking them any of these questions at all. You can just sit back and listen.

a. What was happening to you, moment by moment, as you were reading the piece of writing?

Stop reading after you have read only one or two paragraphs or stanzas.*

1. What was happening to you as you read this opening passage?

2. Tell which words or phrases struck you most or stuck out or had resonance.

3. What has this section just said? What do you now expect the whole piece to say? (In the case of a story: what happened and what are the implications? What do you expect in what follows?)

4. What ideas or beliefs or feelings do you bring to this piece that could influence the way you read it?

5. The writer has just, as it were, introduced himself to you. How did he do it? Formally? Casually? Intimately? Jocularly? Did he thrust out his hand for you to shake? Sidle up to you without looking at you? What sense of the writer do you have now—on the basis of this limited introduction?

---

* You may be reluctant to ask for feedback from a reader who has only read a little bit of your piece. You may feel you'll get nothing but unfounded snap judgments. But first impressions often influence how a reader reacts to the rest of your piece. If you wait for feedback till your reader has finished reading your whole piece you may not learn how your opening section really affected him. You may not learn, for example, that the real reason for his quarrelling with your argument or his failure to experience the main event in your story was because he got irritated at the very start and consequently read the remainder in a resistant, foot-dragging mood. If he had been a cooperative reader he might not have had any of those difficulties. Whether a reader is going to be with you or against you often gets decided in this opening section.

6. At this early stage, are you more *with* the writer or *against* him? dragging your feet or helping pedal?

7. What do you want, need, wish for now? If you are fighting the writer now, what would it take to get you pedaling?

8. Continue reading. If you have a copy in your hand, make light pencil marks to give a fuller record of how you are reacting to the words: put a straight line next to passages and underneath words and phrases that work or please you; a wiggly line in the same way for parts which don't work or bother you in some way.

Stop once again—half or three-quarters through the piece.*

9. What has been happening to you and what is happening to you now? Tell it in the form of a story: first this happened, then I noticed that, then I felt this, and so on. For example:

> First I was open and sympathetic to what I thought you were up to. But then without noticing I drifted into resisting what you've been saying. Something made me feel "Wait a minute! There are things that don't fit!" Somehow I became an adversary, you became my enemy. But now that I stop and think about it, basically I agree with you completely. The trouble is you seem so wide-eyed and innocent and naïve—as though you are always saying "gee, gosh, golly, isn't this idea wonderful and amazing." I want to attack this naïve childish tone. And yet your main assertion is something I agree with. I guess it makes me mad to have my wise sophisticated point of view look silly and naïve.

Make sure to tell everything. Even if it seems irrelevant. If you started daydreaming or thinking about your new shoes, that's feedback. The important thing is to tell the writer where you were in his writing when it happened. All feedback is mixed with subjectivity. Let the writer do the sorting.

10. What changes have occurred in you since before? If you

---

* It's true that you affect the reader's reactions somewhat by stopping him in midcourse and asking him questions. It probably makes him a bit more thoughtful and observant than if he just read through without pause. He will understand some subtleties—and perhaps also notice some ragged edges—that he might otherwise have missed. You may want to ask some readers to read straight through before giving you any feedback at all. But these interim responses solve the most frustrating problem of reader-based feedback, the problem of vaguely global reactions such as "It was pretty good. I liked it a lot." By stopping your reader in the middle you force him to tell you where he is in an unfinished sequence of reactions and thus to talk about your writing as a series of events occuring in time inside a reader's head—which is what any piece of writing is—not as a vague global thingified "it."

were *with* the writer earlier and now resist or doubt him, where did you start to part company? (Or vice versa.) Why? What would the writer have to do to get you back?

11. Point to the sentences or passages you liked especially. Point to the ones you didn't understand or which made you stumble or resist.

12. What do you expect next? What do you need before it ends?

Stop right after you have completed reading it all.

13. What is happening to you now? Changes in reaction or loyalty? What's the most important thing about the piece?

14. How would you instinctively *reply* or *respond* if you weren't trying to give feedback? Would you tell the writer something similar that happened to you? Ask him what was going on in his mind when he wrote? Quarrel with him? Ask for clarification on some issue? Ask: "Did that *really* happen to you?" Ask: "But then what happened after the funeral?" Comment on the meaning of the story? Ask something about technique, such as "What made you decide to start with the shooting instead of the quarrel?" Ask him out for coffee and seek to know him better?*

15. Describe the way the writer ended his piece. Describe it as though he were ending a letter, saying good-bye, ending a telephone conversation: Did he hang up abruptly? Stand around on the doorstep unable to finish his sentence and say good-bye? A sudden gush of warmth? Did he slip out without anyone noticing?

16. Which aspects of *you* does the piece bring out? Your contemplative side? Your childish curiosity or eagerness? Your motherly or fatherly helpfulness ("Let's see how I can help out this nice young writer")?

17. What kind of person has the writer turned out to be? How did he turn out differently from what you had first suspected?

18. What do you like about the piece at this point?

Remain silent and reflective for a few moments.

19. What is happening to you? What delayed reactions or second thoughts do you have? Which parts of the writing seem to have been written in invisible ink and to emerge only slowly as you hold it over a candle? For example,

---

* You may not have to *ask* readers this question. Just notice how they act and what they ask you when they finish reading. Don't get sucked into responding to what they say. Listen to it as feedback.

It's been obvious to me throughout that I disagree with you entirely. But it's only now dawning on me gradually that I haven't been *fighting* you very much. Somehow you manage to give me your meanings as wholly yours. You don't make me feel I have to agree or accept them—or even find them rational. I can be interested and curious from a safe distance. In fact I find my impulse is to come slightly *forward* toward you—not retreat or push you away—because you are giving me a chance to look safely at something I usually fight and push away. It's kind of a relief.

Now read the piece of writing again.

20. Tell the differences between what happens to you on this reading and what happened to you on the first reading.

b. Summarize the writing: give your understanding of what it says or what happened.*

21. Summarize it. If you have difficulty, pretend you only have thirty seconds to tell a friend what this piece is saying. Tell him quickly and informally. You don't have time to get it right or prepare an answer because the train is just getting to his stop. Let the writer hear you fumbling to find the center of gravity. For example, "Well, it's about a trip in the mountains. Or perhaps it's about survival. I guess it's really about the difference between men and women." Then summarize it in a sentence. Then in one word: first a word from the text, then a word not in the text.

22. Summarize what you feel the writer is *trying* but not quite

---

* You may have to push readers to give you summarizing feedback. They often resist it because it feels too simpleminded, too mechanical, too much like they are being given a sixth grade test. It's worth insisting on a summary, however, because without it you may misunderstand everything else you hear. Imagine hearing your reader say "I found your argument irritating and I especially wanted to quarrel with you in the third paragraph and in your conclusion"—and doing your best to stand inside his shoes and find the irritating quality in your words—and all the while not realizing he thought you were saying something entirely different from what you thought you were saying.

Even if you have a poem or story, it's worth getting readers to summarize it; even to summarize the "moral" of the story or "meaning" of the poem. Many readers who consider themselves artistic will scorn to summarize a poem—feeling it is a lowbrow thing to do. But you need to know how your writing has settled or sorted itself out or come to a focus in their heads. You have to give them permission to do what feels crude or imprecise—permission to "do violence" to what you have written. Words won't get into anyone's head without a little twisting. You need to know the nature of the twisting that has occurred.

managing to say. Where is the writing trying to go—perhaps against the writer's will?

23. Summarize what you *wish* it were saying.

24. Give an exaggerated summary. How would you summarize it if you were making fun of it or making a parody of it.*

25. Negative summary. What is it *not* about? What is the opposite of what it is saying? What is it almost saying or refraining from saying? †

c. Make up some images for the writing and the transaction it creates with readers. ‡

26. What other pieces of writing does it remind you of? What *forms* of writing does it remind you of: a love letter? a federal interdepartmental memo? a "why-I-want-to-go-to-college" essay on an application form? a late night diary entry?

27. Tell how someone different from you might react. "If my *mother* read this, she would think it was silly and not very funny." "If John read this, he wouldn't have a *clue* what you were talking

---

* Don't ask for exaggerated summaries if you feel shaky about this piece or generally vulnerable about your writing. They can sting. But they improve the feedback immensely. So many readers beat around the bush and won't come right out and say what they see—they hem and haw and tiptoe around their reactions and they are so afraid of hurting your feelings that you can't even tell what they are saying. They just fill the air with smoke. But when you tell them to *exaggerate* or *make fun of it*, this clears the air and they can just *say* it, *plop* it right down on the table.

And when you get an exaggerated summary you find out how your words will probably be understood by readers who don't read carefully or sympathetically. I got the following parody summary of my earlier book about writing: "Writing is easy. You never have to try, it's never painful, just sit down and write whatever comes to mind and it will always come out just right." It makes me wince. I want to say, "Wait, wait, you made a mistake in your reading," but it's a perfect picture of how the book was perceived by readers with a strong antipathy to what I was trying to say. It would have been helpful to get that feedback before I finished revising the book.

† This sounds odd, but try it on readers and you will sometimes find subtle but important clues about tendencies in your writing and your reader's preconceptions and preoccupations. Sometimes you don't get the benefit of a reader's regular summary (or other feedback) till he gives his version of what your writing is not about or not saying.

‡ Here are some metaphorical questions which will help readers tell you reactions and perceptions they cannot easily express literally, and even some reactions they were not conscious of. Don't push readers too hard to explain or interpret these images. That will hinder them from giving you good ones. Just listen and trust that you will benefit from them even if you cannot understand them or translate them into advice.

about, he'd think you were just describing a dream." "If I were a man, I would feel attacked."*

28. Make up an image for the relationship between the writer and reader. Does the writer seem to have his arm draped familiarly over your shoulder? Is the writer shouting from a cliff to a crowd below? Reading to you from a stage? Sending a letter bomb? Speaking as daddy to his family from the head of the dining room table? Shaking his fist at you?

29. What do you feel the writer is trying to do to you? Beat you over the head? Trap you? Trick you? Surprise you? Make you like him?

30. Is the writer *giving* it? How? On a silver platter? Reverently for your worship—but only from a distance? Laughingly? Is he holding back? Is he giving it and taking it back—coyly giving you glimpses and closing the curtain again? Is he slyly trying to keep his meaning a bit hidden so only the right sort of people will get it—wearing sloppy clothes with hidden signs of taste so that only special people will know that he's special too?

31. Describe the writer's relationship to the reader in terms of *distance*. Close? At arm's length? Distant? Describe *changes* in distance that occur. For example, "I feel the writer backing off toward the end—clamming up, becoming a bit distant or formal— as though he is suddenly embarrassed or awkward at realizing how much of himself he revealed."

32. Find words or metaphors for the *voice* or *tone* in the writing: intimate? shouting? coy? tight-lipped? "I feel the writer being all cheery and jocular but really not letting himself show at all; the joking tone feels like a way of hiding or of not taking his own message seriously. Joe Jokester." Or "I can feel the writer's shyness and self-consciousness coming through the words like a cloud of fog. It's as though he is on stage giving a speech and because he is so nervous he makes *me* feel vicariously nervous. I want to say, 'Forget about us and just concentrate on what you are saying.'" Describe the voice in metaphors of color; of weather (foggy here, sunny there). You can describe voice by comparison, too; for example, like Jack Benny? Kissinger? Edith Bunker? Try not to be

---

*This can be very useful feedback taken at face value—clues to the reactions of different readers. But sometimes an element of make-believe or role-playing permits readers to express some of their own reactions which they weren't aware of or couldn't express.

influenced too much by the way he actually read his words out loud. Perhaps he read them shyly, but there is a domineering voice in the writing itself.

33. Look especially for changes in voice. Perhaps it starts out all stiff, but then loosens up. Where do you see that change? Perhaps it takes on another coloration for the conclusion, for saying good-bye.

34. Try conveying the voice or tone by mimicking it—probably with exaggeration. For example, "Look, buddy, I'm in the know. I've seen it all, I'm a tough guy, you can't fool me." My tone in *Writing Without Teachers* was mimicked in this way: "I'm *really* sincere. You can really believe me. I know just how you feel. I'm a good guy. I wouldn't steer you wrong. Only, don't get mad at me if it doesn't work. I'm really trying as hard as I can. Besides, I'm having a hard time with my writing too."

35. Do you feel a difference between the voice created or implied by these words and the actual writer who wrote them? If you know the writer personally you may hear the difference immediately and vividly: "How come you sound so pompous here when you never talk that way?" But even if you don't know the writer at all, you can still sometimes feel a gap of some sort between the voice *in* the words and the writer *behind* the words—as though the writer is playing some kind of game or being slippery or ironic in the voice he uses. If you can feel this kind of difference, describe it in terms of tone of voice, appearance, personality, whatever. For example, "Behind the sweet and reasonable voice in this essay I sense someone who is actually angry." Make up an image or metaphor for how these two people are relating to each other. (In the D. H. Lawrence passage I cite in Chapter 25 on voice, for example, I feel the author smiling in a somewhat sly and sophisticated way at the ranting and raving voice who speaks the essays.) How do they feel about each other? What would they say to each other if they spoke?

36. What images of the writer come to mind? Hunched over a desk? Sprawled on a divan? Sitting on a beach? How does the writer dress? Hold his body? Wear his hair? Let all images just be intuitive, uncalculated.

37. Use camera metaphors for how the writer handles his material. Where does he move in close, where fade back? Where is it

sharp or fuzzy? What is foreground and background? Is he using special effects or gimmicks? Do they work for you?

38. Whom does the writing seem to address? Strangers? An old friend? Dumbells? Prissy girls? Tough guys? Is it talking *up* or *down?*

39. Describe the punctuation or rhythms (or indeed any tendency in the writing) in terms of a transaction between writer and reader. My wife was once telling me about how I had too many semicolons. I was resisting her advice stoutly, but then she drifted into an image: she felt me trying to keep her, as reader, on a leash, keep her attention on a tight rein, never let her look away from the writing or take a deep breath or relax for a moment—as though I were insecure and afraid to give readers a full stop for fear they would drift off and not come back and pay attention to me. It made her feel continually tugged at. Suddenly I could feel what she was talking about and I had to stop arguing about the rules for legal semicolons and start listening.

40. Try other media. Made a doodle or a picture or a bunch of sounds or a body improvisation to represent the writing or your reaction to the writing.

41. As an alternative to answering any of these specific questions, try just reading the piece and then doing five or ten minutes of fast nonstop writing. You'll find that what you scribble down usually tells a lot about how you experienced the piece. This is a particularly useful procedure when you have gotten used to giving reader-based feedback.

24

Options for Getting Feedback

There is no single or right way to get feedback. In this chapter I will describe the advantages and disadvantages of various options. At the end I will suggest one process I believe is particularly valuable: getting feedback regularly in a writing support group.

• You can get feedback from one person or several. If you really want to know how your words affect readers, you can't trust feedback from just one person, no matter how expert or experienced she is. Besides it is somehow empowering to realize how diverse and even contradictory the reactions are of different readers to your one set of words. It's confusing at first but it releases you from the tyranny of any single reader's or teacher's judgment. It drives home the fact that there's never a single or correct assessment of a piece of writing. When you get conflicting reactions, block your impulse to figure out which reactions are right. Eat like an owl: take in everything and trust your innards to digest what's useful and discard what's not. Try for readers with different tastes and temperaments—especially if you don't have many readers.

But you can get good benefit from just one reader's feedback if you only want criterion-based feedback—if you only want to find out about your organization or logic or grammar, for example—so long as that reader understands those criteria well.* And if you want help on an early weak draft, you can also make good use of

---

*One careful reader can certainly find your mistakes in grammar, usage, and typing—a kind of criterion-based feedback that you should always get on any important piece of writing headed for an audience.

just one reader. You're not so much trying to find out how success-ful your draft is. You know it's inadequate. What you want is to have an interesting discussion about the topic, get your mind jogged, and end up with new insights. Feedback and discussion from one reader—perhaps a friend who is happy to read your rough work simply for the pleasure of hearing your thinking—can go a long way toward turning a shaky first draft into something so solid that others will enjoy reading it for their own benefit, not just as a favor.

• If you get feedback from several people you can get it from them in a group or by meeting with them singly. Usually you learn more in a group. Readers will notice more by hearing what the others say: "I see you are surprised," a reader will say, "by her re-action to that first paragraph, but the same thing happened to me. I hadn't been conscious of it till I heard her tell her response." Or "Her reaction makes me realize I had the opposite feeling when I read that third paragraph." Readers sometimes get into instructive discussions: three people with different perceptions may suddenly put their views together and see something going on in your writ-ing that none of them could have seen alone.

But a group is much more trouble. People have to coordinate their schedules. It takes more of everyone's time (though less of yours). And some people hate groups and clam up—whereas they will give you lots of good feedback if you sit down with them one-to-one. And groups sometimes get sidetracked into useless argu-ments.

• You can get feedback from the same people all the time or use different people on different occasions. There is a great advantage to staying with the same people because they get so much better at giving feedback. And if you use people who want feedback from you in return, that further improves the quality of what you get: people are more honest and open when they need the same gift back from you. But, of course, sometimes you will need one-time-only feedback from particular readers with special knowledge or from readers who are especially like the real audience for your piece.

• Some readers do better if *you* choose the questions. They pre-fer, as it were, to be interviewed. Other readers will give you bet-ter feedback if you hand them the list so they can choose the ones they find most interesting and applicable. You'll have better luck getting these choosey readers to answer particular questions if you give them free rein for a while.

• You can given people copies of your writing (or leave one copy where they can read it at leisure), or you can read it to them out loud. When readers have a copy of your words in their hands, they can often give you more detailed and precise feedback. And it saves time if they can read it before you meet—though they sometimes then don't have it fresh enough in mind when you meet. But in some ways you get more useful feedback when you read your piece out loud. (You must read it twice and leave a minute or two of silence after each reading.) Any passage that is not clear enough to be understood through listening is not really clear enough, even if it can be understood off the page. It is making your reader work harder than she ought to have to work and therefore making her more likely to resist your meaning. And the experience of reading your words out loud to an audience is beneficial in itself.

Since both methods of giving your writing to readers have contrasting advantages, I would advise using each of them at one time or another. It would be almost ideal if readers would read your piece and take notes of their reactions a few days before you meet; and then listen to you read your piece out loud when you meet so it will be fresh in their minds and so they can compare their reactions to the two different experiences.

• If you give readers copies of long pieces instead of reading them out loud, you will save meeting time and readers will probably be able to tell you more reactions. It's hard to listen to and remember something too long. But if that is hard to arrange you can still get very useful feedback if you read out loud just the first few pages of a long piece. If you can get the opening section to work—the introduction and a substantial section of the main body—you've gone a long way toward making the whole piece work.

• You can tell your readers something about your audience, purpose and context *before* they give you feedback: "This memo is meant to give advice to salespeople who will be trying to sell in a very competitive market to resistant customers. I am their supervisor and that makes them often resent my advice. But I want them not to feel any pressure. I want them just to take whatever they find useful in this memo and feel free to ignore what they don't like." If you have a tricky audience problem like this, or if you simply care enormously about the words succeeding with a particular audience (for example, "If this letter doesn't work on her, I don't think I'll get visiting rights for seeing my children"), it is worth explaining the situation at least to some of your readers. They may have some good insights about how your particular audience would react and what that audience needs: insights they would miss if they just reacted as themselves. But if it's really important that your words work with a particular audience, it's worth struggling to find readers like your real audience. Find salespeople or women in a divorce proceeding like yours. Ask favors.

But on the other hand, when readers are busy telling you how they think *other* readers will react, they often miss some of their own reactions. Or they don't tell you some of their own reactions because they have a stereotyped vision of your audience: "Oh well, salesmen don't think about anything except making a sale," or "Women in the middle of divorce proceedings can't listen to reason." It's crucial to get at least some feedback that is not affected by knowledge of your audience and purpose. I always learn most from people's *own* reactions. I'm always saying, "Please don't spend so much time talking about how you think *they* would react, tell me more about how *you* actually did react." You can get the best of both worlds if you keep quiet at first, but then, after getting one round of unchanneled feedback, explain your particular audience situation.

• It's hard not to apologize as you give a piece of writing to your readers: "This is only a second draft and still pretty rough. I was up late last night trying to finish it. I know it's kind of incoherent. I still have lots of revising to do." Sometimes it does no harm and permits readers to be gracious and say things like, "I'm sure it's only because you haven't finished it yet, but I found that opening paragraph very confusing." But sometimes an apology makes readers wonder if you are afraid to hear criticism and afraid to say so. This makes them feel hesitant and uncertain and, as a result, they pussyfoot around. You never learn some of their most interesting reactions. It's usually better to keep your mouth shut and see what they say or else make an unambiguous request for no negative feedback.

• How much negative feedback can you productively use? If too much of it will stop you from working on a piece or slow you down in your writing, you have to be brave enough—and smart enough—to admit it. Until you are secure in your writing—until, that is, you know you can produce lots of writing whenever you need it and that some of it will be good or can be made good—stick with plain sharing and noncritical feedback.

For readers will occasionally hate your piece. Don't ask for full feedback until you are able to *use* negative reactions to see new useful things about your writing—instead of just feeling put down, graded, or judged. Wait till you can say, "I certainly must have gotten something powerful into my words," when readers are angry at what you wrote. Wait till you can refrain from saying, "I answered your objection right there on page three," and instead just nod your head and think to yourself, "Oh, I see. That's helpful. You've shown me that what I say on page three doesn't seem to be working—for you anyway. I wonder if I need to do something about that." Wait till you don't feel you have to *please* readers, just use them. The goal is to hear what your readers tell you and not defend against it, and you can't do that if they have too much power over you. Even after you are used to getting full feedback, you sometimes need to say, for particular pieces of writing, "I'm not ready for criticism on this piece. Tell me what works, what you like, and what you think I'm saying and that's all." I've finally learned to do this.

Readers can give you the kind of feedback you need if you make your request clear and insist on it. Occasionally you need to interrupt them if they forget. And it's perfectly feasible to have a group where some people only share, others call for only noncritical feedback, and others want "the works." And people can change their request from week to week.

• Do you care more about immediately revising this particular piece of writing or more about learning in a long-term way about the reactions of readers to the way you write? When your goal is immediate revising, you will probably be interested in the direct suggestions for fixing your draft that arise from criterion-based feedback. You can frankly pick your readers' minds for advice and for their thinking on the topic. You can even let yourself interrupt them when they trigger a good insight: "Wait a minute! I just realized what I really *meant* to say. . . ." If it's an early rough draft, you may be more interested in discussing the topic and your general approach than in getting much feedback on your actual writing. You may permit yourself to argue with readers about the topic as a way of bringing out new ideas and getting closer to the truth (as long as arguing doesn't make them unwilling to share their ideas and reactions). But don't neglect reader-based feedback. And make sure you spend plenty of time with your mouth shut. Often you write the best revisions only after you finally discover what it *feels* like inside your reader's skin: suddenly you are struck with a much better approach to your topic and a more effective voice—just by listening to someone utterly misunderstand what you were saying.

But perhaps you don't care so much about revising this piece of writing (though you may in fact revise it). What you care about most is developing a better feel for the interaction between your words and the consciousness of readers—a better feel for different fish on your line. When you want feedback for the long haul, you need to get it regularly and to emphasize reader-based feedback. And to listen.

For long-haul learning it pays to get feedback not only on middle and late drafts, but also sometimes on unrevised writing or even freewriting. You will feel naked and vulnerable because such writing has glaring weaknesses you could easily correct. But such feedback will tell you important things about your habitual tones of voice and spontaneous habits of language and thought. Such feedback can lead to deeper and more pervasive improvement in your writing than any other kind.

When you get feedback on unrevised writing, you should ask your readers to tell you about the tones of voice, habits of mind, and ways of relating to readers that they hear in your words—rather than emphasizing whether the words are successful. It is a more personal kind of feedback. In a sense you are inviting them to read your diary. It is crucial that both you and they understand it is fine—beneficial, in fact—for your most unacceptable voices and habits of mind to show. Don't let them make you feel bad when they hear an ugly snarl or hopeless whine in your words, for example, or some habitual verbal fidget. Only by getting better acquainted with such voices or habits of mind, inhabiting them and perhaps even experimentally exaggerating them, will you gradually learn to get control over them so they don't seep into all your writing in subtle forms.*

* "For years I've suffered from male leads in my books being afflicted with selfpity. My leads would whine, beg, play the little boy in ways that seemed to defeat all my.

• How much arguing do you want vs. plain listening? The believing game or the doubting game? (See the appendix essay on these two processes in *Writing Without Teachers*.) I tend to favor the believing game. It's not that readers should try to believe or like the writing. But everyone should try to see the writing through the eyes of whoever is giving feedback at that moment. When it's your turn to give feedback you tell how you saw the words, but while another reader is reacting you never say "Wait a minute, that doesn't make sense because. . . ." By trying to see things through the other readers' eyes you deepen your own reading skills and you help produce an atmosphere of safety and trust that permits others to see and speak better.

But the believing game is not easy. It takes discipline. Some people have a hard time putting their full effort into trying to see through someone else's eyes. Sometimes the energy goes out of a discussion. People are merely putting on their Sunday manners and refraining from argument—not really entering into other people's perceptions. (There is a different kind of energy that occurs when people manage to play the believing game—quieter but no less intense.) And when it's your turn to get feedback on your writing, you need disciplined self-control. Readers will sometimes trick you into talking and not listening by asking you what you really meant here or how you came up with your approach

---

purposes. In my new novel, the same sort of thing began to happen; Buck Ravel fairly pouted all the time I was striving to have him be fairly responsible and self-aware. For six weeks I brought in parts of the book to read, and I kept getting the group more and more pissed off and upset—particularly two gutsy women. They were tired of him, couldn't he buck up, what a baby he was, and who could be attracted to such a pathetic figure? Each week I got more and more depressed over the direction of the book, and I saw that I was going to lose six months of hard work on this book if I didn't handle where Buck was.

"What I did was to sit down and bat out a fast 3,500 words in which I MADE BUCK DO ALL THE THINGS I'D BEEN KEEPING HIM FROM DOING. If I'd been trying to keep him from being a baby, now I made him be a baby. If I'd been trying to keep him from whining, now he whined about everything. And if he was a pathetic figure, I made him more pathetic, till he was nothing but pathetic.

"That broke a dam in the book. Much of what I wrote I found a use for in the book, but much more importantly, I took responsibility for what was oozing out of Buck's skin. Instead of dodging it, I owned it, I made it mine. By HAVING it happen instead of pushing it away, I got in control of it."

Thus Donald Porter to me in a letter about his experiences using a feedback group for his writing. He runs workshops for writers: *The Writing Workshop*, in connection with the Hunter College Center for Lifelong Learning in New York City.

there. You have to turn their questions around into feedback: "What was happening inside you that led you to ask that question?" Readers will also goad you into arguing by misunderstanding what you made *perfectly* clear or criticizing your best passages. You can answer their questions and refute their calumnies after you finish really seeing it their way.

Needless to say, the doubting game can be equally powerful if everyone is up for it. Wrestling can lead to the truth. You can have instructive arguments about the merits of two different ways of organizing some piece of writing or between competing explanations for why most readers ignored the same passage in a piece of writing.

But doubting or believing, it's never useful to let an argument drift into a question of whether a reader was *right* to have the response she had. If readers get the sense that they may be criticized or ridiculed for having peculiar reactions, they will begin to censor and you will no longer get trustworthy feedback. I am leery even of pressing people too hard to *explain* their reactions for fear they will only give reactions they can justify. When you ask a reader to *explain* her reaction it almost always seems as though you are saying, "Prove that it's not wrong or crazy." If you just ask her to tell *more about* her reaction, it feels more like "Help me see the words through your eyes." Value peculiar reactions. They will teach you the most. The best feedback groups I have seen have been characterized by a combination of great frankness and great trust.

• Whether or not you are paying back readers with feedback on their writing, pay them back in other ways. Give them credit. Tell them how helpful they were, and when it fits the kind of writing you are doing, tell in footnotes or introductions that you are indebted to————or that your final version owes much to the helpful feedback of————.

Make sure you give them a manuscript that is neat and easy to read—even if you are asking a good friend for feedback on a very early draft where you haven't even figured out your main idea. It's all right in such a draft to be fumbling for what you want to say as long as your reader can follow you perfectly as you fumble. On the early draft you can help readers immensely by including passages where you talk straight, as though talking directly to them, clarifying your struggle: "What I'm trying to get at in this section is the idea that . . ." or "I'm confused at this point because I argued one way in the first few pages, but here all my evidence is pointing in the opposite direction." (Besides, it helps to get in the habit of writing out these baffled musings as part of your draft—instead of stopping your pencil when they hit you and just thinking them. Writing them out often starts to untangle your confusion.)

You repay readers best by showing them that you actually use them. That doesn't mean always trying to follow their advice (even if they happen to agree with each other, which is rare). It's not their advice which is most valuable, but their perceptions and reactions. You can show them that you not only listen, but actually understand what they are saying. Practice believing it all, even when it's contradictory. Let them see you being shaken loose from your belief in something false or from your preference for a piece of your own weak writing.

Getting Feedback in Writing Support Groups

Adapted from a note to myself, about four years ago:

> I suddenly thought about how I don't have the kind of fear of the unknown I used to have when it comes to writing words down or reacting to words. I know very clearly what has caused this change. It's because I have engaged in feedback workshops over the last few years: getting feedback, giving feedback, hearing others give feedback different from mine; having discussions where the goal was not to agree with each other or figure out what is right, but to see the words through the other person's eyes; constant practice in experiencing and reexperiencing what a set of words can do. Events like this:
> • I hear a particular reaction to a particular word or image and suddenly the whole piece is thrown into a different meaning. Neither mine nor the new one seems better or more complete—merely different.
> • Someone gets mad at a piece of writing. But then, after seeing movies of other readers' minds, he sees something he'd missed and changes his reaction completely. I end up understanding how natural it was to be mad when that piece was missing; and understanding what the writer needs to do to make sure other readers don't miss that piece.
> • I am left cold by a piece of writing and then, through someone else's reading, suddenly the words open up for me and let me enter in, and I see things I hadn't seen. I reflect on what would have had to

be different in the words—or different in me—for the writing to work on me. I conclude that there is only the slimmest chance that such a piece of writing could work for me without the extra help of fellow readers. Yet I can now nevertheless see the virtue of the writing which before I dismissed as poor.

• Someone has a weird reaction to a set of words, but eventually we discover his reaction reflects very accurately some feeling in the writer which had nothing to do with what he was writing. The reader felt the writer mad at him, but it was just a clean, straightforward piece of explanation. No one else felt anything like that. But the writer reveals he was furious at someone at home when he was writing. The rest of us then can get a few whiffs of anger lurking behind the words. We would never have discovered the truth in that strange reaction—the tiny ingredient in the writing that probably affects all readers even subliminally—if we hadn't worked hard to see the words through that one reader's seemingly peculiar eyes.

It must be like what a psychiatrist or therapist might feel after working years and years—if she doesn't go numb or cynical. A sense of having *seen* more of people than most get a chance to see, not being shocked or frightened by what goes on. Nothing human seems alien. Yes, that's what I feel. Not shocked or dismayed at the unexpected things words can do, at the bewildering variety of ways people can react to words. It's a mystery and a mess, but now I can get inside it and see that in fact it makes sense.

I don't run away from the mess any more. I'm more willing to get my hands dirty, to try and make sense of what words actually do to readers, to try and do things to people with words, to try and understand why my words succeed or fail in any given case. From a few years of writing groups I seem to have gotten something I didn't get in many years of study and teaching.

The most effective way to get feedback for overall improvement of your writing and for learning about the effects of words on readers is in a writing support group that meets regularly. This is also the most enjoyable way to get feedback. You need a group of from four to ten people who have promised to come for at least eight meetings—perhaps weekly or biweekly—and bring a piece of writing each time. (It needen't be good writing. If someone says, "I'll bring something if I'm satisfied with it," you haven't got a member.) It takes a while for people to get practice and to trust each other and they need to be able to count on each other to be there.

You can devote all your time to feedback, but I think it helps to give a certain amount of time each meeting to sharing. You could start each session with a quick freewriting exercise and have everyone share some of it; or start with a reading of short pieces people brought with them. A simple method is to have half the group bring pieces for sharing and the other half bring pieces for feedback. This makes it easier to handle writing from a larger group. And it promotes a natural cycle: one week just share an early and perhaps exploratory draft; let it settle and work on it some more; and then get feedback on a revised version the next week. Sometimes people can give particularly helpful feedback because they heard last week's rough writing.

Time. It is hard to give feedback to more than five or six pieces of writing in one sitting. You probably need fifteen minutes per piece—longer if it must be read out loud. And much longer if you want to get into discussions rather than just listen to each other's feedback.

It's important to decide at the start of each meeting how long you have and how many pieces need feedback so you can divide up the time equally. You seldom feel "done" when the time is up so a timekeeper needs to be blunt about calling time, and the group must ruthlessly move on. Otherwise the later people get cheated. You can try giving more time to longer pieces of writing but that leads to tricky computations. There is nothing wrong with the simple proposition that everyone deserves the same amount of time because everyone *gives* the same amount of time. Then each person gets to spend her time as she prefers—on a long piece or a short piece.

Leadership. The best sort of leadership is provided if each writer takes charge of her own time. She needs to say what she wants (for example, no negative feedback, or arguments are welcome, or whatever). It's her job to use her own time best—ensuring, for example, that she hears from each of the readers, or that some important aspect of her writing is not neglected. The writer could, of course, delegate leadership to someone else: "Here, you take charge. I want to be free to listen and take notes." Or you could have people take turns being in charge of each meeting. Or if one person is much more experienced, she could be in charge of all meetings. But I think the writer learns more in the long run—and that is the goal, after all—if she is in charge of the feedback process for her own writing. It helps overcome the main thing that holds people back in writing: feeling helpless or powerless. If a reader doesn't seem to tell you how she reacted to your piece or wastes a lot of time saying almost nothing, or if everyone seems to neglect the aspect of your piece you are most curious about, you might at first feel awkward about pushing them a bit. But you will learn fairly quickly to ask for what you need. And it turns out that people will give it more easily when *you* ask for it than when some "chairman" asks for it.

But even though each writer should *take charge* of her own time it also helps to have someone else (say, the person to the left of the writer) be a kind of *monitor* of certain simple but crucial procedural matters. The group will hold together better and each writer will find it easier to get the feedback she needs if the monitor performs these functions:

- keeps time;
- prevents anyone from talking more than her share of the time;
- stops arguments;
- points out to the writer if she is disagreeing or making excuses instead of just listening.

For the first couple of meetings use very limited feedback if any: just summaries, telling things you liked, and pointing to passages that had resonance. And let readers toss out their feedback in bits and pieces as it occurs to them. People get more comfortable and confident in giving feedback because the spotlight isn't so much on them.

But after a few weeks move to fuller feedback for those who want it and put the spotlight on each reader in turn so she can give as much feedback as possible before the next reader speaks. This is important because you are trying to find out what it is like inside the skin of individual readers, not arrive at some kind of average reaction or consensus opinion. Your message to each reader should be "I need to know what it was like being *you* as you read my words." Don't be satisfied till you get that. After a while you will.

After all the readers have given feedback, they may have more reactions that occur to them on the basis of having heard the others. If there is time and inclination you can have a discussion at this point instead of just individual statements. And the writer can now at last respond and say some things of her own instead of just listening and drawing out readers. For example she might want to talk about the audience and purpose she has in mind for this writing or tell what she was trying to get across or answer some questions that readers asked earlier as part of their feedback.

Put the emphasis on reader-based feedback: finding out what happened in real readers. That doesn't mean you shouldn't sometimes ask for extensive criterion-based feedback (for instance when you are working on something you are about to revise), but make sure to get the reader-based reactions that lie beneath any piece of criterion-based feedback.

No arguments. When people start to argue you know something is wrong because there is nothing to argue about. There is no right answer to defend, no wrong answer to defeat. The only goal is to learn what happened in each reader. Afterward the writer may want to decide for herself which of two conflicting reactions is most likely to occur in her target audience, but right now her job is to learn those reactions and if possible even to experience them. Arguments will interfere with her doing so.

It's worth taking the last five minutes of each session for everyone briefly to tell one thing she liked and one thing she felt could have gone better in the meeting. It's not a time to discuss these things or try to solve problems. But with just these brief comments, most problems about how the group functions will in fact solve themselves.

Summary of Advice for Writing Support Groups

- Insist on a commitment to come and to bring writing.
- Have some sharing in each meeting.
- Give equal time to each writer.
- Let the writer be in charge of her feedback time.
- Use a monitor.
- No arguments.
- No negative feedback for the first few weeks.
- Get each reader to give summary, pointing, and some positive feedback to each piece.
- Get reader-based reactions for all criterion-based feedback.
- Take five minutes at the end for brief positive and negative comments on the meeting itself.

There may be many good reasons why you will depart from these rather strict rules. But if you find your group lagging or get-

ting unpleasant in tone or beginning to fall apart, go back to following these rules. They are designed to maximize trust, support, and
honesty. I believe these are the essential ingredients for a successful writing support group.*

---

*See Chapters 4 and 5 of *Writing Without Teachers* for more about feedback workshops. I would be grateful, by the way, to hear from readers of this book about their
experiences in feedback groups that function on a peer basis—i.e., without being
run by a teacher or writing authority:
- What helps your group function well?
- What impedes it?
- Describe some memorable moments, perplexing episodes, critical incidents.

VI

POWER IN WRITING

INTRODUCTION

A reader has two pieces of writing before her, one by you and one by your friend. Yours is better writing by most standards. It has a clearer and more graceful style, a more logical and coherent organization. It also has more original and better thinking. In addition, your topic interests the reader more than your friend's topic. The reader picks up both pieces to look them over, starts reading yours and notes that she likes it, but starts to look over your friend's piece just to see what it is like. Once she starts reading your friend's piece, however, she keeps on going and never returns to yours. She has been captured and cannot put it down. She is affected deeply by it even though it is not so well written as yours and not what she had wanted to read about.

If this hasn't happened to you, you've probably seen it happen. Some writing has great power over readers even though it is not as "good" by most conventional measures. In this section I seek to know what this deeper power consists of and how to get it.

The most plausible answer is that for words to have power they must fit the reader. You must give readers either the style or the content they want, preferably both. But I'm not satisfied with the answer that says power comes from making your words fit the reader. Is it really power if you just give them what they want? If you write a novel, don't you really want to reach more readers than those who already resonate to your style or who already see things the way you do? Are you willing to talk of the evils of nuclear power only at anti-nuclear rallies to people who already agree with you? Power means the power to make a difference, to make a dent. When people call a piece of writing excellent, sometimes what they really mean is that it made no dent at all: it merely confirmed them in their prior thoughts and feelings.

I assume in this section that of course you will often try to fit your words to your readers. (In Section IV, Audience, I suggest some ways to do so.) Nevertheless when you want power in your words—especially when you want the power of the Ancient Mariner to transfix readers and make them hear what they don't want to hear or give them an experience they didn't set out to have— you must be seeking something other than how to fit words to readers.

The analogy of the Ancient Mariner is appropriate because I think true power in words is a mystery. In the chapters that follow I explore different hypotheses to get closer to this mystery. In Chapters 25 and 26 about voice, I suggest that power comes from the words somehow fitting the *writer* (not necessarily the reader). That good fit between the writer and her words makes for resonance: the words bore through to readers no matter what their disposition. In Chapters 27 and 28 about breathing experience into writing, I suggest that power comes from the words somehow fitting *what they are about*. The words so well *embody* what they express that when readers encounter the words they feel they are encountering the objects or ideas themselves, not words: readers get experiences, nothing is lost in translation. In Chapter 29, "Writing and Magic," I explore the notion that perhaps the writer's job is really to put a hex on words or on readers.

This section is more speculative than the others in the book. I am exploring what can only be called risky hypotheses. But though I am letting myself wax theoretical, I am also deriving a good deal of concrete practical advice from these hypotheses. I believe that if you actually try out the advice you will find the hypotheses themselves more compelling. (The whole section applies to both creative and expository writing except for Chapter 28 which applies especially to expository writing.)

25

Writing and Voice

> A dramatic necessity goes deep into the nature of the sentence. Sentences are not different enough to hold the attention unless they are dramatic. No ingenuity of varying structure will do. All that can save them is the speaking tone of voice somehow entangled in the words and fastened to the page for the ear of the imagination. That is all that can save poetry from sing-song, all that can save prose from itself.
>
> ROBERT FROST, Introduction, *A Way Out*

I am writing here about resonance. I think of a fancy men's room stall with highly polished black marble walls running all the way from floor to ceiling. "They really believe in privacy here," I thought to myself, but as I was humming under my breath without thinking about it, I began to notice that some of the notes seemed too loud. Gradually I figured out—trying different tunes and finally a chromatic scale—that I was sitting in a box that resonated perfectly to one frequency.

That polished black box is the perfect analogy for a clunky violin: a box that resonates to one note and muffles all the rest. The perfect violin, of course, would resonate to all notes richly and equally. But, in fact, no matter how good a violin is, it needs to be "played in"—played long and vigorously—before it resonates well to all its frequencies. It takes weeks or months. And the clunkiest violin can in fact be played in and made to expand its repertoire of resonances. So maybe if I'd sat in that marble stall and sung loudly for days and weeks I could have gotten it to give richness to one or two more notes.

The underlying metaphor for this chapter is that we all have a chest cavity unique in size and shape so that each of us naturally resonates to one pitch alone. Someone is 440 vibrations per second (Concert A), you may be 375, I am perhaps 947. Most of us try to sing the note we like best or the note we've been told to sing, but the sound is usually muffled or inaudible because it's not our note. We are never heard. A few people, it is true, sing with ringing power, but no one seems to understand how they manage this, not even they. In this metaphorical world, then, even if we figure out the system, we are stuck. If we want to be heard we are limited to our single note. If we want to sing other notes, we will not be heard.

And yet, if we are brave and persistent enough to sing our own note at length—to develop our capacity for resonance—gradually we will be able to "sing ourselves in": to get resonance first into one or two more frequencies and then more. Finally, we will be able to sing whatever note we want to sing, even to sing whatever note others want to hear, and to make every note resound with rich power. But we only manage this flowering if we are willing to start off singing our own single tiresome pitch for a long time and in that way gradually teach the stiff cells of our bodies to vibrate and be flexible.

How I Got Interested in Voice

For a long time I had a sense there was something you could call "voice" which was important in writing, but in the last few years I've been impelled to try to think the matter out more fully. What started this round of thinking was teaching a course in autobiography in which I required students to write 15 pages a week. It didn't have to be any particular kind of writing, it could be freewriting, babbling, incoherent. I didn't enforce any definition of autobiographical writing. I didn't grade it. I didn't even think that I would read it: 15 pages a week from 20 students was too much. I had set up the students in pairs where they were supposed to read each other's writing in full each week and then give me only a few pages to read. But these pairs broke down and that left me getting a student's notebook every other week and trying to read 30 pages in it. I found myself reading quickly and intermittently. My standards for reading became fairly selfish: if I was enjoying the words, I kept on; if not, I tended to start skipping. (Students weren't required, by the way, to show me everything—they could signify sections they wanted to keep private.)

But gradually, a new and mysterious standard began to emerge. That writing was most fun and rewarding to read that somehow felt most "real." It had what I am now calling voice. At the time I said things like, "It felt real, it had a kind of resonance, it somehow rang true."

Sometimes these passages were short—a phrase or a sentence in length—a kind of parenthetical aside or a digression in the middle of something else. Sometimes the passages were much longer. Sometimes it was a particular thought that had greater conviction, sometimes it was a particular feeling—an angry, happy, sarcastic, or even self-pitying observation—that somehow rang truer than its surroundings. Sometimes these passages with voice seemed good by other standards, sometimes they were not good writing at all. Sometimes they were bursts of sincerity, but not always. Sometimes I couldn't identify *anything* special about these passages in style or content. It was just that they seemed to jump out at me as though suddenly the writer had switched to a fresh typewriter ribbon.

On some days these passages jumped out at me very clearly: it's as though I could hear a gear being engaged and disengaged. On other days I had no sense of where there was voice and where not: it all seemed alike. I could use all my other standards for writing, but as for realness or resonance or voice I couldn't tell one passage from another.

I began to mark these passages with a line in the margin, and I simply told students that these passages seemed to me to have strength, resonance, power. I said I liked reading them and that something special seemed to be going on. I usually asked whether they also felt something special. Often the students recognized that these passages represented a particular *kind* of writing for them—they could remember a particular feeling or sensation they had as they wrote them. Sometimes not. Often students were surprised at my choices since these passages didn't always feel to them like their best writing. I didn't give any reactions to passages that seemed to lack voice. For the most part I gave only positive feedback. Criticism would have worked against my goals for this course: to get students to write a great deal, to have confidence in their ability to produce writing at will, and to produce in one term such a large pile of autobiographical writing that they wouldn't be able to keep themselves from coming back sometime later to work on it.

A few students seemed to know exactly what I was talking about and value the feedback and want more. A few, at the other end, were very bothered and seemed to use my feedback to prevent themselves from ever doing this kind of writing again. It's as though I'd found a leak and they promptly plugged it.

For most students, however, it was as though I'd planted a seed. They didn't necessarily accept these passages as good writing. I didn't ask them to. I pressed them simply to accept the fact that such passages really did have power for me as one reader. As a result, students seemed to mull the matter over in their minds. They wondered about it as they wrote. They wondered what passages I would pick out next time. Some of them began to get a feel for when they were doing it and when not. They developed a sense of internal cues.

In this process I feel I am giving students permission—indeed an invitation—to move in a direction they've never been invited to move in before. To the extent that they do—that is, to the extent that they begin to listen to my feedback and try to produce some more of what I praise—I think I see a lot of things begin to happen in their writing. Students begin to like writing more, to write about things that are more important to them, and thus to feel a greater connection between their writing and themselves. I think this process leads not just to learning, but to growth or development. Searching for more voice starts them on a journey—a path toward new thoughts, feelings, memories and new modes of seeing and writing. But it is not clear either to the student or to me where the path will lead.

Here are some of the things that seem to happen when students accept even tentatively the invitation to work on voice. First of all, the process affects subject matter. For some students it means writing more about the incidents or observations that were in the marked passages. For others it means exploring those same feelings: perhaps angry feelings, perhaps depressed feelings, perhaps a particular area of their lives. For others it means exploring certain trains of thought. When I give this same kind of feedback in courses that emphasize expository writing, the process often leads students to writing that is autobiographical or self-exploratory—

though not always. But as they explore these areas, character-istically the students come upon more memories, more feelings, more thoughts—often *new* ones. It is not infrequent for a student to say "I've started writing about a part of my life I haven't thought about in years. I'm remembering new things."

My invitation also tends to lead to experimentation: swings of style and mood and mode. It sometimes feels to the student as though I have simply invited *bad* writing since—for some students especially—I find resonance in passages where the writing stops being careful and starts coming apart. Subsequent experiments by the students, then, sometimes lead to writing in which I find nei-ther quality nor voice—merely excessive, dramatized, even hys-terical words with no power at all. But I have an intuition that these experiments are appropriate and useful no matter what the results and so I don't find it hard to refrain from giving negative feedback. I just keep looking for passages that have power. When a student says "What about this?" and points to a passage that ob-viously reflects deep feeling and great excitement at the time of writing but seems completely lacking in power or voice to me, I say I didn't feel power or resonance in it, perhaps even that I didn't like it, but emphasize again that this seems to be a mysteri-ous and subjective business. In a given case I may *feel* certain that the passage lacks quality or power, but on principle I don't believe that any one person's judgment about voice is trustworthy.

My feedback on voice often has yet another effect. Students often come to feel a need to withdraw from writing for an audi-ence. That is, some of the students are quite skilled already and like to write stories, essays, or poems for an audience. But as they explore power in these often new areas of writing, they sometimes don't want to share their writing with anyone—often not even with me. What made these writers skilled was their superior control: the ability to produce just the effect they wanted upon readers. Now they need privacy for experimenting with what is, in effect, an invitation to relinquish control.

Though some of the new memories may be painful, my invita-tion usually leads to more pleasure in writing. It's as though the person has a sense of simply making more *noise* in putting a pencil to paper. It reminds me of a child who gets a loud new toy and just delights in the din. Also of my own sensations when, as I worked on viola bowing exercises, there were brief, round, fat, resonant sounds; brief sheddings of tension in the muscles of my arm and shoulder. I would immediately try to recapture the sound and fail, but over the weeks these interludes of resonance would come more frequently and finally I could usually do it at will and make the instrument and my body resonate together. Then there was a great pleasure just in bowing and bowing—even if it was just one or two notes—to make the roundest, loudest, most ringing sound possible. Similarly, there is a yoga "sound-box" exercise in which you chant a vowel and try to achieve a ringing sound by learning to let the head and chest area resonate.

At first, students can only get this power or voice in the kinds of passages where it first appeared: certain moods, certain memories, certain trains of thought. But, gradually, over weeks and months, if they experiment and try to let this power declare itself and see where it might lead them, it transfers to or becomes available in other areas of writing. For example, perhaps there was a peculiar resonance in passages that were angry or self-pitying—or in descriptions of certain kinds of places. But then, gradually, as the writer does more and more of this particular kind of writing, she gets better at feeling and using this power, and so very slowly the resonance comes to characterize a few more kinds of writing. If at first students could only do it with passages of autobiographical writing that explored certain kinds of incidents, then gradually they could get it in other kinds of incidents, and gradually even in expository writing. For some students, voice came first in certain kinds of expository writing.

It is this experience in the last few years that has impelled me to try to work out a fuller theory of voice. For the power I am seeking, some people use words like *authenticity* or *authority*. Many people call it *sincerity*, but I think that's misleading because this power can be present when the writing is not really sincere and absent when the writing is sincere. I like to call this power *juice*. The metaphor comes to me again and again, I suppose, because I'm trying to get at something mysterious and hard to define. "Juice" combines the qualities of *magic potion, mother's milk*, and *electricity*. Sometimes I fear I will never be clear about what I mean by voice. Certainly I have waxed incoherent on many occasions. One teacher I admire, Ellen Nold, heard me struggling unsuccessfully to explain myself to a meeting of writing teachers at Stanford University. She wrote me:

The voice phenomenon cannot well be discussed in rationalistic terms; every time you tried to define the conditions of it arising, you failed hopelessly. Why not just give up? Why not confront Voice for what it is?

What is It? That's the question Hinduism, Buddhism, Taoism are built around. The very question is a Zen koan. We all know, as Persig in *Zen and the Art of Motorcycle Maintenance* points out, that Quality exists, and we can agree pretty well what writing has Quality and what does not. Quality is the same as Voice is the same as Tao is the same as Self is the same as Atman-Brahman is the same as . . . When I speak with Voice, It's loud because It speaks directly to your Ear, not just to your ear, which is constantly distracted by other voices. . . . You teach writing by pointing out to students when your Ear hears and asking them to do more of That. The rationalists tear their hair out. Can that be teaching? Where is the content? The technique? What is this Voice? Where can I buy an Ear? How do I know that my Ear is like your Ear?

Most teachers have ears, but their Ears are covered. Because they have never thought that Voice is the province of the public school, even if they valued It, they wouldn't ask for It. You ask for It. You tell others that It's there to be sensed and asked for. . . . Don't try to explain it to rationalistic people in rationalistic terms! It is something that ultimately cannot be explained to anyone who hasn't heard. And those who have heard will forgive you for the inadequacy of your words.

But I cannot resist trying to work this thing out more fully and rationally. For one thing I want to be able to explain it to more people—even to people who haven't heard it. Besides, I needed to figure out if voice was the right word. Voice, in writing, implies words that capture the sound of an individual on the page. But though that seems central to what I'm fishing for, sometimes I found passages with this sound—yes, these words had been breathed into—yet the words somehow lacked the deeper power and resonance that had gradually become the object of my quest.

Voice and No Voice

Writing with no voice is dead, mechanical, faceless. It lacks any sound. Writing with no voice *may* by saying something true, important, or new; it may be logically organized; it may even be a work of genius. But it is as though the words came through some kind of mixer rather than being uttered by a person. Extreme lack of voice is characteristic of bureaucratic memos, technical engineering writing, much sociology, many textbooks:

> Tests should reflect changes in learned behavior; the normal utilization of reliability estimates must be revised since it is assumed that we are not measuring a trait or innate mental capacity but rather an acquired skill or concept which can be measured incrementally. Thus scores should reflect changes from one administration to the next. [From an essay about education.]

Nobody is at home here. In its extreme form, no voice is the army-manual style. But the sad truth is that the careful writing of most people lacks voice.

Voice, in contrast, is what most people have in their speech but lack in their writing—namely, a sound or texture—the sound of "them." We recognize most of our friends on the phone before they say who they are. A few people get their voice into their writing. When you read a letter or something else they've written, it has the sound of them. It feels as though writing with voice has life in it. It's almost as though the breath makes the words themselves do some of the work of getting up off the page into our head as we read. We need only pass our eyes, like phonograph needles, along the grooves and magically sounds and meanings will form in our head.

Here is a piece of expository writing in which I find voice.

> The scheme of thought I have outlined in this third lecture explains the balance of faculties that should be cultivated in scientific research. Imaginativeness and a critical temper are both necessary at all times, but neither is sufficient. The most imaginative scientists are by no means the most effective; at their worst, uncensored, they are cranks. Nor are the most critically minded. The man notorious for his dismissive criticisms, strenuous in the pursuit of error, is often unproductive, as if he had scared himself out of his own wits—unless indeed his critical cast of mind was the consequence rather than the cause of his infertility.*

Notice how that jargony piece of educational writing (and perhaps also the final clause in the Medawar excerpt) suffers from the writing process itself. That educational psychologist would never

---

*Induction and Intuition in Scientific Thought, Sir Peter Medawar (Philadelphia, 1968), p. 58.

talk so. She must have had a sense of intended meaning and then *constructed* words to express it. The words lack breath or presence. If she had been talking rather than writing, that same intended meaning would have produced words which were more alive (however lacking in precision or conciseness). It would take her an extra step of revising—and revising consciously for the sake of voice—to change her written words so as to break out of that *language-construction* into a *saying-of-words* on paper.

But just as often it works the other way. You have voice in your first draft and you revise it away. As you clarify your thinking or correct your language you dissipate the breath. We can see that happening in the two paragraphs below. The first one is an early draft in which I find voice. But I think the writer lost that voice when she revised her paragraph in an effort to make it assert one opinion more definitely.

> In the United States there is supposed to be freedom of expression, and yet there are laws against obscenity. No one can say what obscenity really is. And is obscene material really harmful? Maybe some forms of censorship are necessary, but this is just another instance of our country being called free when it is not.
>
> We should admit that freedom of expression is not truly realized in the United States, since the censoring of materials which are considered obscene constitute a definite limitation of this freedom.

In giving a more focused emphasis to the paragraph she lost all the voice, breath, and rhythm that had given life to the first version.

It's not surprising that most people don't get voice into their writing. Writing is so much slower and more troublesome than speaking. So many more decisions have to be made. You must form each word, one letter at a time and figure out the spelling. Writing needs punctuation; it has stricter and less familiar standards of grammar and usage. And in addition to all the extra rules involved in writing, we feel we'll be more harshly judged if we write something foolish or mistaken than if we just say it: "It's down in black and white."

On those speaking occasions when we feel especially judged—for example during a job interview or when we meet a new person we want to impress but fear we won't—even our speech is likely to lose voice: we are likely to speak carefully and even haltingly, choosing our words guardedly, thinking all the while about whether our words are clear, correct, and intelligent. If we heard a recording of our speech in that situation we would probably say that it doesn't sound like us or that it sounds as if we are trying to be someone else or that it doesn't sound like a real person at all.

Imagine if all our speaking were done on occasions like that. Or worse yet, if we were graded and judged and told all our smallest mistakes every time we opened our mouths. We'd get painfully awkward and unnatural in speech. For most people, that is how writing is. They've never written unless required to do so in school, and every mistake on every piece of writing they've ever done was circled in red. No wonder most people's writing doesn't have voice—doesn't sound lively and "like them" the way their speaking usually does.

There are some people, of course, who lack voice even in their speech. They have developed a habit of speaking in a careful or guarded way so that you cannot hear any real rhythm and texture. Their speech sounds wooden, dead, fake. Some people who have sold their soul to a bureaucracy come to talk this way. Some people speak without voice who have immersed themselves in a lifelong effort to think logically or scientifically—who have built up the habit of considering the validity of every word before they utter it. Some people lack voice in their speech who are simply very frightened: they experience all of life as a job interview for a job they doubt they'll get.

It's easy to use this distinction between voice and no voice. We may disagree about borderline cases, but we can probably agree that it's valid and even useful to distinguish writing by whether the author breathed a sound and a human rhythm into it. It's easy to hear voice in this excerpt from *Falconer* by John Cheever (the main character is writing a letter) and lack of voice in the business card message that follows it:

I can remember coming back to the Danieli on the Lido after a great day on the beach when we had both been solicited by practically everybody. It was at that hour when the terrible, the uniquely terrible band began to play terrible, terrible tangos and the beauties of the evening, the girls and boys in their handmade clothes, had begun to emerge. I can remember this but I don't choose to. The landscapes that come to mind are unpleasantly close to what one finds on greeting cards—the snowbound farmhouse is recurrent—but I would like to settle for something inconclusive. It is late in the day. We have spent the day on a beach. I can tell because we are burned from the sun and there is sand in my shoes. A taxi—some hired livery—has brought us to a provincial railroad station, an isolated place, and left us there. The station is locked and there is no town, no farmhouse, no sign of life around the place excepting a stray dog. When I look at the timetable nailed to the station house I realize that we are in Italy although I don't know where. I've chosen this memory because there are few specifics. We have either missed the train or there is no train or the train is late. I don't remember. I can't even remember laughter or a kiss or putting my arm around your shoulder as we sat on a hard bench in an empty provincial railroad station in some country where English was not spoken. The light was going, but going as it so often does, with a fanfare. All I really remember is a sense of your company and a sense of physical contentment.

Jon's Taxi Service

Our motto: To render at all times the most courteous, efficient, dependable and conscientious service human endeavor is able to devise.

The voice/no voice distinction throws light on the odd case of Gertrude Stein. She doesn't just get voice into her writing. She heightens the effect by breaking rules in just such a way that we can't even understand her meaning unless we actually *say* her words. She invents a trick to force us to hear her words, not just read them visually:

> And what does a comma do, a comma does nothing but make easy a thing that if you like it enough is easy enough without the comma. A long complicated sentence should force itself upon you, make you know yourself knowing it and the comma, well at the most a comma is a poor period that it lets you stop and take a breath you ought to know yourself that you want to take a breath. It is not like stopping altogether which is what a period does stopping altogether has something to do with going on, but taking a breath well you are always taking a breath and why emphasize one breath rather than another breath. Anyway that is the way I felt about it and I felt that about it very very strongly. And so I almost never used a comma.
>
> GERTRUDE STEIN, "Poetry and Grammar," from *Lectures in America* (New York, 1935).

Real Voice

Why must I complicate the simple distinction between voice and no voice by introducing a third category, real voice? It's because I think there are some pieces of writing with the liveliness and energy of voice—and in this respect they have a great advantage over writing without voice—yet they lack the power and resonance of the Medawar and the Cheever. The following excerpt is an example (written by a student):

> It always kills me when I see somebody who can take an old toothbrush, a used toilet roll, and a ball of twine, and in ten minutes can whip up a sculpture to rival the beauty of any Da Vinci. Personally I am about as creative as Richard Nixon's joke writer. Something as simple as "Three Dozen Ways with Nylon Net" just flies right over my head. I mean, what would I use nylon net for anyway? To catch praying mantises in my dorm room? Line a shirt with it and wear it when I feel masochistic?
>
> Maybe I'm just frustrated. I just got back from my community kitchen, where my next-door neighbor, Alice Artistic, was cutting partridge-shaped seals from foil Sucrets wrappers to put on the back of her homemade envelopes in which she plans to mail her homemade Christmas cards. My Christmas cards consist of eight-cent postcards with "Noel" written on them in red Bic pen.
>
> I knew I had no artistic talent when my fourth-grade class made maps of Washington out of oatmeal and plywood. I colored mine with pink food coloring, spelled out "Wash" in the middle of it in silver cake-decorating balls and brought it home. My dog ate it for dinner.

This writing has the lively sound of speech. It has good timing. The words seem to issue naturally from a stance and personality. But what strikes me is how little I can feel the reality of any person in these words. I experience this as a lack of any deeper resonance. These words don't give off a solid thump that I can trust.

Consider the speech of certain hyped-up radio or television announcers or slick salesmen or over-earnest preachers: speech that is fluent and without hesitation, full of liveliness and energy, "full of expression" as we say—and yet its voice is blatantly fake. These people are doing some kind of imitation or unconscious parody of how an "expression-filled" voice is supposed to sound.

The speech of such announcers, salesmen, and preachers is merely an extreme example of voice-but-not-real-voice. It serves to illustrate blatantly what everyone sometimes does: adopt a voice in order to face an audience. Since their whole vocation consists of trying to sway an audience with their vocal chords, they are more likely to get trapped in some of these voices: the stakes are higher for them and they are more likely to try too hard and then gradually begin to stop hearing the fakeness. Actors, too, occasionally end up without a solid authenticity in their speech when they are off-stage, though they are usually more subtle than the heavy-handed salesman. They have spent so much time trying to control their voice that they no longer have the knack of just leaving it alone to be itself. But we all adopt less than authentic voices quite often, especially when the demands of a situation are great or our resources seem insufficent. If nervousness doesn't deaden and remove all voice it may make us giddy, talkative, or silly (such as at a party), or we may start sounding solemn and pompous (such as at a job interview). These nervous ways of speaking may have voice: fluency, energy, even individuality. They are gears: we don't have to stop and choose words consciously and pause for decisions. But we can easily see that these nervous voices are not real by a simple observation: if we finally become comfortable at that party or job interview, we stop sounding so giddy or pompous and start sounding like our real self.

Real self. Real voice. I am on slippery ground here. There are layers and layers. For example, if I am teaching a class and feel very insecure or shaky, I am liable to compensate without even thinking about it and adopt a very confident and assured tone of voice. A student who knows me well might sense something fishy in my voice. And if, perhaps, things go so badly that I finally decide to stop in the middle of something I am trying to explain or some activity I am trying to make happen—I explain that I can't really concentrate on what I'm doing and say that I am just going to sit on the sidelines of the discussion—that student might say, "Oh, I see now why he sounded fake, now he sounds more like Peter Elbow." But if I kept up that voice or stance or role for very long—class after class—a student who knew me well personally would be able to say, and correctly too, "Oh, Peter's fallen into his helpless, stuck gear again; that's not him, that's a tiresome habit. He's not daring to be as opinionated and stubborn and pushy as he really is."

Most people make use of various voices as they go through life to deal with particular audiences and situations. Many people speak with artificial sweetness to little children. Many teachers, administrators, doctors and judges adopt a confident, fatherly, competent tone of voice to express their authority or responsibility. If we only know them at work we might say, "That's just what John sounds like," but if he started talking that way at home his wife might say, "Come off it, John, you're not at work now; don't talk to me like I'm one of your clients."

But can I really say that some voices are more "real" than others? What if that really does sound like John. That is, perhaps he *used* to sound different at home and at the office, but gradually over the years his professional tone of voice came to take over all his home talk, too. Or perhaps John was one of those children who talked like a college professor in kindergarten.

Certainly some sociologists interested in role theory would simply insist that we all have a variety of roles at our disposal and that's that. If some "sound realer" than others, it's just that we're better at using those—we have practiced and learned them better. This sophisticated relativist approach may fit the whole range of intermediate voices we use moderately well in our living—the gears or roles we have easily available. But because I'm interested in the extreme cases—the obviously fake voice and especially the rare powerful voice that is somehow deeply authentic or resonant—I cannot stop thinking in terms of real voice. I'm not content to say a real voice is nothing but a well-learned role because when I see people starting to use their real voice I see it is usually *not* well learned. Often it is rusty and halting and they use it badly. And I see that when people start using their real voice, it tends to start them on a train of growth and empowerment in their way of using words—empowerment even in relating to people.

Our less than real voices usually help us to deal with pressures we feel from some audiences and situations, and protect the deeper layers of self. It's no accident that the greatest number of fake-sounding people are in professions where they must constantly meet and impress an audience: salesmen, announcers, politicians, preachers. (Teachers, too.) The pressure of an audience increases our need for privacy. Gears and roles permit us to achieve privacy in public, on the job.

I'm not saying people are wicked if they keep their real voice a secret, but they are neglecting a great source of power. Most of us, even though we don't sound as false as slick salesmen and hyped-up announcers, neglect this power of real voice. Our speech may be lively and fluent and sound just like us; we don't lack voice (not in our speaking, anyway, though we probably lack it badly in our writing). But we seldom use the power of our real voice, and we know it because of the surprising difference we feel on the few occasions when we do—when we get power into our words.

Sometimes it takes a kind of crisis situation for us to take the wraps off our power: perhaps we are backed into a corner and have to speak out to save our self-respect; perhaps it is an important letter; often the words come out late at night or under some other circumstance when the inhibitions of "normal reality" carry less weight. We notice the surprising impact of our words on the listener or reader. For once our words *work*. Often it is startling or even frightening when other people actually feel the full weight of our words: it so seldom happens. Sometimes they are frightened, too. They look at us wide-eyed with surprise and a look that says, "I like you better the regular, ineffectual way."

It may sound as though I'm describing a case where someone finally screams or has a tantrum. Perhaps. But sometimes that frightening power comes when a habitual screamer adopts a quiet whisper. Sometimes, that is, a scream is the sound of someone coming out from hiding, but often words from the center are quiet. Their power comes from inner resonance.

• • •

Some examples. I find real voice in the Medawar and Cheever pieces, above. Here is another piece of fiction—a passage from Section I, "The Window," of Virginia Woolf's *To The Lighthouse:*

The room (she looked round it) was very shabby. There was no beauty anywhere. She forebore to look at Mr. Tansley. Nothing seemed to have merged. They all sat separate. And the whole of the effort of merging and flowing and creating rested on her. Again she felt, as a fact without hostility, the sterility of men, for if she did not do it nobody would do it, and so, giving herself the little shake that one gives a watch that has stopped, the old familiar pulse began beating, as the watch begins ticking—one, two, three, one, two, three. And so on and so on, she repeated, listening to it, sheltering and fostering the still feeble pulse as one might guard a weak flame with a newspaper. And so then, she concluded, addressing herself by bending silently in his direction to William Bankes—poor man! who had no wife, and no children and dined alone in lodgings except for tonight; and in pity for him, life being now strong enough to bear her on again, she began all this business, as a sailor not without weariness sees the wind fill his sail and yet hardly wants to be off again and thinks how, had the ship sunk he would have whirled round and round and found rest on the floor of the sea.

"Did you find your letters? I told them to put them in the hall for you," she said to William Bankes.

Here are four other pieces of writing I have chosen to illustrate real voice.

> *To Be Carved on a Tower at Thoor Ballylee*
> I the poet William Yeats
> With old mill boards and sea-green slates
> And smithy work from the Gort forge
> Restored this tower for my wife George.
> And may these characters remain
> When all is ruin once again.
> WILLIAM BUTLER YEATS

This poem illustrates how words can have real voice without being at all talky or personal. One feels him saying something deeply felt, but it is rather a public, on-stage voice. He is writing, in a sense, through a megaphone.

I went on the job. My father took me. People was very nice. I like them, they like me. I work for a long long time. I used to cook. Lady didn't tell me but I want to learn. So she let me. I cook like I want, eat like I want, and cook for all. There was two other children older than the baby. I was doing fine until my boss' mother came to visit. Then she try to take over. I would cook or help cook and my boss' mother fix my breakfast, my lunch and my dinner on a plate with two biscuit. I took that for a day or so, then I had my clothes packed. Say to my madam that I was leaving. She want to know why. I say my father have plenty food home and I can eat and drink all I want. I say that lady fix my plate. I am used to fixing my own plate. Nobody know my stomach and how much I can eat. My madam say she didn't know that was what she was doing. "I will tell her to stop it." So the lady stop fixing my plate. Then I stay.

ESTELLE JONES, part of
unpublished autobiography

I choose this excerpt to illustrate that I sometimes hear real voice in language that violates some of the patterns of speech. One feels lots of "speech" in it, yet it does not exactly resemble the author's actual speech or anyone else's.

Roses

One day I woke up
and looked out my window
And there were roses all around,
Pink ones and red ones,
I went out and feeled them and feeled them,
And they were nice and soft
Like my sister's velvet dress,
And they smelled like a birthday cake
And like I would be in the woods
When I am walking.
[I have lost the citation for this poem,
    by a child, which appeared in a teachers' magazine.]

I sometimes hear real voice even in words that are themselves vague and trite (for example "and they were nice and soft") when those words somehow manage to be in the right relationship to the writer. I'm not saying, "Isn't it clever considering a child wrote it." And I'm not saying, "Isn't he sincere." The poem is not particularly distinguished on either of those counts. I'm saying, "Look how he could let tired, overused words issue from the center and thereby give them power."

The Perfectibility of Man! Ah heaven, what a dreary theme! The perfectibility of the Ford car! Which of them are you going to perfect? I am not a mechanical contrivance.

Education! Which of the various me's do you propose to educate, and which do you propose to suppress?

Anyhow I defy you. I defy you, oh society, to educate me or to suppress me, according to your dummy standards.

The ideal man! And which is he, if you please? Benjamin Franklin or Abraham Lincoln? The ideal man! Roosevelt or Porfirio Diaz?

There are other men in me, besides this patient ass who sits here in a tweed jacket. What am I doing, playing the patient ass in a tweed jacket? Who am I talking to? Who are you, at the other end of this patience?

Who are you? How many selves have you? And which of these selves do you want to be?

Is Yale College going to educate the self that is in the dark of you, or Harvard College?

The ideal self! Oh, but I have a strange and fugitive self shut out and howling like a wolf or a coyote under the ideal windows. See his red eyes in the dark? This is the self who is coming into his own.

298 Power in Writing

The perfectibility of man, dear God! When every man as long as he remains alive is in himself a multitude of conflicting men. Which of these do you choose to perfect, at the expense of every other?

Old Daddy Franklin will tell you. He'll rig him up for you, the pattern American. Oh, Franklin was the first downright American. He knew what he was about, the sharp little man. He set up the first dummy American.

> D. H. LAWRENCE, *Studies in Classic American Literature*

I sometimes hear real voice in words that are not fully sincere. Lawrence is being kooky and mannered more than earnest and "authentic." Or rather he's turning up the "this-is-really-important" dial so far that it's a bit silly and he knows it. He's fooling around and having fun doing cartwheels and letting on that he knows that we know he looks a bit silly puffing out his chest so far and being so intense. I hear resonance, that is, even in a faint irony which boils down to a certain *absence* of self in the literal meaning. Thus, even in this borderline, tricky case, I would point to the central characteristic of real voice: the words somehow issue from the writer's center—even if in a slippery way—and produce resonance which gets the words more powerfully to a reader's center.

The distinction between voice and real voice helps us understand the tricky relationship between verbal fluency and verbal power. Sometimes they go together but sometimes they are opposed. That is, on the one hand, sometimes fluency is a sign of power: a truly good speaker is never at a loss for words because she has found the door to her best insights and her convictions. But sometimes, on the other hand, we distrust fluent people and call them glib: they speak with lively fluency but they are somehow too smooth. "She spoke so expressively and well but you know I didn't really *believe* her." Such people are good at finding a gear and generating words that fit the situation and the audience; they are never at a loss for words. But somehow all these words—however lively and fluent—don't give us any sense of making contact with the speaker or any sense of knowing her real feelings, attitudes or point of view.

Yet some of those other people who often are at a loss for words—those Billy Budd characters who are tongue-tied and halting in speech, who are always stopping and changing their minds in mid-sentence or breaking off speech as they question what they are engaged in saying—often these very people on certain occasions reveal a gift for speaking with the deepest sort of power and honesty. On the occasions when they actually speak out, they seem to achieve a deeper resonance and authenticity than fluent speakers. Some fluent speakers even find it hard to *know* their real convictions. In some oral cultures, such as some Native American tribes, copiousness itself is distrusted when it comes to speech. There is a sense that authenticity somehow gets dissipated through too many words. Power in speech is rooted in the silence from which it grows.

To summarize, writing *without voice* is wooden or dead because it lacks sound, rhythm, energy, and individuality. Most people's writing lacks voice because they stop so often in mid-sentence and ponder, worry, or change their minds about which word to use or which direction to go in. A few people even speak without voice.

Writing *with voice* is writing into which someone has breathed. It has that fluency, rhythm, and liveliness that exist naturally in the speech of most people when they are enjoying a conversation. Some people who write frequently, copiously, and with confidence manage to get voice into their writing.

Writing with *real voice* has the power to make you pay attention and understand—the words go deep. I don't know the objective characteristics that distinguish writing with real voice from writing with mere voice. For me it is a matter of hearing resonance rather than being able to point to things on the page. I want to say that it has *nothing* to do with the words on the page, only with the relationship of the words to the writer—and therefore that the same words could have real voice when written by one person and lack it when written by someone else. That highlights the mystery, but presumably it is going too far. Perhaps it would be more accurate to say that words contain not just an explicit message ("the sun glints down a pathway of ripples"), but also some kind of implicit message about the condition of the writer (e.g., "I'm curious about that sight" or "I have other things on my mind" or "The sun on the water terrifies me" or "There's no part of me that doesn't see those glints, even the part of me that hates light"). Perhaps when the implicit message reinforces the explicit one in some right way, we get resonance or power. When the implicit message contradicts the main one we get no resonance. But I don't know how to point to these implicit messages on the page and therefore I find it easier to talk about whether the voice "sounds real" or whether the words come in some sense or other "from the center."

I believe, then, that any *kind* of writing can have real voice or lack it—any style, tone, mood, or syntax. The only way we can locate or identify the presence of real voice is through the sensibility of good readers. Since there are no objective criteria, there is no way to verify the judgment of any particular reader. Some people will be better than others at identifying real voice, but in any given instance they may be wrong, no matter how certain they feel. They will hear resonance, but it will be resonance between the words and themselves, not between the words and the writer; or they will hear no resonance, but the interference will come from themselves, not from the writer.

It seems to be no easier to attain real voice in speaking than in writing. In fact some people get real voice in their writing who seldom get it in their speech: powerful writers who talk without power. It is often easier to invest ourselves more deeply and accurately in our words when we are alone with a piece of paper than we can when face to face with an audience.

Real Voice and Bad Writing

As I've been trying to work and rework my thoughts about voice these last four years, I have been nervous about the charge that what I am calling "real voice" is just writing that happens to tickle my feelings or my unconscious concerns and has nothing to do with the words' relationship to the writer. The charge is plausible: if I experience resonance, surely it's more likely to reflect a good fit between the words and *my* self than a good fit between the words and the writer's self; after all, my self is right here, in contact with the words on the page, while the writer's self is nowhere to be found.

Needless to say, I cannot disprove the charge. But I'm not trying to prove that I am right, only to persuade you to adopt a hypothesis—to see if it clarifies your experience of reading and helps you strengthen your writing.

But the charge also made me nervous because I wondered if it showed that my taste is peculiar and defective. The passages I instinctively picked out in a piece of writing were seldom the most skilled or competent writing there; sometimes they were downright terrible. Yet they did in truth appeal to me. And I often get people to do freewriting or I give people exercises in which they turn out careless, excessive, or self-indulgent writing, and I occasionally enjoy reading some of it. And it's true I hate writing that is merely competent. Could it be that I have a peculiar itch for badness?

My theory of voice helps me trust my own taste and deal with the accusation that I don't care about quality. I now see that caring about quality has two different meanings and springs from two different temperamental approaches to writing. On the one hand caring about quality implies a hunger to stamp out terrible writing. A hunger to destroy defects, failure, excess, and ugliness. I don't have this hunger. I am content to let people write much that is bad. I try to let myself write badly too. On the other hand, caring about quality implies hungering for excellence, wanting the real thing, not settling for mere adequacy. That's me. I want the moon. I insist it is attainable: writing that someone would actually want to read by choice, not just for pay or for a favor.

The reason I don't mind badness is that I sense how necessary it is if you want to get beyond mere inoffensive writing to something actually worth a reader's time. I believe it is helpful to develop a taste for real voice because it will not only support your hunger for good writing—your secret feeling that of course you and everyone else can write with power—but it will also help you to be more accepting of the terrible writing it is usually necessary to produce if you want that power.

For the point is that even though real voice brings excellent writing when it is fully developed and under control, it often leads to terrible writing when it is only just emerging and not yet under control. Your most fluent and skillful voice is usually your *acceptable voice*—the voice you develop as you work out an acceptable self. To get it, you probably had to push away feelings, experiences, and tones of voice that felt unacceptable. But these unacceptable elements have energy and power tied up in them that you need to tap if you want to deepen the reasonance of your voice. Yet, of course, you are likely to *hate* these sounds: you have trained yourself to shove them away, you use considerable energy in doing so, they are part of your *anti*-self. When, then, you allow yourself to start using some of these feelings, experiences, and tones of voice in your writing, there is little chance you will be able to use them in a controlled and effective way. Bad writing is almost inevitable.

I am implying, in effect, a roughly Freudian or depth psychology model of a murkey unconscious pool full of powerful, threatening energy. But there is also a less lurid model that underlines what I'm saying about voice—roughly Piagetian: that the attainment of real voice is a matter of growth and development rather than mere learning. In attaining a new stage of development, you move from one mode of functioning to a more complex, sophisticated mode. In the process, skills can fall apart. There are lots of things you did well with that old mode which you now bungle.* A genuine restructuring requires a destructuring. I think I see this happening in writing: many students don't seem to get past certain levels of adequate writing without going through a stage with lots of deteriorated writing.

In short, fear of badness is probably what holds people back most from developing power in writing. Some of that fear is natural in the struggle to develop an acceptable self. But some of it results from teachers who care more about getting rid of badness than about looking for potential excellence. If you care too much about avoiding bad writing, you will be too cautious, too afraid to relinquish control. This may lead to the worst fate that can befall a writer—feedback like this: "It seems pretty good; I liked it fairly well; I can't see anything the matter." What they are really telling you is that they were absolutely unaffected by your words.

If, on the other hand, you really seek excellence, if you seek to write things that others might actually *want* to read, you need to stop playing it safe: go for it, take the plunge, jump over the edge. You won't know where you are going. You will write much that is terrible. It will feel like a much longer path to tread than if you just want to get rid of badness. But you will get rewards. You will get lots of feedback and it will be interesting. People will hate some of what you write and love other parts; some people will love what others hate. If you can put up with all these things, especially the inevitable flops, you will have the satisfaction of knowing that

---

* For example, although children can increase their skill at calculating on their fingers without making new mistakes (a case of plain learning), they will tend to make lots of new mistakes when they start calculating in their head or using abstract unvisualized symbols (a case of development or growth).

something is happening in your writing and that you are on your way to more than mere non-offensiveness.

And in the end it won't be a longer path. Getting rid of badness is an infinite and impossible task. There will always be bits of badness in your writing, lurking here and there for some sharp-eyed reader to find, no matter how hard you try to remove them. Whereas if you go all out for excellence and don't worry about that bad writing that comes with it, before long you will be able to produce some writing that people will really want to read—even to buy.

26

How To Get
Power through Voice

What if this hypothesis about voice is correct? One thing follows from it that's more important than anything else: everyone, however inexperienced or unskilled, has real voice available; everyone can write with power. Even though it may take some people a long time before they can write well about certain complicated topics or write in certain formal styles, and even though it will take some people a long time before they can write without mistakes in spelling and usage, nevertheless, nothing stops anyone from writing words that will make readers listen and be affected. Nothing stops you from writing right now, today, words that people will want to read and even want to publish. Nothing stops you, that is, but your fear or unwillingness or lack of familiarity with what I am calling your real voice.

But this clarion call—for that's what I intend it to be despite my careful qualifiers—immediately raises a simple question: Why doesn't everyone use power if it is sitting there available and why does most writing lack power? There are lots of good reasons. In this section I will give advice about how to get real voice into your writing, but I will present it in terms of an analysis of why people so seldom use that power.

• • •

People often lack any voice at all in their writing, even fake voice, because they stop so often in the act of writing a sentence and worry and change their minds about which words to use. They have none of the natural breath in their writing that they have in speaking because the conditions for writing are so different from the conditions for speaking. The list of conditions is awesome: we have so little practice in writing, but so much more time to stop and fiddle as we write each sentence; we have additional rules of spelling and usage to follow in writing that we don't have in speaking; we feel more culpable for our written foolishness than for what we say; we have been so fully graded, corrected, and given feedback on our mistakes in writing; and we are usually trying to get our words to conform to some (ill-understood) model of "good writing" as we write.

Frequent and regular freewriting exercises are the best way to overcome these conditions of writing and get voice into your words. These exercises should perhaps be called compulsory writing exercises since they are really a way to *compel* yourself to keep putting words down on paper no matter how lost or frustrated you feel. To get voice into your words you need to learn to get each word chosen, as it were, not by you but by the preceding word. Freewriting exercises help you learn to stand out of the way.

In addition to actual exercises in nonstop writing—since it's hard to keep writing *no matter what* for more than fifteen minutes—force yourself simply to write enormous quantities. Try to make up for all the writing you haven't done. Use writing for as many different tasks as you can. Keep a notebook or journal, explore thoughts for yourself, write to yourself when you feel frustrated or want to figure something out. (See Chapter 10 for more ways to use writing.)

Practice revising for voice. A powerful exercise is to write short pieces of prose or poetry that work without any punctuation at all. Get the words so well ordered that punctuation is never missed. The reader must never stumble or have to reread a phrase, not even on first reading—and all without benefit of punctuation. This is really an exercise in adjusting the breath in the words till it guides the reader's voice naturally to each pause and full stop.

Read out loud. This is a good way to exercise the muscle involved in voice and even in real voice. Good reading out loud is not necessarily dramatic. I'm struck with how some good poets or readers get real voice into a monotone or chant. They are trying to let the words' inner resonance come through, not trying to "perform" the words. (Dylan Thomas reads so splendidly that we may make the mistake of calling his technique "dramatic." Really it is a kind of chant or incantation he uses.) But there is no right way. It's a question of steering a path between being too timid and being falsely dramatic. The presence of listeners can sharpen your ear and help you hear when you chicken out or overdramatize.

• • •

Real voice. People often avoid it and drift into fake voices because of the need to face an audience. I have to go to work, I have to make a presentation, ,I have to teach, I have to go to a party, I have to have dinner with friends. Perhaps I feel lost, uncertain, baffled—or else angry—or else uncaring—or else hysterical. I can't sound that way with all these people. They won't understand, they won't know how to deal with me, and I won't accomplish what I need to accomplish. Besides, perhaps I don't even know *how* to sound the way I feel. (When we were little we had no difficulty sounding the way we felt; thus most little children speak and write with real voice.) Therefore I will use some of the voices I have at my disposal that will serve the audience and the situation—voices I've learned by imitation or made up out of desperation or out of my sense of humor. I might as well. By now, those people think those voices are me. If I used my real voice, they might think I was crazy.

For real voice, write a lot without an audience. Do freewritings and throw them away. Remove yourself from the expectations of an audience, the demands of a particular task, the needs of a particular interaction. As you do this, try out many different ways of speaking.

But a certain *kind* of audience can help you toward real voice even though it was probably the pressures of audience that led you to unreal voices in the first place. Find an audience of people also committed to getting power in their writing. Find times when you can write in each other's presence, each working on your own work. Your shared presence and commitment to helping each other will make you more powerful in what you write. Then read your rough writing to each other. No feedback: just welcoming each other to try out anything.

Because you often don't even know what your power or your inner self sounds like, you have to try many different tones and voices. Fool around, jump from one mood or voice to another, mimic, play-act, dramatize and exaggerate. Let your writing be outrageous. Practice relinquishing control. It can help to write in settings where you never write (on the bus? in the bathtub?) or in modes you never use. And if, as sometimes happens, you know you are angry but somehow cannot really feel or inhabit that feeling, play-act and exaggerate it. Write artificially. Sometimes "going through the motions" is the quickest way to "the real thing."

Realize that in the short run there is probably a conflict between developing real voice and producing successful pragmatic writing—polished pieces that work for specific audiences and situations. Keeping an appropriate stance or tone for an audience may prevent you from getting real voice into that piece of writing. Deep personal outrage, for example, may be the only authentic tone of voice you can use in writing to a particular person, yet that voice is neither appropriate nor useful for the actual document you have to write—perhaps an official agency memo or a report to that person about his child. Feedback on whether something works as a finished piece of writing for an audience is often not good feedback on real voice. It is probably important to work on both goals. Work on polishing things and making sure they have the right tone or stance for that audience. Or at least not the wrong one: you may well have to play it safe. But make sure you also work on writing that *doesn't* have to work and doesn't have to be revised and polished for an audience.

And yet you needn't give up on power just because a particular writing situation is very tricky for you. Perhaps you must write an essay for a teacher who never seems to understand you; or a report for a supervisor who never seems able to see things the way you do; or a research report on a topic that has always scared and confused you. If you try to write in the most useful voice for this situation—perhaps cheerful politeness or down-to-business impersonality—the anger will probably show through anyway. It might not show clearly, readers might be unaware of it, yet they will turn out to have the kind of responses they have to angry writing. That is, they will become annoyed with many of the ideas you present, or continually think of arguments against you (which they wouldn't have done to a different voice), or they will turn off, or they will react condescendingly.

To the degree that you keep your anger hidden, you are likely to write words especially lacking in voice—especially dead, fishy, fake-feeling. Or the process of trying to write in a non-angry, down-to-business, impersonal way is so deadening to you that you simply get bored and sleepy and devoid of energy. Your mind shuts off. You cannot think of anything to say.

In a situation like this it helps to take a roundabout approach. First do lots of freewriting where you are angry and tell your reader all your feelings in whatever voices come. Then get back to the real topic. Do lots of freewriting and raw writing and exploration of the topic—writing still in whatever style comes out. Put all your effort into finding the best ideas and arguments you can, and don't worry about your tone. After you express the feelings and voices swirling around in you, and after you get all the insights you can while not having to worry about the audience and the tone, then you will find it relatively easy to revise and rewrite something powerful and effective for that reader. That is, you can get past the anger and confusion, but keep the good ideas and the energy. As you rewrite for the real audience, you can generally use large chunks of what you have already written with only minor cosmetic changes. (You don't necessarily have to write out *all* the anger you have. It may be that you have three hundred pages of angry words you need to say to someone, but if you can get *one* page that really opens the door all the way, that can be enough. But if this is something new to you, you may find you cannot do it in one page—you need to rant and rave for five or ten pages. It may seem like a waste of time, but it isn't. Gradually you will get more economical.)

By taking this roundabout path, you will find more energy and better thinking. And through the process of starting with the voices that just happen and seeing where they lead, often you will come to a *new* voice which is appropriate to this reader but also rings deeply. You won't have to choose between something self-defeatingly angry that will simply turn off the reader or something pussy-footing, polite, and full of fog—and boring for you to write.

A long and messy path is common and beneficial, but you can get some of the benefits quicker if you are in a hurry. Just set yourself strict time limits for the early writing and force yourself to write without stopping throughout the early stages. When I have to write an evaluation of a student I am annoyed at, I force myself to write a quick freewriting letter to the student telling him everything on my mind. I make this uncensored, extreme, exaggerated, sometimes even deliberately unfair—but very short. And it's for the wastepaper basket. Having done this, I can turn to my official evaluation and find it much easier to write something fair in a suitable tone of voice (for a document that becomes part of the student's transcript). I finish these two pieces of writing much more quickly than if I just tried to write the official document and pick my way gingerly through my feelings.

• • •

Another reason people don't use real voice is that it makes them feel exposed and vulnerable. I don't so much mind if someone dislikes my writing when I am merely using an acceptable voice, but if I use my real voice and they don't like it—which of course is very possible—that hurts. The more criticism people get on their writing, the more they tend to use fake voices. To use real voice feels like bringing yourself into contact with the reader. It's the same kind of phenomenon that happens when there is real eye contact and each person experiences the presence of the other; or when two or more people stop talking and wait in silence while something in the air gets itself clear. Writing of almost any kind is exhibitionistic; writing with real voice is more so. Many professional writers feel a special need for privacy. It will help you, then, to get together with one or more others who are interested in recovering their power. Feeling vulnerable or exposed with them is not so difficult.

Another reason people don't use their real voice is that it means having feelings and memories they would rather not have. When you write in your real voice, it often brings tears or shaking—though laughter too. Using real voice may even mean finding you *believe* things you don't wish to believe. For all these reasons, you need to write for no audience and to write for an audience that's safe. And you need faith in yourself that you will gradually sort things out and that it doesn't matter if it takes time.

Most children have real voice but then lose it. It is often just plain loud: like screeching or banging a drum. It can be annoying or wearing for others. "Shhh" is the response we often get to the power of our real voice. But, in addition, much of what we say with real voice is difficult for those around us to deal with: anger, grief, self-pity, even love for the wrong people. When we are hushed up from those expressions, we lose real voice.

In addition, we lose real voice when we are persuaded to give up some of our natural responses to inauthenticity and injustice. Almost any child can feel inauthenticity in the voices of many TV figures or politicians. Many grown-ups can't hear it so well—or drown out their distrust. It is difficult to get along in the world if you hear all the inauthenticity: it makes you feel alone, depressed, hopeless. We need to belong, and society offers us membership if we stop hearing inauthenticity.

Children can usually feel when things are unfair, but they are often persuaded to go along because they need to belong and to be loved. To get back to those feelings in later life leads to rage, grief, aloneness and—since one has gone along—guilt. Real voice is often buried in all of that. If you want to recover it, you do well to build in special support from people you can trust so you don't feel so alone or threatened by all these feelings.

Another reason people don't use real voice is that they run away from their power. There's something scary about being as strong as you are, about wielding the force you actually have. It means taking a lot more responsibility and credit than you are used to. If you write with real voice, people will say "You did this to me" and try to make you feel responsible for some of their actions. Besides, the effect of your power is liable to be different from what you intended. Especially at first. You cause explosions when you thought you were just asking for the salt or saying hello. In effect I'm saying, "Why don't you shoot that gun you have? Oh yes, by the way, I can't tell you how to aim it." The standard approach in writing is to say you mustn't pull the trigger until you can aim it well. But how can you learn to aim well till you start pulling the trigger? If you start letting your writing lead you to real voice, you'll discover some thoughts and feelings you didn't know you had.

Therefore, practice shooting the gun off in safe places. First with no one around. Then with people you know and trust deeply. Find people who are willing to be in the same room with you while you pull the trigger. Try using the power in ways where the results don't matter. Write letters to people that don't matter to you. You'll discover that the gun doesn't kill but that you have more power than you are comfortable with.

Of course you may accept your power but still want to disguise it. That is, you may find it convenient, if you are in a large organization, to be able to write about an event in a fuzzy, passive "It has

come to our attention that . . ." kind of language, so you disguise
not only the fact that it was an action performed by a human being
with a free will but indeed that *you did it.* But it would be incorrect to conclude, as some people do, that all bureaucratic, organizational, and governmental writing needs to lack the resonance of
real voice. Most often it could do its work perfectly well even if it
were strong and clear. It is the *personal, individualistic,* or *per-
sonality-filled* voice that is inappropriate in much organizational
writing, but you can write with power in the impersonal, public,
and corporate voice. You can avoid "I" and its flavor, and talk entirely in terms of "we" and "they" and even "it," and still achieve
the resonance of real voice. Real voice is not the sound of an *individual personality* redolent with vibes, it is the sound of *a meaning*
resonating because the individual consciousness of the writer is
somehow fully behind or in tune with or in participation with that
meaning.

I have stressed the importance of sharing writing without any
feedback at all. What about asking people to give you feedback
specifically on real voice? I think that such feedback can be useful,
but I am leery of it. It's so hard to know whether someone's perception of real voice is accurate. If you want this feedback, don't
get it early in your writing development, make sure you get it from
very different kinds of people, and make sure not to put too much
trust in it. The safest method is to get them to read a piece and
then ask them a week later what they remember. Passages they
dislike often have the most real voice.

But here is a specific exercise for getting feedback on real voice.
It grows out of one of the first experiences that made me think
consciously about this matter. As an applicant for conscientious objector status, and then later as a draft counselor, I discovered that
the writing task set by Selective Service was very interesting and
perplexing. An applicant had to write why he was opposed to fighting in wars, but there was no right or wrong answer. The draft
board would accept any reasons (within certain broad limits); they
would accept any style, any level of skill. Their only criterion was
whether *they* believed that the *writer* believed his own words. (I
am describing how it worked when board members were in good
faith.)

Applicants, especially college students, often started with writing that didn't work. I could infer from all the arguments and com-

motion and from conversations with them that they were sincere but as they wrote they got so preoccupied with theories, argument, and reasoning that in the end there was no conviction on paper. When I gave someone this feedback and he was willing to try and try again till at last the words began to ring true, all of a sudden the writing got powerful and even skillful in other ways.

The exercise I suggest to anybody, then, is simply to write about some belief you have—or even some experience or perception—but to get readers to give you this limited, peculiar, draft-board-like feedback: where do they really believe that you believe it, and where do they have doubts? The useful thing about this exercise is discovering how often words that ring true are not especially full of feeling, not heavy with conviction. Too much "sincerity" and quivering often sounds fake and makes readers doubt that you really believe what you are saying. I stress this because I fear I have made real voice sound as though it is always full of loud emotion. It is often quiet.

● ● ●

In the end, what may be as important as these specific exercises is adopting the right frame of mind.

Look for real voice and realize it is there in everyone waiting to be used. Yet remember, too, that you are looking for something mysterious and hidden. There are no outward linguistic characteristics to point to in writing with real voice. Resonance or impact on readers is all there is. But you can't count on readers to notice it or to agree about whether it is there because of all the other criteria they use in evaluating writing (e.g., polished style, correct reasoning, good insights, truth-to-life, deep feelings), and because of the negative qualities that sometimes accompany real voice as it is emerging. And you, as writer, may be wrong about the presence or absence of real voice in your writing—at least until you finally develop a trustworthy sense of it. You have to be willing to work in the dark, not be in a hurry, and have faith. The best clue I know is that as you begin to develop real voice, your writing will probably cause more comment from readers than before (though not necessarily more favorable comment).

If you seek real voice you should realize that you probably face a dilemma. You probably have only one real voice—at first anyway—and it is likely to feel childish or distasteful or ugly to you. But you are stuck. You can either use voices you like or you can be heard. For a while, you can't have it both ways.

But if you do have the courage to use and inhabit that real voice, you will get the knack of resonance, you will learn to expand its range and eventually make more voices real. This of course is the skill of great literary artists: the ability to give resonance to many voices.

It's important to stress, at the end, this fact of many voices. Partly to reassure you that you are not ultimately stuck with just one voice forever. But also because it highlights the mystery. Real voice is not necessarily personal or sincere. Writing about your own personal concerns is only one way and not necessarily the best. Such writing can lead to gushy or analytical words about how angry you are today: useful to write, an expression of strong feelings, a possible *source* of future powerful writing, but not resonant or powerful for readers as it stands. Real voice is whatever yields resonance, whatever makes the words bore through. Some writers get real voice through pure fantasy, lies, imitation of utterly different writers, or trance-writing. It may be possible to get real voice by merging in your mind with another personality, pretending to be someone else. *Shedding* the self's concerns and point of view can be a good way to get real voice—thus writing fiction and playing roles are powerful tools. Many good literary artists sound least convincing when they speak for themselves. The important thing is simply to know that power is available and to figure out through experimentation the best way for you to attain it.

27

Breathing Experience
into Words

Go to the pine if you want to learn about the pine, or to the bamboo
if you want to learn about the bamboo. And in doing so, you must
leave your subjective preoccupation with yourself. Otherwise you impose yourself on the object and do not learn. Your poetry issues of its
own accord when you and the object have become one. . . .*

"Leave your subjective preoccupation with yourself." I've been
talking so much about *self, self, self* in the chapters on voice. What
if that's all wrong: incorrect; immoral. I don't think it is, but since
what I am seeking in this section of the book is a central mystery—
life or power or magic in words—there is probably more than one
path to it. I pursue now another approach, another line of attack, a
different set of terms.

Reading and Really Reading

Writing is hard, mysterious work. Of course. That's what this book
is all about. But if we stop shaking our finger at the writer for a
moment and stress instead what a hard and mysterious job the
reader has, we will end up learning something important about
writing.

To get meaning out of a set of words, a reader must build mean-

*From *Basho. The Narrow Road to the Deep North and Other Sketches*, Nobuyuki
Yuasa, *ed.* (New York, 1966), p. 33. Quoted by John Balaban in his "South of Pompeii the Helmsman Balked," *College English*, vol. 39, no. 4, December 1977.

ing in. When you come to a word you don't know in your reading, you may have to look it up in the dictionary and then try out the different definitions to see which one is intended here. This is much more work than you usually have to do when you read, but it serves to illustrate a basic fact about reading: for everything you read, you must *bring* meanings to the words, not take meanings from them. Meanings are in readers, not in words. When the page says *chat*, English readers bring thoughts of a cozy conversation; French readers bring thoughts about cats. Readers build meanings; words just sit there.

Think what this means for you as a writer. You have these thoughts you want to communicate, but you can't just give them to readers, you must get readers to construct them. You must walk up to readers and say, "Let's go for a ride. You pedal, I'll steer." You are saying, "Here's a beautiful sculpture for you," but it is just a pile of limp balloons intricately arranged on a rack. In order to see the sculpture, readers first must blow them up—and blow them up right, too. They must provide *pneuma*—breath-spirit. "Here's a lovely painting," you say, but it's just lines and numbers and readers must paint in the colors. You don't even supply the key which tells which color is designated by which number. Readers must bring that knowledge: that's what it means to know how to read.

You can't give readers a finished product no matter how much you want to—any more than a playwright can actually send a live play through the mail. She can only send the script—a set of directions for producing a play. The best you can do is make sure you have overhauled the bicycle so that the pedalling isn't harder than necessary. You can promise not to go up unnecessary hills. You can make sure there aren't any holes in the balloons or misprints in the paint-by-numbers picture that would make the tree come out purple—unless you want it purple. But no matter how good a job you do of *preparing* the piece of writing, still the reader has to do all the work of pedalling, blowing, or painting-by-numbers.

If that makes reading sound like a lot of work, there's worse to come. For I've only been talking about getting *meaning* out of words. But the real topic here is power in language. That means we must talk about readers getting an *experience* out of words, not just a meaning.

I remember the occasion when I first realized that the reader has this second layer of work to do if the words are going to have power. I was reading a novel and I came to this sentence:

> Now this night the sun had left the sky in a cascade of magenta over pale blue, and the autumn moon nearly full had begun to illuminate the huge dark clouds piling on the horizon.

It stopped me. I had been having some difficulty or resistance since the beginning, but I'd sort of pushed it away from consciousness and kept on reading. With this sentence I suddenly realized that I couldn't *see* that sky—and that there'd been lots I hadn't been seeing all along.

Now perhaps I would have seen the sky without any effort if the writing had been clearer. One gets a bit mixed up about where the moon and sun and clouds are in relation to each other. Or perhaps I would have seen the sky if it hadn't been the creation of a student, for credit, and therefore constituted required reading for me when I felt like doing something else. Or perhaps the image might have jumped into my head if I hadn't been irritated with the student. For I guess I better admit that I was already annoyed with her even before I started reading her words—for reasons that had nothing to do with her writing.

But however ample these explanations might be for my failure to see her sky, they do not in the slightest undermine what I suddenly realized: that no matter how good the writing, no matter how freely I am reading, no matter how well liked the writer, the fact remains that whenever I actually *see* or *experience* something in a set of words, I must consent to do so, and I must in addition supply the imaginative or psychic energy that is required to form that image in my head. (I am talking in this chapter, by the way, about descriptive and narrative writing. I will consider expository writing in the following chapter.)

Whenever in the past I had stopped reading because of this kind of frustration, I had tended to describe it as a case of the writing "not working." For the first time I now realized that beneath most cases of words not working lies an act of refusal by the reader. (There are, I admit, some cases where the reader doesn't refuse and tries as hard as she can and still gets no meaning or experience. But readers usually refuse to try any more long before they've really given their all.)

Of course, I'd many times previously been aware of an *out and out* refusal: refusal to read altogether, refusal to pedal at all, refusal to keep on reading or go any further. But this was different. I kept on reading that novel. It was, in this case, my paid duty. I kept on understanding what she was saying in virtually every sentence and, to a large extent, recognizing the skill and experience and sophistication she often displayed (for the sentence I quoted above was one of the least skillful of all). And I was able to make judgments about one passage or phrase being stronger than another, and so on and so on. I kept right on and performed what must be called a conscientious job of reading—going on afterwards to make some written comments to the student.

What emerged finally was this distinction which now seems so important to me: I allowed that writer access to my *mind,* but I didn't allow her access to my *experience.* It's as though I were a musician reading the score for a symphony on paper in silence. I was looking at it, seeing what key it was in, seeing what kinds of melodies and harmonies it uses, how it blends winds and brass, seeing where it is loud, dramatic, quiet, and so on—all without hearing any sounds in my head. I was doing a competent job of reading the directions for the production of music, but it would have taken an extra piece of effort, an additional investment of self—however automatic or subliminal that effort might be for a good musician who enjoys what she is reading—actually to *hear* the sounds, to *experience* the music. If I content myself with merely reading I can usually make judgments—"Yes, that is a well-formed melody; yes, that is a clever alternation of strings and brass; no, that is an ungainly harmonic progression"—based on my past experience with music. These may be astute judgments or not, but they are made without hearing the music. Perhaps, then, my comments to this student were sound or perhaps not, but the fact remains that I made them without experiencing her words— only understanding them.

The crucial fact about reading, then, is that the reader is engaged at every moment in making a choice of whether to invest the energy required to *have* the actual experience implied in the words, or merely to *read the directions* for constructing an experience. It may not feel as though I am making that choice or investing that extra effort when I am reading something I find powerful. It feels as though I am just sitting back and letting the writer do it to me—as though she is *giving me* experience. It feels as though I can just relax and purr and say "Yes, I love it, do it to me again." But that feeling is misleading. Really I had to supply both the consent and the energy. What the writer gave me was the kind of directions that made it seem fun and easy. I guess the reason it doesn't feel like work to construct experiences from good writing is that we never do it unless we want to. They can't make us do something that internal. They can make us read, but they can't make us experience. (Thus, my act of refusal came to my attention in a piece of required reading.)

Another example from required reading. Teachers are always complaining that students don't "follow directions" even though the students did read and understand those directions perfectly well. Or employers require us to read memos or instructions, and we do so, yet we go on to act as though we hadn't read them: following the wrong procedure, breaking equipment, forgetting the essential step. The answer is that we read, but we didn't really read. If we were given a straight-forward test on our understanding of what we had read, we would probably pass the test. We did understand; we can recall. It's just that we didn't have the *experience* it would have taken to make a dent on our unselfconscious behavior.

Even our failure to assemble a toy or appliance according to its "simple instructions" is illuminated by this question of whether we build an experience out of words—whether we hear music as we silently read. It's not usually that we didn't comprehend the directions, but rather that we didn't *remember* to put in that damn bolt or bend that strut over to the left even though at the moment of reading those words we understood them. That piece of advice simply passed through us because there was so utterly little sense of *experiencing, visualizing, hearing* what the words were saying. The writer failed utterly to get us to *participate* in any feeling of what it would be like to put that bolt on or bend that strut over.

Since I've come to notice how the reader must supply both the consent and the energy for any powerful writing, I see more clearly what often really happens when I am not satisfied with a novel or poem or story. Instead of just saying, "Oh, the writing doesn't work," or "I guess I'm not interested enough in that subject"—and those judgments may be correct—now I often notice something else: I don't *trust* the writer enough and I'm damned if I'm going to have the experiences she wants me to have. There are lots of experiences that I won't let writers persuade me to create for myself till I trust them. No one can make me feel terrified or make me cry unless somehow she wins my trust. Thus, a piece of writing is likely to fail with me if someone tries to put an intensely scary or sad scene right at the beginning. I simply won't row if she steers me toward that waterfall. I won't let her play with my feelings. Yet, often the very experience I refuse to create for myself in the opening page or two is one that I am willing to have later on, after I have become involved—which is the same as saying after I have come to trust the writer.

The kinds of experiences I am willing to have at the start of a piece of writing are milder. I'll let the writer tell me an interesting idea or start a narrative going (as long as it's not too strange). I'm open to hearing the sound of a voice talking or a mind working; to seeing a view of a house or room or landscape. I suspect this is one of the reasons why stories and novels so often start with description: it's not that we need to start with images—plenty of writing succeeds without much description at all—but that description is a good way for the writer to show the texture of her mind so we can build up some trust.

This tells me more about the writer's task. The writer steers, sitting in the stern, facing forward; the reader does all the work, rowing and also facing backwards without even knowing where she is going till she gets there. To change metaphors yet again, as writer you must say to your reader, "Why don't you take off your clothes and let me play with your body." Is it any less of an invasion to play with peoples' minds than to play with their bodies? Yes, perhaps they will *read* what you write—if they have to or if they are curious—but they won't *really* read you, they won't expend the additional energy required to have the experience you are trying to convey unless they trust you.

How, then, do you win a reader's trust or permission? I think that writers win my trust when they are completely focused on the experience they want me to have. I'm not talking about getting me to *believe* them. That is really less important. I'm talking about the ability to get me to experience what they are talking about.

When writers fail to win my trust or consent, it is often because I sense them trying to manipulate me, or at least I feel some of their energy and attention not on the experience, but on what they want to do to me. That's what I feel in the magenta sunset piece.

"Manipulative" is too strong a word, but you can feel some of the writer's attention taken away from the image itself and given over to the fanciness of her language and the impressive effect it is intended to have.

Here is a milder example:

> The sun shone through all the tiny driplets of water clinging to the trees as though each one was a tiny prism and surrounded us with sparks. We were really glad to see the sun after our long wait, and what a beautiful reward it was.

The first sentence wins my trust and makes me at least begin to see the image, but there is a letdown in the second sentence, particularly the last half of it, because the writer stopped being wrapped up in the experience itself and started trying, as it were, to urge me to have it.

Another way writers try to gain our trust is by coming on all sincere and honest—proclaiming by their manner, "Trust me, I'm a nice person, I'll be straight with you." With some readers this works, but, in the long run, they wonder, "Why is she *trying* so hard to be honest? What is she hiding or trying to sell?" If someone is trying too hard to be honest, she probably doesn't trust herself—at some level. One of the qualities that distinguishes people we trust is simply that they really do trust themselves. They trust that what they have to say *is* important and that you will listen. It's a quality that undamaged children have, and it rivets the attention of a listener. When a writer is too worried about whether you will listen, whether what she is saying is really right or important, this lack of trust takes the form of a fine cloud of fog or static in the air. Sometimes it makes you feel faintly uncomfortable, the way you feel at a party when the person you are talking to is nervous or wonders if she is okay or wishes she could move on to talk to someone else: you *feel* her leakage of attention away from what she is actually saying off into her distracting inner thoughts and feelings. A good talker believes fully in what she is saying and can put *all* her attention into her words, even when the situation is distracting. That second sentence above, "What a beautiful reward it was to see the sun," is really a piece of insecurity on the writer's part.

Sometimes, of course, it seems as though a writer *overpowers* us. We don't happily consent to row while she steers, we have our breath taken away and feel we have no choice. But really the writer has wrung a genuine consent from us: the same kind of consent we grant when someone tricks us or "commands" us through sheer tone of voice. Sometimes the writer gains unwilling consent by dangling a taboo subject that secretly fascinates, such as sex or torture. (Thus, the power of taboo subjects usually declines after awhile—after we enjoy it enough that it isn't so taboo—and so we become bored with what used to tingle us. Writers must constantly escalate sensationalism to recapture bored readers.) More often, writers overpower us simply by their *authority:* pervasive confidence in themselves, utter conviction about what they are saying, complete command over their craft. But even though we may *feel* overwhelmed, the truth is that we are really consenting to put ourselves in such powerful hands. Besides, it's just reading, after all, not real life. We can afford to let someone snatch us completely into her power in books, even if we have learned to resist it in real life.

Some readers are more likely to be overwhelmed than others. Children, for example, may be more prey to this authority than adults, more apt to go along. That is why we tend to be more sympathetic to the idea of shielding children from certain kinds of reading. They seem more "impressionable," literally, in that they seem more likely to create the impression or experience in themselves. Children seem more apt to have nightmares about something they have read or seen than adults. In a sense, then, they are better readers: they subject themselves more completely to the words.

But as children get older and more sophisticated, they get better at making the kind of *refusal* to experience that most adults are good at. At a certain age—often adolescence—we see a child working overtime to strengthen these refusal muscles. The child takes a delight in deflating all experience from that romantic or scary movie scene: she sees the special artificial lights shining on the faces, imagines the big cameras and dollies moving around, notices the special effects, and sees *through* the mysterious moonlight with clouds scudding across the sky to a broad sunny day of filming with the camera lens stopped down. It may be many years before that adolescent will actually let herself feel deeply thrilled or scared by what's on the screen. And some people, of course, stay numbed. (I wonder if the taste for sensationalist books and movies might not be a healthy, if misguided, attempt on the part of numbed people to prove themselves alive enough to breathe experience into words.)

It is this mysterious event, then, this difference between reading and really reading, this breathing of life into words, this construction of an experience out of our own materials by someone else's blueprint, this thing we do that we don't usually notice ourselves doing—not just reading the notes, but hearing the music in our heads: this is what I am trying to explore in this chapter. But however mysterious or unconscious the event is, we can often hear it easily. Most everyone has heard it, especially as a child. When someone is reading out loud to us and breathing experience into the words, we can usually hear their investment. It's especially audible to us when that reader, while reading out loud, suddenly stops hearing the music in what she is reading:

> What happened? I was there in the forest. It was happening to me. There was no bed, no crack in the ceiling, no wallpaper stripes, no mommy reading to me. I didn't have to go to bed. Now I'm listening to mommy read me the story. Now I have to go to bed. She still reads with all that expression in her voice, she reads just like she was reading before, but now she's thinking about daddy or about having a fight or about going downstairs to do the dishes. We were there in the forest. Then she stopped trying and we fell back here.

The Writer's Job

I emphasize the complexity of reading because I think that what you must do as writer, if you want power in your words, is equally complex, mysterious, and hard to define. But it's simple to say. My entire advice for this chapter—though I will spell it out more fully and practically at the end—can be boiled down to this: if you want readers to breathe life into your writing so that they get a powerful experience from it, then you must breathe experience into your words as you write. I don't know why it should be the case that if you experience what you are writing about—if you go to the bamboo—it increases the chances of the reader's experiencing the bamboo. But that's the way it seems to work. The more you try out this hypothesis about reading and writing, the more you will see it confirmed.

I can illustrate the process most vividly with a workshop game where you try to tell images so that others actually see them.* What often happens is that the student describes something, perhaps a maple tree in the middle of the front lawn with flowers growing around the trunk. But it doesn't quite work. It doesn't make me *see* it. I say, "Wait. I can't see it. *You* must not have seen it. Close your eyes and wait till you really see it. Stop looking for words, look for the vision itself. Don't hurry." And we wait a bit while the speaker closes her eyes and tries to see the image clearly, and then she says, "I can see it now, but it's a little bit different now." And she tells her image, but the tree isn't in the middle of the lawn. It's really near the sidewalk. And it doesn't have flowers around it, it has long strands of scraggly grass that the lawnmower didn't get. And as she tells it, it *does* work, we all see it clearly. It's as though her first image was an imperfect or distorted view of the "real" image, the second one. The first time she was trying to see it through a poor telescope so she had to invent some details. When I push, she focuses the lens better and can finally see the image clearly.

Of course there is no reason, theoretically, why the speaker couldn't *see* the original image of the tree in the middle of the lawn with flowers around it. And it's a perfectly good image. That's what characterizes a good writer: the ability to see anything. But this inexperienced writer needed to put all her efforts into having an experience instead of trying to stick with any particular image, and when she did so, she got more experience into her words, but the tree moved near to the sidewalk and the flowers changed to scraggly grass. Probably that first image was "constructed" on the basis of a half-remembered scene while the improved image goes back and taps that memory itself. Or perhaps neither image is an exact memory, but the second one makes more use of memory fragments than the first one did. The first one was too much of an idea or conception, not enough of an experience.

I seem to be saying that if you could actually *go* to the bamboo and stand there looking at it—if you could suddenly be transported back to your old childhood bedroom which you are trying to write about now—your words would automatically have more power. And, of course, they probably would. But I can get closer to the

---

* Part of an approach called "Story Workshop" developed by John Schultz and his associates. See "The Story Workshop Method: Writing from Start to Finish," *College English*, vol. 39, no. 4, December, 1977.

heart of what I mean by "breathing experience into words" by pointing out that actually looking at the bamboo with your own eyes is not necessarily enough. This is the lesson you learn in a drawing class where they have you do push-ups in really seeing, not just looking. You must do the classic Nicolaides * drawing exercise where you are not allowed to take your eyes off the object for the entire time of the drawing, not allowed to look at your paper at all. The goal is to learn to really see—to pour all your energy into your eyes and into the object. Not to let any of your attention leak away from the object you are drawing to anything else, such as whether your drawing looks right.

The drawings people produce when they can't look at their paper are very instructive. They are liable to have obvious distortions of one sort or another. But they usually have more life, energy, and experience in them than drawings produced when you keep looking back to your paper and correcting your line and thereby achieving more accuracy. They give the viewer more of the *experience* of that torso or apple. (I remember a drawing of a nude I made this way, and it was really quite good; I was proud of it and wanted to show it off, but the genitals were embarrassingly large. With this method, you tend to enlarge what you pay good attention to.)

It may be complicated for psychologists or philosophers to deal with this distinction between seeing and really seeing, but it's simple enough to notice it on certain occasions: you stand there on the lawn and really see that beech tree and somehow the perception fills you or fully occupies you—the tree is wholly present to you. Or else, you stand there and, yes, you see it, but somehow you don't see it fully, for you are slightly distracted or numb or unable to focus your attention. Some of your energy or attention is elsewhere. There is incomplete impact or commerce between you and the tree. (Obviously this isn't really a binary distinction between "merely seeing" and "really seeing," but rather a gradual continuum that stretches from pathological distractedness up to mystic participation.)

The principle that emerges, especially after many image workshops, is simple. If you want your words to make a reader have an experience, you have to have an experience yourself—not just deal

---

* See *The Natural Way to Draw*, Kimon Nicolaides (New York, 1941).

in ideas or concepts. (I will talk about conceptual or idea-writing in the next chapter.) What that means in practice is that you have to put all your energy into seeing—into connecting or making contact or participating with what you are writing about—into being there or having the hallucination. And no effort at all into searching for words. When you *have* the experience, when you have gotten to the bamboo, you can just open your mouth and the words that emerge will be what you need. (In the case of writing, though, you will have to revise later.)

It is probably easier to really experience something if you are actually standing there looking at it. But not necessarily. And it is probably easier to really experience something if you have actually seen it—that is, you will probably do better writing about memories than about made-up events. But not necessarily. For the essential act in experiencing something is wholly internal: the opening of some slippery gland or the clenching of some hidden muscle to allow a full participation between one's self and the object (or event or experience or sensation). To achieve this act of full experience, sometimes it feels as though we must do something positive: clench or scrunch or try harder to focus all our energy. But sometimes, on the other hand, the essential act feels like a letting go. We must learn to release something and just *allow* the perception to fill us up.

I permit myself a grand vagueness here. I think the subject warrants it if we talk at the level of theory. But, in practice, things are simple. When I read a piece of imaginative writing that doesn't work—doesn't give me the experience it is talking about (such as the magenta clouds piece), I have learned that I can tell the student, "I can't *see* it! I don't believe you are really seeing or hearing it as you write. Don't think about words. Go back and experience it. Then see what words come." This advice usually helps.

For you as writer, then, the crucial distinction is between trying to experience your subject fully versus trying to find the right words. In the one activity your energy and attention are directed wholeheartedly to what you are describing, in the other your energy is directed at your language or at your reader or at considerations of what kind of writing you are doing.*

---

* William Byrd, the Elizabethan composer, said that the right *notes* would come without effort to a composer of religious music who succeeded in wholly fastening his mind upon the divine subject:

I don't mean that you should *never* turn your attention to the words or the audience, or never try to figure out whether you are saying the right thing in the right way. You can and should do exactly that—just as wholeheartedly—during a later revising process. You can make drastic changes as you revise and still win readers to create powerful experiences in their heads, so long as the ingredients you are revising grew out of a full experience of your subject. When you devote all your energy to having an experience, the words that come to you may be a great mess. For one thing, there may be too many words. When you try to experience your subject and let the words come as they please, you often find yourself wordily taking two and three shots at the same target. During revising, you will need to omit many of these words. In addition, you may have to rearrange many things—even make drastic changes of shape. Sometimes there are fewer words because you don't feel obliged to spell out everything you see in your raw version.

If you revise only by cutting and rearranging elements in your raw writing, you end up with a revision made only of first-draft words—words written while you were experiencing your subject matter and not thinking about writing. But you can also add new words and passages as you revise—self-consciously and critically making judgments about what the style, context, audience, and meaning demand. When your raw writing grows directly out of full experience of your subject, the life entrapped in these words enables you to generate more words during the revising process that also contain life. The life in those original words keeps you in touch with the experience and enables you to dart back into it even if only for a moment as you search for a better word or phrase—even though you are engaged in the cold, calculating process of revising.

There is such a profound and hidden power to sacred words that to one thinking upon things divine, diligently and earnestly pondering them, the most suitable of all musical measures occur (I know not how) as of themselves, and suggest themselves spontaneously to the mind that is not indolent and inert.

From the dedication to *Gradualia,* quoted by Joseph Kerman, in "William Byrd and the Catholics," *New York Review of Books,* May 17, 1979.

Some Examples

Consider this story by Chris Magson:

Bill and I were friends, closer than brothers. We grew up on farms next to each other, near Keene. Our families were close, too. When the war broke out, we both signed up, rather than being drafted. We went through basic training, and were assigned to the same unit. We fought for two years on the Pacific atolls and islands. It became hard to remember the days before, in New Hampshire.

One day while establishing a beach-head on some God-forsaken atoll, our unit was wiped out. Bill and me were all that was left. No wounded. I never have figured out what happened. One moment, we were ducking our heads to dodge the flying ammunition, and the next moment everything was quiet, except for the sounds of bloated flies feasting on the sores of the corpses. We kept our heads down, not daring to twitch.

After a while, Bill stuck his head above the mound of sand we were hiding behind. "Frank," he whispered to me, "there's nothing out there." When he said that, I took a peek. Nothing but the mangled bodies strewn on the sand. I recognized a few. Silent, we gathered up the dog tags. Most of them were discolored. We didn't see a sign of the enemy. Not alive, anyway. We took all the water and food we could carry and set off to find the highest part of the small isle. The growth was stunted, and yellow. We didn't say much. We heard nothing, not even a bird.

Bill was walking in front of me about twenty paces, but when he stepped on the mine, it sent me flying. I fetched up against a tree. When I came to, the first thing I saw was the bloody bundle of rags that was Bill. He had no legs or arms anymore. I went over to him. He was alive, but just barely. Numbly, I tourniquetted his seeping stumps and shot an ampule of morphine into his shattered hip. I looked at his face, and turned away again. He was trying to speak, so I leant near his mouth. "Frank," he said, his breath flagging, "don't leave me like this . . . rifle." I knew what he wanted, and I put my gun next to his ear, but I couldn't squeeze the trigger. Blood came out of his mouth and I thought he was dead. I left him, and stumbled weeping uphill. I walked until I noticed that the plants were getting green, and I could hear a bird. I stopped and sat. I poured a little warm water from the canteen over my hair, and wondered what to do next. The sun was white, and it bounced off the rocks nearby and struck my wet eyes.

I got up and walked some more, hoping to find shade. I didn't find any, so I kept walking. I stumbled into a glade without noticing. I looked down, and the grass under my dusty boots looked trimmed. I sat down and wondered about it. Anything to keep my mind off of Bill. It was about then that I saw something in the middle of the opening. It looked like a bank safe without a door or handle. On the top of it, there was something like a funnel tilted off to one side. The object was a dull grey, and the funnel-thing looked like an old gramo-phone trumpet. There was no grass around it, just a circle of yellow dust. It hurt my eyes to look at the thing. It made a noise just then, a sound like a pulse beat. I couldn't hear it exactly, but I could feel it in my bones. The pulse got louder, and more vibrant, and it kept in-creasing until my eyes watered. It went THUM THUM THUM and then, out of the funnel, shapes in dark smoke erupted. They rolled into themselves like furry smoke rings. I remember Bill's grandfather used to delight us when we were little by making them, his creased face working. But it wasn't smoke rings that came out of the thing, but shapes, rectangles, smoky pyramids and perfect spheres. I watched it, not believing. The shapes curled out, and instead of fad-ing, they came to the ground and flattened out, while retaining their shape. The thing let out an anvil-shaped burst, and stopped.

"Hello, I've been waiting so long," something in back of me said. I whirled around, and stood facing the lady. She was dressed in a knee-length black skirt and there were pearls clustered round her throat. She was about fifty, or maybe forty. It was hard to tell. She spoke again. "Now, I can leave. Thank you so much for coming." She held her hands out by her side and closed them, saying, "Come children, we must go now." She walked away, her arms positioned like she was holding hands with two children. She looked back at me smiling, and said, "You must understand. I know they are gone, but the delusion is enough for me." I shouted at her as she left the clearing. "What do you mean! Please!" The thing in the center THRUMed again, and I turned around. Bill was walking toward me, waving his arm and smiling. He broke into a trot.

There are three passages which I feel trying hardest to be pow-erful: the early silent moment with flies and corpses, the death of the buddy, and the final pathos of the woman's feeling for her children. But though these passages tug at me and ask me to have a powerful experience, I find I refuse. I hold back from putting myself in and constructing the feelings asked for by the words. His rendering of the smoke machine, on the other hand, seems power-ful. I experience it vividly. I'm taken out of myself and given a kind of participation in that strange series of images and in this way I am genuinely moved by it.

My hypothesis is that the writer *experienced* that machine more wholeheartedly, with better focus of attention, than he did any other part of the story. When I spoke to him I discovered that the machine, exactly as he described it, had appeared to him in a dream the night before he wrote the story and that it had indeed been the germ that gave rise to the whole story. He was, in effect, starting off from a powerful experience and I would say that he managed well, as he wrote, to put himself back into that experience, to connect with those perceptions in his dream.

Let me contrast this powerful passage with the other three that are trying but not fully succeeding in making me construct an experience in my head. The final one with the woman and children seems particularly weak. It seems generated almost entirely by a clever (though obscure) *idea* the writer had—a gimmick almost—as he cogitated a way to end the story. He didn't let the story end itself; he had to figure out and manipulate an ending.

The middle passage about the death of the buddy, I would guess, does to some degree grow out of an experience, but I sense it also grows out of the *idea* of this event: it is a conceptualized event as much as it is an *experienced* event. My guess is that the writer had an experience of sorts—some kind of losing of a buddy, yes—but really wasn't willing to pay anywhere near the price in emotional investment it would have taken to go past the feelings to the event itself and experience precisely *this* loss of a buddy through gruesome, close-up death.

That early moment of silence with flies and corpses is an interesting borderline case. It is a powerful sentence with its sudden contrast: "One moment we were ducking our heads to dodge the flying ammunition and the next moment everything was quiet except for the sounds of the bloated flies feasting on the sores of the corpses." It doesn't quite win me to have the experience it is talking about, but I may be more finicky here than some readers: I think my refusal comes as much as anything from the fact that he is trying to make me have such a strong experience so early in the story. If I came on these words later in the story, after I had built up more trust for him (which I do build up—until the gimmicky ending, where I lose it) probably I would consent automatically to build for myself the experience he was trying to convey. (My hunch is that he was experiencing the time-lapse—a striking psychological event that probably intrigued him in his own experience—more than the gruesome physical details.)

Since I started looking at writing and my reactions in this way, I have begun to sense a kind of small-is-powerful principle. That is, often I find the most powerful parts of a story to be renderings of smaller, less intense experiences. Writers often fail when they try to render deep, harrowing ones. They run into a double barrier. Not only is it harder for them as writers to put themselves wholeheartedly into such strong experiences; but even if they do so, they are asking for an enormous expenditure on the part of the reader.

Of course, it can work the other way around: a powerful or harrowing experience, because of its impact on the writer, can lead her to focus better all her attention upon it so that she experiences it fully again as she sits down to her desk two months or two years later. Notice, however, that bigger is only likely to be better if it is an experience you have actually had. When you try to *make up* intensely powerful events, you are especially likely to fall on your face. And, in general, as I see writers learning really to experience what they are rendering in words, I see them tending to de-escalate the emotional scale, and focus on smaller, humbler events than they used to try for. It is the hallmark of inexperienced writers—corny *True Magazine* writers—constantly to clutch for more and more "powerful" experiences. Since they don't really experience all these harrowing events as they write, they don't come up with words which inspire a reader to do so either.

Consider this short piece by Randy Silverman:

Snaggle-toothed, crouched in a hall that is dimly lit, draped in a non-descript raincoat, stands a man. He is drunk, he's not a poet. Like a dream on a moonless night, he stands there and does not think. He is the remains of a life he would rather not remember. Lost behind the bloodshot doors of misery lay a man of heart. In the eyes of this stranger was no sign of recognition that a rather large, green, iguana was scampering up the hall towards him. The iguana's tail brushed his shoe as it ran down the hall, followed closely by three or four excited children. The iguana scurried in an open door down the hall, and the kids disappeared close behind it. The door slammed, and the hall was again thrown into dim-lit silence.

The snaggle-toothed man, now leaning against a door frame, gurgled to himself a song he no longer remembered. His eyes wandered around the hall, taking in the old paint and plaster. He caught a glimpse of his reflection in the glass window of the door across the hall, and he paused. A faint recognition ran through his mind, like a hedgehog moving in its tunnel. He remembered his wife, Mira, as she looked at him with her deep penetrating eyes, so serious. Her mouth showed no sign of a smile or ripple of a frown, a Mona Lisa mouth. Her hat was cloth and fit close to her head, turned up at the edges. One shoulder was bare.

The man looked away from the glass and down to the floor. He hunched his head over and heaved a sob of grief, then another, and another, until his eyes burst into tears. His head bobbed up and down like a cork for a few minutes, then the tears subsided into a calm stream, washing his face and beard.

Suddenly he noticed a tugging at his pants leg. Looking down, he discovered the tugging was coming from a little girl of no more than four, standing there next to him in her nightgown. In her left hand she was holding out a napkin for him to take. He reached out his hand and took the napkin from her and put it to his face.

These words have the power of making me construct the experiences rather than just reading the directions. I hear the music. I believe that in the act of writing, Silverman managed to focus wholeheartedly on the events or images, to participate in the experience he is rendering. There is no energy leaking off to the side in a search for words or concern for the reader or doubt about the value of what he is describing. (Of course, he may have thought about all these things while he revised.)

I sense a slight lessening of power in this early passage: "He is the remains of a life he would rather not remember. Lost behind the bloodshot doors of misery lay a man of heart." The passage *interprets* the scene—*tells* us how to feel—rather than just *giving* us the scene. In contrast, however, the very next sentence about the iguana represents for me a surge of greater than usual experience. In the later simile about the hedgehog and the memory of the wife, I feel a better than usual ability to let the words grow out of experience.

My hypothesis is that Silverman managed in this story, and especially in those strong passages, to stand out of the way—to keep his *self* or *mere thinking* or *feeling* out of the way—and to let the experiences somehow find their way into words under their own steam. (It is interesting to note that just as when you read something good you don't feel you are expending any effort, so, too, when your writing goes particularly well, you may not feel you are expending effort either. When you make a good enough connection with the bamboo, neither you nor your reader has to do any work; all the energy comes from the bamboo, from the gods, from fission. All the same, you may feel drained and tired at the end of one of these lucky writing sessions.)

My emphasis on the need to *have* the experience is just another way of giving the old traditional writing advice: show, don't tell. That is, if you want readers to feel something, it's no good telling them how to feel ("it was simply *terrifying*"). You have to show them things that will terrify them. When I feel a writer trying to convey an experience by intoning "nevermore" or "ineluctable" or "chthonic," I resist her and do not get the experience: she is taking her attention away from her perception of the bamboo and becoming preoccupied with trying to make an effect. Explaining or trying too hard for fancy language is like holding up laugh cards to the studio audience at a radio or TV show: we resist when they try to *tell* us how to feel.

The advice here is *almost* (but not quite) the same as that other traditional advice: to give lots of specific sensory details and avoid generalizations. That is, if I persuade you to be specific in describing the tree and not just gush about how beautiful it is—to give the color of its leaves and the texture of its bark and the sound of its leaves in the wind—that will probably force you to go back and re-experience that tree. But it is not the sensory details in themselves that will make your description work, it is your experience of the tree that does it.

Sometimes when people are advised again and again to put specific details in their writing, they start to make them up without experiencing them. Here at the end of this passage is a particularly lifeless-because-not-experienced sensory detail.

After work, Don went to a show he had seen advertised in the newspaper. It was in a hotel ballroom not far from the shop. Don went into the main showroom, his feet tipping into the thick crimson carpet.

This was written by a student who seemed to me to suffer from a tendency to write from ideas and conceptions rather than from experience. I was searching for something to praise—something where I could say, "Do more of this," not just "Don't do that"—and I lit on the bit about the feet hitting the carpet. And "tipping into" is an interesting metaphor. I ended up saying, "Do more of that," but, in truth, I suspect that the whole detail of the feet hitting the red carpet grew out of an idea or a ready-made phrase-and-idea that the writer had encountered in her reading, not out of experience. I couldn't really feel any experience of feet hitting carpet. (Of course, reading is a source of real experience, too: one can borrow phrases and even long passages out of one's reading—as many great writers have done—so long as you *experience them* and thereby make them yours.) In short, "See the tree!" or "Experience the tree!" is better advice than "Give more specific details about the tree!" Experiencing the tree can, in fact, lead to *unspecific* writing that is nevertheless powerful—as the following passage illustrates:

> We drank in the garden. It was a spring day—one of those green-gold Sundays that excite our incredulity. Everything was blooming, opening, burgeoning. There was more than one could see—prismatic lights, prismatic smells, something that sets one's teeth on edge with pleasure—but it was the shadow that was most mysterious and exciting, the light one could not define. We sat under a big maple, its leaves not yet fully formed but formed enough to hold the light, and it was astounding in its beauty, and seemed not like a single tree but one of a million, a link in a long train of leafy trees beginning in childhood.
>
> JOHN CHEEVER, "The Lowboy,"
> *The Stories of John Cheever* (New York, 1978)

A Warning about Feelings

"If you want to write well, make sure that you have lots of strong feelings." That may seem to be my message here, but it is not. I have purposely used the word "experience" for what the writer needs—no doubt till you are very tired of it—and avoided as much as possible the word "feelings" or "emotions."

But our language is fuzzy in distinguishing the different things people have inside: feelings, experiences, conceptions, ideas. When I say that the writer "should experience" what she is writing about, I mean something much closer to "should see and hear" than "should feel strongly." Feelings get confused with experiences because, when we experience something fully, feelings occur, too: real experiences hit us hard. But strong feelings, in themselves, don't help you breathe experience into words. In fact, some of the worst writing fails precisely because it comes too much out of feelings rather than out of the event or scene itself—out of the bamboo.

Consider, for example, what happens if you decide to write about that car accident you were in. You will find that there is a huge difference between the words that grow out of your *experience* of the accident and those that grow out of your *feelings* about it. To experience it, you have to go back and be there—see, smell, and hear everything. But the feelings you end up with—"It was so *awful*" or whatever—may well impede you from re-experiencing the accident. (And happy feelings can also block full experience of an event. "It was so wonderful, so glorious, I felt like I'd never felt before" is sometimes all the inexperienced writer can say when she gives in to her *feelings* about an event she wants to write about.)

Of course, it wasn't just sights and sounds you were experiencing during the car accident, you were probably experiencing feelings, too. So, when you let words grow out of the experience itself—when you manage to go back and connect with or relive the accident—you will have words that issue not only from sensory experiences, but also from feelings, too. As well you should. But it's not that these are *feelings* that makes them the right source for your words, it's that they are part of the experience of the accident. What causes so much bad writing is the flood of *later feelings* that tend to follow, if only by an instant or two, any strong experience. These later feelings tend to dominate our memory and, as we write, rush in to monopolize our attention. The reason they do so, I think, is that they are a kind of short cut that saves us from actually re-experiencing the event itself.

In either case feelings, as feelings, are of no value for writing. They are of value only insofar as they are part of the original experience itself that you are trying to render in words. Therefore, you should probably lean a bit away from them since they have such a tendency to numb or mush or blot out the rest of your experiencing. Thus teachers are sometimes led to make an extreme though perhaps useful blanket rule: no feelings! Stick to sense data.

Notice how few feelings there are in the Silverman piece about the drunk (though it creates feelings in the reader). The weakest sentence results from a slide into telling feelings about how pathetic this man is. Silverman's strength was his ability to zero in on the object and not his feelings about it. The Magson war story is weakest at the three emotional moments and strongest in the smoke machine which is rendered without feelings. In short, having feelings about the bamboo is not the same as going to the bamboo.

You can, of course, write powerfully not about the car accident, but about the feelings you have as a result of it—the funk, the jitters, or whatever. Fine. In that case you should try to let your words grow out of those feelings, or if you are writing much later, you should try to get back and re-experience them. But don't pretend you are writing about a car accident. You are writing about the emotional aftermath of a car accident.

Advice

The goal is to get power into words. If I am right, that means getting your reader to breathe experience into what you write: get her to pedal while you steer, get her to let you play with her mind, get her to hear music and not just read notes. To make this happen, *you* must breathe experience into your words. You must go to the bamboo. But what does this mean in practice?

• Direct all your efforts into experiencing—or re-experiencing—what you are writing about. Put all your energy into connecting with the object. Be there. See it. *Participate* in whatever you are writing about and then just let the words come of their own accord.

• You can fix the words later when you revise. That's when you can be savage: cut, correct, clarify, rearrange entirely. That's when you can and should think carefully about your audience and what style is appropriate; about your topic and what approach will work best. It's easy as you revise to make enormous changes in style, tone, approach, and structure and still keep life in your words.

• In your raw writing, don't let your words grow out of a conception or idea. It's *possible* to start with a conception—"Let's see. What about a story of someone who marries his mother by mistake"—as long as you are then willing to move past your clever idea into actually experiencing the events that are entailed by it.

But that is a dangerous route unless you are a very skilled writer. When you start out from an idea or scheme or gimmick, it is usually harder to *have* the experiences.

• Use memories. It is usually easier to experience things that actually happened to you than to experience made-up events or scenes.

• Write about what is important to you. If it is important, you will probably find the psychic energy you need to really connect with it or open yourself to it. But don't rely on intensity to arouse yourself or your reader. Intensity is often a prophylactic against experience. And peak experiences that never happened to you are especially hard to relive. But I mustn't be dogmatic about these subsidiary rules. Sometimes you can connect better with a big event, sometimes a little one. And some people actually connect better with fantasy events than with remembered ones. It's the main rule that is important: wherever the experience is, go there.

• I suggested earlier that if you want the reader to trust you or give consent to having an experience at your hands, you must trust yourself and not think too calculatingly about what you want to do to her. This may sound like impossible advice ("Don't think about sex" or "Don't put beans up your nose"). But if you follow the main advice in this chapter, you can achieve the purity of heart you need. If you just put all your energy into actually seeing what you are talking about, you won't have any attention left over for creating that distracting fog of self-doubt or manipulativeness.

• Don't ask for too big an experience from your reader too soon.

• Learn to coach yourself, to give yourself pep talks as you write—especially if you sense yourself losing contact with what you are trying to write about:

Be there! See it! Hallucinate! Hear it! Feel it! Be that person!

Close your eyes and don't let yourself write down any words until you can actually see and hear and touch what you are writing about.

To hell with words, *see* something!

• Read out loud as much as you can: your own writing and that of others. It develops the crucial muscle you need for learning to focus your attention wholeheartedly upon the meaning of words as you emit them. Listeners can actually hear it when you let even a tiny bit of your attention leak away, and this will help you gradually to gain control over this slippery inner putting-experience-into-words muscle.

• Whenever you get feedback, always ask readers to point out the bits that actually made them see something or hear something or experience something. Insist on the real thing: not just what feels to them like impressive or earnest writing, but passages that actually caused movies in their heads. It is rare. Much of your writing will cause no movies at all. That's par. But when feedback shows you even a few short passages that actually do it, you will be able to think yourself back into what it felt like as you wrote them. This will give you a seat-of-the-pants feeling for what you must do to get power into your words—what muscle you have to scrunch or let go of to breathe life into your writing.

• Play the image game—with one other person or with a small group. Take turns giving each other images. If the listener doesn't actually *see* the image, then you must stop, stop trying to say words, and go back inside to work harder at actually seeing the image. Others must wait patiently for you to get there. They must allow you the time and silence and concentration you need to tune out your present surroundings and focus all your attention on the image you are trying to experience.

This game helps you most effectively if you start small. Focus only on a couple of objects. Instead of trying to describe that whole scene on the terrace, focus down on the small table next to the canvas chair: the number 2 pencil with a broken point touching a moist ring left by a cold drink on a plastic table.* And don't use narrative. Restrict yourself to what can be captured by a still photograph. Narrative is a way to get your reader's attention, but it is a rudimentary kind of attention, mere curiosity about what happens next. It doesn't make her actually build an experience in her head. Narrative is powerful but you need to have it *in addition* to experience in your words, not as a crutch or substitute for experience.

---

*It's by illuminating a tiny fragment of a scene and just suggesting the rest of it in a minimal way that you are most likely to get listeners to recreate the scene for themselves. One tiny detail serves as a kind of dust particle that listeners need in order to crystallize a snowflake out of their own imaginations. Trying to describe *everything* usually means that nothing really comes alive. And by zeroing in on just a detail or two, you establish your point of view.

These are good rules of thumb: start small, focus your attention on only a few details, let them be the spark for the listener's more elaborate creation. But the process isn't the same for everyone. The main thing is for the listeners to stop you if they don't get movies in their heads from your words; and your response should not be to search for better words, but to increase your efforts actually to see what you are describing.

• Don't let this chapter trick you back into your worst habits: "No, I'm not ready to write yet. I don't *see* it clearly enough in my head. I'm not having a *real* experience. I'd better go and look through some old photos I have. I will experience things better if I do some research or take a long walk or lie down on the sofa and close my eyes." Sometimes the best way to get to the experience of what you are writing about is through nonstop writing, even if at first the words seem dead, mechanical, and unfelt. It's all right to close your eyes and stop putting out words when you are playing the image game, with a live audience right there listening to you. The presence of others will ensure that you will come up with words before long. And if you happen to be someone who writes easily and is already turning out pages and pages and pages of writing that somehow lack power, *perhaps* it will help you to sit longer in silence before actually putting words to paper. But for most people, the important thing is to keep writing.

28

Breathing Experience into Expository Writing

What about expository writing: essays, reports, articles, memos, and other conceptual writing? They usually grow more out of thinking than out of sights, sounds, smells, or touch. Must they then fail to have power? fail to make the reader hear music? fail, that is, to make the reader construct an experience for himself? When we look for power in writing we certainly look more often to creative writing—narrative and descriptive and poetic writing—than to expository writing.

But there is the same distinction to be made for expository writing that I made above for descriptive or narrative writing: the distinction between words that have power because they grow out of experience and words that lack power because they do not. For the fact is that thinking about the bamboo is just as much an experience as seeing the bamboo. And just as people sometimes describe a remembered tree without fully experiencing it (thus the weaker image of the tree with flowers in the middle of the lawn)—indeed, people sometimes even describe the tree right in front of them without fully experiencing it—so too people can describe a *thought* without fully experiencing it. In short, seeing a tree, imagining a tree and having a thought about a tree are all mental events that one can experience fully or not so fully. And the problem in giving power to conceptual writing is the same as it is for giving power to descriptive or narrative writing: if you want your reader to *experience* your thinking and not just manage to understand it—if you want him to feel your thoughts alive inside him or

339

hear the music of your ideas—then *you* must experience your thoughts fully as you write.

But it's not so easy to describe the difference between "really experiencing" a thought and "sort of experiencing" it. For descriptive writing I could just say "See it!" and "Forget about language!" but you can't see thoughts and they only exist in the form of words—for many people at least. It usually helps to say "Feel it!" but feelings are not really the point. The essential act is participating fully in the thought. We say someone "believes what he's saying" or "speaks with conviction" and those phrases probably indicate that the speaker is experiencing his thought. But you don't really have to believe or have conviction about an idea to put your whole self into it—you just have to make some kind of inner investment or concentration of energy.

But in practice the situation turns out to be much the same for expository writing as for descriptive or narrative writing. The same kind of effort is needed: put all your attention into connecting wholeheartedly with your thoughts and get inside them instead of trying so hard to find the right language for communicating them. The same kind of advice makes it happen: "Close your eyes and go there! Be there! Stop worrying so much about describing your thoughts clearly or well!" Most people, in fact, benefit from being told "See it! Hear it! Feel its texture!"

If you are not really experiencing your thoughts as you write, pretend you are the first person who ever had that thought and write excitedly about your new breakthrough. Pretend perhaps that the idea is dangerous and write arguments against it. These are ways to connect with thoughts as though they really matter when you have lost your focus or concentration.

It also helps to put your body into it. Let your *muscles* react in some way as you say or write your thought. See which part of your body the thought wants to erupt through. Some researchers have found that children have a physical reaction—a piece of tension-release in some part of their body, a shiver or jiggle—when they figure something out. What's special about figuring something out is that it always consists of a *new* thought or a *new* connection, and you can't have a new thought without really experiencing it.

Thus you usually get more experience into your words when you are figuring something out for the first time than when you write about an old idea you've long understood. You see more in it and write more vividly. Watch someone give a lecture he has given many times before. You can tell very easily whether or not he manages to re-experience the ideas as he explains them again.

If we ask why people should do this peculiar thing of "having a thought" enough to remember or explain it, yet not experience it fully, the answer is the same as for why people should describe images without really seeing them in the mind's eye: it's easier. You have to put out energy to experience something—even if it seems to happen without effort under ideal conditions. For example you might have had an important idea or train of thought last week which you want to write about. But now you are very tired or in a completely different frame of mind. You will tend to drift into telling your thinking more or less from memory. Your words will essentially be a reconstruction of a past event. It will take extra effort and investment to put yourself back again fully into last week's thinking, start it up again as a *present* event. If you do so and manage fully to experience your thinking, that will sometimes make your writing clearer ("Oh, *now* I see how I got from P to Q."). But sometimes it will make your writing messier ("This exciting idea seems to lead me in all directions at once. I can't stay on one track."). Coherence is not the goal of raw writing, life is. Coherence is what you must impose on raw writing as you revise.

Much of the writing we are asked to do in school or work involves explaining someone else's thinking. To do this well we must get inside that other person's idea. That's the mark of good popularizers of science, such as Isaac Asimov and Arthur Koestler. Perhaps they are describing what Kepler thought or explaining a basic fact of chemistry, but they manage better than most others to get themselves to *have* the ideas they want to convey. When we have to write about the thinking of others, we are especially likely to slip into the path of least resistance, the energy-efficient method: we summarize the ideas without really being there. That's why children who are never asked in school to write about their own thinking often get worse and worse at experiencing thought.

It's often some kind of distraction or confusion that keeps us from experiencing fully what we are writing about. If you are worried about your writing or about your audience's reaction you cannot keep your whole attention on what you are trying to say. I think of the classic scene where the student comes in to the teacher about a bad grade on an essay. The teacher says, "I got confused. Tell me what you were driving at," and as the student gets involved in explaining his idea, his meaning gets clearer and his words more alive. "Why didn't you *write* it that way?" the teacher asks, and the student doesn't know why. But the act of writing an essay for the teacher took so much attention away from *experiencing* his idea—attention given to worrying about whether he was saying the right thing and saying it right—that his words ended up dead and dull and probably unclear. Note, however, that his spoken words were not, strictly speaking, *clear* or *coherent*. A transcript would show them as a mess. The teacher praised them because they managed finally to state the essential idea in a pointed and felt way—probably through some crucial distinctions. But this main idea and these distinctions were scattered here and there in a pudding of language which was a mess—but felt and alive. Notice, then, how this is a picture of exactly what that student should have written for a rough draft. The teacher is really praising a messy but lively first draft that the student probably didn't dare write.

In summary, then, I can make the same statements about expository and creative writing. Even though experiencing requires more energy than not experiencing, if things go well you naturally and easily do experience what you are writing about. To experience fully is natural, human, and alive. But when you are tired, under pressure, scared, or distracted, it takes an act of special effort and self-management to get yourself to experience fully what you are writing about. You need to learn to stop, concentrate your energy, and focus your attention wholeheartedly on your meaning—and do it so vigorously that you don't have any energy or attention left over for worries or distractions.

The Special Difficulty of Expository Writing

It seems especially rare to find essays and reports that take you past an understanding of the ideas actually to hear the music of those ideas. Teachers can usually get more power out of their students by asking them to write stories and descriptions from personal experience than by asking them to write from their thinking. Why should this be?

The answer is that it's not good enough to breathe real, experienced thinking into your expository writing; that thinking must also be *disciplined*. Thoughts are supposed to be coherent, that is, to begin at the beginning and follow along a single track and end up at the end or conclusion. And there aren't supposed to be any mistakes in logic. But that's not a picture of how the mind usually experiences thoughts. Our habitual thinking is seldom strictly logical but rather associational, analogical, metaphorical. We think and we experience our thoughts, but those thoughts are often rambling or even jumpy—and mixed up with feelings and stories and descriptions. To think three or eleven thoughts in a row, follow logic, and come out with the right answer at the end is something our minds can be trained to do, but we seldom do it out of school or work. Seeing and hearing we do all the time.

No wonder it seems harder to give readers an experience with reports and essays than with creative writing. You must *translate* more. There is a longer path you must travel from experienced thinking to acceptable expository writing than you need to travel from experienced sensation to acceptable creative writing. To take this longer path, either you must manipulate and censor your thought-experiences more as you try to write down correct thoughts in the right order; or else you must revise more as you transform your raw, uncensored writing into logical coherence. Either way—whether you practice internal manipulation or external revising—you are likely to lose more of your *experience of thinking* during the writing process. Hence the final piece of expository writing is likely to fail to make the reader hear music.

Expository writing *harder* than creative writing? It is usually assumed that anyone can learn to write acceptable expository prose but that only gifted or special people can learn to write creatively. "Oh, I can't write stories, I'm not a creative person, I'm just a normal person" is the assumed logic here. But this common assumption involves a double standard. More is demanded of creative writing than of expository writing. Creative writing must actually make the reader experience the sights and sounds and feelings it is trying to get across, not just communicate them. Otherwise it's felt as not worth reading, not worth writing. Expository writing on the other hand is called acceptable or even good if it does no more than make its ideas clear—even if the reader doesn't experience or feel those ideas at all. Try saying this sentence to a creative writer after you have read his story or poem: "I understand *perfectly* just what you were trying to get across." He is liable to be crushed. "Didn't you feel anything? SEE anything?" It's a much worse put-down than if you just said "Huh?" But if you say exactly the same sentence to an expository writer after you read his essay or report, he will take it as praise. For the creative writer to "get something across," he must get the reader to feel it. For the expository writer to "get something across," he need only get the reader to know what it is.

This double standard can be defended, I suppose. After all, we only read creative writing for fun. If it doesn't give us an experience we put it down. It is a reader's market. But when it comes to expository writing it is often a writer's market. No matter how badly written that report or article is, often we may *not* put it down, we must keep on reading it and try to digest its ideas for our jobs or for our own needs. One might also argue that since everyone has to write expository prose for many tasks in life, but not creative writing, it is unfair to insist on talent. Mere adequacy should be called good enough.

But I object to this double standard. Speaking as a reader, I call it tyranny. We don't have to accept all this dead expository writing without fighting back. We can demand that it have experience in it. Of course a change in expectations will not automatically improve all expository writing. People write plenty of dead creative writing now even though they understand that it must have life in it or they have failed. But it would make an enormous difference if we could change people's attitudes and convince expository writers that their job is to make readers experience their thinking, not merely understand it.

I know it sounds crazy to talk of raising standards for expository writing when it is now so terrible in most realms of public and professional life. But look for a moment at what is terrible about it. Not just that it is unclear or full of jargon and formulas. The real problem is writers' refusal to take full and open responsibility for what they are saying. If a writer is willing to say, in effect, "I'm *me*, I'm saying *this*, and I'm saying it to *you*," his words will not just have more life in them, they will also be clearer and more coherent. The worst and most pervasive form of bad writing is some form of hiding or chickening-out. "The great enemy of clear language is insincerity," writes George Orwell in "Politics and the English Language." Memo and report writers could no longer refuse to take responsibility for their words if they were really trying to get readers to experience what they were saying. Writing in this fashion they would have to invest themselves more in what they write, and as a result they would have more fun and not hate writing so much.

Perhaps I exaggerate. There is, it is true, a certain amount of expository writing that does make us hear the music of the ideas when we read it:

> "The question is very simple. I requested the court to appoint me attorney and the court refused." So Gideon had written to the Supreme Court in support of his claim that the Constitution entitled the poor man charged with crime to have a lawyer at his side. Most Americans would probably have agreed with him. To even the best informed person unfamiliar with the law it seemed inconceivable, in the year 1962, that the Constitution would allow a man to be tried without a lawyer because he could not afford one.
>
> But the question was really as far from simple as it could imaginably be. Behind it there was a long history—a history, that until recently had seemed resolutely opposed to Gideon's claim but now had started to turn and move in his direction. The question that Gideon presented could not be resolved without reference to issues that had been fought over by judges and statesmen and political philosophers—issues going to the nature of our constitutional system and to the role played in it by the Supreme Court.
>
> We have come to take it for granted in this country that courts, especially the Supreme Court, have the power to review the actions of governors, legislators, even Presidents, and set them aside as unconstitutional. But this power of judicial review, as it is called, has been given to judges in few other countries—and nowhere, at any time, to the extent that our history has confided it in the Supreme Court. In the guise of legal questions there come to the Supreme Court many of the most fundamental and divisive issues of every era, issues which judges in other lands would never dream of having to decide.
>
> The consequences are great for Court and country. For the justices power means responsibility, a responsibility the more weighty because the Supreme Court so often has the last word. Deciding cases is never easy, but a judge may sleep more soundly after sentencing a

man to death—or invalidating a President's seizure of the nation's steel mills—if he knows there is an appeal to a higher court. Justices of the Supreme Court do not have that luxury.

ANTHONY LEWIS, *Gideon's Trumpet*,
Chapter 6 (New York, 1964)

And our minds are naturally logical too, not just associational. For although Socrates doesn't prove in the *Meno* that the uneducated slave boy already knows the Pythagorean theorem from a previous existence, he does drive home that brute fact about all human minds: we cannot quarrel with correct logic once we understand it. Logic is built into us. Logic may even give deeper excitement than seeing and hearing. Certainly for many people the most intense music is the music of the spheres—the perception of built-in coherence in nature—and that is the music of pure ideas. We all have the capacity to hear it.

But the truth is that we don't hear it much these days as we read our allotment of expository writing. We could blame ourselves: if only we listened harder as Plato asked us to listen. But Plato didn't have to read most of the expository writing that comes into our hands either. (Socrates himself didn't believe in writing words down at all. He didn't think juice could be transmitted to paper.)

In any event my point still stands about the difficulty of giving readers a powerful experience with expository writing, and this difficulty can be restated in simple commonsense terms: for creative writing to be good, it has only to make the reader hear music; for expository writing to be good, it also has to be correctly reasoned and true. When you are writing about sensations in a story, you get to tell them any way you want, so long as you make readers feel them. You get to decide how you perceived them and what it was like and what order to tell them in. But if you are writing your thinking, everyone seems to have automatic permission to tell you whether it is true and what order it should go in. Since expository prose will probably be judged more for its truth and correctness than for its power, it is virtually impossible to write it without paying great attention to whether it is true and correct. How, then, can you possibly give all your energy and attention to experiencing that thought?

So why try? Why take all this energy away from the serious task of making your reasoning true and correct, and squander it on getting your writing to pulse with life, if that only gives readers a more palpable experience of the muddle in your mind? Why not simply accept the fact that of course conceptual writing requires disciplined thinking; that of course discipline means following more rules than you must follow for creative writing. (That's why people who hate rules prefer to write creatively.) And therefore accept the obvious conclusion: to *experience* disciplined thinking, you have to *do* more of it. It's not enough just to invest yourself in your own muddled thoughts.

But when I look around at people who do a lot of disciplined thinking—people who are especially good at getting correctness and truth into their writing—I see that they are not necessarily better for that reason at breathing life into their essays or reports. Some are good at it, many are not. Philosophers, logicians, and mathematicians are probably the most disciplined of all thinkers, yet they are not better, as a class, than other writers at getting readers to feel their ideas. When, on the other hand, I look at people who are good at getting readers to feel their ideas, I see that they are not necessarily more disciplined as thinkers.

As far as I can see then, the ability to discipline your thinking and the ability to make readers *experience* your thinking do not necessarily correlate with each other. My conclusion is that learning to discipline your thinking is a good thing: it will improve your life in many ways; it will make your writing truer and more vigorous. Most of the suggestions in this book, especially in the revising section, are designed to help you get more disciplined thinking into your prose and will probably do so more effectively than if you took a course in logic. But learning to discipline your thinking won't, in itself, get you any closer to the goal of *this* chapter: making readers *experience* what you tell them.

Look at good popular expository prose in magazines and nonfiction books; even at good academic or professional writing (except for what appears in scholarly journals). Such writing often violates the rules for expository writing that are taught in school. It violates those rules so that the writing will resemble more closely the way people experience thinking. If we list some of the striking characteristics of how people experience thinking we will be describing characteristics found in much good published expository writing:

• We often experience our thinking with lots of "I, I, I" in it. The agent who is having these thoughts is often at the center of awareness. So, too, a good professional writer often explains his ideas in terms of how he arrived at them or how he understands them.

• Trains of thought as we experience them usually do not start at the beginning, logically speaking, but rather at some perplexing dilemma or some striking fact or example that captured our attention and made us start to wonder about this whole issue. From this arresting detail we must often fight a long way backward to the logical beginning of the matter and forward to the concluding "answer." That's just how good writers often structure their essays.

• The mind often takes three or four different approaches to a problem before coming up with one that succeeds. So, too, will some good writers carry you through a few failed attempts before getting to an approach that succeeds. Theoretically this takes longer but sometimes it is the best way to help the reader really understand the problem.

• The mind often works by association, analogy, digression: we get lost and sometimes seem to lose or forget the thread of our quest even though, deep down, we are still working on the problem. A good professional writer sometimes permits digressions during which the reader may even forget the main point or question. Indeed, sometimes you can't get readers to reconceptualize something till you get them to forget about it for a little while and come upon it unexpectedly from a new direction.

Natural thinking is often characterized by incoherence and error, too, of course, while good writing embodies disciplined thinking. But disciplined thinking need not be so different—in *style* and *structure*—from the way the mind operates naturally. That is, the thinking needs to be correct, but the writing can still seem more like someone puzzling something out or talking to you than like logical syllogisms or mathematical equations.

I don't mean to say that it is impossible to breathe experience into the most strict, formal expository prose. But it is harder. The strictest, most formal expository prose I know is in academic journals, and writing there is notable for its deadness. The problem is not that these academics don't understand what they are talking about nor even that they are undisciplined in their thinking. (Plenty are undisciplined, of course, but even the disciplined ones usually fail to get power into their articles.) But as professionals or academics writing in their official journals to their most rigorous colleagues, too often they—or I should say "we" since I also write these articles—too often we allow ourselves to be too preoccupied as we write with whether we might be found wrong or with what a published, professional, learned essay ought to look like. When people try to conform to the strictest canons of expository writing, they seldom permit themselves to generate words out of a full and wholehearted experience of their thinking. Sometimes you can compare the same train of thought in a journal article and in a book by the same writer. The book version usually has a bit more life in it (whether it was written before or after the article) because the writer felt more as though he was following his *own* rules in the book.

The Dialectic of Attention

But even though the strictest rules for expository prose seem unnecessary to me, and even though you can probably write more informally for many audiences than some of your teachers have led you to believe, that is not my main point in this chapter. My main point is that if you want to breathe experience into your expository writing—to make your readers feel your ideas—you have an extra layer of difficulty that you don't have with creative writing. To breathe experience into your words, you have to pour all your energy into just experiencing the thought, yet in order to make it disciplined thought—however informal—you must also pour enormous energy into getting your thinking straight. These two goals conflict with each other.

Whenever you have to attain two conflicting goals, the best approach is to pay wholehearted attention first to one and then to the other in a dialectical alternation. If you try to reach for both goals at once—in this case experiencing your thinking and getting your thinking straight—you allow yourself to be tugged in opposite directions at the same time and you will just end up doing a mediocre job at both.

When I am writing something difficult for me—and this chapter is an example—I often have to switch my focus of attention back and forth more than once. That is, I start by putting all my energy into trying to experience my thinking as I write fast and uncritically: I try for total immersion in my thinking wherever it goes. But then during the next stage as I am critically revising and shaping my words and trying to make my thinking disciplined, I sometimes seem to lose touch with my ideas. As I try to remove blunders, to add clarifications, to deal with exceptions or counterarguments, and to construct a logical order for my thoughts, I slowly sag, and the energy seeps out of my words, and the writing gradually gets more complicated or wooden or dead. I become very discouraged where originally I had been excited. And sometimes it's not just the language that begins to feel dead but the ideas, too: "How could I ever have been so excited about these ideas? They are so tiresome or so obvious or so wrong-headed or so merely-intricate," my feelings tell me. It's only after I have brought more discipline to my thinking (though I may hate it more)—and usually I have to retype everything because it has become such a mess—that I finally realize I must go *back* and put all my effort into *feeling* those thoughts. As I do this I find I can gradually remove dead language and put in live language, words that I can feel, words that have breath in them. This process of reinvestment usually involves trying to *speak* the sentences I find on the page, feeling how awful they are, and then trying to *say* the thought in language I believe. Having, in effect, examined this creature for defects, now I can let myself fall in love with it again, become vulnerable to it or feel its power, and thereby invest myself linguistically in it again. Only then can I dare let my real words come out, the words that actually have my breath in them. During that intermediate period of detached critical examination I had, without realizing it, retracted or hidden or fogged over the words that were actually part of me. But since this process of reinvestment gives birth to lots of *new* words—and often brand new trains of thought are sparked off—I usually have to turn my energy back to critical revising once again. And so forth and so on, till I have a set of words that will pass muster with both of my consciousnesses.

I make this story sound a bit neater than what often happens with me. The truth is more ragged: piling up a lot of writing with parts that excite me; trying next to shape and revise it and as I do so gradually getting lost, thrashing around in a swamp, sunk, discouraged; and then by a dogged sweaty process I don't clearly see, finally getting out of my dilemma to a draft I believe in. For I am now just beginning to understand this dialectic of attention—just now beginning to to realize consciously that when I get too sagging and discouraged during the revising process, I need to start putting all my effort back again into the process of simply experiencing my words. What this means in practice is that I need to go back and read over the good bits of my raw writing to get in touch with them, perhaps read over some revised sections that I feel pleased with, and perhaps do some more raw writing. When I am reinvested, then I can turn back to revising with critical consciousness.

Sometimes when I am working on something I have already revised and clarified and struggled with, I glance back at something in my original pile of raw writing and I am surprised: "Hey, none of my revised versions has the power and life—even crispness—of this original passage. I didn't know where I was going, I didn't understand the main point, I didn't see it as part of a sustained train of thought, but I stated this particular idea with more *juice* here than I've managed to give it in any later clarification." The point is, I now realize, that it's hard during revising to *enter into* that idea with the wholeheartedness that I had the first time. Some of my attention is dissipated on considerations of where it goes, how it fits, and how to say it best. And also, I'm simply not *trying* as hard—not pouring myself into it—since I feel I already know that idea, I've already stated it, I've already got it in hand. Therefore I don't need to *put out* so much. If you want to play tennis well you have to pour your attention into looking at the ball. You lose that concentration or focus or full participation in the ball when you feel, "Oh yes, I see this ball, I know where it's going, I've got this thing in hand." That's when you are apt to miss the ball or hit it wrong.

Advice

• When you have expository writing to do—essays, memos, reports, or whatever—start by putting all your energy into experiencing your thinking. If you don't *have* much thinking yet—if you don't yet know much of what you want to say—experiencing your thinking turns out to be the best way to get more. That is, let your early writing be raw. Use whatever trains of thought you have as they occur to you, including digressions, frustrations, and doubts. In addition use the words themselves that simply come out of your mouth as you open it and force yourself to write even if they seem wrong or stupid or unsuitable. You will have raw writing that contains, much of it, the breath of experience. But of course it may have other characteristics of spontaneous thinking: its connections may be associational and analogical more often than logical; it may have mistakes in logic even where you tried to be logical; it may have many false starts and digressions; it may start somewhere in the middle—or rather it will start and restart in different places and tend to go in different directions at once; the language may be unclear or unsuitable. And it may lack any clear conclusion. But if you simply pile up all your thinking as it comes to you, you can produce many good ideas and much writing with life in it. That's exactly what you need for a first draft. Next, as you shape and revise this raw writing, you can give it clarity and coherence. Finally you can end up with writing that is coherent and logical but also makes the reader experience your ideas.

• On some occasions, however, you will already know almost everything you want to say before you sit down to write. You can start then by getting your thinking straight rather than experiencing your thinking. Start, that is, by making an outline (full sentences), since that is the best way to cross-examine, correct and organize your thinking. With the structure and security this outline gives you, you can engage in the writing itself and as you do so pour all your energy into experiencing your ideas. But if you find that sticking to your outline somehow drains life and experience from your writing, then I would advise skipping the outline and following the words where they go and using the outline later for organizing your raw writing.

• You can give yourself pep-talks as you write expository prose: "Feel it! Am I really experiencing it or just settling for describing it from memory? Be someone who cares deeply about this idea!"

• Role playing as you write is one of the best ways to breathe experience into words. If you are writing about someone else's ideas or explaining information you don't care about, pretending to *be* someone else will help you get more involved. For example, if you have to write a report explaining the three policies that your committee must choose from, pretend as you explain each policy that you are the person who invented it. Tell the idea in the first person: "First I realized this, then that . . ." As you revise you can make the few changes needed to put it back into your voice, but the ideas will have life. If you must write about thinking that feels ancient, strange, or tiresome to you—if you feel you can't get within a hundred miles of what you are writing about—pretend you are the first person who has ever had these thoughts and write an excited letter about your breakthrough. It can also help to be someone who *disagrees* with what you are trying to explain: "Yes, Mr. Darwin, that's an interesting idea you have there, but I'm very upset by what follows from your irresponsible speculation."

We are likely to assume that expository writing ought to emulate the kind of communication used by God and the angels: they communicate with each other directly, purely, all in one gulp. Humans, on the other hand, because our reason is clouded with mortality, must use discursive reason which gets at truth only gradually, step by step, imperfectly—often by means of a crooked path. Good expository writing—we feel—should be pure and direct and distilled. Or it should be like mathematics. There should only be the essence, none of the dross. Role-playing helps knock this assumption out of you. It makes you *talk onto paper*. Powerful conceptual writing is usually more like talking than like mathematics or telegrams between angels. It usually has lots of clayey, mortal imperfection about it: the writer is standing there in front of you and he has to explain one point at a time, sometimes back up to repeat something important, not be a in a hurry, and sometimes pause and look around. When your expository writing goes particularly well, it is often because you have drifted into actually *speaking* to someone as you write. Later, during the revising process, you can remove some of the speech habits—"Oh yes, there's something else I suddenly realized is very important to tell you"—that may make a written piece feel too chatty or cute. But you don't have to hurry to remove them as long as you get them out eventually. The speaking *mode* of writing helps to breathe experience into words. Only speech has breath in it. (The role-playing suggestions in the Loop Writing Process, Chapter 8, though they are exercises for generating *new* thinking, are also ways to get more experience into your words. You cannot have new thoughts without experiencing them.)

• Give yourself as much practice as you can at putting experienced thinking on paper. That means keeping a diary or journal or folder for your thoughts and reactions. Have a place where you talk to yourself on paper and aren't afraid to explore thoughts as well as feelings.

• But it also means writing down thoughts *when they strike you*.

Even if you are doing something else. If an idea seems important to you or if it relates to an important project, it is especially useful to write it down at the time. Allow yourself to find a scrap of paper now—or within five minutes—and write it down briefly. When a thought first intrudes on you, you can be sure you are experiencing it. Don't settle for saying, "I'll have to sit down and write about this idea when I get home." You may well be out of touch with it by then.

This method is important for me. It means sometimes getting out of bed for five minutes after I have turned out the light, or retreating to the bathroom if I'm in a public situation where it's inappropriate to write myself a note, or writing on the back of a blank check when no other paper is handy, or tuning out in the middle of a meeting while I write down my own idea which the conversation somehow triggered. (It looks as if I am diligently taking notes on the meeting.) I find that many of my best ideas about X come after I have put it out of my mind and I'm thinking about Y.

Therefore, if there's something you know you have to write, it pays to *start* it as early as you can—that is, to sit down and do four or five pages of free exploration to fertilize your mind. Having done this, you'll find that many extraneous events during the next few days or weeks will trigger new thinking about your topic.

It's not much trouble. You'll be surprised by how quickly you can get down a rich train of thought when you are in the middle of something else or waiting to go back to bed—especially if writing has always been a slow ordeal for you. You aren't trying to write it well or completely, you're just trying to *capture* the experience of your thought. You'll feel enormously grateful when you do sit down later to write a full draft because you will have a little pile of thoughts to start from. Felt thoughts. Even as few as three are a fruitful pile because they were jotted down in different mental contexts so that when you set them to interacting among themselves—when you try, that is, to figure out how they relate to each other or which of them is true—showers of other ideas will come to you.

But don't just jot down key words or phrases, write a short note. Pure or distilled information usually won't carry experience. You need your information in the form of speech or syntax. It needn't be lengthy speech or correct syntax but it needs breath in it. Just write quickly out of the feeling and drama of your sudden thought instead of translating into "essay language." Here is a note I wrote myself on a little scrap of paper when I was in the middle of something else (think I was listening to a lecture that was difficult to follow):

> Do you want your reader to have to struggle to figure out what you are saying? Damn right! I had to work to figure it out. Why shouldn't he? Besides, if it's too easy for him, he won't appreciate it.

• Do as much reading out loud as you can. Of others' writing and of your own. It exercises the putting-experience-into-words muscle.

• Put your body into it as you write. Clench your fist, bang your hand on the desk, stamp your feet, make faces. When you connect wholeheartedly with what you are trying to say you may well find yourself crying or giggling or shaking. Let your body react just as it wants, and keep on writing, even if it feels peculiar. (It's not.) If you try to stop the tears or giggling you just make it harder to stay in contact with your thinking.

• Get a feeling, finally, for this dialectic of attention: since you need to invest singlemindedly in experiencing your thinking but also to invest singlemindedly in disciplining your thinking, the only way of doing so is to alternate between the two. Learn to notice cues that tell you when your attention is divided or when you are distracted or worried or pulled out of focus. Learn to make yourself *do* something about it. Stop, look around, and then pour your attention into experiencing or disciplining.

And even when your attention *is* focused one way or the other, learn to notice cues that tell you when you need to switch your attention to the other. Switch to disciplining your thinking when you feel a cycle of investment and raw writing is finished, when you are just covering the same ground over and over, circling unproductively back on your old ideas, or when a deadline is approaching. When, on the other hand, you notice you are getting too discouraged and stale as you revise—perhaps even making things worse rather than better, throwing away good bits, making needless changes, taking all the energy out of your language—switch away from disciplining your thinking back to experiencing it. Here are the best ways I know for reinvesting yourself in your thinking:

- Go back to your raw writing and read over the good bits.
- Read over revised sections that work well.
- Do new raw writing.
- Force yourself to *say out loud* your thoughts in words you would use in talking to a friend.

Writing and Magic

29

I seem to have drifted into a magical view of writing. In the last two chapters about experience I say that you must have a real experience for the words to have power, but it is almost as though I am saying that you must magically devour what you are writing about if you want to put a successful hex on the reader—must enter into the thing or merge your soul with the soul of the thing. In the two voice chapters I say you must be in the right relationship with yourself, but it is almost as though I am saying you must purify yourself in a blameless holy rite or else your words will not have grace. When you have gotten all the steps right in the magic dance, *bang*, your words have life, they "take." When you miss some step in the dance, you can't find the right words, or else you find the right *words*, but they lack inner juice and just buzz buzz fog static in the reader's head. I seem to talk, in short, as though what's important is not the set of words on the page—the only thing that the reader ever encounters—but rather something *not* on the page, something the reader never encounters, namely the writer's mental/spiritual/characterological condition or the *way* she wrote down the words. A given set of words can be powerful or weak, can "take" or not take, as with a potion, according to whether the writer did the right dance or performed correctly some other purification ceremony before writing them down.

Could I really believe something this irrational? Surely not.

I guess.

But what if I really let myself take this magical view? What if I persuaded you to abandon your scruples, too, and give way to the childish or irrational or primitive modes of thought that lie so near the surface in us all? What would we discover? I think we would discover a useful way to regard the writing process and some good practical advice. And some danger.

The magical view of language, in a nutshell, is that the word is a *part* of the thing it stands for—the word *contains* some of the juice or essence or soul of the *thing* it points to. If I write down someone's name on a piece of paper and then stick pins through these written words or burn them up I can thereby visit misfortune on that person. If I pronounce a curse on someone, pronouncing her name in just the right way, I can bring her bad luck. (Words, in this view, are no different from other symbolic objects: we can stick pins in a doll to kill someone; we can eat wolf for ferocity.)

When I let myself enter into this allegedly aberrant way of looking at language, the first thing I notice is how common it is. Few people, perhaps, *act* on the basis of magic or superstition, but most people feel its gentle tug. "Maybe it was sunny *because* I wore my raincoat." Few can prevent the occurrence of such thoughts. Magic is a powerful form of thinking, and few minds can turn off one mode of thinking just because it is discredited. When someone says, "I hope we don't get a flat tire," as everyone piles into the car, it is not so unlikely to hear someone else answer, "Oh don't *say* that, you'll give us one." More people leave off the last phrase and content themselves with "Don't *say* that," but this phrase carries the same implication that words *do* exert a pull on things.

There is something else I notice when I let myself take a magical view of language, and that is how many serious, professional, and otherwise rational writers dally with magic in their writing. They have to get the right pencil or chair or paper. If they get any steps wrong in the ritual dance they use in writing, they feel as though words won't come or that the wrong words will come or that the words won't be effective. In addition writers often have a great fear of *talking about* something they are writing or planning to write. It's as though talking will put a jinx on it. This implies various conscious or unconscious modes of thinking:

• The words will be ruined if they come out of the mouth instead of on paper. Speaking uses up or dissipates one's vital fluids for writing.

• If people hear the ideas, that will somehow suck them away.

- If writers *say* what they are trying to write before it is fully cooked, that will somehow fix it in the wrong language or structure. It mustn't see the light of day in any form till it has gone full term in the womb and been fully born.
- Effective spells must be prepared in secrecy and solitude.

I don't find any of this odd at all. If you invest yourself deeply in something as mysterious as writing, it's hard to avoid magical thinking.

Moderate Magic

But to get the benefit of a magical view of language, we don't have to go overboard. Let's be reasonably magical. I'm admitting, that is, that of course language usually functions just as the rationalists say it does. Of course a word doesn't have any of the thing's juice in it; it's just an arbitrary sign. We could just as well hang the sign D O G around the neck of cats. A dog is no more *like* D O G than a cat is. I am Peter but they could have named me Bill and I'd still be me. It's an irrational fidget to think of me as "Peter-like" and my brother as "Bill-like."

So much for most language. But I insist on exceptions. A few parents on a few occasions manage to name their children *right* so that the name really does make a difference. Some writers on some occasions really do restore magic to language. They somehow put juice into words and thereby cast a long-distance spell over readers. When readers cast their eyes on these rare magical marks they are made happy, they are galvanized into action, they are turned to stone or madness. And so here is the first dividend of adopting my reasonably magical view of language: it lets me state the writer's goal with utter simplicity, namely, the ability to write "flat tire" in such a way that air whooshes out of the left front U. S. Royal and the steering wheel tugs in the driver's hands.

For the magic used to be there. It was there for earlier societies and for each of us as children. Words were once connected in a more primary way with *experience* or *things*. That's why primitive people make mistakes in logic. Even Socrates, smarter than most of us, can make a silly mistake that we wouldn't make and base an argument, for example, on the idea that the shorter man has more shortness in him that the taller man. Logic had to be gradually developed and honed *out of* language. It took a ceaseless using and overusing of words—words rubbing and rubbing against each other till they gradually get rounded and smoothed and unhooked from *things* and *experience*. That's why numbers and algebriac symbols are better for doing logic than words are. Words have to become less loaded, less magical, mere instruments of pragmatic use before people stop being fooled by them. Magic came first, logic later. Poetry came first, prose was a late development. Metaphor came first, literal language had to be invented.

Scholars and rationalists like to tell the history of language as a story of things we gained that our forebears lacked—in terms of the stupid mistakes the ancients made. But how about what we lack and what they had? They had power in language that's hard to capture now. In Homer and so-called primitive poetry and chants, we see how people in a pre-literature society seemed to have an easier time making good poetry out of simple and straightforward words. It's as though they had the knack of getting more juice into a set of utterly unprepossessing pragmatic words than we can do now even if we utter the same words—or at least only the greatest writer can now do it.

So, too, with children. They make mistakes because they use language magically. They say that dogs are called *dog* because they have dogness in them or look like *dog*, or because *dog* sounds like a dog. But children have more real voice. They talk poetically more easily than adults do. Yet what they make poetical—when you stop and look at it—often seems merely simple and straightforward. I'm not talking about the child's utterance that is clever "considering he's only a child"—which of course is charming in its own way.* I'm thinking about the child's words that are utterly simple. Children have available the gift of wholeheartedness, complete intentionality. That, perhaps, is one definition of innocence: meaning 100 percent what you say, not holding back, not leaking attention off to the side. As a child sitting in your lap will reach up and grab your chin and pull it around to make you pay attention to her when you are trying to talk to someone else, so the child has the gift of uttering words which force you with an equally graphic forcefulness to pay attention, the gift of writing words which force you as you read them to say them with full meaning and attention.

* Shakespeare loved this charm and often put witty clever words into the mouths of little children in his plays. But, interestingly, little children are among the least powerful of his characters in the impact of their language.

Children can command us. (People wouldn't have to resort to beating children if there weren't this awesome power in them.)

For adults in a modern literate sophisticated culture, words are cheap. Images, too. It used to be that a printed word compelled belief and an image gave experience. To be able to show the word or image in a book constituted proof. Words used to be expensive, images precious. Now they are often tiresome noise.

Must we then choose? Power or rational intelligence? Must we give up one or the other? It can seem that way. One thinks about modern academics, especially philosophers and sociologists. Their language is often voiceless and without power because it is so utterly cut off from experience and things. There is no sense of words carrying experiences, only of reflecting relationships between other words or between "concepts." There is no sense of an actual self seeing a thing or having an experience. Of course all language is just categories, strictly speaking, but this magical train of thought helps you realize that some language is more second-hand or thrice-percolated than other language. Sociology—by its very nature?—seems to be an enterprise whose practitioners cut themselves off from experience and things and deal entirely with categories about categories. As a result sociologists, more even than writers in other disciplines, often write language which has utterly died.

But of course there are academics, philosophers—even sociologists—who can write with real power. We can be sophisticated and still get magic into language. But the suspicion lingers that perhaps it is harder, it involves swimming against the tide.

This magical view of language explains an otherwise odd phenomenon in writing. You can tell immediately when a wrong name is used in a story by someone who is not a good writer. "*Harry* stood on one leg trying to get the chewing gum off his shoe." Perhaps everything so far has been skilled and compelling, but when you read "Harry" you *know* that the writer stopped and made up a false name. She was too timid to use her own name or whatever the real name was. It wasn't Harry. Everything else you believe, but "Harry" you don't believe.

Why should this be? It's mysterious. And not just for less common names like *Harry* or out of the way names like *Trevor*. Even if she had used *Bob* instead of the real name, it would still feel wrong—unless she had the truly good writer's trick of somehow investing *Bob* with juice. But then she could have called him *Egbert*.

The same thing happens with swear words. " 'Damn!' he muttered when a piece of bubble gum got stuck under his fingernail." You know he didn't say "damn." And it's not just because it's too mild a curse. Sometimes the inexperienced writer uses the naughtiest swear he knows but that too fails when it is invented rather than heard. There seems to be a bit of room for error when it comes to everything else in writing. You can get the color of the pond slightly wrong or the angle of the hair on her forehead. But names and swear words have to be just right or they light up and say tilt.

Really good writers, of course, can use made-up names and make them ring true, but unless you are terrific, you better have the courage to use your own name if you are talking about yourself in your story, or get your roommate's or your mother's permission. Or skip their permission. Otherwise, the wrong name will let the air out of your whole story. You can't make magic yet, so you better settle for the truth. Or rather you can get magic only through truth. Eventually, you will be able to get magic into lies.

This is a curious business, but it helps me notice that there are still traces of magic left in language. It gives a glimpse of what it might have been like when there was magic in all language—when we used gold rather than "legal tender." For names and curses are two *cul-de-sacs* of language. While most language has been grinding away for centuries into smooth, round, pragmatic symbols, semiotic chips, like pebbles being worn smooth by the sea, names and curses still have juice—they don't feel like purely arbitrary signs like red and green for stop and go, like · · · --- · · · for SOS. Yes, they might have named me *Bill* instead of *Peter*, but once I'm Peter for a while, hooks seem to sprout between that name and the real me. We see it with national flags: the flag burner demonstrates her faith in juice as much as does the outraged onlooker. What if someone took your name and wrote it on a piece of lovely white paper, spit on it, crumpled it up, put it in the toilet, peed on it, and then flushed it down? Names and curses, then, remind us of what was there and what can be put back if we write well.

It is interesting that among modern theories of language, the one that fits best with this magical view is the most mechanical, scientific, prosaic, and least romantic: the behaviorist or stimulus-response theory of language. It tells us that we learn to talk the way that Pavlov's dog learned to drool when the bell rang. That is, after Pavlov rang the bell to announce dinner, day after day, the response to dinner gradually began to generalize and become, in addition, the response to the bell. In the end, the bell alone was enough to elicit the saliva.

So, too, this theory says, when it happens enough that the child sees the ball and simultaneously hears people say *ball*, the response to the real ball slops over onto the sound, and gradually the sound *ball*, by itself elicits . . . what? a seeing? a sensing? a thinking about? an impulse to pick up and bounce? For here is where the critics of the theory pounce: "How absurd! Your theory says that I will behave in the presence of that mere sound *ball* just as I behave in the presence of the real red round bouncing thing itself." Which of course no one does.

But the sophisticates of the stimulus-response school have an answer. They reply that the response to the meat or to the ball is not so entirely generalized that we actually mistake the bell or the word *ball* for the real thing. They point out that not even Pavlov's dog *mistakes* a bell for dinner. He doesn't chew and swallow or try to eat the bell, he just drools. It's only a small portion of the response to the thing that slops over onto the sign of the thing. In fact, as we use a word more and more, as we become more knowledgeable ourselves in our use of language, a smaller and smaller trace of the response to the original object gets elicited by the word. Presumably a child just learning language is likely actually to see movies of a ball in her mind's eye when she hears the word *ball* or someone says "Where's your ball?"—and not just movies of any ball but *the* ball that she learned the word from. But as this child uses more words and more balls, the sound of the word *ball* elicits something more like what we would call an idea of balls in general rather than movies of her particular favorite old ball. (What you need to remember as a writer, though, is that there *are* movies of her deeply loved ball stored in her head and ready for screening any time, if only you can say the word *ball* right or say it in the right context.)

There is no lack of scholarly objection to this behavioral view of language. It is not now fashionable. But it does have a charm when you are trying to figure out power in writing. It suggests the very historical and cultural process we have noted: a gradual separation of word from thing. As people use language more they learn to make fewer of those mistakes that come from confusing the word and the thing, yet they see fewer movies as they listen and read. In addition, the stimulus-response model of language fits nicely with the way people seem to respond to names and curses. In the case of names and curses—the least frequently used words—you see people going some distance toward actually mistaking the word for the thing. Perhaps the most extreme example is with the name of God. The Old Testament Jews were not to write or say His Name: that name itself contained part of God's holiness. And still, it is not uncommon for people to feel that by pronouncing the name of God or Jesus or Christ they make present a piece of God's holiness: an attitude of reverence is called for in the presence of the word, perhaps even a slight bow of the head. Certainly a capital letter in writing. And cursing with the name of God feels to them like an act of serious desecration.

So, too, with excremental and copulatory words. The horror of some people at hearing or reading those words shows that the sign elicits in them a substantial portion of their response to the thing itself. Many people, of course, are not quite so horrified; a much more fractional portion of their response to the thing is elicited by those words, but they are made vaguely uncomfortable, nevertheless. These people are not chewing and swallowing at the sound of the bell, not even drooling, but they are getting a whiff. And finally there are those sophisticates who feel that excremental and copulatory words are no more "loaded" than any other words. But those enlightened souls can probably remember precisely the time and place in their lives—often the army or camp or a boarding school—when those words were used so much—rolled around and bounced against each other and against the rest of language and experience so much—that they came to be "just like any other words." Fond memory: that wonderful first time in the linoleum floored hallway when you were able to say "shit" without the slightest internal quiver—just like the big girls. Here then, we see a reenactment in later life of that progression in children from a fuller response to the word *ball* to a more fractional response.

Names, too. The bit of God's essence in God's name is perhaps more obvious than the bit of me in my name, but we can feel it in certain circumstances. For example, if we are in a group from which one member is absent for some rather loaded reason—perhaps she has been expelled in an unpleasant way or she quit with great anger, or the group is meeting secretly to plot against her or she recently died—the mere mention of her name is likely to carry enough juice to give those present a tiny shiver. Special circumstances make her absence so pervasive or deep that we can feel a trace of her presence in the sound of her name. We see the same thing when the lovesick girl or boy can't keep from repeating again and again the name of the beloved. I have learned—for another example—that people are more fully present in a group if they have introduced themselves by saying their name out loud. Once they have done so—even though they know their names cannot yet actually be remembered along with all the other new names introduced—they are more likely to feel part of the group and therefore to speak and respond to others or to feel that their absence will be noticed. If you want someone's full presence, it helps to ask for her name. When people only give their first name, as many young people now do, I believe they are really holding back just a little of their essence—just in case.

In our rational and sophisticated culture, then, names and swearing remind us that all language used to be loaded but now juice is in only a few corners. But the phenomenon of good writing—the fact that a good writer can christen her character "Trevelyn," a huge trucker, and have Trevelyn say "Pshaw!" when he steps in a dog turd, and have it all feel real and give us movies in our head—this reminds us that magic can be restored to words. You can learn to give to readers an experience equivalent to when the little old lady sees "****" in print. You can make your reader react to the *word* as though you had thrown the thing itself right there in her lap.

Escape Route

But seriously now, can words *really* carry some magical essence of the thing? A thought experiment suggests an escape route if the magical view is too unsettling. Imagine a whole pile of bank checks written by different people. Perhaps you hijacked the mail truck and you have them all in your hand. There is no way to know from looking at the checks whether they are any good—whether there is money in the various accounts to cover them. But imagine that as you look at all these checks, suddenly one catches your eye. In some way you can *feel* with certainty that this one particular $100 check is good, valid, solid. From looking only at the words before you on the paper, you can experience the existence of money somewhere in a bank. The check writer did what we all want to do as writers.

But imagine, now, getting a check for $100 with a 10-page letter from the person who signed the check, explaining why she is giving you the money. From such a full explanation you might well be able to know with assurance that the writer really meant to give you the money and, had made sure that the check would not bounce. After reading such a letter you would, when you turned to look at the check itself, feel the cash behind it. These mere words on paper, "one hundred dollars" would elicit from you much or most of the response you would have to the thing itself, the cash. But, of course, it is not the words on the check itself, alone, that give you this experience of cash in your hand, but rather the words on the check *in the context of* the letter. Maybe it's this kind of thing that happens when we feel words "carrying" some of what's not there. (Our response to real cash illustrates again the fact that "mere words" can carry juice—since real cash is nothing but words on paper, too.)

So maybe that's where the power in writing comes from that I want to call magic: context. For, in fact, it usually takes a longish piece of writing to give us the magic of a real experience—a passage long enough to carry a lot of context. A short passage or excerpt alone usually won't carry the magic you felt in those very same words as you were reading the whole thing. Perhaps it is all a trick of context that makes us know and feel when there is "money in the bank" for a particular story or poem or essay. You can, thus, write the word "ball" and make me see movies of my favorite old childhood toy, but only if you surround it with a bunch of other words that are just right.

We see it in lying. Most people don't lie well. It flusters them and makes some kind of tension in the body. They probably don't look the listener in the eye in the same way, or there are other little telltale movements in the body that somehow manifest discomfort. Thus the context makes a sensitive listener feel something fishy in what she is hearing, a note somehow not to be trusted.

So, too, perhaps with writing. Perhaps when we write something false—perhaps even when we write something slightly out of tune with our "real self" so that it goes against the grain of some thoughts and feelings in our unconscious—we are just the tiniest bit flustered and uncomfortable and even though the reader is not there to notice a slipperiness in our eye movements or a restlessness in our hands, still there are comparable micro-fidgets in our syntax and diction. Inauthenticity will out.

And then, of course, there is the fact that some people are good liars. They can tell whoppers without any of those telltale signs. Besides writing a handsome $100 check, they can also write that 10-page letter that makes you feel the cash in your hand. That's the ability that enables people to write great stories, poems, plays, and essays. "The truest poetry is the most feigning," says Shakespeare—and Auden echoes in a good poem about writing. It's the ability that frees the Shakespeares from having to write about what actually happened to them—writers who have "negative capability" and can create for the reader a seemingly limitless range of experiences they never had.

But that's the question. Is it really true that Shakespeare never experienced what it was like to be Miranda—a girl who'd never seen a man other than her father? Somehow he must have created that experience for himself. When someone who has never seen the sea writes powerfully about it, she must somehow or other have experienced it in her head. She could create it for herself even if she'd never lived it in the flesh. Presumably the trick of the good liar is somehow to get yourself to feel in some sense or other the reality of what you are saying. Of course you know it's a lie, but you are better than the rest of us at pushing that awareness off into one convenient insulated pouch at the moment of lying and somehow getting your mind and feelings—or your voice—to enter into these false words in some kind of act of "meaning it."

So if the magical view of language makes us nervous we can see our way clear now to abandoning it. Of course the words don't really carry any of the thing's inner juice, it's just a matter of the naïveté of listeners or the trickiness of speakers. Of course the check doesn't have any of the $100 in it, it's just the accompanying letter. Of course there is none of me present when they meet without me and say my name. It's just that some people are susceptible to primitive reactions, perhaps because they feel guilty or bothered. It's true that old responses can be reawakened. They are there inside, waiting. We all have it in us to respond like the primitive, like the child, like the little old lady—to have a spell cast over us by mere marks on paper. It happens when the writer is good enough. But there is no magic. There is just the cleverness of good liars and the eternal susceptibility of humans to respond magically. There is nothing but the effect of tiny, subtle cues in the context.

How disappointing.

But we don't have to abandon the magical view. My hunch is that the writer should keep it. That is, even though we could, like clever carnival swindlers, analyze the susceptibilities of readers (suckers!) and even though we could, like careful, white-coated, empirical scientists, hook readers up to wires and study which cues on the page make for magical responses—just as we could study how to lie well by analyzing the wrong movements that give most of us away and the right ones of the masters, nevertheless we'd be better doing what I'll bet master-swindlers and liars really do: they put their focal attention on their *meaning* rather than on their movements or those of their victims.

It's all analogous to learning to use a cane if you are blind or blindfolded. In truth, the borderline between yourself and the outside world is where your hand touches the cane. The farthest outpost of sensation or awareness is your hand. Yet it is useful—and it turns out to be natural with almost everyone—to permit a more magical view and slide your awareness past your hand down the cane to its lower tip. By putting the focus of attention on the place where the street bumps against the cane, instead of the place where the cane bumps against your hand, you learn to behave as though the stick is part of your body: you can learn to feel not the pressure of the cane on your hand but the pressure of the curb on the cane.* If you make this act of putting-yourself-in and learn to treat the stick as part of yourself rather than part of the outside world, then the stick does become part of you. You will feel that familiar shudder when the cane touches the fresh dog turd, even though strictly speaking you didn't touch it at all.

The writer, then, writes well by putting magic *into* words just as the blind person sees well by putting herself into the cane. If the writer is putting her attention on subtle reactions in readers and subtle telltale syntactic qualities in her writing, she will be as inefficient as the blind person who tries to read the street by restricting her attention to the actual pressures in her hand caused by the

---

*This example comes from Michael Polanyi's *Personal Knowledge: Toward A Post Critical Philosophy* (Chicago, 1974).

cane. Such an approach requires so much *translation*—"Let's see, if this effect, then that cause, and therefore I should make the following move . . ." —which, in turn, causes a cloud of self-consciousness and fog, in the behavior of the writer or the cane-wielder.

You need to be like the ancient mariner who has the power simply to look the reader in the eye and start talking and thereby paralyze her: prevent her from moving away, compel her to listen, and compel her to experience everything you are saying. This will come quickest by concentrating not on the details of your technique, but on the importance of your tale. If you succeed in *really* believing your tale is deeply important, you already and automatically believe in magic without giving the matter any awareness at all.

All the rituals that writers perform, then—"I've got to have a number 2 pencil with a perfect point. I must work at certain times and places, I must never read over what I've written on the same day I write it, and if I talk to anyone about what I'm writing, it will be ruined"—these rituals and fetishes are testaments to belief. Belief in the magic of getting words to come out of one's guts and a belief in the power of words to hit readers in the gut.

Belief produces that universal injustice proclaimed by Christ: the rich get richer and the poor poorer. Someone who manages to have success in writing tends to write suddenly better. She's finally learned to believe that she *can* wield magic. She half-doubted it before. With her success comes belief and with that comes a sudden infusion of new power. Belief is the source of a child's power. The child *commands* our attention because it doesn't enter her head that we could do anything else but pay full attention. One of the saddest sights of all is that spunkless child who lacks this power to command attention: she's gotten so little trustworthy attention that she's lost her knowledge that of course her words have power.

But most of us somewhere on the way to adulthood also lost our knowledge that of course our words have power. "Naturally," explains the realist. "That's what we mean by being an adult. Tiny children cannot help thinking that their words—even their unspoken wishes—magically cause events. But if children want to grow up they must learn to see cause-and-effect accurately and forsake primitive wishful thinking." Yes, I reply from my moderate magical view, we must learn enough realism to understand that our every wish and word do not cause action in the world. But we must not go as far in our "learning" as most people go when they end up feeling they cannot put magic into words. If it is childish to believe that our every wish causes action in the world, it is equally childish to sulk at the loss of omnipotence and conclude that individuals are helpless to change the world and that words cannot move mountains. They can. A few people have power all the time; most people have it occasionally (though they tend to forget about it or try to explain it away); and everyone has power available.

The agenda for the writer then is clear: to regain that ability to put magic into words. It takes more, of course, than merely believing in magic. It takes practice and skill. But belief is necessary, and the amazing thing is how far belief can take you toward doing it—especially if you have already worked hard on your writing.

What does this mean, then, in practice? I think it means the kinds of advice I gave in the Voice and Experience chapters. The activities I advised there are activities of really *doing* it: putting your awareness all the way out to the end of the cane, not merely to the end of your fingers. In a sense, you can only send your experience as far as the page, but you need to *think* your experiences all the way through to the inside of your reader's skull.

More advice. Use the truth wherever possible. Real events. Real names. In addition, however, practice lying whenever possible. The entrance into magic is through the truth. By putting real experiences and your real self into words you will get a feeling for what it is like to wield magic, and with this feeling you can begin to practice telling lies—practice "having" experiences you've never had, practice getting your real self or whole self entirely behind words that are false, ironic, ambivalent, or even evasive. (Some people, of course, cannot tell the truth convincingly, but they can tell lies or wishes or dreams with compelling power. To be strictly accurate, then, I should not advise so unqualifiedly to start with truth. The best advice is simply to believe in magic and find where your magic lies readiest to hand. Once you get a feeling for your ability to put magic into words, then you can learn gradually—don't hurry—to expand the range.)

More advice. Magic is catching. It can help enormously to put yourself in the company of people who are succeeding in using their magic. Read their words. Listen to them read their words out loud. Write in the same room or the same building with them; write when they write; look for chances to go off with them for a day's or a week's work-play of writing and sharing. Read your words out loud to them. (Try to avoid two dangers: don't get negative feedback from them on your writing if you are not genuinely ready for it or if they give it destructively. Just insist that they listen and praise the bits they like. Secondly, don't let yourself be intimidated: "Oh dear, they can do it, I'll never be able to do it." Try to keep these helpless feelings from depriving you of the enormous boost you get from being with people who are using their magic.)

You can catch magic even from yourself. That is, it can help a lot to read over pieces of your own writing that you know are successful and powerful. Read your good words silently; better yet out loud. This gives you the actual psycho-muscular feeling for what it was like to put juice into words. By reawakening this memory/feeling, you can more easily get into that gear again. Reading over your own good work is particularly useful when you are having a hard time getting warmed up—perhaps after a long period of nonwriting.

Success is infectious. Don't therefore start by trying to write the Great American Novel and sending it off to the best publishers, or sending poems off to the *New Yorker*. Instead of inviting continual rejection, insist at all costs on being published and read. Find small or informal magazines, presses, publications; if necessary, crank it out yourself on a mimeograph machine and distribute it to readers you know. Write for audiences you can actually reach: people who know you and like you, people who will understand you, people for whom your words will work.

I can't decide whether my reasonably magical view of writing is literally true or not, or whether the stimulus-response account of language is the correct one or not. I don't quite know how one might settle the question once and for all. But the magical view is useful. For teachers, critics, and theorists will always be tempted to try to specify exactly what characterizes good writing. Some talk about certain kinds of syntactic complexity (certain numbers of words per "T-Unit," for example), some talk about sensory specificity or the absence of generalizations, some talk about unity or coherence or ambiguity or tone. It's inevitable. If I had some good ideas about what constituted good writing I would get excited and try to tell everyone. But the magical view saves us from these precise specifications. And that is a good thing for two reasons. First, I think they are false: whenever I see an abstract description of what makes good writing, I always think of actual cases of good writing that violate it. Secondly, such descriptions take your attention to the wrong place as you write. They make you think about the writing as you write instead of about your meaning or topic—they preoccupy you with making sure your words have the right characteristics instead of whether you can really see the bamboo; they make you look at the glass in the window instead of through to the view. Most of all, the magical view of writing helps you believe what is necessary and true: that your words can have enormous power.

But the magical view has dangers. It can trick many people into believing what is false and destructive: that the *source* of this power is entirely outside you, that power comes from stern-eyed gods or fickle muses or from the state of your soul (which you can't see or judge), or from "it," or from standing out of the way, or from getting all the steps right in some mysterious ritual dance. The magical view can reinforce helplessness and lead to feelings like these:

- I don't know where the power comes from. All I can do is hope and pray. Nothing I *do* makes any difference.
- What I've written is worthless because I've been using the wrong colored 3 by 5 cards or writing at the wrong time of day. There's nothing I can do to improve it now.
- I've talked too much about this piece and frittered away all its vital juices. There's nothing to do but give up on it.
- I can't revise or improve this piece; the words just came to me because I stood out of the way, they're not *my* words. If I make any change the whole thing will come entirely apart and I won't be able to put anything back together again.
- If I ever lose what I've written I can never rewrite or reconstruct it.
- I can't write today; my focus is all wrong and besides I've missed the fruitful time of day.

Thinking in terms of magic can also trip you up by making you *want* magic too badly—make you unwilling to slog along writing mediocre, dead, even terrible words. Everyone has the impulse to put off writing till the mood is right. Mere laziness, perhaps, but also it reflects a truth—sometimes you have magic and sometimes you haven't—*and a falsehood*—that when you haven't got it, no amount of effort or shrewdness will do any good.*

But magic isn't everything. Sometimes what you need most is just to get something written, and wanting magic too badly will keep you from doing so. Often you can write something that is true and clear and important—but lacks magic. If you had insisted on magic you would have written nothing at all.

I return here, then, to the main theme of my book. You must learn—and for some reason you often have to relearn—how to churn out words whether or not you feel in tune with what you are writing. The precondition for writing well is being able to write badly and to write when you are not in the mood. Sometimes you cannot get to the magic except through a long valley of fake, dead writing. Though you must believe in magic, then, often you must be willing to do without it.

---

* "You can create magic by disciplining yourself to write and work and concentrate. Like the medicine man, you can do it on command. (Professional writers do, and have the appropriate accompanying rituals.) It's not just waiting for it to happen to you, on the one hand, or pouring out words on the paper hoping it will come, on the other hand. It's some way, through ritual, concentrating, working very hard, of getting yourself into *that state*. You can force yourself to *see*. The way may be long—lots of dead words or cigarette butts—but if you've once experienced it you'll try for it again." Margaret Proctor, a good writing teacher, commenting on a draft of this chapter.

A SELECT ANNOTATED BIBLIOGRAPHY ON PUBLISHING

Prepared by J. C. Armbruster

Bowker Catalog. R. R. Bowker, 1180 Avenue of the Americas, New York, N. Y. 10036. Free.

This outstanding selection of books on book publishing introduces you to major channels of contemporary publishing, as well as standard references on publishing markets.

Coda: Poets & Writers Newsletter. Poets & Writers, Inc., 201 West 54th Street, New York, N. Y. 10019.

This monthly newsletter is a primary guide to contests, grants, scholarships, and other recently created writing opportunities. It also profiles new magazines, and features short articles on current publishing trends in fiction and poetry writing.

Directory of Little Magazines, Small Presses, and Underground Newspapers. Edited by Len Fulton and James Boyer May. Dustbooks, 5218 Scottwood Road, Paradise, Calif. 94969. 1979.

The acknowledged reference for writers starting into the little magazine or self-publishing markets. These listings are especially useful for the beginning writer seeking reviews of a self-publishing book.

Guide to Women's Publishing. Women Writing Press, R. D. 3, Newfield, N. Y. 14867. 1978.

A cataloged listing of women's presses and other non-sexist publishing groups, this publication provides a good contact list for women breaking into print.

How To Get Happily Published. Nancy Evans and Judith Appelbaum. Harper and Row, 10 East 53rd Street, New York, N. Y. 10022. 1978.

The best introductory guide for the new writer. Professional editors Evans and Appelbaum unveil the basic steps to getting published: developing your writing; where, to whom, and how to submit manuscripts; following up on initial sales; supporting yourself while writing, and publishing vs. self-publishing. The appended resource directory is a cornucopia of books, people, and organizations aiding both experienced and new writers.

Literary Agents, A Complete Guide. Poets & Writers, Inc., 201 West 54th Street, New York, N. Y. 10019. 1978.

It tells most things you would want to know, such as when you need one, how to get one, how much to pay, who they are.

Literary Market Place: The Directory of American Book Publishing; with Names and Numbers. R. R. Bowker, 1180 Avenue of the Americas, New York, N. Y. 10036. Published annually.

An essential reference with excellent sections covering different publishing and writing preparation and placement sources. Especially useful are the sections on "U. S. Book Publishers" (with geographical location listings) and "Reference Books of the Trade."

Printing It. Clifford Burke. Ballantine Books, Inc., Div. of Random House, Inc., 201 East 50th Street, New York, N. Y. 10022. 1974.

Burke presents several methods of designing, composing, and printing your books. The techniques are within the capabilities and price-range of even the most modest self-publisher.

The Publish-It-Yourself Handbook: Literary Tradition and How-To. Edited by Bill Henderson. The Pushcart Press, Box 845, Yonkers, N. Y. 10701. Revised annually.

Personal experiences in self-publishing are presented by such diverse essayists as Anaïs Nin and Stewart Brand. A how-to section in the back give clearsighted steps to putting out your book, and is followed by a sterling annotated bibliography. A must for those committed to self-publishing.

Writer's Digest. 9933 Alliance Road, Cincinnati, Ohio 45242.

A monthly magazine full of articles, stories, and advertisements that will interest writers of all sorts.

Writer's Market. Writer's Digest, 9933 Alliance Road, Cincinnati, Ohio 45242. Published annually.

This volume contains thousands of listings under 169 categories, starting with Audiovisual and ending at Water Supply and Sewage Disposal. Writer's Market provides writers with each publication's specific interests in freelance submissions, word pay rates, and the volume of freelance material they publish. However, they do not list all publishers, and must not be considered an all-encompassing source for freelance writing markets.

Writing To Sell. Scott Meredith, ed. Harper & Row. 1974.

One of the important literary agents of our era talks about writing and selling fiction.

Index

Subjects

Advice, 17, 30-1, 38, 44-6, 94-100, 175, 188-90, 197-8, 205-6, 208-9, 214-15, 226-35, 280, 304-13, 332-3, 335-8, 351-6, 358, 370

Attention, 177-8, 183-90, 237, 255, 320, 326, 336, 338, 368-70
  Dialectic of attention, 349-51

Audience, sections iv (177-235), v (237-77); 4, 6, 26, 30, 32, 33, 35-6, 38, 40-41, 44, 55, 71-7, 80, 95, 100, 122, 126, 128, 135-6, 139-45, 152-3, 168-9, 200, 280, 285, 293-5, 306-9, 312, 326
  Audience-oriented writing, *see* Writing
  Dangerous audience, 179, 184-90, 200
  Real vs. imagined audience, 186-90, 192, 220-24
  Safe audience, 21, 179, 184-90
  Teachers as audience, chap. **20** (216-35); 179, 189, 196, 307, 341-2, 347, 349

Autobiography, *see* Biography

Beginning, *see* Starting to write; Opening section

Behaviorist theory of language, 362-5, 371

Believing game, 50, 201, 203, 270-72

Biography, 82-84, 149, 204, 282, 284, 286

Basics, 184

Blocked, being blocked, 9-19, 41, 43, 122
  see Freeing the writing process

Brainstorming, 8, 10

Case studies, 78

Children's stories, 194, 247

Collaboration: collaborative writing, 116, 124-5
  Collaborative revising, chap. **13** (139-45); 123-25, 306
  see also Feedback; Support group

Collage, 148-9
  Collage essay, 150-66

Coming apart, writing comes apart, 131-4, 138, 174

Conscientious objector application, 311-12

Control, chap. **6** (39-46); 18-19, 59, 285, 302, 307
  see also Taking charge

Correctness, *see* Grammar and usage

Criterion-based feedback, *see* Feedback

Cutting, *see* Pruning

Creating and criticizing as the two mentalities central to the writing process, 7-12, 14, 121, 130, 134, 136, 170, 173, 199

Names